SECONDARY MATHEMATICS INSTRUCTION
An Integrated Approach

SECONDARY MATHEMATICS INSTRUCTION

An Integrated Approach

Margaret A. Farrell
State University of New York at Albany

Walter A. Farmer
State University of New York at Albany

 JANSON PUBLICATIONS, INC. Providence, Rhode Island

ACKNOWLEDGMENTS

The authors wish to thank the copyright holders for permission to reprint in this text the following figures:

Fig. 3.7: From *Science teaching and the development of reasoning* (Volumes for Biology, Chemistry, Earth Science, General Science and Physics), by Karplus, R., Lawson, A. E., Wollman, W., Appel, M., Bernoff, R., Howe, A., Rusch, J. J., & Sullivan, F. (Berkeley, CA: The University of California, 1977). By permission of The Regents of the University of California.

Fig. 9.3, 9.4, 9.5: From Book H of the School Mathematics Project, by Harris, J., Hobbs, D. A., Lewis, K., Strong, R. W., & Wilson, T. (New York: Cambridge University Press, 1972), pp. 111, 112, and 114. Reproduced by permission of Cambridge University Press.

Fig. 10.7: From "Ratios and Proportions," New York State Mathematics Teachers' Journal, 27 (Winter 1977). By permission of the editor, Stanley Taback, and the author, Constance C. Feldt.

Library of Congress Cataloging-in-Publication Data

Farrell, Margaret A.
    Secondary mathematics instruction: an integrated approach /
Margaret A. Farrell and Walter A. Farmer.
      p. cm.
    Rev. ed. of: Systematic instruction in mathematics for the middle
and high school years. c1980.
    Bibliography: p.
    Includes indexes.
    ISBN 0-939765-26-8: $40.00 (est.)
    1. Mathematics—Study and teaching (Secondary) I. Farmer, Walter
A. II. Farrell, Margaret A. Systematic instruction in mathematics
for the middle and high school years. III. Title.
QA11.F37 1988
510'.712—dc19
                88-28231
                CIP

Secondary Mathematics Instruction: An Integrated Approach is a completely revised edition of *Systematic Instruction in Mathematics for the Middle and High School Years*, copyright © 1980 by Addison-Wesley Publishing Company, Reading Massachusetts.

*To Our Students Who Continue To Be
Students of Teaching*

CONTENTS

TO THE STUDENT   xiii

PREFACE   xvii

**CHAPTER 1 MODES OF INSTRUCTION: INSTRUCTIONAL
              MOVES BY THE TEACHER**   1

    1.1 Definitions of common instructional modes   3

    1.2 Introductory activity   6

    1.3 Uses of modes   7

    1.4 Summary and self-check   25

    1.5 Simulation/practice activities   26

    Suggestions for further study   27

CHAPTER 2 FEEDBACK: THE HEART OF INSTRUCTION   28

    2.1 Definitions   29

    2.2 Introductory activity   30

    2.3 Feedback: Getting, using, and giving   31

    2.4 Summary and self-check   42

    2.5 Simulation/practice activities   43

    Suggestions for further study   44

CHAPTER 3 THE INTELLECTUAL DEVELOPMENT
OF STUDENTS: ADOLESCENT REASONING
PATTERNS 45

3.1 Introductory activity 46

3.2 Cognitive development from a Piagetian perspective 48

3.3 Research on reasoning about mathematics topics 60

3.4 Individual differences 63

3.5 Summary and self-check 68

3.6 Simulation/practice activities 69

Suggestions for further study 70

CHAPTER 4 THE STRUCTURE OF MATHEMATICS:
PRODUCTS AND PROCESSES 72

4.1 Introductory activity 74

4.2 Product aspects of mathematics 75

4.3 Process aspects of mathematics 80

4.4 A model of the nature of mathematics 88

4.5 Instruction and the dynamic nature of mathematics 90

4.6 Summary and self-check 100

4.7 Simulation/practice activities 100

Suggestions for further study 103

CHAPTER 5 INSTRUCTIONAL OBJECTIVES:
TARGETS OF INSTRUCTION 105

5.1 Introductory activity 107

5.2 Instructional objectives versus other kinds of
goal statements 108

5.3 Domains of instructional objectives 111

5.4 Summary and self-check 122

5.5 Simulation/practice activities 123

Suggestions for further study 124

CHAPTER 6 THE LEARNING OF MATHEMATICS:
STEPPING STONES TO PLANNING 126

6.1 Introductory activity 128

6.2	Meaningful learning	129
6.3	Categories of human learning	132
6.4	Task analysis	142
6.5	Concept mapping	143
6.6	Advance organizers	145
6.7	Retention, transfer and practice	146
6.8	Summary and self-check	152
6.9	Simulation/practice activities	153
	Suggestions for further study	155
CHAPTER 7	**DESIGN OF INSTRUCTIONAL STRATEGIES: THE GAME PLAN**	**156**
7.1	Introductory activity	158
7.2	Daily planning based on the instructional model	158
7.3	Putting it all together	188
7.4	Long-range planning	192
7.5	Summary and self-check	199
7.6	Simulation/practice activities	200
	Suggestions for further study	201
CHAPTER 8	**EVALUATION OF INSTRUCTION: THE PROOF OF THE PUDDING**	**203**
8.1	Evaluation versus testing	205
8.2	Introductory activity	207
8.3	Assessment of cognitive objectives	208
8.4	Assessment of affective objectives	233
8.5	Assessment of psychomotor objectives	236
8.6	Report cards and final grades	236
8.7	Summary and self-check	240
8.8	Simulation/practice activities	241
	Suggestions for further study	243

CHAPTER 9 PERSPECTIVES OF MATHEMATICS
EDUCATION: LEARNING FROM THE PAST 245

9.1 Introductory activity 246

9.2 From the three R's to The Standards 247

9.3 Implications for the mathematics teacher 260

9.4 Summary and self-check 265

9.5 Simulation/practice activities 266

Suggestions for further study 267

CHAPTER 10 THE MATHEMATICS, SCIENCE, AND
EVERYDAY WORLD INTERFACE:
COMMUNICATION AND COOPERATION 268

10.1 Introductory activity 270

10.2 Mathematics through science 271

10.3 Mathematics and the everyday world 282

10.4 Summary and self-check 287

10.5 Simulation/practice activities 288

Suggestions for further study 290

CHAPTER 11 RESOURCES FOR MATHEMATICS
INSTRUCTION: GOLD IS WHERE YOU FIND IT 292

11.1 Introductory activity 294

11.2 Inexpensive equipment and supplies 294

11.3 Uses of collectibles in the mathematics classroom 297

11.4 Nontypical uses of audiovisual and technological aids 304

11.5 Field trips 306

11.6 Human resources 307

11.7 Safety and legal aspects 307

11.8 Differentiating instruction 308

11.9 The mathematics teacher is a learner, too 309

11.10 Summary and self-check 311

11.11 Simulation/practice activities 311

Suggestions for further study 313

**CHAPTER 12   DISCIPLINE: CONTROL OR CHAOS IN YOUR
CLASSROOM   318**

   12.1   Attention versus noise   319

   12.2   Introductory activity   321

   12.3   An ounce of prevention   321

   12.4   The big culprits   328

   12.5   A pound of cure   332

   12.6   So you're a teacher   336

   12.7   Summary and self-check   339

   12.8   Simulation/practice activities   339

        Suggestions for further study   341

APPENDIX   MODULAR ASSIGNMENTS   342

        Resource File Module   342

        Learning Hierarchy Module   344

REFERENCES   346

NAME INDEX   353

SUBJECT INDEX   356

TO THE STUDENT

(This introduction was written with the preservice teacher in mind. Inservice teachers might compare our list of the basic ingredients needed to enter mathematics teaching with their own experience. The final paragraphs on the instructional model serve as an introduction to the text itself. We recommend that all readers carefully review that section.)

So you want to be a teacher? Are you *sure* that secondary school mathematics teaching is for you and that you are for it? No expert can tell you the answer. Nor is there any evidence to support the notion that teaching skills are passed on by heredity. The fact that Dad and Aunt Sally are teachers is in the realm of interesting, but unrelated information. Neither will the mere reading of this book in and of itself provide you with the answer. What this book is designed to do is to promote an interaction of your talents with real-world classroom situations in a systematic way so that you will find an answer and so that you will know when you have found it.

The term *interaction* was deliberately chosen. Becoming a teacher depends on your willingness and ability to learn the complex background necessary for teaching and to implement that background in meaningful ways in the classroom. A mathematics methods instructor, a college supervisor of student teaching, and a school cooperating teacher can and will help in many important ways and at crucial points in the process. However, no one person or combination of these persons can do your part. What is your part? Our cumulative experience in working with hundreds of young men and women in methods courses and student teaching points to several things *you must bring* to the situation.

Comprehension of subject matter is certainly one key ingredient. No one expects you to recall all the detailed information you have learned in many semester hours of coursework in mathematics. In fact, much of this information will find only the most limited use in teaching secondary school students. What is important is that your command of the fundamental concepts and basic principles enables you to apply those concepts to unique or novel situations and to treat them on various levels of sophistication while maintaining the integrity of the academic content.

Courage is also vital. Inexperienced teachers are generally "tested" by secondary school students who want to determine what they can get away with in class. Novice teachers who cannot bring themselves to consistently insist on adherence to some simple rules of conduct—and thus risk temporary dislike by their students—don't last very long. Little things overlooked in the hope that they will go away soon grow into big things; confrontations follow, and growing disrespect for the teacher breeds overt hatred. When situations progress to this point, the odds (25 students versus 1 teacher) are almost always insurmountable, and another teacher is lost to the profession.

You must genuinely like young people! Even the dullest of students can sense a teacher's dislike in spite of the teacher's best efforts to conceal the feeling. Even professional actors or actresses would be hard pressed to present a facade for five class periods a day, five days a week, throughout the entire school year. When students perceive a teacher's dislike of them as young people, problems are certain to develop. Then, too, consider how such teachers must feel having to work closely for extended periods of time each day with age groups they do not like. The start of each teaching day must seem like the beginning of a familiar bad dream.

Physical endurance is often overlooked. Beginning teachers are constantly amazed to discover how physically exhausted they are at the end of a teaching day. All the years you spent sitting in class as a student have done little to prepare your muscles for the amount of standing and walking required by teaching. On top of physical strain in the classroom, teachers have to face correction of papers and preparation of lesson materials after dinner. This proves too much for some to endure.

A realistic view of self is another prerequisite for success. All of us bring strengths and weaknesses to the teaching situation. You must learn how to capitalize on your strengths and be determined to shore up your weaknesses as rapidly as possible. This means that you must learn to be receptive to constructive criticism offered by supervisors and you must develop the skills of self-criticism. After all, shouldn't the main goal of teacher education be to help novices progress to the point where they can succeed in the classroom and continue to learn about instruction on their own throughout their teaching careers? Because we firmly believe that it is, the main purpose of this book is to assist you in becoming a life-long student of teaching.

If what we have said thus far makes sense to you and if you are determined to give teaching your best shot, you are our kind of person and this book was written with you in mind. Teaching can and should be an intellectually stimulating and ever-changing challenge. It should also be an endless source of satisfaction.

Note that the word *instruction* instead of the word *teaching* appears in the title of this book. Our choice of words indicates emphasis on producing learning according to specific intents of the teacher (objectives) by purposefully controlling those variables known to affect various types of learning. No doubt your students will learn in your classes things other than those you intended to convey. We pay some attention to these byproducts of instruction, but we decided to focus on an integrated approach to instruction in mathematics.

Obviously, there are many aspects of instruction that generalize across any subject matter. However, our experience indicates that novices learn best by starting to think about the specifics of their own discipline, to apply these specifics in particular instances, and to reach generalizations *after* a critical mass of first-hand experience has been accumulated. Further, each subject matter discipline has its own type of conceptual framework (structure of ideas) and its own kinds of processes for generating ways of finding out that system of ideas. Analyzing the discipline in terms of these process and product aspects reveals its potential as a source of objectives (specific goals to be attained by learners).

Does one teach *content* or *kids*? Think this over for a minute and see if you believe that question is really worth considering as an either/or proposition. Practitioners almost universally agree on a response such as "Both," or "One teaches subject matter to students," or "One teaches students the subject matter." As experienced secondary school teachers, we long ago abandoned any inclination to consider either/or responses to this perennial question. This point of view should be obvious in the instructional model schema that precedes each chapter of the text.

Note that this schematic model incorporates both a planning and an implementation vector. Both the nature of the content to be learned and the intellectual development of students are treated as essential prerequisites to the specification of objectives. Once realistic and valid aims have been specified, knowledge about how humans learn various categories of content can be used as a basis for designing instructional strategies. The strategies must include plans for *giving feedback to students* so they will know how they are progressing toward the objectives during the implementation stage. It is also vital to *plan for and collect feedback from students* so that planned strategies can be intelligently altered during the same stage. Similarly, the feedback loop that goes back to the specified objectives can function only if knowledge of student attainment of these objectives is obtained regularly and systematically.

Does this model of instruction make some sense to you? It should, because we have developed it by working with hundreds of preservice and inservice teachers. However, don't worry if all its ramifications are not clear at this point. That's what this book is all about. Read it, but don't stop there. Interact with the ideas, perform the activities, then apply the integrated approach with your students and *believe the data.*

PREFACE

The first edition of this text evolved over a ten year period as we collaborated to improve key parts of the undergraduate program for the education of mathematics and science teachers. Sample chapters were used in an intensive professional semester program in which special methodology and clinical experiences reflected the emphasis on the integration of theory, research, and practice. The book also has been used as a source book, or required text, in graduate mathematics education curriculum, supervision, and perspectives of mathematics education courses. Secondary school department chairs have used it to assist their new teachers and experienced teachers have praised the text for serving as a catalyst to help them reflect on their own teaching. Doctoral students have found that the integration of psychology and mathematics instruction, as well as the emphasis on the structure of the discipline of mathematics, serves as a good basis for their research in mathematics education.

We have been gratified by these postive responses to the first edition. In the second edition, we used the word *integrated* in the title of the text to highlight the integration of theory, practice and research that occur at several levels. There is the thought model of instruction on the first page of each chapter. In each chapter, we relate one or more components of that thought model to the subject of the chapter and, always to the real world of teaching. The schema of the thought model of the discipline of mathematics found in Chapter 4 is of major importance. That model reflects a dynamic view of mathematics, its products and processes. We emphasize the simple mathematical models that can be introduced by the teacher and encourage the reader to contrast the model of mathematics with its sister discipline, science. Thought models are used to illustrate aspects of psychology, as in the nested stages model in Chapter 3 and the information processing model in Chapter 6. Yet, with this emphasis on theory and research, a hallmark of the text is its practical validity as a guide to the mathematics teacher who is in the real world of the classroom. We take the approach that learning is a constructivist activity and thus, the text is written in an interactive manner. We also take the view that teaching is a complex, problem-solving task and we continually challenge the reader to reflect on the nature of this task.

In this second edition, we have included many references to research supporting specific suggestions or results. All of these sources are listed at the end of the text in a single list, References. We have updated the Suggestions for Further Study section at the end of each chapter, but have continued to try to keep these of the kind that could be read with profit by the preservice teacher and the inservice teacher new to the topic. Expanded indices, both name and subject, are responses to needs voiced by students who used the first edition. There are major revisions in some chapters, particularly Chapter 3, where we no longer introduce Piagetian psychology as if to a beginner. The emphasis is now on the application of research and theory in cognitive developmental psychology to instruction in mathematics. Next, we consider recent research on the learning of mathematics by secondary school students and also introduce the reader to individual differences, under the categories of cognitive style, information processing, gender differences, and the talented and the slow learner. Chapter 9 has also been substantively rewritten and now provides a more extensive base on historical perspectives that affect instruction and curriculum in mathematics, as well as a look at the future implications of issues such as the integration of information technology into the classroom. Throughout the text, attention has been given to the integration of calculators and microcomputers into the mathematics classroom. All other chapters have been updated.

Each chapter begins with an introductory section written with the college student in mind; we later characterize these sections as *advance organizers*. A few chapters have a section on definitions, and all have an introductory activity that we have found indispensable to learning. Some are paper-and-pencil activities, but most are laboratory or interview tasks. Each chapter concludes with a summary and self-check, a set of simulation or practice activities and a collection of annotated readings.

There are several possible orderings of chapters that might be used by an instructor of a mathematics methods class. We have found that Chapter 1 is an ideal place to start since college students relate to the material in that chapter. Since our students concurrently spend part of their time in a clinical experience, we like to move rather quickly to Chapter 3. Because they are observing and working with adolescents, they have a base of data to reflect on as they study Chapter 3. Chapters 7 and 8 include sections on short- and long- range planning and testing. We have found that it makes little sense to study the later sections until our students need to work with long-range activities. Chapter 10 and parts of 11 can be threaded throughout the course. In fact, we assign the Resource File Module in the Appendix on the first day of class and check parts of it at various times throughout the course. When we use the text as a source in a graduate course, we use other orderings of chapters to fit the needs and the expertise of the audience.

We appreciate the helpful comments and suggestions of colleagues who read some of the revised chapters, Ms. Constance Feldt, Dr. Vicky Kouba and Dr. Jan McDonald. We are especially grateful to Mrs. Norah Davis who mastered the MAC to type first drafts of the text in a short time period, to Mrs. Carolyn Richbart who began the work on the index for us, and to Ms. Constance Feldt who completed work on the index so that we could make our deadlines.

Delmar, NY   M. A. Farrell
July, 1988   W. A. Farmer

CHAPTER ONE

MODES OF INSTRUCTION

Instructional Moves by the Teacher

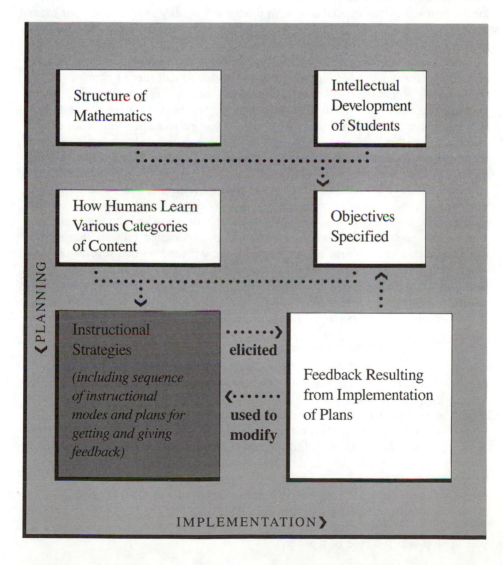

As explained in the introduction, we view teaching as a complex problem-solving task, one whose components are highlighted by the instructional model on the title page of this chapter. Note the shaded box that illustrates the place where *Modes of Instruction* fit into the total picture. Why begin with components of instructional strategies? Certainly there are several logical alternatives. Why was the decision made to begin with modes?

We begin with modes of instruction because we believe it is the most psychologically sound beginning point for students who are preparing to teach. It is an area where you have a wealth of concrete experiences upon which to draw. Your teachers have used some or all of these modes since the day you entered kindergarten, so your experiences with modes are readily available in your memory and will enable you to interact with the information and ideas to be presented in this section.

Before proceeding any further, let's be sure the phrase *Modes of Instruction* communicates the idea intended. Some prefer to call these behaviors *Teaching/Learning Activities*. Either term means essentially the same thing. Just ask yourself the question, "What kinds of things do teachers do in an effort to help students learn the content of mathematics?" If you reflect upon your own experiences as a student, certain things are sure to come to mind. Most students recall lecture, discussion, homework, and question/answer. Some of you will also recall hands-on activities (maybe your teachers called this laboratory work), demonstrations, audiovisual aids, or computer-related activities. If you came up with an assortment similar to these, we are off to a good start. Now consider whether you, each of your classmates, and your instructor all mean exactly the same time when using each of these labels or terms. Our experience tells us that such is not the case. This is not at all surprising, since we tend to use several of these terms very loosely in our speech and since most textbooks do little better on this point. If we are to communicate ideas effectively, we must first give operational definitions of the key terms to be used.

Let's begin with an operational definition of *operational*. A definition is of the *operational* type if *it refers to key observable traits and, wherever possible and appropriate, how these are measured*. Unlike most dictionary definitions, our definition does not describe the new entity in terms of abstractions (nonobservables). Do you have the idea? The only way to be sure is to try to use that idea in appropriate ways.

You will get feedback as you interact with the main part of the next section, where we consider the most commonly employed modes, their operational definitions, their uses in instruction, and their potential for getting and giving feedback (knowledge of results). We begin with the lecture mode because it is the one that college students have experienced most frequently. The sequence of others that follow was selected according to a preconceived pattern of verbal interaction. See if you can detect this pattern as you read. Above all else, be sure to interact with the material, as rote memorization will be of no use when the time comes for you to step into the role of teacher.

1.1 DEFINITIONS OF COMMON INSTRUCTIONAL MODES

Lecture   During most of the time you spent in college classrooms you were expected to sit quietly and listen to the professor talk about the subject matter. Often you were expected to take notes, and sometimes your teacher used the chalkboard. Frequently at the end of such a class period the teacher asked, "Any questions?" Questions from students may not have been either expected or desired, and such questions were seldom forthcoming. What, then, is a brief operational definition for *lecture*? *The teacher talks, perhaps with some use of the chalkboard, while the students listen quietly and sometimes take notes.* Check this definition to be sure that it communicates meaning in terms of observables. Can you tell one when you see one? If so, this is a bona fide operational definition. Note that no time requirement is made in the definition, so this mode may occur for either an entire class period (as is frequently the case in college classes) or for smaller segments of a class session (as is more frequently the case in secondary schools).

Question/Answer   This is one of the most common modes employed at the secondary school level. Novice observers are usually amazed at the results of keeping tally of the number of questions asked by the teacher during a 40-minute class period. The total often exceeds one hundred and not infrequently approaches two hundred! The pattern typically begins with the teacher asking a question and then recognizing one student, who answers. Next the teacher reacts verbally in some way to the student's response and asks a questions of another student, who then responds. Again the teacher handles the student's response and poses another question, which in turn is answered by a third student, and so the pattern continues. As in the lecture mode, the teacher may write some things on the chalkboard and the students may take notes. Thus the operational definition for *question/answer* is: *The teacher asks a question; one student answers; the teacher reacts and asks another question which is responded to by a second student, and so forth.* Again note that the definition does *not* specify a time limit, so the mode may continue for all or any part of a class period.

Discussion   This term is used very loosely by many teachers, students, and textbook writers. We have all observed instructors who began class with "Today we are going to discuss the very important applications of _____ " and who then followed with 40 minutes of lecture on the topic. Textbook writers are also prone to make the same error, as evidenced by a host of chapters that begin with something akin to "The following topics will be *discussed*."

Throughout this book we use the term *discuss* to refer to *planned student-to-student talk with occasional verbal intervention by the teacher*. Think back to the last time you were involved in a buzz-group session. Your most recent participation was probably in the dorm rather than in a college classroom, for this mode is rarely employed by college teachers. If your last experience was an actual discussion, most or all of the participants contributed information and ideas *without* filtering them through the leader of the group every time. Have you caught the essential difference that discriminates this mode from the question/answer mode? If so, you are doing well. If you are not so sure, talk it out with a few classmates and refer back to the operational definition. Note that no time limit is implied, nor is the size of the group narrowly prescribed. However, the entire class is rarely involved as a single discussion group. On the other hand, one person can hardly constitute a discussion group. A group consisting of five to seven participants is the size recommended as optimal for effective discussion. Have you caught on to the pattern we had in mind as we sequenced the presentation of the three modes defined (not *discussed*) thus far? If so, try to verify your conjecture as you read about the next three modes.

Demonstration   The literal meaning of this word is "show" and that meaning pinpoints the operational definition of the mode. Typically, but not always, *the teacher shows something, such as a model of a geodesic dome, or how a set of gears moves, while students watch.* In some instances, one student may do the showing while other students and the teacher watch. You may be thinking at this point that usually some talking (such as lecture or question/answer) is used with a demonstration. Some talking usually is involved, but silent demonstrations can be used very effectively. What do we call a situation where demonstration, short lecture, and question/answer are used in an integrated fashion? This is one example of an *instructional strategy*.

We consider the design of strategies in Chapter 7. If you reflect on your own experiences as a secondary school student, you are probably about to conclude that, with rare exceptions, modes are usually combined into a strategy. This is good thinking. For now, however, let's focus attention on the individual modes, since this background will serve you well when all other prerequisites to strategy design have been mastered.

Laboratory   This mode does not refer to a place nor a special class period in the weekly schedule, but to an activity. This activity may occur in a regular classroom, a specially equipped room, at home, or outdoors. The key idea is that *students manipulate concrete objects or equipment under the direction of the teacher*. Junior high students may be taking samples of ten M and M's from a large bag and counting the number of brown, green, yellow and red candies in each sample as part of a probability lab. Geometry students may be engaged in a paper-folding task and asked to observe and write down the names and properties of all the shapes and special line segments they think are formed. This is in clear contrast to demonstrations in which only one individual does the manipulation and in which all others watch. (The word *manipulation* is frequently used by mathematics teachers to mean "calculation." This is not the sense in which we refer to manipulative tasks.)

The three modes that follow include other activities used by teachers to help students achieve objectives. While these are not completely distinct from the five presented earlier, they have their own advantages and limitations that need to be emphasized.

Individual student projects   At first glance, this may look like the laboratory mode. The critical differences are that here the *students are all doing different manipulative activities or varied library research, or different problem-solving tasks on an individual basis.* Note that all students are not doing the same things in the same place at the same time as so often is the case in the laboratory mode. Some student choice of activity is also implied by this mode.

By now you have probably discerned the pattern of sequencing of modes presented thus far. We began with the "talking" modes, placing the most teacher-dominated mode first (lecture) and moving through to the least teacher-dominated mode (discussion). Next we considered the "showing" and "doing" modes, again moving from the most to the least teacher-dominated mode.

Audiovisual and technological activities (ATAs)   Actually all modes involve hearing, seeing, or both and a few involve touching in combination with seeing, and sometimes hearing. However, this mode typically means that *students look at, listen to, or touch specific kinds of equipment. Equipment typically known as audiovisual includes projectors for films, film strips or loop films, video cassette recorders, audio tape recorders and compact disc recorders, and overhead or opaque projectors. Equipment that is usually classified as technological includes mini, micro, and mainframe computers and programmable and non-programmable calculators.* It is easy to think of examples of this mode being used as an integral part of another mode, rather than in addition to it. For example, an algebra teacher may demonstrate the effect of changing the value of a on the graph of the equation $y = ax^2 + bx + c$ by showing successive graphs on the screen of a computer.

Supervised practice   This mode involves having *students try to perform some practice tasks, often at their seats or at the chalkboard, while the teacher observes their progress and gives help and reinforcement as needed.* Like all other modes, this one has an important role to play in effective and efficient strategy design. However, novices often either overlook its importance or carry out this mode in an ineffective manner. We outline more about this later, but think about the relationship of this mode to the mode that follows. Perhaps you can get the jump on us.

Homework   "Boo, Hiss!" is the typical student reaction to homework. Could this be due in part to the narrow definition given to the mode by typical teacher use? Let's not limit the possibilities to the odd-numbered problems for tonight. (Guess what is coming for tomorrow night?) We prefer to define the homework mode as *any activity relevant to the achievement of objectives, that students perform outside of the scheduled class sessions.* This definition encompasses such potentially meaningful activities as spending 15 minutes in the supermarket after school to get data from labels on competing brands of the same product, getting data for growth curves on plants grown over a two-week period, and interviewing a random sample of people to elicit their beliefs on a mathematics-related topic. It also leaves room for doing the even-numbered problems from a textbook when this makes pedagogical sense.

Although we might try to identify and operationally define a few more modes, the nine defined thus far are the common ones and will suffice for our purposes. By now if you have been interacting with the text, you should be anxious to get on to meatier questions of what each mode has to offer as input into strategy design and what the potential of each mode is for getting feedback (finding out how well each student is doing) and giving feedback (letting students know how they are progressing).

1.2 INTRODUCTORY ACTIVITY

There's no observation without an observer.

A. With at least one other classmate, observe a junior high or senior high mathematics class. As the class progresses, record data following the format shown in Figure 1.1. Record instances of feedback the teacher got and any reactions by the teacher to that feedback. Be specific—for instance, list the approximate number of hands raised.

Use of the following shorthand will save time:

T: teacher Q/A: question/answer
S(Ss): student (students) Demo: demonstration
HWPM: Homework post-mortem ("going over" last night's homework)

Time	Subject/Grade: **Algebra 2** Names of modes observed	Topic: **Quadratic Function** Samples of feedback observed during the use of each mode
8:10 am to 8:15 am	1. T lectures on relationship between function and relation; sketches examples of function and relation on the board	1. 3 Ss have heads on desk; all others look front, are quiet, and take notes.
8:15 am to 8:20 am	2. T: Q/A on content of lecture	2. 10–12 Ss volunteer and T calls on 4 in front, praises ans., and clarifies.

Fig. 1.1

B. Meet with one or more of your classmates who observed the same lesson. Compare the data collected and check for agreements/disagreements as to the modes observed and the related feedback. Account for any discrepancies in the data that might have resulted from lack of consistency in use of the operational definitions of the modes (consult Section 1.1).

C. Consult with classmates who observed other lessons and look for any common patterns, such as number of changes of modes used within a single class period and amount and kinds of feedback given or received by the teacher. (Note: This activity can be carried out in a live classroom or while viewing a videotape of a class.)

1.3 USES OF MODES

Lecture

This mode provides an opportunity for the teacher to give verbal input at key times during the class period. (Remember, there is no time requirement in the definition of this mode.) Introduction to lessons, summaries of problem-solving strategies, information on the history of mathematics or on applications of some mathematical concept—all of these are important instances of times that the lecture mode might be used effectively. It is assumed that the words of the lecturer convey substantively the same meaning to all of the students. (Reflect on this assumption when you study differences in adolescent reasoning in Chapter 3.) It is also assumed that the students are listening with the intent to comprehend and remember, not just displaying the "lecture syndrome" (eye movements following the teacher, smiles on faces when the teacher tells a joke, and so on). Since it is difficult for most secondary school students to remain passive listeners for long periods of time, the lecturer should either keep it short or be a dynamic lecturer, or both. Few novices, if our experience is any guide, are dynamic lecturers. What has been your personal experience with lectures that extend for long periods of time? How long can you pay rapt attention? Does the lecturer seem to know when you are confused on a point, or does he or she continue to retread the same ground while you are anxious to get on to the next idea? What feedback is available to the lecturer? How can he or she interpret the feedback signs, particuarly if the group is sophisticated in playing the game of school? Further, how do students find out if they are following the thinking of the lecturer? Obviously the feedback-giving and -getting potential of this mode is minimal and, along with the limited attention span problem, it is a strong argument for using lecture selectively and for brief time spans.

Question/Answer

Many novices, and some veterans, believe question/answer is a mode that enables the teacher to find out who knows what. Is it? Only one student responds at a time, a sample of only one out of twenty-five or thirty! So much for feedback potential—better than lecture, but still extremely limited. Furthermore, many a novice has been misled by apparently positive feedback from one segment of a diverse group of students in a question/answer sequence. Quiz scores subsequently reveal far less success with the topic. Consider the following illustration: Jack answered question 1; Mary, question 2; Sam, question 3; and so on. That's right! Mary and Sam may have been cued in by Jack's response, but may be unable to *begin* the problem. Other students may be unable to *complete* the solution. What, then, is the *forte* of question/answer?

The question/answer mode is extremely valuable as a way to guide developmental thinking, to stimulate creative problem solving, to initiate discussions, and to stimulate quick recall of prerequisites needed for the day's lesson. Indeed, the question/answer mode can be used effectively in combination with every other mode. The kind of question asked, the preamble to the question posed, and the variety of ways used to encourage and accept responses are all skills that make the difference between thoughtful interaction and humdrum, dull sequences.

There are three major components of the question/answer mode that need special attention: the questions themselves, the ways in which student responses can be obtained, and the ways in which student responses can be handled. Beginners can get disastrous results from trying to use the question/answer mode when a complex question is dropped on the class like a bomb. Lack of student response may also be a function of the teacher's inability to handle earlier responses. Ms. Goldberg complains that only Bill and Sara ever respond to her questions, but in Mr. Boswell's class, most or all members of the class mumble something whenever he asks a question. What can be done to help either of these teachers? A lot! But let's start at the beginning.

The following do's and don'ts are intended for the teacher whose difficulty seems to be related to the nature of the questions asked.

The question—do's and don'ts

1. Write down the major question in a developmental sequence and analyze the possible responses ahead of time.

2. Precede a question/answer by a brief lecture or demonstration designed to set the stage for the sequence.

3. Do not ask frequent yes-no questions or fill-in-the-blank questions, such as "Does anyone know the answer to number five?" (Students who answer "No" or "Yes" have answered the question.)

4. Increase the number of questions requiring a phrase or a sentence in response.

5. Do not try to elicit developmental thinking by the all-encompassing "What about" questions, such as "What about the circle?"

6. Use a variety of opening question-phrases, such as "How? Who knows? When is ... true? What is ... ? What seems to be ... ? Why?

Notice that suggestion 1 refers to your planning, as does suggestion 2; but all the other suggestions require some on-the-spot analysis. An observer can help gather appropriate data; so can a tape recorder. In either case, a teacher can begin to alter his or her questioning skills over time. Why is suggestion 2 made? As you read the section on the discussion mode, look for a parallel guideline. Try to imagine a classroom where the teacher regularly disregards suggestion 3. What kind of class response is likely to occur? If you conjectured that something like mumbled responses (or shouted responses) from a few would probably happen, then your conjecture matches reality. Now suggestion 3 takes on more significance, for even the newest student of teaching realizes that if wide and specific interaction does not occur, the teacher has no way of immediately assessing the extent to which the question/answer mode guided developmental thinking.

How do you get specific and wide interaction from students? The second set of suggestions deals with diverse ways of *getting* responses from students (the second critical ingredient in an effective question/answer mode); none should be used exclusively.

Getting responses from students—do's and don'ts

1. Pose the question *before* you call on someone.

2. Do not call on students in the same area of the room for all answers.

3. Help shyer or slower students gain confidence by asking them easy questions at first.

4. Don't bore bright students by always asking them recall questions.

5. Do not direct a series of quick questions to students row by row (or in any clear pattern).

6. Do not call *only* on students who volunteer.

7. Wait at least three to five seconds prior to accepting responses to high-level questions. Inform the students that you are going to do this.

8. Tell the students that there is no penalty for incorrect or partially correct answers. Tell them it is not a quiz, but a learning experience.

Several of the suggestions are again a part of your planning. Suggestions 3, 4, and 7 refer to easy and higher level questions. A careful analysis of the mathematics content *before* you begin the class will help you to plan several high-level questions. For example, in a lesson on the trigonometric functions, an algebra teacher might ask students to describe how to use a translation to map the sine curve onto the cosine curve. Depending on the quality of the answer, backup questions on the justification for the described procedure could help students to go beyond memorized routines. Beginning teachers have found that suggestion 7 is difficult to implement until they have established some control in the classroom. However, researchers (Budd-Rowe, 1978) have found that its effective use with a thought-provoking question has turned many a passive class into one which volunteers. One way to introduce a class to this questioning technique might be to say something like: "I am going to ask you a thought question and I won't take any answers for five seconds. Here's the question ... "

Since the teacher wants to optimize both the number and the quality of responses from the students, many of these suggestions must be used in combination with one another. Occasionally, the teacher should violate one of the guidelines to achieve an optimum result. For example, Mrs. Frost cannot implement suggestion 1 from the responses list. As soon as the end of her question is heard and before she is able to call on a student, her seventh-grade class shouts out responses. What should Mrs. Frost do? See if the next set of suggestions helps.

These suggestions deal with the third component of the question/answer mode—handling student responses.

Handling student responses—do's and don'ts

1. Ask another student to agree or disagree and give his or her reasons for doing so.

2. Take a "straw vote" ("Let me see the hands of those who agree with Jack, those who disagree, those who aren't sure."), and follow up with a request for justification.

3. Frown a bit and ask, "Are you sure?"

4. Ask other students to add to the answer of the first student.

5. Ask a student to explain how he or she arrived at the solution.

6. Ask if there is another way to solve the problem.

7. Do not accept *mixed* chorus responses.

8. If a student cannot answer a difficult question, ask a contingency (backup) question on a lower level.

9. Refuse to accept responses that are not audible to all students.

10. Give praise for partially correct responses to complicated questions.

Mrs. Frost, who has to deal with a "too eager" class, may now use one of these suggestions to direct attention to one student. One clear way to convince a class of the limitations of the mixed chorus response is to use suggestion 1 from this set of guidelines. That student's confusion as to what he or she is asked to defend is more convincing than a hundred reminders from the teacher. These suggestions must be used with some care and in combination with those listed earlier.

In addition to all the concerns noted so far, the physical location of the teacher can greatly influence the nature of the verbal interaction. Look at Figure 1.2 and analyze the flow of verbal interaction. Each number represents either a question or an answer, and it is clear that a large number of these occurred, but where? Why? Where was the teacher? (*T* designates teacher location.)

```
┌─────────────────────────────────────────┐
│                Chalkboard                │
└─────────────────────────────────────────┘
                     T
┌─────────────────────────────────────────┐
│  1,  3,  5,  7, 10, 13, 15, 17, 19, 21, 23, 25,  │
│ 27, 29, 31, 33, 35, 38, 41, 43, 45, 47, 49, 51,  │
│ 53, 55, 57, 59, 61, 63, 65, 67, 69, 71, 73, 76, 79 │
└─────────────────────────────────────────┘
```

	66	4, 64, 68	18, 34, 52, 54, 56	14, 32, 42, 44, 46, 48, 50
		24, 28	8, 11, 58, 70	9, 12, 26, 37, 40
2		30	36, 39, 74, 78	16, 60, 62, 75, 77
	6		72	20, 22

20 students present

Fig. 1.2 Flow of verbal interaction.

Now analyze Figure 1.3.

There is still only one teacher in the classroom, but that teacher has moved to four different locations during the sequence. Why? Compare the sequence of numerals in the box designated as teacher responses in each case. A different pattern of verbal interaction is occurring in these two classrooms.

To what extent can the teacher control this pattern so that the broadest possible feedback sampling can occur? The teacher who stands next to a timid, soft-spoken student can encourage a louder voice by moving away from the speaker. The right-handed teacher may find that he or she frequently calls on students to the left of the teacher's desk. Your position is important and must be consciously varied to achieve optimum results.

Discussion

As noted earlier, most activities labeled "discussion" are really lecture or question/answer. In a discussion, as defined here, the teacher usually initiates the interaction, but is only sporadically heard from after that. What, then, is the first essential ingredient for a discussion? There must be a topic—a question, a problem, or a situation in which the students can share ideas and compare or contrast views. What are some suitable topics or situations that have been used effectively by mathematics teachers in initiating discussion?

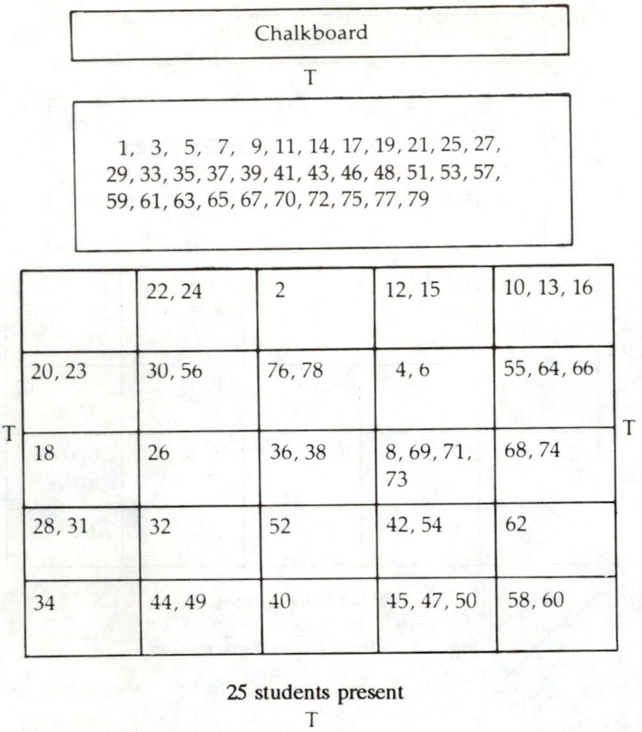
Chalkboard
T
1, 3, 5, 7, 9, 11, 14, 17, 19, 21, 25, 27,
29, 33, 35, 37, 39, 41, 43, 46, 48, 51, 53, 57,
59, 61, 63, 65, 67, 70, 72, 75, 77, 79
22, 24
2
12, 15
10, 13, 16
20, 23
30, 56
76, 78
4, 6
55, 64, 66
T
18
26
36, 38
8, 69, 71, 73
68, 74
T
28, 31
32
52
42, 54
62
34
44, 49
40
45, 47, 50
58, 60
25 students present
T

Fig. 1.3 Flow of verbal interaction.

Class	*Topic*	*Procedure/Purposes*
1. Geometry	Original proofs	Small groups seek varied methods of proof, contrast efficiency, difficulty level of each, advantages of one over the other.
2. General math	Traffic pattern in school corridor	Groups to discuss ways of reducing congestion in school corridors by establishing new traffic pattern; must design plan to get all needed data.
3. Any subject level	Test post-mortem when results range from very good to poor	Each group to be arranged by the teacher to reflect the range. Group to discuss all problems on which any member needs help, consider reasons behind errors, pinpoint strategies for correct solutions.

4. Math lab   Results of   Groups to compare results,
                 individual or   conjecture possible generalizations
                 group lab work   based on lab work, pose questions,
                                         analyze reasons for varied results.

Obviously, a second major ingredient for a successful discussion is appropriate student prerequisites. In the first illustration, students who know only enough geometry to obtain one solution to the proof-problems will have nothing to compare. If all or most students in the class are at this level, the "discussion" will degenerate into a practice session. For a similar reason the teacher must structure heterogeneous groups in the third illustration just given. If all the failing students are in the same group, you have the blind leading the blind. Of course, a teacher who attempts a discussion on traffic congestion models before the students have learned simple sampling procedures and ways to collect and relate data on number of students and size of corridor is asking for a shared ignorance pool on the topic. (You may have experienced such ignorance pools in many out-of-school discussions.) Even given all of the student prerequisites mentioned with respect to the traffic pattern problem, the wise teacher would also prepare the way for an effective discussion by an appropriate pre-class assignment. In this case, the students might be asked to observe the corridors at least two days before the planned discussion so that they can identify two of the areas which are most crowded in the class passing times. Such an assignment "sets up" the class with a common area of concern, on which each has gathered some recent observational data. Some discussions need this kind of pre-class assignment where a reading, the completion of a set of structured exercises, or the collection of survey data provides everyone with a common set of initial information to serve as a basis for discussion questions.

The necessary ingredients for the effective use of the discussion mode, then, are the suitability of the topic, the students' grasp of needed prerequisites, and pre-class assignments, when needed. But even with the presence of all of these, many discussions slump because the teacher ignores a simple structural ingredient. Compare Figures 1.2 and 1.3 with Figure 1.4. Students who see only their nearest neighbors and only the backs of heads are not likely to engage in useful interaction. Seating arrangement becomes of prime importance. Figure 1.4 offers two possible seating arrangements for the discussion mode. A teacher who makes considerable use of discussion may want to explore alternative seating arrangements *within* subgroups. Some guidelines that make a lot of sense have been verified by practitioners in the area of group interaction (Kell & Corts, 1980).

1.   Communication tends to flow *across* a circle, not around it. Remember that a massive amount of communication is nonverbal and we can see more clearly the facial expressions of the person across the circle or table.

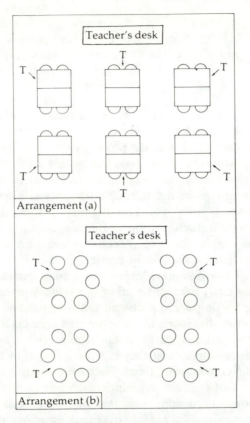

Fig. 1.4 Arrangements for discussion.

2. A corollary to the above guideline is the principle that communication is maximized between students who sit opposite each other and lessened between those who sit side by side.

Although it is probably impractical to assign each student to a seat, you can use the above guidelines to encourage a shy student to participate, or to discourage an overtalkative student from monopolizing the group.

Finally, where should you be during the discussion? To find the answer to that question, you must first answer several more important questions. What can a teacher find out *during* a discussion? How can a teacher contribute without altering the mode to Q/A?

If you've prepared the class for the discussion, carefully selected a suitable topic, structured the groups and seating arrangements thoughtfully, and clearly given all instructions *before* the students move into their groups, then your role in the first few minutes is that of a helpful overseer. You are making sure that all students follow those initial instructions by making a quick tour around the perimeter of the groups.

What next? If you're only interested in the end product of the discussion, you can hire a babysitter and take some time off. Be careful! You may scoff at that idea, and yet some teachers reward only the end product and neither attend to, nor reward, the steps students take to get to that end. You want to get feedback on each group's work and on as many individuals' work as possible. Who is contributing? How? Who agrees, disagrees? You must systematically circulate and look and listen carefully to get this kind of feedback. Furthermore, if students are to believe that their efforts in the discussion are worthwhile, you must give verbal and nonverbal praise to individuals and groups for such things as creativity, thoughtfulness, intelligent skepticism, and efficiency. However, you must be cautious that your praise isn't misconstrued as a closing off of discussion, because your other major role is to sustain the discussion by cuing students as to potentially useful avenues by answering some questions and by posing other questions. Take a long careful look at the various positions of the teacher in Figure 1.4 and notice the directions the teacher faces. Why are these directions and positions recommended? In what areas is the teacher never found in these diagrams?

When does a discussion end? When the attention of subgroup members starts wandering, the discussion mode has already continued too long. You should call a halt when all groups have made some inroads on the topic and when sharing of ideas seems desirable. After all the students have responded to the signal to end the discussion, each spokesperson can report on that group's findings. Then students from other groups can be asked to indicate agreements or disagreements. Finally, you can help all to summarize class results.

Notice that the feedback getting and giving of this mode has high potential. You may sample everyone a number of times under optimum conditions. The discussion mode also has been found to be especially effective in promoting the learning of problem solving in mathematics classes (Davidson, 1980). We'll reconsider the unique contribution of this mode and others where students interact with other students in Chapter 3, when we study adolescent reasoning.

Demonstration

Used in combination with lecture, question/answer, or laboratory, this mode can be remarkably effective. The following examples illustrate just a few of the ways in which demonstrations can be used to enhance mathematics instruction. (See Chapters 10 and 11 for many more examples.)

Examples of effective demonstrations

Class (topic)	Demo	Use
1. Math 7 (Symmetry in Living Things)	T cuts grapefruit in half	To show model of radial symmetry

2. Math 8 (Units of Measure)	T holds up can of soup, box of cereal	To get attention on all the diverse units on the labels
3. Geometry (Locus)	T stretches and shrinks shape on large geoboard	To illustrate the paths of moving points
4. Algebra 2 (Conic Sections)	T produces shadow images of a metal ring by tilting the ring between the wall and a powerful bulb	To illustrate the conic sections using a "cone" of light rays

To focus student attention on a demonstration, you must first be sure that the object can be seen. (You'd be surprised at the number of teachers who ignore this "common sense" maxim!) The model or apparatus must be large enough to be visible from the rear, or the teacher must move about the room with a smaller object. White cardboard sheets or the overhead screen can provide an effective backdrop. A calculator designed for use on the overhead projector may be used to demonstrate proper keystroke sequence by a student who has figured out how to raise a base to a power. A model of the hyperboloid or a dissectable cone can be highlighted by placing either of them on the stage of the overhead. The overhead light in a darkened room shines on the object as in a theater. What are the students to see? Do they know where to look and why? If not, the effectiveness of the demonstration will suffer.

Although demonstration is often used simultaneously with other modes, a silent demonstration can be very effective. Such a demonstration might be used either to set the stage for, or to further develop, a topic. One teacher had a computer demonstration of continuously changing designs showing on a large screen throughout the first half of the class, while the students were engaged in other activities. By the time she specifically directed their attention to the screen, all were intrigued by the patterns they had seen and many had conjectures about the mathematical transformations which were being used.

What is the potential of this mode for feedback getting? Almost zero. Oh, experienced teachers learn to "read" the nonverbal signs—the alert gazes, the "aha" expressions, the scowl, or the worried look. Unfortunately, experienced students have also learned to play the game of school and many manage to put on the face the teacher wants to see.

Laboratory

Since the students are manipulating equipment or material in this mode, they are doing so to collect data. Therefore, you might employ this mode to help students reach a generalization, test a conjecture, observe the application of a rule, or learn and practice a psychomotor skill. Some examples follow.

Examples of effective laboratory exercises

Class	Materials	Activity	Purpose
1. Math 7	String, meter stick, cans of different shapes and sizes	Students measure circumference and diameter, record data, and calculate C/d.	To obtain the generalization that the calculated C/d appears to be a little more than 3.14.
2. Algebra 2	Wax paper with a fixed line drawn and a point placed above it	Students fold the paper so that the point coincides with the line; they obtain a large number of folds.	To observe the evolving parabolic shape and construct the definition of parabola.
3. Geometry	Geoboards, rubber bands	Students place two different trapezoids with diagnals on the geoboard and find the areas of the 8 triangles formed in each case; compare results.	To generalize about the equal areas and to use geoboard rules to verify the conjectures. (A geoboard *proof* can follow if geoboard axioms are identified.)
4. Math 7, 8	Poker chips	Students move chips to form rectangular and, where possible, square shapes using $1, 2, 3, 4, 5, 6, \ldots, 24$ chips; they record numbers which can be represented by squares, by only a row of chips, or by one or more rectangular shapes.	To form concept of prime and composite numbers, of perfect squares.

How does a teacher implement the laboratory mode? Perhaps more than any other mode, this one requires careful preparation of materials, instruction in safety precautions, organization of equipment, and possible reorganization of the usual physical facilities in the classroom. Directions need to be pre-planned. Some teachers write directions on an overhead projection sheet so that all students can refer to them repeatedly. If the laboratory activity involves small groups, the teacher must decide on the nature of the groups. Again, it may save time to list group names and locations on an acetate sheet or the chalkboard. Don't forget the need to survive! If Marc and Tom fight continually, you're asking for trouble if you place them in the same group.

Is grouping a necessary part of the laboratory mode? In example 1, group work may be essential, with members of the group alternating the jobs of measuring, checking, recording and calculating. In example 2, on the other hand, each student needs to work independently on the paper-folding task and there is no real advantage in grouping. In either case, beware of being hypnotized by eager, active students who never attain the purpose of the lab because you forgot the most important ingredient of all. You must tell the students where they're headed, emphasize the need to look for patterns (as in example 3), insist on careful recording of data, and structure the follow-up to the lab so that the different observations can be shared. Here is a place where developmental questioning combined with lab can be used with profit.

What feedback potential is possible with this mode? Little or none if you are ill-prepared, must repeat directions often, or must continue to carry materials to different students. However, if you have done your job well, the students should be busy with the materials in a matter of minutes. Now you can move systematically to each individual or group, listening, asking questions, and observing the way in which the students are proceeding. In addition, you have unlimited opportunities to praise, to cue, and to correct intermediate errors.

Why use the lab mode with bright, older students who are well motivated? Isn't it a waste of time? Recall your own experience in recent college classes when a new concept was defined for you. Did you always grasp the concept? Have you sometimes been helped to understand the concept by a concrete example furnished by a peer? If so, then you already can appreciate the potential importance of the lab mode for all students. Indeed, it has been found that even the brightest students in advanced classes profit from well-designed hands-on activities introducing them to an unfamiliar, complex concept. There is much more about this in Chapter 3.

Some references to help the mathematics teacher design interesting laboratory activities will be found in Chapter 11, and the emphasis on the use of the laboratory mode in various curriculum projects is described in Chapter 9.

Individual Student Projects

Projects can be initiated by students or by the teacher. Projects may be used to explore some topic in depth, to introduce relevant applications of the mathematics topic being studied, or to investigate the historical background of the topic. Project work may occur during the class period, but most of the project work is usually carried on outside of class time. Student reports may be shared with the class, and student productions can be displayed.

Here are two examples of project directions used in senior high school mathematics classes.

1. *Math 10 Project*   *Date*: February 8

   A. Choose one of the following topics:
   Linkages; Space-filling; Curve stitching; Polyhedral decorations

   B. Design an original model. Check out the mathematics of your design with the teacher. Then build a durable, attractive model and be prepared to explain its properties to the class.

   C. Submit your plan on a five-by-eight-inch index card by February 15. Completed projects are due February 22, and class time will be reserved for reports the week of February 25.

2. *Math 12 Project*   *Date*: October 1

   A. Choose *one* of the following topics:
   Algebraic Balancing of Chemical Equations
   Algebraic Solution to Electrical Circuits
   Minimal Surface Area Experiments with Soap Films
   Numerology
   Ciphers, Codes, and the Way They Are Broken
   Mathematical Aspects of Population Growth
   Statistical Study of Finger Length Variation in Adolescent Hands
   Mathematics in Sound and Music
   Function Before Fashion—Mathematical Designs
   Timetables, Calendars, and Clocks
   Analysis of Hurricane Paths

   B. Research the topic and prepare an 8- to 10-page typed paper on the results of your findings. Include a bibliography of at least four references. You may *not* include an encyclopedia as one of the four sources! Be sure to cite these references in the format given in class.

   C. Submit a one-page outline by October 15.

   D. Completed papers are due November 1.

If students complain of the extra work involved in a project, then the teacher has goofed somewhere along the line. The project should be threaded into the coursework. It is up to the teacher to design assignments and daily work so that students see this mode as an alternative, but different, way of learning relevant aspects of mathematics. The students soon learn that the teacher doesn't mean what is said if no class time is reserved for reports, or if the end of the project means little more than a grade in the teacher's record book.

Because much of the project work is completed outside of class time, the feedback potential prior to project completion is limited. However, the teacher is able to gather feedback on a host of student capabilities upon completion of the project, and can give feedback in the form of written or oral comments. Project work affords an excellent opportunity to encourage students to give feedback to each other—formally during oral reports, and informally as they inspect posted projects.

The first time students hand in completed projects, the teacher is faced with a new problem. How will the projects be graded? Twenty-four reports, models or posters may exhibit considerable artistic talent, or none at all. The teacher who hasn't thought about the evaluation aspect of the project work may be faced with a barrage of student criticism when the graded material is returned to the class. "This isn't art class!" "How did you judge the projects?" "What's my grade?" These are not easy questions to answer, but you must answer them if you assign projects. See if the material on all aspects of evaluation found later in this book meshes with your present response.

Audiovisual and Technological Activities (ATAs)

Lights out! Is it a signal for paper-wad battles or siesta time? All too often, even in an interested class, ATA time means neither the battle nor the nap but an extraneous short feature that is clever but hasn't much to do with the topic. Again teacher preparation is critical if this mode is to help students learn.

There are four major areas of preparation in the use of ATAs: (1) use of the equipment; (2) quality and suitability of the tape, slide, film, filmstrip, computer program, transparency, or video; (3) preparation of the students; and (4) followup and integration of the ATA into other modes.

The suggestions listed below may seem to include the obvious, but our experience in the classrooms of novice teachers convinces us that the obvious is often overlooked.

ATAs—do's and don'ts

1. Use of the equipment:
   a) Check out your school's rules and regulations and follow them. (Some schools have student operators of equipment.)
   b) Dry-run equipment you will operate *in the classroom in which it will be used*. Check visibility and/or audibility from various areas of the room.
   c) When the equipment consists of multiple microcomputers and software to be used by students, there is a need not only to dry-run the equipment, but to teach the students to observe certain routines and precautions. The "Suggestions for Further Study" section at the end of this chapter includes a recent text that provides information on some of these cautions. However, given the constantly changing state of technology, we

recommend that teachers take one of the many courses on the incorporation of the microcomputer into mathematics instruction and follow that up by reading of relevant articles in professional journals (see Chapter 11).

d) If your school does not provide calculators for each of your students, you will need to check on whether the students own calculators and, if so, whether the calculators have some important differences in the way they operate. This kind of "dry-run" could be accomplished by asking students, in a class or as a homework assignment, to perform certain keystroke sequences and record the results. For example, does the calculator handle order of operations $(5 + 3 \times 7)$ correctly if the numbers are entered from left to right? See the "Suggestions for Further Study" section for a source on calculator use in the mathematics classroom.

2. Quality and suitability of the materials:

a) Review all material you hope to use and *do not* use material of poor quality or limited applicability, even if last year's teacher did order it.

b) Be a ruler of, not a slave to, equipment and materials! If parts of a computer program are excellent for your purposes, run only those parts. (Be sure that you have keyboard control over such programs.) If you wonder how the students would have considered a question heard on a film before they hear the answer, stop the film, engage in Q/A, then start the film, and let it provide the reinforcement. The possibilities are unlimited.

3. Preparation of the students:

a) Provide an introduction and an overview. Let the students know where and how this ATA contributes to the topic being studied.

b) Explain to the students their responsibilities. Will you ask questions during, and/or after, the viewing/listening? Should they take notes? If so, make sure they can see. (Obvious, isn't it? But how many pitchblack classes have you sat in and been expected to take notes?)

4. Follow-up and integration of ATA mode:

a) Plan alternative ways of combining this mode with others to get feedback, to give feedback, and to promote attention to the task. One route, the interspersing of Q/A with the ATA, was alluded to in 2b. Another effective route is to prepare an outline with questions or problems to be responded to either during the viewing/listening or after, or both. Hand this outline to the students prior to the viewing/listening.

b) Keep the particular ATA material alive after the lights go on. Conduct Q/A or small-group discussions if suitable. Future lessons, assignments, tests, and quizzes should refer to examples from this use of an ATA whenever possible.

It is clear that all this time and effort should not be wasted on worthless materials. But the old saying, "A picture is worth a thousand words," has been proven true too often for you to ignore the immense potential of the ATA mode. However, suppose you have equipment available for either a lab or a demo and have a video cassette or a computer program that portrays the same lesson. On what basis would you make a choice of mode? How would you rate this mode as to feedback potential? Why? Check out your conjectures against the ideas presented in Chapter 2.

Supervised Practice

Practice makes perfect—or does it? Have you ever practiced a golf swing with little improvement in your drive? It's probable that you learned an error to perfection. That's right. Practice must follow *relevant* instruction. You must know how to get feedback on the results of that instruction before and during the *supervised* practice. In fact, the word supervised suggests that intimate tie between this mode and feedback. In Chapter 2, several suggestions aimed at feedback getting and giving are detailed.

Here are a few suggestions that should help you implement supervised practice:

1. Use several short periods rather than one long, marathon session at the end of class. (Of course, this will keep students busy; but there is a more important reason. It has to do with feedback and learning. (Chapters 2, 6, and 7 have more on this.)

2. Sequence and cluster your practice examples so that all or almost all students can begin the work and so that no one is finished before you have some time to make a tour of most of the room. Tour of the room? That's right. "Supervise" does not mean that you monitor the group as if you were the guard in the tower of a prison yard.

3. Follow the arrows in Figure 1.5 *after* all the students are at work. The arrows illustrate the direction you should face. Why is it a good move to turn the body as diagrammed here? Remember, there are 25 students in those seats, and they are not all like thee or me. The tour should be quick and complete. So try not to interrupt the tour to spend time with a single student. If you haven't guessed why, the next chapter offers some reasons.

4. Systematically move into the room to check the work of individual students. But five hands are up! Use verbal and nonverbal signals to let students know you see their hands and will be with them in order. In the meantime, they could try another easier problem or be directed to share their question with another student.

5. Be aware of the entire class even while helping one student. Turn to face most of the class. Bend at the knees, rather than the waist. (It's good for posture, too!) Give a cue, but insist on student responsibility to try. Students soon learn that some teachers will do the work for them if asked.

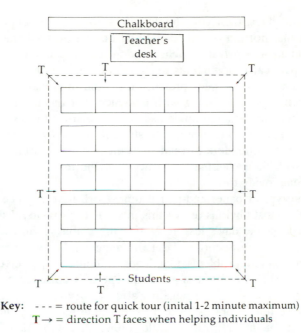

Key: - - - = route for quick tour (inital 1-2 minute maximum)
        T→ = direction T faces when helping individuals

Fig. 1.5 Positioning of teacher during supervised practice.

Supervised practice is such a critical mode that more attention is paid to it in later chapters. For now, we leave you with questions. When should a teacher end a supervised practice session? Do honor-level twelfth-graders need supervised practice?

Homework

Three examples of nonroutine homework assignments were described in Section 1.1. Refer back to these examples and consider how the teacher would make use of the products of the students' efforts during the subsequent day's lesson. You should be able to think of several good possibilities. However, actually making use of the homework is based upon the assumption that nearly all students have done the assigned task. How can the teacher ensure that such will be the case? One often-overlooked technique is to inform students how data from an assignment will be used. This technique encourages students to view homework as an important part of the course rather than simply as "busy work." However, in spite of your best efforts to head-off the problem, you must be prepared to cope with the reality that one or two students will come to class unprepared. What alternatives exist to handle this kind of problem? Shouting, screaming, and idle threats will do nothing to salvage the situation nor will they prevent its recurrence. Positive action, which demonstrates the consequences of students' failure to prepare, is needed. For example, if your plan calls for a question/answer session based on the collected data, then you should refuse to allow unprepared students to participate in that portion of the lesson and emphasize to them the importance of the assignment in a private teacher/student conference after class. However, perhaps your plan calls for students to share and analyze data in small groups. In the case of older students, peer pressure from the unprepared students is often the most effective remedy, along with evidence that the teacher is alert to the problem. Suppose unprepared students begin to disrupt the work of the group? Then, you must step in so that prepared students are not penalized. One alternative is to direct the offenders to read relevant material in other texts instead of participating with their classmates. Notice that the teacher must have alternate class assignments ready to use, as needed.

Does the typical paper-and-pencil homework have a place in instruction? Yes. In fact, the most obvious use of this mode is to provide *relevant* practice on skills introduced in the day's lesson. Notice the emphasis on the word *relevant*. Recall the statement in Section 1.1 on the danger inherent in routine selection of the even-numbered problems that leads students to perceive homework as mindless practice. But caution is advised! There is considerable evidence that practice has no effect—or even negative effects—beyond a certain point. When students perceive homework as a way to keep them busy, they tune out. The key to this is to err on the side of too little, rather than too much, of this kind of homework. Choose only a few exercises or activities, and make sure the ones you choose make sense to the students.

Another sure way to turn off the class is to use homework as a punishment. If your class has already learned to associate homework with punishment, you will need to be particularly thoughtful about your use of this mode. Resource books are filled with appropriate possibilities: open-ended questions, practice in coded or puzzle form, take-home labs. See Chapter 11 for specific references.

A less often used, but effective, approach to get the most out of relevant paper-and-pencil exercises is to build the foundation of tomorrow's lesson into today's homework. For example, a carefully structured sequence of quadratic equations could be assigned to give practice in use of the quadratic formula. Then if the roots range from real, rational roots to imaginary roots, the students can be asked to look for a pattern relating the kind of roots to the value of the expression $b^2 - 4ac$. The teacher now has an entrée to the topic: the nature of the discriminant. A teacher who comprehends and analyzes subject matter is at a distinct advantage in designing such assignments.

The "what" of homework is crucial; the "how" is equally important. When possible, let students begin work on exercises in class, and *don't call it homework*! The alert student often has his or her own definition of homework, and will tell you that it is to be done at home. There are a variety of reasons for allowing students to start such work in class. One of these has to do with feedback. By now you probably have some idea what that is. Think of some other advantages of an early start.

"How" also refers to the post-mortem procedure (the day after). Will you collect the homework every day in every class? Why? When? Will you take class time to check on the results of the class work? How? When? The answers depend to an extent on your need to get and give immediate feedback to the class. There are some specific post-mortem procedures suggested in Chapter 2, but two rules of thumb are basic. First, don't do the homework for the students. Second, don't ignore the homework. If it can be ignored, it wasn't worth doing.

You've heard the expression, "Different strokes for different folks." Can you think of any implications of this saying for use of the homework mode? If not, you are typical of most people with long careers as students who have seldom, if ever, experienced differentiated assignments. Do those students who whiz through five typical application problems at the end of today's lesson need to do more of the same for homework? Then, too, consider that small group of students who could solve none of the problems by the end of the lesson. Diverse feedback of this kind is a clue that different homework assignments need to be designed and matched to various student needs. Think of other situation where it makes maximum instructional sense to ask that different students pursue varied tasks as homework.

As is the case with all instructional modes, effective and efficient use of homework requires careful consideration of alternatives and thoughtful planning by the teacher. *Effective* and *efficient* are key ideas you will find emphasized throughout this text. One of the greatest rewards of teaching is evidence of student learning as a result of teacher attention to these ideas.

1.4 SUMMARY AND SELF-CHECK

Where have we been and where are we going? We began with the consideration of a model of instruction and devoted our initial attention to that part to which novices typically bring the greatest range of personal experience. We asked you to reflect on the component labeled "Instructional Strategies" and to begin identifying the ways teachers promote student learning—modes. These are important parts but *only parts* of what is meant by the term *strategy* (overall plans targeting on the achievement of an objective). Nine typical modes were identified and defined operationally. Common uses and abuses of each were explained, and you were introduced to the feedback-getting and -giving potential of each of these modes. More questions were raised than were fully answered; and that was by design rather than by accident. Some of the answers depend on the exploration of other components of the model in later chapters.

Right now, however, you should be able to:

1. Name and operationally define nine common instructional modes.

2. Identify modes being employed during either a "live" or recorded lesson.

3. List at least two uses and two abuses of each mode and provide reasoned justification for your choices.

The exercises in the next section are designed to test your understanding of some of these modes as they relate to your role as a teacher of mathematics. Your understanding of the content of your subject matter discipline will be put to the test, as well as your ability to move from the role of a student to that of a teacher. These situations are based on actual classroom happenings, and the content analysis exercises have been used by classroom teachers to improve instruction. Give all of them your best efforts. Then go back and check your responses against your experience and your learning as you progress through other sections of the text.

1.5 SIMULATION/PRACTICE ACTIVITIES

A. Each of the following questions is defective in its potential for eliciting unambiguous evidence of student learning. Identify the defect and construct a more effective question.

1. How about the circle?

2. Is 22/7 equal to π?

3. Can you tell me how to differentiate $f(x) = x^2 + 3$?

4. Does everybody understand the law of sines?

5. "Where do you want me to put the decimal point?" (Hint: While we were observing a class, a student teacher asked this question. A response by students, inaudible to the student teacher, was rather specific in terms of an anatomical reference.)

B. As soon as the teacher started a demonstration, several students began to stretch to the right and the left in their seats; three students in the last row stood up. This teacher probably ignored the need to have demonstrations visible to the class. Suggest two or three ways of overcoming this problem if the physical object is small or cannot be moved.

C. Select one of the following topics: probability, volume, congruence, ratio, fraction. Describe a demonstration that would help teach the central idea. Be specific about the material(s) you would use, how you would manipulate them, and other modes you would use in connection with the demonstration. Limit this teaching segment to a five- to ten-minute portion of the class period.

D. During successive periods you observed the same laboratory taught to comparable groups by two different teachers. Teacher A's class paired off quietly, got their materials quickly, returned to their desks, and immediately begin to work along the lines directed by the teacher. In Teacher B's class, students jammed up at the front of the room and began jostling and making extraneous noise. The students returned to their desks with needed materials only after a period of several minutes, during which there were frequent loud reprimands by the teacher. Next there was a rapid series of requests for the teacher's help from various parts of the room and sporadic verbal commands by the teacher to "follow directions," "get to work," "stop wasting time."

List at least three variables in teacher behavior that could account for the differences in the students' performance in the classes. Defend your selections.

E. Choose any topic from the content of secondary school mathematics and design a homework assignment to serve two purposes: (1) It should provide relevant practice of some skill. Identify the skill. (2) It should be structured to allow you to elicit a subsequent idea or skill.

Provide answers to the exercises, and write a brief justification of the ways in which your assignment meets both of the above purposes.

SUGGESTIONS FOR FURTHER STUDY

Carin, A., & Sund, R. (1971). *Developing questioning techniques: A concept approach.* Columbus, Ohio: Charles E. Merrill.

The aim of this book is to help classroom teachers select and use questioning techniques not only to promote cognitive development, but also as a way of building student self-esteem. This goal is realized to a high degree. The taxonomies of the cognitive and affective domains (Bloom and Krathwohl) are used throughout, and numerous examples are provided to illustrate the ideas presented. The relevance of the work of well-known cognitive psychologists (Bruner, Gagne and Piaget) is shown and Budd-Rowe's research on the effects of "wait-time" is used effectively. The chapters on creativity and the construction of guided discovery lessons are highlights of this book.

Goldberg, K. P. (1982). *Pushbutton mathematics.* Englewood Cliffs, NJ: Prentice-Hall.

Although Goldberg's book contains many valuable uses of calculators in various areas of mathematics, it is cited in this section for the pedagogical and technical information in the first two chapters and Chapter 10. In the first two chapters, the author suggests ways the teacher can help students to "dry-run" (our language) their calculators, explains some limitations of particular types of calculators, and gives specific kinds of preparation needed in order to make calculator lessons work. Chapter 10 is entitled "Programmable Calculators" and contains a short lesson for the teacher on these more expensive and more complex calculators.

Harper, D. O., & Stewart, J. H. (Ed.). (1986). *Run: Computer education* (2nd ed.). Monterey, CA.: Brooks/Cole.

This collection of short essays contains a wealth of practical information, as well as presentations of issues related to computer education. We recommend the selection by Andrew :Yeaman, "Put Your Computers in the Most Efficient Environment (pp. 130–131) for hints on the ergonomic arrangement of computer furniture and computers, with attention to alleviating fatigue, eye strain and stress. Equity issues related to computer-access are also affected by arrangement and location of computers, as well as by scheduling of computer time. See Marlaine Lockheed and Steven Frakt's article, " Sex Equity: Increasing Girls' Use of Computers" (pp. 237–240), for valuable information on this issue and ways the teacher can help to provide equal access to boys and girls.

Hunkins, F. P. (1972). *Questioning strategies and techniques.* Boston: Allyn and Bacon.

This very useful paperback assumes no previous knowledge of techniques and attempts to deal with all aspects of the subject in a clear but concise way. For the most part, the author has accomplished these goals quite well. The entire presentation is made within the frame of reference of curriculum study groups in mathematics. Sufficient examples are included to illustrate the major points, and frequent ties are made to Bloom's Taxonomy. Novice teachers would do well to skip over the detailed treatment of various categorizing schemes (such as those of Taba, Suchman, and Hunkins) and to concentrate their attention on the other parts of the book.

CHAPTER TWO

FEEDBACK

The Heart of Instruction

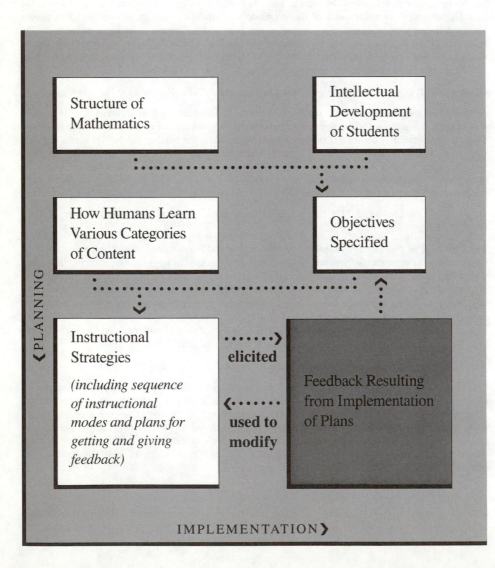

Many teachers assess their effectiveness in the classroom in terms of student reaction. Some teachers do this sporadically; some, naively; a few, regularly and systematically. Yet this kind of assessment, the *getting of feedback*, is the basis of all learning theories and the core of all attempts to communicate with others.

Some college instructors are notorious ignorers of feedback procedures, according to students who sit through lectures where no questions are asked or answered and no recognition of student attention or confusion occurs. In these cases, students learn to psyche out the instructor on the basis of feedback unknowingly given them. In contrast, when instructors consciously and systematically provide feedback, students learn whether their performance is correct, nearly correct, or totally incorrect both from the feedback provided by the instructor and from the built-in feedback components of the content.

In nonschool areas of life, people get and give feedback regularly. The mechanic who diagnoses a car's malfunction does so by testing and then observing a reaction, subsequently modifying the test and performance on that basis, and so on. The doctor, the lawyer, and the golfer—all with varying degrees of success—use feedback to modify their performance so that they may reach some goal. The systematic approach exemplified by computer work and characteristic of analysis of all kinds of complex systems requires the feedback loop. Notice the position of the feedback box in the instructional model on the chapter opening page. Follow the arrowheads, and analyze the reasons for the multiple connections of this component to others in the model. Your reading in Chapter 1 has already introduced you to the connecting link between modes and feedback. The following reading and activities spell out those connections and engage you in the problem-solving task of interpreting and analyzing feedback.

2.1 DEFINITIONS

Feedback The student gets feedback when the teacher says "incorrect" in response to a student's answer; the teacher gets feedback when he or she notes that a student has written the correct solution to a problem posed by the textbook; a student gets feedback while checking the results of a solution to a problem. Therefore, an operational definition of *feedback* is *any information, verbal or nonverbal, communicated to teacher or student, on the results of instruction.*

Notice that the definition of feedback makes it clear that both the teacher and the student need to *get* feedback if instruction is to be both efficient and effective. From the teacher's point of view, plans must be made to *get* feedback and to *give* feedback. Now you've guessed it; we've spiraled back to modes. *When the teacher uses a sequence of two or more modes with the planned intention of getting and/or giving feedback, that type of sequence is referred to as a feedback strategy.* Feedback often appears in subtle forms and can be easily overlooked. In the following activity you will be introduced to one such aspect of feedback.

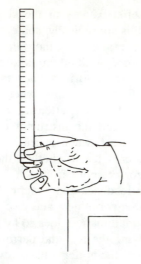

Fig. 2.1

Results for P_1

Trial #	1	2	3	4	5	6	7	8	9	10
Ruler mark										

Fig. 2.2

2.2 INTRODUCTORY ACTIVITY

A two-person team is needed for this activity. One person, P_1, rests one arm on a table so that the heel of the hand is on the edge of the table. P_1 should turn that hand sideways and prepare to catch an object between the thumb and the index finger. The other partner, P_2, holds the object, a 30-cm ruler, at the 30-cm mark between the thumb and index finger of one hand. P_2 then positions the ruler so that it is almost entirely above P_1's hand—actually with the 1-cm mark at the level of P_1's thumb (see Figure 2.1). When P_2 drops the ruler, P_1 tries to catch it. The measurement at which P_1 caught it is recorded.

A. Repeat the procedure ten times, and record P_1's results in a table such as the one shown in Figure 2.2.

B. Switch roles and record P_2's results in a similar table.

C. Identify the various kinds of feedback that were observed throughout the entire activity. Describe the changing nature of the feedback. Who got feedback? Who (what) gave feedback? Account for any improved performance on the basis of feedback received by the "catcher." What other variables may have interfered with an improvement in performance?

Activities such as the ruler activity are specifically designed to teach students the nature of feedback in tasks involving motor reflexes, such as braking a car suddenly. The popular computer video games, such as the PACMAN series, are certainly teaching players about the use of feedback and its relation to hand-eye coordination, as well as about certain types of problem- solving strategies.

2.3 FEEDBACK: GETTING, USING, AND GIVING

Assumptions

The major assumption that forms the theme of this chapter is that feedback is a key part of all instruction.

The byproducts of this general assumption are four specific assumptions:

1. Feedback should be given to, and elicited from, the widest possible sampling of students.

2. Feedback strategies should be implemented frequently and at key points during *each* instructional period.

3. Feedback should be interpreted and used to pace instruction and/or to alter the sequence of instruction.

4. Feedback should also be used to assess the feasibility of the stated objectives.

Getting Feedback

Throughout the previous chapter, you were urged to consider each mode's feedback potential. Check your understanding of this against Figure 2.3. If you do not agree, it may be due to the fact that you are thinking about various forms of nonverbal feedback while we are considering only verbal feedback at the moment. On the other hand, disagreement might indicate a need to review operational definitions of the various instructional modes. In any case, try to resolve this matter in your mind before reading any further.

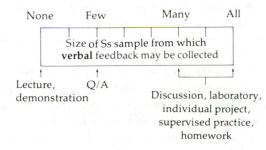

Fig. 2.3 Verbal feedback potential for various instructional modes.

Since each mode does have unique purposes in instruction, modes with zero verbal feedback-getting potential need to be followed by and interspersed with positively valued feedback strategies in order to assess the effects of instruction and modify it when necessary. For example, a short lecture can be followed by questions specifically designed to assess the listener's grasp of the lecture. Questions can range all the way from the "What did I say" type to the more meaningful "How" or "Why" types. At all costs the lecturer should avoid the "Any questions" habit unless the typical silence from the class response is quickly followed by a specific question from the teacher. Most students have learned to shrug off "Any questions?" as merely rhetorical. Further, sometimes the student who is confused and knows that the teacher is willing to field questions just can't phrase a sensible question and doesn't want to admit it! Such a student profits from class reactions to thoughtful teacher-constructed questions on the content of the lecture. The teacher might ask students to write the answers to appropriate questions then and there. Feedback from many students can then be obtained as the teacher quickly tours the room. Such a procedure might be followed by a *straw vote* (poll).

The straw vote is one of the most useful techniques for efficiently obtaining feedback. The teacher asks to see the hands of those who agree, who disagree, who aren't sure (or any analogous classification). The procedure takes less than a minute and provides information to the teacher on the diversity of class views. However, the teacher who immediately begins to reteach the topic or to quickly move on to the next topic on the sole basis of a straw vote may be in for a shock. Why? Suppose that one-third of the class disagreed with the expected answer, but that all of these students had simply misinterpreted one minor aspect of the question!

You can probably imagine many other possible reasons for diverse feedback. Therefore, straw votes should frequently be followed by a more sophisticated kind of feedback strategy—for example, a series of questions to members of each faction probing the reason(s) behind their response, or a quick tour around the room sampling papers of members of each group, or a student demonstration in defense of a response. The alternatives are many, but the teacher must plan these alternatives based on the likely stumbling blocks in the lesson and the teacher's knowledge of the needed prerequisites for subsequent phases of the lesson.

All of the preceding suggestions could be adapted easily for use during or after the other modes that have little or no feedback potential. It is particularly important to intersperse higher-rated modes to get feedback *after* a sequence of developmental questions has been used. There is a serious caution to be observed here. Suppose your class was being led through a careful sequence of developmental questions that was interspersed with straw votes at every third question. You've got it! Many students would stop voting and would probably stop thinking—about the lesson. Developmental questions must flow as smoothly as possible with members of the class learning from one another's answers as well as from the teacher's cues. With the modes rated high in feedback potential, the teacher can get a broad sampling of specific feedback if the modes are being used in appropriate ways.

Two of these higher-rated modes, laboratory and supervised practice, are critical in feedback getting. However, most novices and some experienced teachers frequently overlook the enormous potential these modes possess for improving instruction. The two illustrations that follow include elements of feedback getting, using, and giving.

Supervised practice sample

T has just completed a lecture and Q/A sequence on procedures for rewriting equations of functions in standard form. A straw vote on a single practice example showed most Ss with the correct answer. Therefore, T directs the Ss to begin working on the rest of the examples. Before T moves from the front, T checks to make sure that all Ss have started and tells a S whose hand is raised for help to reread notes until T has had a chance to check on others' progress. All others are now at work. T tours the room (as suggested in Chapter 1) and sees that only a few Ss are having difficulty with examples 5 and 8. T praises individual Ss quietly, indicates in a clear voice that many Ss are making good progress, quietly gives a cue to one S in difficulty, then moves to a second S and notices that some Ss have almost finished all nine examples. T sends selected Ss to the board, asks one S to serve as tutor for any S needing help, assists another S, and checks progress of class. (T has to decide if enough Ss are far enough along to stop the practice and look at the models of correct performance on the board. T must also decide if progress was sporadic or substantial. Do the Ss need additional practice on the same kind of examples or on a more complex set, or should T begin displaying a sequence of computer graphs so that Ss can check the equations in standard form against these graphs?) T calls the class to attention, tells them to compare their work with the board work and to be prepared to identify areas of difficulty. T stands in the rear quietly while this occurs and then takes straw votes on the number of Ss who agree or disagree with board work and seeks corrections where needed. Ss are frequently asked to respond to Q from other Ss.

Notice that the teacher refused to immediately move to the first student who raised a hand. Why? Suppose the quick tour had uncovered a far different story? If most students were blithely working away on the basis of a misconception, the delay caused by the teacher's conversation with an individual could lead to, at least, wasted time and, at worst, chaos. The same kind of rationale can be advanced for not interrupting the tour. (Remember the question asked of you in Chapter 1?) This teacher was also alert to differential progress and tried to use positive feedback in more than one way. Students were used as individual tutors and were asked to display their work on the board so that all other students could get feedback on the nature of the completed work. The other instances of feedback getting and giving in this sample are numerous. After you read the next section on feedback giving, check this illustration again for specific examples.

Laboratory sample

T begins with a ten-minute lecture with demo related to finding the empirical probability of an event. A three minute Q/A session, in which T sampled eight students, provided positive feedback on Ss understanding of (1) the empirical techniques used to obtain number of favorable ways the event could happen, (2) the "sample space" method used to record data, (3) the location of the various games of chance and problem cards, and (4) the roles of each lab partner.

T then gives the signal to begin work and takes a position in the room from which the Ss collection of materials and equipment can be observed. All Ss gather materials quickly and quietly, then return to their assigned laboratory places. At this point, T begins to move quickly and systematically from group to group. T notes that the first four groups visited are proceeding exactly as directed but just as T reached the fifth group, loud voices were heard coming from the opposite corner of the room.

T moves quickly to the loud group, touches one S on the shoulder, and uses the finger-across-the-lips signal when the S looks up. Both partners quiet immediately and T asks if they are having a problem with the exercise. Both partners start to talk at once, each complaining that the other is misinterpreting the card problem. (The problem is: What is the probability that two jacks will be drawn from a standard deck of 52 cards, when two cards are drawn without replacement?) "Herman is drawing the cards one at a time," complains Yvonne. T holds up one hand in a "stop" gesture; the Ss quiet down; and T uses Q/A with each in turn to clarify the procedure . The partners return to work; T observes they are now working amiably, and T moves on to other groups that are all proceeding in an orderly fashion.

As T continues to move from group to group, observations indicate that all Ss are now interpreting the directions correctly in the case of the coin, dice, card, marbles,and the roulette wheel events. However, the first three groups to progress as far as the event using the roulette wheel and the spinner have difficulty agreeing on the nature of the events that are to occur. T turns off the lights for three seconds. All the Ss quickly stop whatever they're doing and look at T, who then turns the lights back on and gives a lecture-demo on these particular events. All groups then return to work at T's signal, and T's subsequent observations while touring groups indicate all are now obtaining appropriate data.

With about five minutes of work time left in the class period, T overheard the following conversation among one pair of partners:

Saul: *"We calculated the probability of a black number showing on the roulette wheel as 42/100 and of a 2 occurring on a spin as 3/100. If we want the probability of both happening at the same time, we would have a combined probability equal to the product of 42/100 and 3/100."*

Alice: *"No, we wouldn't! We would just be adding one event to another, so the total probability would be the sum of 42/100 and 3/100."*

Saul: *"Look, think of it this way. The chance that both events will occur at the same time is less likely than for just one to occur. A sum would signify just the opposite."*

T praises Saul and Alice privately for thinking ahead and gives each credit for having a certain amount of logic. A short Q/A sequence by T gets Saul and Alice to compare this problem with the card problem where two jacks had to be drawn. T asks both to rethink the definition of probability based on sample space usage. Then T goes to the chalkboard, writes a brief statement of the problem posed by Saul and Alice, and for the evening's assignment asks each student to write out a sample space using ordered pairs to solve this problem. Then each student is to arrive at a generalization for the $P(A \cap B)$ and to obtain the probability of the first event or the second happening, given the same data. A brief flickering of the lights signals "cleanup," which progresses smoothly and quickly. T calls attention to the assignment, publicly gives credit to Saul and Alice for thinking ahead, and praises all for their very good work during the period. The bell rings, the Ss leave, and T checks to see that all is in readiness for the next class, which is to begin in four minutes.

Note the highly positive feedback the teacher received on the effectiveness of the introduction to this laboratory exercise. Identify all the things the teacher did to ensure that all students would begin the laboratory work effectively and efficiently. Also note how the teacher found out that only one group was encountering difficulty with the card problem and how this problem was handled without interrupting the other students who were proceeding without problems. Nonverbal feedback giving, as well as feedback getting, is highly effective for all who learn how to use it.

Apparently the teacher was quick to read the negative feedback collected on the roulette wheel/spinner problem and made use of it to reorient the entire class. If the teacher had failed to interpret this as a widespread problem, no doubt it would have been necessary to treat the same problem over and over in successive individual visits to nearly all the groups.

The student-to-student discussion between Alice and Saul not only provided the teacher with valuable feedback, but also presented a golden opportunity to reinforce prior learning on the nature of the mathematical enterprise and to provide for an in-context extension of that learning by means of a relevant homework assignment.

Most of us are quick to criticize and slow to praise. Note that the teacher in this instance did find numerous opportunities and ways to give well-deserved praise to individuals as well as to the entire class. In the long run, this approach yields big dividends for all and helps put in proper perspective those occasions when a teacher must offer constructive criticism as part of instruction. It will be well worth the effort to reread the entire description of this laboratory class and recount the occasions and techniques of praise-giving that occurred.

In addition to the specific modes referred to in this section thus far, there are two other common instructional situations that are frequently mismanaged because the teacher ignores available feedback. The two situations are labeled homework post-mortem (HWPM) and test or quiz post-mortem (T/QPM). In the former case, post-mortem refers to what the teacher plans to do about yesterday's homework. In the latter case, post-mortem refers to the return of a test or quiz and the teacher's plans for "going over it." Unfortunately, "going over it" is literally what happens in many classrooms. In the case of a test or quiz that has been corrected and analyzed, there is no excuse for boring the class by requiring everyone to sit through a rehash of each answer regardless of class performance. The teacher already has specific feedback from every student. Feedback so general that the teacher is still not sure where the students' learning problems are signifies a defect in test construction (more on that in Chapter 8).

Homework post-mortems are a somewhat different kind of beast. The teacher who let the students start the homework in yesterday's class may have some feedback on the initial success of the students, but many teachers are misled by this and assume far too much. At other times, teachers can receive useful feedback from students who come in for extra help after class. But once again, it would be a mistake not to check out the generalizability of the data before acting on it. So Mary, Jim, and Abby had trouble with example 5! So what?! Why should the teacher assume that the other 23 students need to sit through a lecture on the ins and outs of this question? What can you do to avoid these pitfalls and others like these?

Several illustrations of feedback strategies used in both homework post-mortem and test or quiz post-mortem are detailed next. Identify the ways in which the teacher gets, gives, and uses feedback not only at the start of the post-mortem, but during it.

Homework post-mortem   If a teacher wishes to ascertain the extent of student mastery of homework tasks, both of the following illustrations have proved useful.

1.   In a class of 24, T sends 6 Ss to the board (at or prior to the opening bell) to put answers to 6 questions on the board *without* taking homework papers with them. T instructs Ss at seats to check their solutions against work as it is being put on board. T then tells the seated Ss that they will be required to talk through one of the examples, agree and tell why, correct errors and give reasons, or explain alternative correct solutions as soon as Ss at the board finish. Meanwhile, T walks around, makes a quick check of homework

papers, identifies (a) those papers that are complete, (b) those on which various problems have been left out, and (c) types of errors made. Then T sends 6 *other* Ss to the board to critique the earlier work. Next, a third set of 6 students may be used to settle disagreements among the previous 2 Ss who worked at a problem.

or

2. T distributes copies with answers, or solutions and answers (overhead may be substituted for individual copies) *as Ss* enter the room. Ss are directed to check their work against the standard displayed by the copy or on the overhead while T walks around to check as in example 1 above. Then T selects Ss to explain typical errors T has detected from papers.

If the teacher is satisfied that most students have achieved mastery of the task but wishes to provide feedback in an efficient way on details of the procedure, the teacher may:

1. Check papers as Ss walk in, identify correct answers, and instruct Ss with correct models to put work on board. Then, direct Ss to stay there to explain and to answer questions from other Ss.

or

2. Give selected Ss acetate sheets to take home. Then tell them to do the assigned problem on acetate for projection the next day. Also, inform them that they will be expected to explain and answer the questions of other Ss.

Test or quiz post-mortem   After a full-period test has been given and graded, the teacher does an item analysis (see Chapter 8) *prior* to handing back papers and uses the results to:

1. Identify those problems that will be treated in class. Procedures similar to those detailed in the section on homework post-mortem might be followed.

or

2. Make an instructional decision to completely reteach selected parts of the content.

or

3. Divide class into groups of five Ss whose grades were distributed over the range. Instruct Ss to work cooperatively until all students in the group can do each problem. Walk around and act as a resource person.

After giving a short quiz and collecting papers, the teacher may display answers on overhead immediately if major disagreement is not expected; materials tested are prerequisite to next topic; and/or little time remains in the instructional period.

Perhaps at no other time in the classroom is the teacher's identification of positive and negative feedback and use of both so crucial to attention keeping and to promoting time-on-task. In the interest of calling on everyone, teachers sometimes ask students to read answers to homework or test questions. If this can be done quickly and efficiently, the practice has some merit. But read the conversational sequence that follows.

T: "Question 5. Rachel."
Rachel: "I didn't get it."
T: "Why?"
Rachel: "I just didn't try."
T: "Jack? 5?"
Jack: "3057?"
T: "Is that what all of you got?"
Ss (mixed chorus of shouts): "No," "Yes," "I don't know," "Who cares?"

Variations of the above conversation have occurred with disturbing frequency in some of the classes we've observed. However, effective teachers try to avoid this kind of time wasting. They provide the feedback needed by the students who tried to do the homework in one or more of the following ways:

1. T reads all answers and tells Ss to record them and check their responses.

2. T projects a prepared acetate with answers and proceeds as in 1 above.

3. T has answers posted on the bulletin board for Ss to check during supervised practice time.

As soon as the class has seen or heard the correct answers, it then makes sense for the teacher to take a straw vote on the total number of correct answers or on examples most often missed. Here you must be alert to both positive and negative feedback.

When should the class wait for one or two students to be helped? If all but three students got examples 5 and 7 correct, how can the teacher differentiate subsequent instruction? If many students missed all of the examples, what factors might cause the teacher to decide to reconsider only one example? These questions and others like these are representative of the need for intelligent decisions by the teacher during ongoing instruction.

Take another look at the instructional model that appears at the beginning of this and every other chapter. Notice the arrows leading *from* the Instructional Strategies box *to* the Feedback box. As a result of planned feedback strategies, the teacher gets feedback on the effectiveness of the instruction thus far. Now the teacher must use that feedback and may need to alter the planned instructional strategies—the arrows leading *to* the Instructional Strategies box *from* the Feedback box. The loop continues as long as instruction continues and will be used effectively to the extent that the teacher gets feedback, can interpret feedback, and can draw on background knowledge to generate immediate modifications of planned strategies.

These are some aspects of feedback use that depend on an analysis of the subject being taught, or the intended objectives, or the intent of the planned strategies. You should be prepared to make more sophisticated decisions on these aspects after working through Chapters 4, 5, 6, and 7. However, even at this point in the text, you have read enough about modes and feedback to make some tentative hypotheses about next steps. See if your conjectures are included in the next section.

Using Feedback

Sometimes the best immediate use of feedback is to get more feedback. More feedback may imply a larger or broader sampling of students, or it may refer to the nature of the responses and the need to obtain more specific or more extensive responses. More extensive feedback getting is essential if instructional strategies are to be implemented.

Some of the more common uses of feedback are listed below.

1. After obtaining feedback on the number of students who possess the prerequisite learning for the next topic, T may:

    a) Reteach the prerequisite material if all or most Ss have given negative feedback to T. If T has received positive feedback from a few Ss, they may be encouraged to help T in the instruction by demonstrating, justifying correct answers, analyzing the reasons behind the misconceptions. In any case, T should reteach the topic in some novel way. The original set of strategies obviously failed!

    b) Ask Ss to try a practice example (while T makes a quick tour of the room) if there seems to be ambiguous feedback.

    c) Use appropriate recall Q/A and lecture to weave specific instances of the prerequisites into the ongoing lesson if only a few Ss give negative feedback on the prerequisites. Tell the Ss that you will be doing this, and reinforce the "old" when it occurs.

2. When beginning HWPM, T displays or reads the answers and then gets feedback (in one of the ways suggested earlier) on the extent of the students' problems with homework.

    a) If only a few Ss give T negative feedback, T may:

        (1) Use Q/A with members of the rest of the class assisting *if* the analysis can be accomplished in a short period of time and *if* it can be made meaningful to the rest of the class.

        (2) Work with the small group of Ss while putting the large group to work on other materials.

        (3) Tell the small group of Ss that they will be helped later in the class when supervised practice occurs, or after class in a remedial period.

    b) If a diverse number of examples were missed by varying numbers of Ss, T may:

        (1) Tell Ss only example 5 will be treated at this time, since all other examples are simply variations of example 5. T can then follow the

reconsideration of example 5 by supervised practice of one or more of the other examples.

(2) Group Ss by cluster of examples missed *if* there are some Ss who got most or all of the examples correct. These latter Ss will serve as teachers of the small groups.

(3) Reteach the basic idea underlying the homework *if* the nature of the feedback suggests serious learning problems. T may use one of the homework examples in this set of teaching strategies and should include a supervised practice session on one or more of the remaining examples.

(4) Tell Ss to hand in the papers so that T can locate the sources of the errors *if* T has noticed that diverse, careless errors seem to be common. T should return the papers the next day and may add some general oral comments to the individual written comments.

Many of the suggestions given on the preceding pages could be used in other instructional situations—after a sequence of developmental questions, during a lab, or during the use of an ATA, for example. Notice the recurrence of "ifs" in almost every statement. There is no recipe for perfect teaching. In each case you must consider the consequences of your actions and make those moves that seem most promising in relation to your objectives.

One of the important characteristics of any of the preceding suggestions is letting the students know what to expect. Suggestion 2a(3) spells this out, but you should add similar notes to each of the suggestions. Students can get the impression that their successes and failures are being ignored or dismissed as unimportant if you don't *give* explicit feedback on your expectations. You should have noticed many examples of feedback giving in earlier sections. In the following paragraphs, specific attention is paid to this important topic.

Giving Feedback

If the reading thus far has seemed to de-emphasize nonverbal feedback, you might ask yourself why. Are there modes where nonverbal feedback may be especially misleading and others where it provides information not otherwise available to the teacher? Check out your ideas on this with classmates, then reread the introductory section of this chapter and the sample practice and lab situations in Section 2.3.

However, if nonverbal feedback is sometimes misleading when the teacher gets it and tries to interpret it, it is often doubly misleading when the teacher *unconsciously* gives such feedback. For this reason, it is often asserted that we teach students many things in addition to those we intend. Teachers give students feedback on the importance they attach to a topic by verbal emphasis, projected seriousness of purpose, and time spent in instruction or in correcting students' misconceptions. Teachers convey to students that they are progressing toward the intended objectives by smiling, giving a "thumbs up" signal, or patting a student on the back during supervised practice. It is important that the nonverbal feedback given by teachers parallels the verbal feedback. How would you feel if an employer verbally praised your work but *looked* disgusted at the same time? Imagine the confusion of a toddler who has just said a four-letter word and been scolded verbally by chuckling parents. No wonder the tot repeats the word for more laughs!

Feedback giving needs to be incorporated in all instructional strategies. If we follow the events of instruction in a typical lesson, we can pinpoint places where the teacher must *plan* to give feedback.

The events of instruction* and feedback giving

1. *Gaining and controlling attention.* T gives Ss feedback on what to observe, its relevance to past work, and so on.

2. *Informing the student of expected outcomes.* T tells Ss whether they will be expected to reproduce a derivation, apply a rule to typical problems, or write down observations made during a film.

3. *Stimulating recall of prerequisites.* T may tell Ss the relevant aspects of prerequisites needed today.

4. *Presenting the new material.*

5. *Guiding the new material.*

6. *Providing feedback.* T praises correct responses, modifies partially correct ones, and clarifies in case of errors. T has Ss copy a sample problem with its solution.

7. *Appraising performance.* As the Ss check out their learning in supervised practice, Q/A, or discussion, T gives feedback as in event 6.

Two categories of feedback giving that are especially important are: providing a model of correct performance and praise. As noted in the events of instruction, one time when the teacher must provide a model of correct performance is in the teaching of type problems (see event 6). The teacher does this when he or she puts type problems on the board (overhead), shows correct procedure step-by-step *after* appropriate rule teaching has occurred, and emphasizes format or labeling that is acceptable. Now the students have a model against which they can compare their efforts on similar problems. The teacher should give praise to individual students for correct alternative solutions, for fast as well as correct work, for good questions about the procedures, or for improvement toward a solution even if the solution has not yet been obtained. Some teachers have learned to effectively use nonverbal as well as verbal signals to give feedback to students on their efforts. Feedback often needs to be provided by immediate reinforcement for correct verbal and nonverbal responses from an individual

---

*The "events of instruction" used here are an adaptation of Gagné's (1970, p. 304) description of the events of instruction.

student, from small groups of students, or from the entire class. This kind of positive feedback (or praise) should occur during supervised practice, when Ss ask good questions, for S responses that show connections, after quizzes or tests, and during homework review.

There are also times when the teacher must give feedback in response to an incorrect answer. A mistaken interpretation of discovery teaching leaves some teachers with the impression that they should never give students this kind of information. As a result, students try to guess what is in the instructor's mind. Experienced teachers learn to give this kind of feedback by means of contingency questions or by using analogy, a physical model, or a numerical illustration. In these ways students "read" the indirect feedback and conclude for themselves that their original response was in error.

A similar kind of feedback is inherent in a design or puzzle based on the coding of the correct answers to a set of exercises. The students note the existence of an error when the design is lopsided and most, if not all, students will then attempt to eliminate the error. Such built-in feedback systems are a tremendous aid to both the teacher and the student. Connect-the-dot pictures, used in children's coloring books, have often been adapted for this kind of mathematics practice. If your students have access to microcomputers, they will surely be interacting with computer programs designed to give feedback on correct and incorrect results, to praise efforts and even, to provide cues or remediation in the case of errors. Thus, computers, as well as interactive videodiscs, can be powerful aids to the teacher in giving immediate feedback to individual students. The teacher should be on the alert for courseware that also collects feedback for later analysis—perhaps in the form of the amount of time that particular students worked at problems, or in the form of a record of all strategies used by each student. You will find some sources of all of these built-in feedback systems in Chapter ll, and many more in the experienced teacher's files. Finally, teachers provide feedback on written work by writing comments on test papers, homework papers, projects, and so on.

From our point of view, it would be hard to overemphasize the importance of feedback. We're willing to bet that you, as we, have sat in classes where the ineffective and the inefficient use of feedback was a central problem. Without the collection, interpretation, and use of feedback, the assessment of classroom activities must fall back on unreliable factors such as the desires of a supervisor, the gut feelings of the teacher next door, or the words of wisdom of some quasi-expert enshrined in a textbook.

2.4 SUMMARY AND SELF-CHECK

In the present chapter, we elaborated on the concept of feedback and considered specific strategies for getting, using, and giving both verbal and nonverbal feedback. Several illustrations of instructional situations were described and analyzed in detail to focus attention on the crucial importance of feedback. A host of specific recommendations for getting, using, and giving feedback were incorporated throughout. Novices would be well advised to heed these carefully, since many of our former students have confided that they reread this material several times with increasing profit as they progressed through student teaching and even after they had taught for one or more years. We consider this to be excellent evidence that feedback is indeed the heart of instruction.

Right now you should be able to:

1. Operationally define feedback, feedback getting, feedback using, and feedback giving and describe several classroom illustrations of each.

2. Identify instances of effective versus ineffective feedback getting, using, and giving occurring during either a "live" or taped lesson and state reasons for your judgments.

3. Design effective feedback strategies that can be incorporated into actual lessons that you will present to students.

The exercises that follow are designed to test your comprehension of feedback as it relates to your role as a teacher of mathematics. These situations are based on actual secondary school classroom situations typical of those we have regularly observed. Give them your best efforts. Then compare your proposed solutions with those of your colleagues, instructor, college supervisor of student teaching, cooperating public school teacher, and/or other experienced teachers. Discuss all differences in proposed solutions thoroughly, and reconsider and amend your responses where this seems appropriate. However, defend your ideas vigorously wherever evidence and reason support your views and resist the temptation to react only on the basis of gut feelings and established tradition.

2.5 SIMULATION/PRACTICE ACTIVITIES

A. T follows homework strategy of checking all papers at seats while Ss work on a review problem. T collects the following feedback:

1. Four Ss have perfect papers in every respect.

2. Six Ss either have no papers or papers with little work done on the assignment. (Two of these Ss rarely bother to do homework.)

3. Ten Ss have most of the assignment correct. There is no common pattern in types of errors made and no common pattern of missed problems.

Design a promising strategy that makes use of the positive and negative feedback described.

B. T has just taught a rule and received some feedback that a variety of Ss could apply the formula in stereotype situations. Now T gives Ss three or four examples to do in an eight-minute supervised practice session. T begins the supervised practice in the fashion outlined in Chapter 1. When T collects initial feedback, T finds that 8 Ss can't even begin the work while the other 17 Ss seem to be progressing very well.

Design a promising strategy for using this positive and negative feedback.

C. T administered a ten-minute surprise quiz at the beginning of the period. T observed from the rear of the classroom and noticed that several Ss just sat and stared for the last three minutes while others seemed to finish during the last minute. T collected papers systematically. Some Ss complained that the quiz was too long. Some asked: "How much is this going to count?" and "Can I take a makeup?"

Interpret the feedback and outline the T's immediate strategy for handling the situation.

D. T planned to introduce a complex rule by a carefully designed sequence of developmental questions. Some Ss moved quickly from correct responses, to the early easy questions, to a correct generalization before T had asked all of the planned intermediate questions. T asked a sample of other Ss questions designed to diagnose whether they also accepted the generalization. This feedback and a straw vote gave T feedback that the class had moved faster than expected.

The next step in T's plan for the day called for several short practice sessions with problem sets of gradually increasing difficulty. Use the feedback described above as the basis for suggesting an appropriate change in the spacing of T's planned practice sessions.

SUGGESTIONS FOR FURTHER STUDY

Abbey, D. S. (1973). *Now see hear! Applying communications to teaching.* Toronto, Ontario: The Ontario Institute for Studies in Education.

This little paperback is filled with practical ways to improve feedback giving and getting. Abbey included sections on body language, listening skills, uses of media, and ways to provide positive reinforcement.

Gagné, R. M. (1975). *Essentials of learning for instruction.* Hinsdale, IL: Dryden Press.

This brief paperback incorporates a presentation of Gagné's views on the place and importance of feedback in human learning. His model of the act of learning phases depicts feedback (reinforcement) as the final phase in any act of learning, and the author explains its interrelationship with other components of the model. The need to involve a large sampling of students in both feedback getting and giving is stressed, and some specific techniques for achieving this end are included.

CHAPTER THREE

THE INTELLECTUAL DEVELOPMENT OF STUDENTS

Adolescent Reasoning Patterns

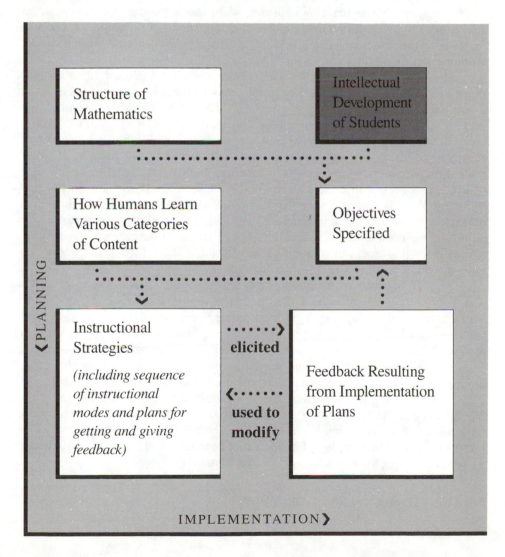

At the turn of the century, magazine pictures of children depicted them as shrunken adults. The pictures were a fairly accurate representation of the belief that children reason in the same way as adolescents and adults. Although some early psychologists, such as G. Stanley Hall (1883), were interested in the development of children, the emphasis was primarily on *quantitative* rather than *qualitative* differences in intellectual development. As a result of this view of mind, many teachers approached all age groups the same way—lecture and then set all students to work copying and practicing. Differentiate instruction between younger and older students by giving younger students smaller doses of ideas. Unfortunately, some teachers still behave this way. Even teachers of honors classes unwittingly imitate this teaching behavior, when they equate *differentiation* of instruction with giving these more capable students "more of the same." If you had the latter experience, you know that this approach placed a new burden on the memory, but didn't help you understand.

How do secondary school students reason? What preconceptions do they bring to the classroom? When they think about mathematics, what do they think it involves? The most promising source of help on all of these questions begins with the work of the Swiss genetic epistemologist, Jean Piaget. His massive collection of data puts to eternal rest the myth that children are intellectually shrunken adults. A four-year-old boy asks "Why do the clouds move?" or "Why is the grass green?" A tenth-grader thinks that doubling the length of each edge of a cube will result in doubling the volume of the cube. How is each of them thinking? What factors will alter the four-year-old's approach to his world? What obstacle is confusing the tenth-grader? Piaget directed our attention to the active nature of the human intellect. The key both to cognitive development and to apparent stumbling blocks in reasoning seems to be in the nature of the *interaction* between the individual and the environment.

Piaget's rejection of the mind as a blank paper on which the teacher writes was not new. Others in mathematics education from Warren Colburn in 1829 to William Brownell in the 1930's, as well as prominent educational philosophers, such as John Dewey, as early as his Pedagogic Creed of 1897, had argued that meaningful knowledge is *constructed* by the student. More recently, Romberg and Carpenter (1986) emphasized the need for teaching that focuses on the active nature of the learner of mathematics and the dynamic nature of mathematics itself. We're getting ahead of our story. What exactly did Piaget find out? How did he explain his findings? What additional analyses of adolescent reasoning have been completed by more recent researchers? What is the relevance of all of these findings to the teaching of mathematics to middle and high school students? These are the questions we address in this chapter.

3.1 INTRODUCTORY ACTIVITY

I hear and I forget; I see and I remember;
I do and I understand.

A.   Although this activity can be completed by one person, it will be more effective if it is completed by several students who can then discuss the analysis questions. It is appropriate for either novice or more experienced teachers of mathematics.

B.   Each person needs a sheet of wax paper approximately 30 cm on each edge. Draw a straight line, *l*, about 5 cm from one edge. Then place a point, *P*, about 8 cm from the same edge and halfway from the sides of the sheet (Figure 3.1). Label the point and the drawn line. Map *P* to any point on *l*, fold and then open the paper. (Be sure the fold, or crease, is evident.) Next map *P* to a different point on *l* and again fold and open the paper. Continue the mapping, folding and opening steps and look for a pattern (Figure 3.2).

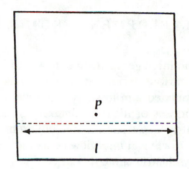

Fig. 3.1   First step in parabola construction.

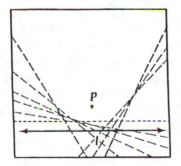

Fig. 3.2   Wax paper parabola.

C.   Respond to the questions in this section individually and then talk about your answers with others doing the activity.

   1.   What kind of curve seems to have been constructed by this process of mapping a single fixed point to a set of other points along a fixed line? Explain why the construction of lines of reflection in this manner should yield this curve. (Refer to Section 11.3, Chapter 11 for more information on paper-folding and conics.)

   2.   Reflect on your thinking as you completed three folds, then four, ... When did you decide that the pattern being constructed was a representation of a parabola? Did you have any early ideas that were shown to be incorrect after further investigation? In what ways does this construction with all its folds help to make visual various properties of the parabola? You've studied the parabola before. If this was a novel experience for you, in what way(s) did it clarify or strengthen your concept of parabola?

D. You were literally constructing a parabolic representation in this activity. If you were following the directions in B mechanically, you were only interacting with materials. If you were thinking about the emerging pattern, making tentative conjectures and testing them, you were mentally active and there was a dynamic interplay between your mind and the activity. Then, when you were asked to reflect on your earlier thoughts, you were mentally active at another level, one that researchers call the "metacognitive" level—thinking about your own thinking.

3.2 COGNITIVE DEVELOPMENT FROM A PIAGETIAN PERSPECTIVE

While doing some routine intelligence testing in Alfred Binet's laboratory school in Paris, Piaget became curious about the answers children gave—especially the wrong answers. This stimulated him to study cognitive development by systematically observing the responses of his own children to various real world stimuli and to tasks that he contrived. As soon as the children were able to respond to questions, he used the semi-clinical interview he had learned while serving a brief internship at Bleuler's pyschiatric clinic in Zurich. He reported the results of his studies in books such as *The Origins of Intelligence in Children*, *The Reconstruction of Reality in the Child*, and *Play, Dreams and Imitation in Childhood*. The interviews were replicated with other children by collaborators of Piaget. Eventually he and his collaborators added tasks involving manipulation of physical materials or equipment to the semi-clinical interview in order to assess reasoning, not only by what the youngsters said, but also by observing what the youngsters did with the equipment. Piaget's written reports of the data collected in the interviews, the reasoning patterns revealed by the data and his analysis of patterns of cognitive development eventually resulted in over thirty books and hundreds of articles. During the 20 years between the two world wars, Piaget's colleagues, along with psychologists in France, Russia and Great Britain, replicated and extended Piaget's research efforts with hundreds of people from birth to ages 16 or 17. After World War II, American psychologists became more aware of, and more interested in, Piaget's work. Behaviorists and, later, neo-behaviorists were critical of his qualitative methodology and skeptical about the generalizibility of his results. Logicians and some mathematics educators questioned the closeness of fit of the mathematical models he chose to explain his data. Over the decades, however, one major result was confirmed. When the Piagetian tasks were replicated faithfully, youngsters in diverse cultures and social strata responded with predictable reasoning patterns and provided justifications in almost the same words.

What patterns did Piaget claim existed? What qualitative differences did he find as children moved from primary to secondary school age? Inhelder and Piaget (1958) described responses to fifteen tasks that illustrated the changes in reasoning patterns for youngsters ranging in age from five years to seventeen years. An excellent illustration comes from a task that involves the law of floating bodies. Recall that concepts of volume (liquid and solid), weight, and specific gravity and density are involved. Students are given various objects to place in a container of water and asked to predict whether the objects will float or not, and why. After some preliminary tests, the youngest children incorrectly predict that a coin will float because it is "little" or that a wooden plank will sink because it is "heavy." Individual perceptual characteristics of the objects are cited as causal factors. The next stage in reasoning is shown by the more advanced youngsters who take into account the level of the water, the volume of the object, or even the weight of the object, all of which are quantifiable variables. Still this group of youngsters cannot solve the problem because they seem to be limited to reasoning about observables. Finally, the next stage of reasoning is characterized by responses in which the students hypothesize about a situation that is not directly observable, such as the comparison of the weight of the object with the weight of an equal volume of water. For although the entire volume of water in the container can be observed, the volume of water equal to that of the object in question has no observable shape. Thus it is necessary that an abstraction be conceptualized. This last illustration is an example of the kind of reasoning in the most sophisticated stage of reasoning, labeled the "formal" stage by Piaget. The label "formal" suggests freedom from the constraints of the concrete world as well as the ability to reason about the form apart from the substance that the form might represent. It is the kind of reasoning we regularly need in many areas of mathematics, such as probability theory, group theory or symbolic logic.

Piaget and his colleagues devised and administered multiple tasks across domains such as number, geometry, and probability. The data they collected formed clusters of similar reasoning responses to these tasks; and their analysis of all of these clusters of responses resulted in a more general set of reasoning patterns. These more general reasoning patterns always appeared in an *invariant sequence* that Piaget conceptualized as consisting of four major stages. Because Piaget asserted that even our earliest abilities are not eradicated but serve as a basis for later abilities, teachers at all levels need to be aware of the major characteristics of all of the stages of cognitive development.

The Stages of Cognitive Development

The first stage (usually birth to about 2 years) is characterized by the gradual refinement of motor reflexes as the child begins to "know" the world by using the five senses. Infants touch, taste, smell, listen to, and look at everything within range. Piaget called this stage *sensori-motor*.

In the second stage, language development increases children's ability to represent things in a variety of ways. Pots and pans become cars and trucks and a child may become upset if one of his or her "cars" is put in the micro-wave. Labels, to this reasoner, are literally what they name. Perception develops further and notions of large, small, wide, hot, cold and so on are refined. However, it

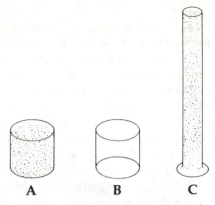

Fig. 3.3   Conservation of liquid capacity.

is perception that sometimes leads youngsters of this stage of cognitive development to make decisions that seem unreasonable to the adult. The response of six-year-old Mary to one of the conservation tasks graphically illustrates this dependence on perception. Mary was shown two jars of identical capacity and shape (Figure 3.3) and allowed to fill each with limeade. She agreed that both jars contained the same amount of limeade. However, when the limeade from container B was poured into container C—a taller, thinner jar with the same capacity as the other two jars—Mary no longer agreed that the amount of limeade remained the same (i.e. was *conserved*). Her justification was that jar C has more limeade because it's taller. (Another child distracted by a different perceptual change might have said jar C is thinner and thus, holds less limeade.) Mary's inability to divorce her thinking from a perceptual change, to consider the two compensating perceptual changes simultaneously, or to mentally reverse the action of pouring limeade from one jar to another are all characteristics peculiar to this second stage, which Piaget called *pre-operational*. The label he chose comes from the meaning he gave to the term "operation"—an action that is mentally internalized, reversible and organized in a complex system.

The third and fourth stages are both characterized by operational thinking but are differentiated from one another by the nature of the reality about which youngsters are able to reason, as well as by the form of their reasoning. Piaget called the third stage *concrete operational*. By using the term "concrete" he emphasized these youngsters' dependence on reality concrete to themselves, for example, a familiar experience or a hands-on activity. In contrast, in the fourth stage, the formal operational stage, the more advanced reasoners are relatively free from the restrictions of their senses. These youngsters can imagine the possible as containing the real so hypotheses may be based on non-observed and non-experienced phenomena, as they were in the floating bodies task outlined earlier. For the formal students, the real is a subset of the possible.

Reasoning patterns of the concrete and formal stages   The major contrasting reasoning patterns of the concrete and formal stages are outlined in Table 3.1.

Table 3.1
Reasoning Patterns of Concrete and Formal Operational Students

Concrete	Formal
Needs reference to concrete experiences, familiar objects or events.	Also reasons with concepts and indirect relationships, assumptions and theories.
Is restricted to reasoning inductively (generalizes on the basis of data).	Also uses hypothetico-deductive reasoning.
Needs step-by-step instructions in a lengthy procedure.	Plans a lengthy procedure and tends to use systematic approaches in recording data and in deciding next steps.
Does not attempt to check conclusions; seems unaware of inconsistencies in own reasoning.	Reflects on own reasoning and tries to resolve inconsistencies; seeks necessary, as well as sufficient, conditions for a conclusion.

The reasoning patterns of the formal reasoner, listed in Table 3.1, correspond to the four characteristics of the formal operational stage: (1) the treatment of the real as a subset of the possible; (2) the ability to use hypothetico-deductive reasoning; (3) the ability to use combinatorial reasoning; and (4) second-level or propositional thinking (Piaget & Inhelder, 1969). The abilities of the concrete operational student include important building blocks for the subsequent stage. For example, the ability to generalize is a very powerful intellectual skill. However, if many adolescents are still limited to the reasoning patterns of the concrete operational stage (and we will see later that a substantial number do exhibit, at most, concrete reasoning skills), it is not surprising that many students find proof-skills difficult to attain. These skills require the ability to think in the hypothetico-deductive mode—"*If* this triangle *were* similar to the given triangle, then .... " Students who are restricted to deductions based solely on experience ("If it rains tomorrow, then the ground will be wet.") are puzzled and frustrated by the kind of "If, then" reasoning required in constructing a proof. As you continue to study the relationships between cognitive development and prerequisite mathematical reasoning skills, watch for instances of hypothetico-deductive reasoning, problems in which both a general and a necessary conclusion is required. Ask yourself why so many mathematics students have difficulty understanding the difference between necessary conditions and sufficient conditions. Study the following statements.

1. A sufficient condition for a quadrilateral to be a rectangle is that it is a square.

2. A necessary condition for a quadrilateral to be a rectangle is that it is a square.

Which of these statements is true? Why? Teachers often resort to Venn diagrams showing squares as a subset of rectangles to help students understand that statement (1) is true and statement (2) is false. Reflect on your own cognitive processing when you compared statements (1) and (2). Now consider the comparative difficulty of verifying a rule by finding one instance that works versus proving that a statement is true. We think you'll agree that the reasoning involved in verifying for one case is much easier than that involved in proof-constructing.

There are also specific reasoning patterns, intellectual skills or, more properly, schemata that develop in either the concrete or formal stage. Some of these are summarized in Table 3.2 along with descriptive comments about the nature of these schemata.

The single asterisk (*) in Table 3.2 indicates that there is a developmental lag between understanding conservation of area itself and understanding how area is measured. Why should there be a lag? Isn't this a fairly obvious formula? Let's reflect on a typical developmental approach to the teaching of the formula and see if that sheds any light on the conceptual difficulty. Area measure is often introduced by drawing a rectangular shape on a grid, counting the squares in the grid and calling that result the area. Then, the students are shown that the total number of squares can also be obtained by multiplying the number of squares on the width by the number of squares on the length. All too often, the teacher immediately sets the students at work practicing examples where they are given lengths and widths of rectangles and asked to compute areas. What's wrong with this sequence of events? Here is a typical set of practice examples:

1. $l = 5$ cm and $w = 4$ cm   4. $l = 4.5$ cm and $w = 2.5$ cm

2. $l = 12$ cm and $w = 3$ cm   5. $l = 7/2$ cm and $w = 2$ cm

3. $l = 14$ cm and $w = 10$ cm

Notice that there are at least two conceptual leaps from the counting of squares lesson to these examples. One is the fact that the number of squares on the length and width are no longer mentioned; instead the continuous measure of each of those dimensions is given. Can you find the other conceptual leap? If you identified the difficulty of thinking about parts of squares as represented in the last two examples, you're beginning to think about the learner's problems. Suppose that most students *succeed* (get the correct numerical answer) on these practice exercises. Does this positive feedback mean that the use of the area formula has been understood by this students? An example like the one that follows is one way to get more specific feedback on the level of understanding.

> Mr. Allsop plans to tile the floor in his bathroom with Armstrong vinyl tiles. The floor is rectangular in shape. The tiles he has decided to buy are shaped like squares and are 6 inches on an edge. Describe the steps Mr. Allsop might take to find out how many tiles he needs to buy. What are some of the problems he might face?

Notice that this problem requires that the students reverse the developmental lesson and actually come up with a count of the square tiles. In a class

Table 3.2
Selected Schemata of the Concrete and Formal Stages

Concrete Stage	
Schemata	**Description**
Classification simple	Distinguishes between familiar objects (e.g. squares and circles)
Classification hierarchical	Applies class-inclusion concept to construct classification trees (e.g. tree of parallelogram family)
Seriation or Ordering simple	Arranges a collection of ordered objects (e.g. $-4 < -2 < 2$)
Seriation or Ordering complex	Solves ordered relationship problems in concrete way (e.g. Draw graphs of $M < 3$ and $N > 1$ on the same number line. When does $M = N$?)
Conservation of number, weight, length mass, area*, volume**	Knows that measure (e.g. weight) does not change even if the form of that being measured is perceptually altered.
*Determination of area by use of length and width multiplication	Knows why the area formula results in an estimate of "covering"

Formal Stage	
Schemata	**Description**
Combinatorial operations	Considers and acts on all possible combinations, given 4 or more variables (Already noted in Table 3.1)
Proportional reasoning	Solves ratio and simple direct proportion problems. By the end of this stage, the ability to solve inverse proportion problems develops.
Probability	Concepts of randomness and of compound probability develop late in the stage.
Correlational reasoning	Understands correlation statements and the distinction between these and causal statements.
Multiplicative compensations determination of volume** by multiplication of length, width and height.	Understands why the formula results in an estimate of capacity and that a change in one dimension requires a compensating multiplicative change in one or both of the other dimensions in order to maintain a constant volume.

question/answer session, the teacher can find out whether the students realize that measuring the length and width in inches and computing the area will also provide a count of the number of tiles. Dimensions for the bathroom floor were deliberately omitted from the problem statement to avoid blind application of a rule. By suggesting different possible measures for the length and width of the floor, the teacher can also find out whether the students realize that the results might point to a need to purchase tiles and cut these into fractional parts.

Ms. Blumenstalk approached the sequence of area proofs in geometry by having her tenth grade students estimate the area of irregular shapes in a lab activity. They covered the shapes with different congruent real world objects from pennies to bananas. Then the students used some of the more interesting Escher patterns, perhaps a tile like the ones in Figure 3.4 (see others in Ranucci & Teeters, 1977). They worked in groups and discussed the advantages and disadvantages of the different shapes as area unit figures. Eventually, they worked on grids, triangular and parallelogram, as well as square grids and came to an understanding of the usefulness of square grids. When Ms. Blumenstalk turned to a consideration of the proofs for the well-known area formulas, she found that these tenth graders had a new appreciation of the relationship of those formulas to the area concept and possessed the concrete prerequisites to suggest transformations of the figures to get equivalent areas.

Look back at Table 3.2 and notice that there is a double asterisk (**) in two places. Try to work out for yourself the developmental issues represented here. If you've forgotten the typical presentation method for volume, look through both junior high texts and a senior high geometry text. Talk over your ideas with another student of teaching.

The nested stages and the secondary school student   Throughout all of Piaget's work, the concept of developmental stages includes the notion that early intellectual abilities are built upon, modified and extended by later ones, rather than eradicated by them. The diagram which follows is an attempt to illustrate this relationship, as well as the complex one of individual differences within stages and across stages (Figure 3.5). The *nesting* illustrates, for example, the formal operational student's ability to use intellectual skills of an earlier stage when needed, while the crevices in the schema illustrate that same student's inability to reason formally about tasks for which he or she lacks concrete prerequisite experiences. College students who were talented and highly abstract reasoners in the field of literature have reported their frustration and anxiety when faced with a symbolic approach to a mathematics topic (Buerk, 1982). For these students, past experiences in mathematics classrooms had convinced them that mathematics is a collection of rules to be memorized. They needed a concrete basis to help them to make sense of particular topics, and their instructors didn't provide that basis. Some college mathematics majors have had a similar experience when taught differentiation and integration processes without any reference to a developmental, concrete basis. Perhaps you were one of them. How did you overcome the

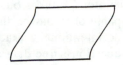

Fig. 3.4

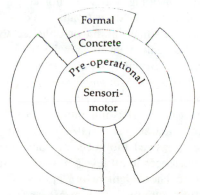

Fig. 3.5 The nested stages model.

problem? Are there some aspects of the calculus that are still semi-mysteries to you?

The nested stages model is suggestive of considerable diversity in reasoning ability among students of the same age group. It is clear that much depends on the prior experiences, both in and out of school, with which the students interacted. Furthermore, there is a substantial body of evidence that even students who are capable of formal reasoning in a particular topic area may choose not to operate at a formal level. (Neimark, DeLisi & Newman, 1985). Some of these differences betwen competence and behavior may be due to preferred learning style, a topic we'll consider in the section on individual differences. Some of the differences may be a response to the kind of questions asked in school. For example, if the problems are simple, if students are never asked to predict or if the teacher always demonstrates the solution, then students need not use formal operational reasoning. The unintentional discouragement of formal operational thinking in those who are capable of it may be the most disastrous result of this kind of teaching. Teachers who intentionally attack this problem use some or all of the following: "What if" questions; tree diagrams to encourage a systematic approach to many combinations; a "Predict, explain your prediction, now verify, modify predictions" sequence; or classwork on a problem for which the teacher has no answer.

How does the teacher decide whether the students in a particular course are likely to be primarily concrete operational or formal operational reasoners? From the many studies of reasoning, especially those related to mathematics and science (e.g. Farrell and Farmer, 1985; McDonald, 1982; Shayer & Wylam, 1978), we can conclude that even among the "college-bound" students from middle school through college, there will be a mix of concrete and formal reasoners in *all* classes. In group tests of college bound tenth graders, from 30 to 40 percent have reasoned at the concrete level. Another approximately 30 percent showed some evidence of formal reasoning, but were not consistent, even in the same topic area. These reasoners, called "transitional thinkers," are of special interest because classroom experiences may inhibit or enhance their progress to formal reasoning. Even among the seniors in advanced mathematics classes, there are students who do not exhibit formal reasoning in areas such as proportions, a major conceptual strand throughout secondary school mathematics classes. Thus, the teacher must analyze the subject matter for clues as to the kind of reasoning it implies and be cognizant of the reasoning abilities of the students who are expected to learn the subject matter. Piaget (1935), referring to the highly abstract nature of mathematics, emphasized the need for concrete (perhaps visual, familiar, and/or hands-on) experiences at all levels in the teaching of mathematics.

Thus, a senior high teacher might plan a laboratory, such as the M and M activity found in Simulation Activity F, before presenting concepts of theoretical probability. Even if the students have had previous experience calculating the probability for various rolls of the dice in middle school mathematics classes or biology classes, it is unlikely that this concrete activity was a sufficient basis for the transition to the concepts of theoretical probability.

Well-structured concrete activities, even for less formal content, are not wasted on formal reasoners. Ms. Sosnick, a geometry student teacher, planned a strategy using several modes with a concrete basis in her lesson on congruence proofs for overlapping triangles. She constructed a large poster paper model of a triangle and used paper clips to attach smaller varicolored triangular cutouts to the master figure. After using the demonstration model to illustrate coincident sides, corresponding angles, and so on, then Ms. Sosnick gave each student a smaller version of the model to use, "*if needed*," while working on several proofs. After a few minutes of pseudosophisticated remarks about the cutouts, *all* students were observed making use of the individual models. Some used a model to verify a conjecture; some, to locate corresponding parts; and some, to suggest a potential problem-solving strategy. The concrete models with their dynamic potential not only got and kept attention but served as a stimulus to novel problem solving.

These illustrations are samples of the many ways in which instructional modes may be used to help adolescent reasoners at various levels of cognitive development. Reconsider the potential of these teaching ideas for enhancing interaction after studying the next section.

Process of Cognitive Development

How did Piaget explain the transition from one stage to another? Piaget identified four factors, all of which were assumed to affect cognitive development. These are: (1) maturation (2) experience (3) social interaction and (4) equilibration (Piaget, 1964). According to the first two factors, a person's genetic makeup as well as the environmental stimuli with which he or she is faced are important mediators of development. Equilibration, the fourth factor, and the most controversial of Piaget's constructs, might be thought of as the tendency of a complex cybernetic system, the human mind, to adjust and restructure in response to apparent aberrations. We've left consideration of the factor of social interaction for last because this factor deserves particular attention in terms of instructional implications.

Cognitive and social interaction   Piaget insisted that knowledge is active: that to *know* an idea or an object required that the person manipulate it physically and mentally and thereby transform it. At different developmental stages, the activity of transformation takes on different forms. Nine-month-old Marcy shakes a toy, tastes it, looks at it, and listens to it. In her own way, through her senses she transforms the object and so "knows" it to the extent that these actions transform it for her. In the Introductory Activity, you performed a paper-folding task and were asked to respond to questions about it and to reflect on your thinking. You physically transformed the wax paper and, it is assumed, mentally transformed (perhaps enhanced?) your prior knowledge about a parabola as well as your ideas about the nature of knowledge. Notice that "to transform" doesn't necessarily mean to radically change; it may mean to become more sure of concepts. The cognitive interaction occurred when you were *mentally* active.

Social interaction occurred when you discussed your ideas with other students. For Piaget, this aspect of working out ideas by talking them over with others is a major mediator of development. Think about your own strategies when you have to solve real world problems. If you're working on a computer program, trying to master advanced techniques on the ski slope, or muddling through a personal dilemma, you will spontaneously and actively think about those characteristics of the real situation that you perceive as relevant to your problem.

For example, Tony, a ski instructor, can easily identify the external characteristics of your interaction as he watches you systematically trying to weight and unweight your skis across a steep slope in response to slides and skids. If you are unable to correct your parallel turns, Tony will try to create a new mental model for you to reflect on. Whether Tony knows the theory or not, he instinctively recognizes the necessity of cognitive interaction managing the physical interaction on the slope. There is also bound to be social interaction in the ski school as you and Tony, and perhaps you and other skiers, talk about the lesson, translate Tony's instructions in different ways, and praise and encourage each other.

On the other hand, you may solve your computer programming problem by yourself. There does not need to be social interaction in all cases for development to proceed. Without it, according to Piaget, development is hindered; and with social interaction, development is enhanced. Perhaps discussion of the computer programming problem would have led to deeper insights, not just a solution for the specific case.

Think through your own school instruction and consider when interaction seemed to be enhanced. Which teaching/learning modes were used often, seldom, or not at all? The answer we often are given is that listening to lecture was emphasized; small-group discussions were minimized and laboratory, outside of science class, was never used after the elementary grades. Might there be some connection between the mode used and failure to retain the ideas in any meaningful way for very long? Are there times when listening is an appropriate way to introduce ideas? Are there times when reading can be said to encourage interaction? You can answer that last question now. Do you recall reading an article throughout which you were struggling with the ideas being communicated? You may have even felt impelled to argue with the author. Have you also had the experience of reading an article and not being able to recall its major theme a few hours later? What were the characteristics of each article, the differences in the knowledge you brought to the task, the differences in your desire to "know"?

In many of your college classes, listening is expected to be the student's major role. What do you find are essential prerequisites for you, the listener, if listening is to result in knowledge, not just memorized bits and pieces? Suppose you, the listener, have all the needed prerequisites. What is required of the lecturer? Must the lecturer also write on the board (overhead acetate) or provide handout notes? If you haven't already done so, compare your answers to these questions with those of two other readers of this section. Try to come to some consensus on major points. In a later section, we'll reconsider the questions raised here.

Adaptation Piaget provided us with other constructs that explain the functioning of cognitive interaction. Consider your own mental activity as you read these paragraphs. Each reader comes to the reading with different experiences, differing degrees of understanding of Piaget, and different retention of past school learning. You read the same words. Some of the words may be familiar, but may be used in a slightly novel way. Some of the ideas may be, for you, old friends; for another reader, the same ideas might present a totally new notion. If you were to talk out your mental activity as you read for understanding (We all know that it's possible to read just to finish an assignment and then wind up with a cognitive residue of zero!), you might describe it as a *matching-patching* task. You may try to *match* the inferred ideas to ones you possess that seem to be similar, or you may *patch* previous cognitive knowledge on the basis of a new twist. It is important to realize that 30 readers may conclude the same reading with 30 different shades of meaning. It must be obvious that if you possess no conceptual glue with which to do the matching-patching, then no meaningful knowledge will be added to your cognitive structure.

Piaget had specific labels for the match-patch function described here. He labeled the process where an individual interacts with an experience (a real object, a situation, inferred ideas through reading, listening, or seeing) *adaptation*. He described adaptation in terms of two concurrent functions: *assimilation* and *accommodation*. In the illustration we used, the reader *assimilates* (matches) the ideas inferred from the paragraphs as he or she simultaneously *accommodates* (patches) prior cognitive structures to the new input. Notice that when adaptation (matching-patching) occurs, the individual is changed in a cognitive sense while he or she changes the experience.

There are some clear signals to the teacher in the functioning of adaptation. First, if assimilation-accommodation is to occur, the gap between the new experience and past knowledge cannot be too large. How large? There is no easy answer, but there are hints. If you analyze the nature of the content and search for prerequisites, some obvious prior needs will be identified. Then you can informally diagnose through homework assignments, or a short question/answer period or any number of other modes.

Warning: We've already seen that what students were exposed to is not necessarily what they've learned! What's between the covers of a syllabus or text may or may not have been included in instruction. Even if it were, you now know enough about the variable potential on the receiving end of instruction to question the probable retention of that base. What are we proposing here? Assume ignorance? Reteach everything needed? Certainly not! If you do, you'll bore a great many capable students. However, we are back to the necessity of getting feedback on the nature and extent of prerequisite knowledge. Diagnosis!

Now we're ready to respond to the earlier questions as to the roles of the lecturer and the listener in an effective college class. The lecturer has to know his or her "stuff." Equally important, though, the listener has to have enough background knowledge so that the spoken words trigger meaningful associations.

Also the lecturer has to capture the listener's attention at the start and keep it throughout. Is the listener expected to recall data and to dig into the lecture for deeper meanings? If so, the listener will probably need to take notes and the lecturer may need to facilitate the note taking with a written aid and possibly, a demonstration, e.g. a dissectable solid, or a paper folding model. Notice how much more is demanded of the lecturer if listening is to be active. Regardless of the lecturer's oratorical charms, notice how difficult it is to keep the atmosphere right for interaction on the part of the listener! Perhaps this is why most college students take notes during a lecture. That physical activity may be a stimulus to mental activity, although sometimes note taking can be done automatically with the more complex areas of the brain tuned out.

3.3 RESEARCH ON REASONING ABOUT MATHEMATICS TOPICS

Much of the research on cognitive development completed by Piaget and his colleagues related to reasoning about mathematical concepts. More recent research by mathematics educators interested primarily in school learning complements the Piagetian research and provides the mathematics teacher with more insights into adolescent reasoning. In this section, we have included selected studies relevant to middle and high school mathematics.

Wagner, Rachlin and Jensen (1984) studied the strategies used by a sample of twelve students in the first level high school algebra course. They found that the students shared several basic misconceptions about the nature of algebraic concepts. Most of the students believed that the symbol $-x$ must represent a negative number and that variable expressions such as $x + 1$ don't really represent numbers. For example, the students were asked to solve three equations that were structurally the same, but in which the form of the variable was changed.

$$\text{Solve for } s: \quad \frac{s}{8} - 3 = 14. \tag{1}$$

$$\text{Solve for } t: \quad \frac{t}{8} - 3 = 14. \tag{2}$$

$$\text{Solve for } t + 1: \quad \frac{t+1}{8} - 3 = 14 \tag{3}$$

Eight of the 12 students recognized that equation 2 was basically the same as equation 1 and simply gave the answer of 136, that they had obtained for s. The remaining four students re-solved the equation, "just to check." However, most of the students found it much more difficult to recognize that equation 3 was just another form of both 1 and 2. Only four students said that $t + 1$ must be equal to 136; but even these continued the process and found a value for t, which had not been requested. The other students re-solved the equation and most of them solved for t and then found $t + 1$.

This misconception may account for the common difficulty algebra students have whenever they are faced with examples that don't seem to fit the stereotypical pattern they have "learned." For example, students memorize the pattern for factoring the difference of two squares:

$$(a^2 - b^2) = (a + b)(a - b)$$

and can be quite successful with problems of the form $(x^2 - y^2)$, but quite unsuccessful with an example like $(a^2 b^4 - 9c^2)$. Perhaps what these students stored in memory was the simple literal pattern; so that only an almost exact fit is recognized by them as conforming to the pattern (Davis, 1984). W. W. Sawyer (1964) made suggestions of various visual and pictorial ways to represent algebraic expressions that might help the concrete thinker with these algebraic generalizations. For example, geometric shapes could be used in the general formula-like statement (Figure 3.6) These shapes could then be shown to represent a variety of algebraic expressions

(i) $\quad (\triangle^2 - \square^2) = (\triangle + \square)(\triangle - \square)$

(ii) $\quad (a^2 - b^2) = (a + b)(a - b)$

(iii) $\quad ([5x]^2 - [6y]^2) = (5x + 6y)(5x - 6y)$

Fig. 3.6   The difference between two squares.

Notice the sequence of replacements for the geometric shapes in Figure 3.6. The student who learns the formula pattern in (i) has a pictorial image to store—an image which is both concrete and general.

The concept of ratio and proportion has been the subject of intensive study by researchers in both mathematics education and science education (Fajemidagba, 1983; Farrell & Farmer, 1985; Hart, 1978; Karplus & Karplus, 1972; Karplus, Pulos & Stage, 1983). Early concrete thinkers have shown little understanding of either ratio or proportion. They sometimes succeed on proportion problems involving doubling, but they use an additive strategy to get the answer. Late concrete or early formal reasoners (a group often called "transitional" reasoners) have some success in solving problems involving first order direct proportions if the word problems are about familiar experiences and if pictorial representations or some kind of concrete references are included.

Farrell and Farmer (1985) in a study involving over 900 tenth, eleventh and twelfth grade students in college-bound mathematics and/or science classes, found that approximately 47% of the students could not solve a puzzle problem involving a simple direct proportion, where the variables were related in a $2:3$ ratio. The puzzle problem, which we called Mr. Tall and Mr. Short (see Figure 3.7), was developed by Robert Karplus and used both in multiple research studies, some of which have been cited earlier, and in inservice workshop materials (Karplus, R., Lawson, A. E., Wollman, W., Appel, M., Bernoff, R., Howe, A., Rusch,

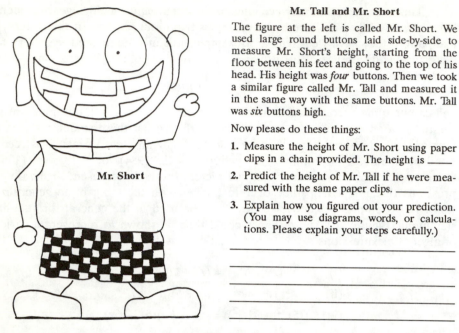

Mr. Tall and Mr. Short

The figure at the left is called Mr. Short. We used large round buttons laid side-by-side to measure Mr. Short's height, starting from the floor between his feet and going to the top of his head. His height was *four* buttons. Then we took a similar figure called Mr. Tall and measured it in the same way with the same buttons. Mr. Tall was *six* buttons high.

Now please do these things:

1. Measure the height of Mr. Short using paper clips in a chain provided. The height is ____

2. Predict the height of Mr. Tall if he were measured with the same paper clips. _____

3. Explain how you figured out your prediction. (You may use diagrams, words, or calculations. Please explain your steps carefully.)

_____

_____

_____

_____

Fig. 3.7

J. J., & Sullivan, F., 1977, p. 1–6). The common erroneous strategy was an additive one. Such students said that because Mr. Tall was two buttons taller than Mr. Short, he should be two paper clips taller. When a random sample of the successful students were interviewed on a hands-on proportionality task involving direct as well as inverse proportions (Inhelder and Piaget's [1958] projection of shadows task), only 24% were able to demonstrate successful reasoning. They were unable to correctly apply inverse proportional reasoning. The evidence supports Piaget's contention that proportional reasoning is a late acquisition of the formal stage of reasoning. That explains the difficulty teachers report with the teaching of fractions, percents, conversion from one system of measurement to another and other diverse topics requiring the understanding of proportions. In fact, Mc Bride and Chiapetta (1978), who studied ninth graders' understanding of equivalent fractions, concluded that ability to use that concept improved as proportional reasoning developed. Some mathematics educators have suggested that teachers should not move too quickly to the algorithm used to solve proportions: the product of the means equals the product of the extremes. Students seize on this easily memorized strategy statement and misapply it throughout their secondary school mathematics and science courses. Instead, it is recommended that tables of data be examined; that students get practice constructing equal ratios in different forms; and that concrete, geometric examples of proportion, such as enlarging and shrinking exercises, be included in instruction.

Another area of concern of secondary mathematics teachers is the learning of proof. The classic study of teaching axiomatics in America was Harold Fawcett's (1938) year-long course in geometry. In his class, students were expected to invent the axioms of the course and work together in a problem-solving mode. He reported considerable success with these students in understanding the nature of proof and in transferring some of the logical skills used in proof to real world situations. It seems that he anticipated the work of Piaget, doesn't it?

As you re-examine the reasoning patterns of the concrete and the formal reasoners in Table 3.1, you'll notice that the ability to produce a deductive proof requires the reasoning of the formal operational student. Among the areas studied by researchers are the theoretical nature of proof (Farrell, 1967), the development of the concept of proof (Lovell, 1971); the misconceptions underlying students' errors in proofwriting (Senk, 1985), and instruction to bridge the gap between student understanding and proving skills (e.g. Krist, 1981; Libeskind, 1980). Lovell found that when students between the ages of 16 and 18 were asked: "What do we mean by a hypothesis?" more than 20% of them thought a hypothesis is a true statement, or a proved statement, or one that cannot be proved. Lovell concluded that if the misconceptions of these students are not corrected, there is no way they can develop an understanding of the nature of proof. Some of the instructional research has provided suggestions for high school teachers, much of which is incorporated into the work in Chapter 7 on proofs in geometry. Some of the more recent work has made use of the microcomputer to give students practice and feedback with hypothesizing and the effect of hypothesizing in geometry (see Simulation/Practice exercise B).

These are only a few of the sample topics being studied by mathematics education researchers. The message is that mathematics teachers must realize that mistakes, especially consistent ones, need to be analyzed carefully rather than dismissed as evidence of failure to listen or failure to study. Very often the developmental differences among the students are the underlying sources of inability to understand a teacher's explanation.

3.4 INDIVIDUAL DIFFERENCES

We have already talked about the individual differences in cognitive development in a typical middle school or high school class. However, there are factors other than cognitive development that result in individual differences in reasoning performance. One such factor is called "cognitive style."

Cognitive Style

Cognitive style is usually described in terms of the two opposite ends of a continuum. Does a student seem to respond to problems quickly with the first idea associated with the problem (an example of impulsivity) or does he or she think about the problem and consider it from several angles before responding (an example of reflection)? Teachers have to be aware of these differences that adolescents may have developed over time and that affect how they respond to questions and thought activities in the classroom. If you pose a complex thought question, you may have to provide special cues for students on the impulsivity end of the continuum—("This is a question that I want everyone to have a chance to consider. No responses until I give a signal.").

Another way of considering cognitive style is in terms of a continuum with poles of field independence and field dependence. Field independent students are more flexible, are aware of the parts of a problem and tend to be analytical, while field dependent students attend to the global picture or the total environment. This aspect of cognitive style may explain why some students refuse to give up a problem-solving strategy even when it is not working. Adi and Pulos (1980) found that the field independent students were more likely than field dependent students to try a new strategy in problem-solving.

Processing Information

There are also differences in how students process information—the way they put ideas together mentally to help them recall the information or the application process. High performing students seem to seek efficient ways to *chunk* information. They seem to store organized structures, which Davis (1984) calls *frames*, in which rules and concepts are linked together. McDonald (1982) found that formal operational tenth graders had concept maps (ways of interrelating concepts and principles) very similar to those of experts in geometry and significantly different from those of the concrete operational students.

Differences in processing information may also be affected by differences in the ways student represent problems mentally. For example, a problem situation might be represented in a physical or visual way, an informal linguistic way, or an algebraic manner. Secondary school students vary in their ability to use all three ways effectively. Middle school students are just learning the connection between ordinary language and the language of symbols, whereas senior high students who are skilled symbol-manipulators have difficulty understanding the relationship between an algebraic statement and the real world situation modeled by it. From a developmental perspective, secondary students need visual and hands-on experiences to help them form the mental representations most likely to be retained in long-term memory. More generally, classroom experience with all three kinds of representation is needed to help students move gradually from one kind of representation to another (Resnick & Ford, 1981, p. 217).

Gender Differences

Gender differences in mathematics achievement have been studied by a number of mathematics educators (Fennema, 1975; Fennema & Sherman, 1978; Peterson & Fennema, 1985; Reyes, 1984). There appears to be no significant difference between the genders until middle school when girls outperform boys on calculation exercises and boys begin to outperform girls on problem solving exercises. Later differences, in favor of the males, have been partially attributed to the effect of stereotyping about mathematics as a subject. Youngsters in middle school and the first level high school classes have been found to hold the view that mathematics is a male-oriented subject. Probably as one result, adolescent girls have reported more math anxiety than adolescent boys and, thus, tend not to persevere in mathematics courses in the same numbers as boys. When these young women are in required mathematics classes, they avoid risks (or are victims of "learned helplessness") by seldom responding to complex questions. Instead, they resort to a learning style that depends on memorizing information. Thus, reasoning ability, performance, and eventual career choices can be affected by learned attitudes related to gender-stereotyping. Performance in mathematics may also be related to prior experiences of boys and girls outside of school in developing abilities needed to learn mathematics. For example, some girls have been found to outperform most boys in linguistic tasks and some boys, to outperform most girls in spatial tasks. These differences may result from the mass of experiences typically built up by boys in games, hobbies and out-of school work experiences that use spatial abilities and the contrasting experiences of girls with verbal tasks. Whatever the causes, mathematics teachers need to be conscious of the need to reverse this trend, which is already quite advanced by secondary school. Introduction of female and male role models in mathematics careers and reports on female and male mathematicians (See sources in Chapter 4) are two specific ways to begin to show that mathematics is a subject area open to women and men. It is important to monitor laboratory work and computer area use to ensure that males and females get equal access and are equally involved. Most important, the teacher has to demonstrate equal expectations for the males and females in the class. There is a growing set of resources in this area. See Chapter 11 for some of these resource books for teachers.

Slow Learners and Academically Talented Students

These two groups of students have been the subject of articles, yearbook chapters and research studies. As a result, we have learned about some of the most common reasoning and learning patterns of each group.

The slow learner   The "reluctant learner," the "underachiever"—these are some of the labels used to designate students who achieve below some minimum standard (Callahan & MacMillan, 1981; Lowry, 1972). When these labels are used to designate students at the **lowest** range of achievement they refer to students who tend to have poor study habits and learning difficulties. Their reasoning patterns are, at best, concrete operational, and, even then, restricted to the simplest reasoning of the concrete operational student. On tests of reading, listening and speaking, they score far below grade level. These adolescent students chunk in small bits and consequently score below criterion on retention tests. They try to represent information exactly as presented and, therefore, memory overload occurs very quickly. It is no surprise that these lowest achievers do not persevere in tasks, are motivated by short-range rather than long-range goals and have little self-confidence in their ability to learn.

Typical classroom instruction seems to fly in the face of these characteristics. Repetitious drill on arrays of meaningless (to the student) information is bound to fail with students whose memory skills are poor. What they do need is a variety of concrete, everyday activities presented in a meaningful manner to help them make sense out of schoolwork. They need many experiences with hands-on materials, careful step-by-step directions, intermittent reinforcement for progress and praise at each completed stage of the learning. Notice that there's little difference between this suggestion and those given for the concrete operational reasoner at any age. The chief difference is the need for strategies to combat the failure syndrome these learners have acquired. There must be built-in opportunities for deserved praise and positive reinforcement; the rate of presentation needs to be matched to the attention span and reading/listening levels of the students and problem situations must be in terms of real world experiences relevant to this age group. These adolescents may read at the second grade level and reason like fifth or sixth graders, but their interests are those of sixteen or seventeen year olds. The illustrations that follow illustrate some of the adaptations the teacher might use.

Omit the reading in a creatively designed worksheet and audiotape the directions, being careful to speak slowly, to repeat and to avoid complicated words. Arrange individual projects cooperatively with the industrial arts teacher, the coach or the art teacher. Teach the students to use calculators in lessons on problem situations and thus, remove one of their excuses for failure (*"I never could divide!"*). Engage them in the building of physical models to help them learn and practice measuring skills. Help them to construct a survey that they will use to interview other students and adults on a topic of interest to them (e.g. AIDS-literacy or teenage pregnancy) and teach them how to present the data in a table and on a graph. Ask the social studies teacher, the school nurse and, perhaps, the science teacher to work in conjunction with you on the discussion of such value-laden issues. Warning! Also first discuss the entire project with your cooperating teacher or department head.

It should be clear that we believe that these students can learn if taught in a meaningful way with many concrete experiences. What's all-important is that the teacher demonstrate the same belief. You do slow learners no service by passing them on despite inability to meet standards. However, reasonable standards, interesting and challenging activities, and the atmosphere promoted by a thoughtful teacher will help give the slow learner confidence and an appreciation of the accessibility of mathematics.

The academically talented   These students are not always those with the highest grades, nor even those who speed through exercise material. The young Galois was considered mediocre by his teachers, who advised that he be demoted. Bored and disinterested, he gave only passing attention to his studies. Subsequently, he amazed all by winning the prize in the general examinations despite his barely adequate results in traditional school work. An encounter with Legendre's geometry had aroused his enthusiasm, and he began to apply his intellectual talents to geometry and then to algebra. His contribution to the contemporary view of fundamental structures, such as group and field, is considered one of the milestones in the development of abstract algebra. History is replete with similar tales of intellectual giants who in their youth were considered stupid, recalcitrant, and unmotivated. Yet even in their youth, a discerning teacher would have been able to collect clues as to their capability.

What are the characteristics of this group of students? Their reasoning patterns develop more quickly than those of their age group and they process information in very efficient ways. Thus, they have well-developed memory skills. In fact, their excellent memory sometimes misleads teachers into assuming that they understand everything they can memorize (Ridge & Renzulli, 1981). Farmer (1983) tested a group of thirty academically talented middle school youngsters involved in a summer mathematics and science program who demonstrated superb memory skills and insightful responses to problems. It was tempting to assume that they would reason formally. In fact, their reasoning ranged from concrete to transitional and formal. Twenty-six out of the thirty students succeeded on the Tall-Short task depicted in Figure 3.7, but only eight were able to respond at the formal level to an inverse proportional reasoning task (the projection of shadows task).

While repetitious drill is wasted on the slow learner for one reason, it is an anathema to the academically talented for another reason. Bright students need less practice than the average student. However, bright students are able to go deeper and further into a problem situation than others in their age group. These academically talented students generalize after fewer hands-on activities. Notice that we aren't saying that the concrete basis can be omitted. (Think back to the nested stages model.) Given their capabilities, these academically talented students have more self-confidence and will persist in a task interesting to them over long periods of time. Thus, teachers can make excellent use of individualized projects.

In a twelfth-grade mathematics class, three gifted students had capabilities far beyond the rest of the class. By group consent, a special Friday class was designed. The three students worked in the room or the library reading and studying a topic external to the course while the rest of the students worked with the teacher on trouble spots identified during the week. Occasional teacher conferences with the talented students gave them a chance to report on progress.

Freedom to explore an interest, to use different methods of solution, and to seek answers to atypical questions is what the talented student needs. That doesn't mean that the teacher isn't needed, or that anything goes, or that the rest of the class can be ignored. Students who are working at an individual project while the rest of the class is pursuing a lesson should have clearly defined responsibilities. A teacher may "contract" with such students as to both the quality and the amount of work to be completed by a deadline. If talented students enjoy helping other students, they can, under careful supervision, become teacher aides. Some students find this role an exciting way of increasing their own depth in mathematics, but don't assume that all do. Diversity is the norm among humans.

3.5 SUMMARY AND SELF-CHECK

The subtitle of this chapter, "Adolescent Reasoning Patterns," was selected to emphasize the intellectual gap between you and your students. You presumably, have learned the subject matter you will be teaching. However, you have transformed it so completely from your initial experience with it that your resulting knowledge is now in a form inappropriate for the initial learning of your students. Somehow you have to retrieve that initial experience and help your students to transform knowledge successfully. To do this, you must first learn all you can about the adolescent intellect, their particular reasoning patterns in areas of mathematics, and the individual differences that affect the development of their reasoning. How do your students learn? What has been their history of knowing? What do their questions and errors tell you? What differences can you expect in a typical classroom? These and related questions have been the subject matter of this chapter.

In this chapter, secondary students' reasoning was described as an active, constructive process. The development of reasoning from sensori-motor to pre-operational to concrete and, then, formal reasoning was outlined, with special emphasis on the reasoning of the concrete and formal operational thinkers. The importance of interaction, in particular social interaction, in cognitive development was described. The way in which all of us develop our reasoning abilities by interacting with environmental stimuli was pictured as a matching-patching analogy (adaptation). Recent research results related to reasoning problems in particular secondary mathematics areas were described. Individual cognitive differences that have an effect on the reasoning of adolescents about mathematics were presented and special attention was given to low achievers and academically talented students. Throughout the chapter, specific implications for mathematics instruction were provided.

The title of this chapter is repeated in the shaded component of the instructional model on the title page of the chapter. Notice the connecting link between that box and the "Structure of Mathematics" component. Although there have been continuous references to student reasoning about mathematics in this chapter, the emphasis has been on the student. It is now important to highlight mathematics itself—the subject of the next chapter.

Now you should be able to:

1. Operationally define cognitive interaction, social interaction, adaptation, accommodation, and assimilation.

2. Contrast the abilities of the concrete operational reasoner with those of the formal operational reasoner.

3. Explain the significance of the nested stages model.

4. Give at least two types of individual differences which could have an effect on reasoning.

5. Rank instructional modes from most to least promising in terms of research on the cognitive development of adolescents, given a specific set of modes and a description of the students.

6. Classify student behavior in terms of research on adolescent reasoning after viewing a "live" or video-taped lesson in which students were involved in a laboratory problem-solving activity.

7. Suggest at least three different methods that could be used to obtain some initial clues as to your students' cognitive development.

The exercises that follow include some additional ways to deepen your understanding of the theory and research on adolescents' reasoning and help you apply that understanding to issues of instruction in mathematics.

3.6 SIMULATION/PRACTICE ACTIVITIES

A. Ms. Pringle told her eighth-grade class to cut out the three squares constructed on the sides of a right triangle (see Figure 3.8). Then they were directed to cut the smaller squares into five sections using the dashed lines and to try to "cover" the largest square with these five pieces. Eventually all the students were able to complete the task. Next she asked the class to imagine cutting one or more of the five sections so as to obtain six (or eight or ten) total sections. "Would we still be able to 'cover' the large square if we used the new set of six (or eight or ten) sections? Why or why not? " Most students agreed that the square would still be covered with six sections, but as Ms. Pringle increased the number of sections they were to think about, some weren't sure what would happen. Two students argued loudly that if the pieces were small enough, there would be so many of them that they would overlap the largest square.

    Explain the reaction of these two students and the confusion of others in the light of Piagetian theory.

B. Obtain a copy of "The Geometric Supposers: Triangles" and review its uses on an available microcomputer. (This courseware has versions for the 64K Apple II family, the 128K IBM PC or PCjr., and the 256K Tandy 1000.) Study the teacher's guide and try out some of the activities. Be prepared to talk about the reasoning needed to succeed on the various activities.

C. Make copies of the TALL-SHORT puzzle (Figure 3.7) and prepare chains of ten #1 paper clips. Then try out the puzzle on a sample of volunteer junior high and senior high students. Be prepared to talk about the data.

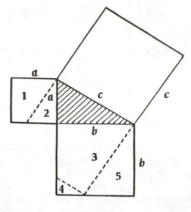

Fig. 3.8

D. Prepare a geoboard with a square outlined in rubber band, so that the sides of the square are parallel to the edges of the geoboard. Prepare a second geoboard with a square outlined in rubber band, so that the sides of the square are not parallel to the edges of the geoboard. Then try this "test" on some adolescents or adults. Show them each geoboard in turn and ask what kind of figure is outlined by the rubber band; but be sure to hold each geoboard so that one pair of edges is parallel to the floor. (Be prepared for responses of "square" and "diamond.") If the respondent says "diamond" to the figure on the second geoboard, slowly turn the board so that the square is oriented in *typical* fashion, i.e. with one pair of sides parallel to the floor. Then ask the question again. What is the relationship of these kinds of responses to the reasoning patterns presented in this chapter?

E. The M & M lab described here was used by a junior high teacher. After reading about the lab, identify the ways in which the lesson incorporates aspects of research and theory on the reasoning of junior high students.

LAB: The teacher divided the class into pairs and gave each pair a small bag of M & M's (20 brown, 8 yellow, 8 orange and 4 green in each bag).The students were to predict how many M & M's of each color were in the bag without looking. After demonstrating how to carefully shake the bag and how to draw without looking, the teacher told the groups to draw one candy, record its color, return it to the bag, draw, record and return that candy to the bag, and so on until each pair had completed 40 draws. Each pair's totals were recorded on the board and a class set of totals was obtained. The ensuing discussion included a consideration of empirical probability, the comparison of the results with the actual contents of the bags, and a consideration of theoretical probability. (Farmer & Farrell, 1986).

SUGGESTIONS FOR FURTHER STUDY

Adler, I. (1966). "Mental growth and the art of teaching." *Mathematics Teacher*, **59**, 706–715.

Adler's article has become a classic introduction to Piaget's theory. It has the advantage of focusing on highlights, identifying and disposing of major misconceptions about the theory, and specifically pinpointing implications for all teachers in both the choice of strategy and of content. Since all the examples are from mathematics or science, the article can be read with most profit by teachers of those disciplines. The reader will do well to obtain a basic understanding of Piagetian theory from *other* sources and to read Adler for his interpretation of Piagetian contributions to the "Art of Teaching." They are excellent!

Glennon, V. J. (Ed.). (1981). *The mathematical education of exceptional children and youth: An inter-disciplinary approach.* Reston, VA: National Council of Teachers of Mathematics.

This professional reference source uses the term "exceptional" in the contemporary sense. The term refers to all those youth who deviate from the "average or normal" youth in mental characteristics, sensory abilities, neuromuscular or physical characteristics, social or emotional behavior, communication abilities, or in multiple handicaps to the extent that they require some modification of school practices in order to reach their potential. Two chapters are of particular relevance in terms of the introduction to the slow learner and the academically talented in Chapter 3 of this text. In Chapter 5, Callahan and MacMillan describe the particular characteristics of slow-learning or mentally retarded children and suggest appropriate modifications to be made in teaching mathematics to them. In Chapter 6, Ridge & Renzulli give an extensive treatment of the issue of teaching mathematics to talented or gifted students and include many excellent classroom illustrations. Experienced teachers will find all of the remaining chapters of this text to be useful as each of the other types of exceptionality is explored and the implications for mathematics teaching, based on research and theoretical concerns, are presented.

Gorman, R. M. (1972). *Discovering Piaget: A guide for teachers.* Columbus, Ohio: Charles E. Merrill.

This small paperback is still the best introduction to Piaget on the market. The author intends that the book will promote a guided discovery approach and so encourage that interaction at the core of Piaget's theory. For this reason, much of the material is read with ease. The exception is the section on the INRC group (pages 44–57), which is highly technical and could well be omitted in favor of concentration on other sections.

Jacob, S. A. (1984). *Foundation for Piagetian education.* Lanham, MD: University of America Press.

This book is highly recommended for both beginners and those with some background in the developmental psychology of Piaget. The author has succeeded in accurately reflecting Piaget's work and in developing educational practices related directly from his epistemology. The result is a very readable and valuable source for teachers.

Lowry, William C. (Ed.). (1972). *The slow learner in mathematics* (Thirty-fifth yearbook), Reston, VA: National Council of Teachers of Mathematics.

This yearbook contains chapters written by different authors on the characteristics of the slow learner, the ways to provide a promising instructional environment, and some specific suggestions for classroom use. Some of the chapters are directed at teachers of primary grades, but others contain ideas of interest across the middle and senior high years. Of particular interest to secondary school mathematics teachers are the descriptions of promising programs and practices found in Chapter 11. Don't be surprised if many of the activities and games found in Appendix A seem appropriate for the average middle school youngster.

CHAPTER FOUR

THE STRUCTURE
OF MATHEMATICS

Products and Processes

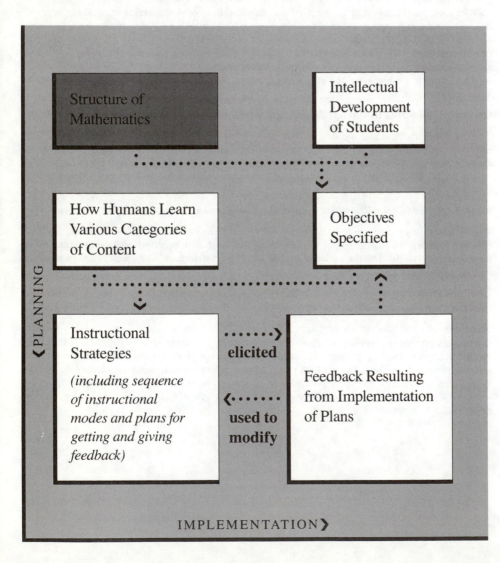

It is a truism that we learn more about a subject when we teach it. Every tutor, swimming coach, and scout leader knows the experience. So be prepared for some rude shocks to your mathematical belief system. Such shocks are part of teaching and can be learned from and capitalized on. In this chapter we'll pose a range of questions designed to help you learn (and relearn) mathematics from views other than that of a student.

Why is a thorough analysis of subject matter content and structure so important? Why pursue this matter at this particular point in our study of teaching? Let's see if you can begin to formulate answers to these questions by looking back at the opening page of this chapter. Note that the shaded box, "Structure of Mathematics," couples with the previously treated "Intellectual Development of Students" portion of the instructional model to form the bases for specifying objectives. In any thoughtful approach to instruction it is vital to formulate clear objectives that closely match both the students they are presumed to affect and the subject matter content they are claimed to represent. Why vital? As the rest of the model depicts, these objectives will be used to design instructional strategies, guide the collection of feedback, and then be reassessed in light of resultant learning. Thus the teacher's comprehension of the subject matter of mathematics will have profound effects on all aspects of instruction. Now is the time to face the issues. College students typically have spent nearly all of their time in three to four years of mathematics courses committing to memory the mechanics of the subject, dutifully completing exercises in how to obtain the correct answers and learning how to prepare for final examinations. A few college students have experienced courses in the history, philosophy, or structure of the discipline of mathematics where the focus has been on the analysis of various subcategories of knowledge within the subject matter and the interdependence of the processes used to generate knowledge within this specialized field. If you are one of the fortunate few with this type of background, a quick reading of the early sections of this chapter should suffice to check the completeness of your own comprehension. If you are one of the great majority who have not yet concerned yourself with the structure of mathematical knowledge and the processes used to generate it, you will need to give immediate and concentrated attention to this chapter.

We begin by asking you to take a stand on an issue that intrigued scholars for centuries. The issue is phrased as an either/or, but not both statement.

Mathematics was invented

or

Mathematics was discovered

You must choose a stance now. So stop and consider the implications of each statement. Let's be clear about the meaning assigned to the key words. *Invented* is to be thought of as it is used in a sentence such as "Alexander Graham Bell invented the telephone," while *discovered* is to be used in the sense of "Mary discovered her diamond ring under the counter." Notice that in both cases the person may have had an insightful idea, but in Mary's search the product—a ring—was not altered or brought into being by her activity. Take a few minutes of thinking time to decide on your position before reading any further.

Did you choose "invented"? Then how do you explain the novel work in the calculus by both Newton and Leibniz, who independently came to similar conclusions? There was much bitterness in seventeenth-century England when Leibniz published his findings first and thus received acclaim throughout Europe. Perhaps the basic concepts of the calculus always existed and were waiting for the insightful searching of Newton and Leibniz? However, if the concepts existed in some "discoverable" sense, like Mary's ring, they could be seen, touched, or perhaps heard. However, Newton's formulation of the concept of an "infinitesmal" was startling to him and to mathematicians for the next two centuries. After all, all basic concepts were, they thought, supposed to be self-evident truths and there just was no way in which the infinitesmal corresponded to the physical world. Thus Newton "invented" the concept of the infinitesmal.

If the cornerstones of mathematics were invented to satisfy a practical or theoretical need, then the teacher must point out the reasons behind a definition, a label, or a rule, explore with students alternative beginnings, and encourage mathematizing. Why is 5/0 undefined? Mr. Harris might say, "That's just the way it is. We must accept it as fact." Ms. Marple might say, "Let's see what division means. What do you think the answer should be? If 0 is the answer, it should check. Let's try it. Let's try Jack's idea, too. Does 5 check? Now will any number times 0 equal 5? You see, that's the reason: because our definition of division is such that none of the numbers will work."

What stance do you think Ms. Marple or Mr. Harris would have taken on the invented/discovered question? What is your stance now? The question is not closed. There is much more to learn. In the next sections you'll do some mathematizing yourself. That should help you assess and, possibly, redefine your thoughts on this matter.

4.1 INTRODUCTORY ACTIVITY

Mathematics is a verb, as well as a noun.

What do we do when we mathematize? What do we obtain? In this activity you are asked to identify as many processes and products of mathematics as you can. Think junior/senior high mathematics, and complete a chart like the one portrayed by Figure 4.1 Write nouns under the "products" column and the "ing" form of verbs under the "processes" column.

Products of mathematics	Processes of mathematics
Corollary	Generalizing
Formula	Computing
Number	Assuming

Fig. 4.1

A. Think geometry, algebra, arithmetic, and so on and try to formulate as complete a list as possible.

B. Compare your chart with those of at least two other classmates and try to resolve any differences you have found.

C. Which of the listed processes are employed primarily by the user of established mathematics? Which are used primarily by the person who needs to develop novel mathematics?

D. Try to rank, or to classify, both the products and the processes in the order in which they might occur in the development of mathematics. (Did you remember to include deducing and inducing?)

E. Which of the processes are likely to be emphasized in junior high mathematics? Which in senior high mathematics?

As you read through this chapter, you may want to revise your original chart. In this and later chapters we'll consider ways of teaching these aspects of the subject matter.

4.2 PRODUCT ASPECTS OF MATHEMATICS

If you included postulate and theorem in your list of products, you were probably thinking of high school geometry. However, some of you may have learned that there are postulates and theorems in arithmetic and algebra. Most contemporary high-school texts are designed to introduce students to theorems in the real number system, such as $(-a)(-b) = ab$. This emphasis on structure in which many general results are deduced from a small number of accepted statements is a key aspect of the nature of mathematics. Since you will be teaching about structure in algebra, geometry, and even in junior high mathematics classes, it is important that the nature of the products directly related to structure be crystal clear. That's "old hat" to a mathematics major, isn't it? Maybe it should be, but if you're not quite ready to distinguish postulate from theorem, don't be discouraged. Even Euclid, the genius of geometry, found that these distinctions were not easily made. We'll review just a few of his decisions and their consequences.

Don't get the wrong idea! Euclid was, indeed, a genius who is credited with the initial, monumental task of systematizing much of the mathematics used in his time. Thus, he might be considered the father of the present-day emphasis on structure. Strange though it seems now, most of the relationships in Euclidean geometry were known and used *before* Euclid. A cuneiform tablet dating from 1900 B.C. to 1600 B.C. provides evidence that the Babylonians were familiar with at least 15 sets of what are now called "Pythagorean Triples" (NCTM, 1969). However, Euclid accomplished the creative work of arranging these results in a hierarchical fashion, in which d followed c if d could be derived from c alone or else from c and any of a and b.

Nevertheless, one of Euclid's first mistakes was that he tried to define everything—an impossibility that yielded some ridiculous results. Here is his "definition" of a point. *A point is that which has no part.* It was not until the work of nineteenth-century mathematicians, such as Gauss, Bolyai, Lobachevsky, and

Riemann, who initiated a re-examination of the foundations of mathematics, that the necessity for beginning with *undefined concepts* was universally accepted. If you wrote point, straight line, or plane in your list of products, you were identifying *undefined concepts* from plane Euclidean geometry. We can give meaning to such concepts by asserting relationships that we wish to exist among them. For example, a familiar relationship called a *postulate* is: Two points determine a straight line. That postulate asserts something about the nature of a straight line. Other postulates add different shades of meaning to the notion we wish everyone to share. We no longer try to define *straight line*. (Unfortunately, there are still some junior and senior high texts that include so-called definitions of *each* of these terms. One of your responsibilities as a mathematics teacher will be to correct errors such as this in instructional materials.)

The second "error" made by Euclid would seem completely reasonable if you were one of his contemporaries. Postulates were considered self-evident truths and, thus, were accepted without proof. As history makes clear, Euclid's view of the nature of postulates (and the nature of mathematics) was upheld by most mathematicians until the nineteenth century. The famous story of the "parallel postulate" reads like science fiction. We can only highlight a small portion of it here, but we urge you to read the entire tale.

Euclid's fifth postulate is wordy and sounds complicated. Surely a postulate ought to be a *simple* statement of the self-evident! Something so complicated should be proved, so throughout the centuries, famous mathematicians tried to prove the fifth postulate (or an equivalent version of it). Nothing worked! The attempt of Saccheri, who used the indirect method of proof, is an object lesson. It is said that Saccheri, who was not able to deduce a contradiction from both of his negations of the postulate, ignored the possibility that perhaps there was no contradiction and altered his work so that it would seem to "vindicate Euclid."

What is Euclid's fifth postulate? Most of you learned it in the form proposed by Playfair: On a plane, through a point external to a given line, there is one and only one line parallel to the given line. The statement seems obvious and is a good match to experience. It is not surprising that mathematicians hesitated to consider alternatives—none of them had your vantage point. You have vicariously traveled in spaceships and have seen (via television) that the earth is not a good physical model of the Euclidean plane. It is all the more remarkable that three nineteenth-century mathematicians turned their attention from trying to prove the fifth postulate to instead proposing substitute postulates.

When Bolyai proposed his substitute postulate—that through a point not on a line *infinitely many* lines may be drawn in the plane, each parallel to the given line—the geometry he derived from this postulate and other postulates was ridiculed by many as the work of a madman. Such was also the case with Riemann's non-Euclidean geometry, which was based on another substitute postulate: Through a point not on a line, *no line* may be drawn parallel to the given line. Yet Riemann's geometry later was used in the theory of relativity developed by Einstein.

What is the nature of postulates? *Postulates* are, indeed, *statements accepted without proof, which together with defined and undefined concepts are used to prove theorems by means of deductive logic*. Some may seem obvious, but others may appear to flaunt the evidence of our senses. That possibility makes mathematics seem very much like mental gymnastics. Is Bertrand Russell's comment that mathematics is a game, "where we never know what we are talking about, nor whether what we are saying is true" (Russell, 1929, p. 75) a correct description of mathematics? It's not quite that capricious a subject. The criteria for a mathematical system, criteria built into Euclid's formulation, are simplicity, parsimony, sufficiency, and consistency. The choice of postulates should not violate these criteria. Above all, a set of postulates must be consistent.

When we defined *postulate*, we, at the same time, defined *theorem*. Why can we make that claim? Take a second look at the definition of *postulate* and convert it into one which begins: *A theorem is*... You should have obtained a statement equivalent to the following: *A theorem is a statement that is proved by deductive logic on the basis of postulates, defined concepts, undefined concepts, and other theorems*. Notice that we did not use the verb form *can be proved*. Sometimes mathematicians and textbook writers assert statements that *can* be proved as postulates. Proof may not be included for reasons such as simplicity or efficiency (or even because the mathematician has not yet been able to contrive a proof). Theorems are remarkable products of mathematics. Given the same set of postulates and concepts, they are statements that are true for all time.

> *The area of a triangle is equal to one-half the product of its base and the height to that base.*

This theorem holds for all triangles and will never be rejected on the basis of future research in mathematics. To put it another way, the probability that some future researcher will find a triangle (remember, we must agree to accept the postulates and concepts on which this proof is based) whose area isn't equal to $(\frac{1}{2})bh$ is zero. Why are we so certain? If you're struggling with an answer like "You can't *find* a triangle!" or "A triangle isn't something you can touch or see," you've correctly identified the source of our certainty—the nature of mathematical concepts. Without saying much about it so far, we've been gradually introducing you to this other major product of mathematics.

What is a concept, whether defined or undefined? If you included terms such as *triangle, integer, pi, locus, congruence, set,* and *inequality* in your products list, you were referring to a few of the defined concepts of mathematics. When you learned the concept of triangle, you may have been shown triangular shapes—cardboard cutouts, three pipe cleaners tied together, or pictures of triangular grids on bridges. Eventually, you learned that all these objects and drawings were representations or physical models of a triangle, not the triangle itself. In fact, you probably learned the concept of triangle before you were taught to recite a definition, and you may have even learned quite a bit about the concept

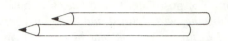

Fig. 4.2   Bella's model of two intersecting lines.

before anyone told you its name. So a concept is not its label, nor is it any physical model or single example.

What is a concept? Some people use as synonyms words such as *idea*,
thought model, and *classification*. We prefer *classification*, since the first two terms
have meanings broader than that of *concept*. We have synthesized the following
definition as one that seems consistent with psychology of learning usage and, at
the same time, applicable to mathematics content. A *concept* is *a classification of
objects, object-properties, or events into a set by the process of abstraction*.

The concept itself, then, exists in the mind as an abstraction. Mathematical
concepts, as we've seen, can be only imperfectly represented by physical models.
Therein lies one of the challenging instructional problems for you as a teacher.
Bella insists that two different lines can intersect in more than one point and
demonstrates that concept by placing two pencils together, as shown in Figure
4.2. Think about Piaget's description of intellectual development as you reflect
on Bella's conclusions.

Bella has a confused concept of line, and perhaps of intersection. It will be
difficult to make her realize that distinct lines, whether parallel or not, occupy
distinct locations in the plane if Bella is totally reliant on concrete objects for
learning. A variety of physical representations, analogies, and questions will help
to disturb her complacence and are the best hope for helping to correct her view
of these mathematical concepts.

Have you learned the concept of a concept? Test yourself on a novel instance. Which of the following would you classify as concepts?

1. tangent lines

2. isosceles trapezoid

3. $C = \pi d$

4. greater than

5. infinite

6. area

You should have selected all but item 3 as concepts. Notice that items 1 and 2
are formed by adding another essential attribute to an existing concept. Item 4
describes a relationship between members of another concept (for example, 7
is greater than 2). Sometimes this kind of concept is called a *relational concept*.
Why is item 3 rejected? Although several concepts (diameter, π, equals, circumference) are referred to, this statement is more than the sum of these concepts.
When concepts are chained together to result in a standard procedure, the result is known as a rule or a principle. All theorems and postulates fall into this
category. Some are abbreviated into statements called formulas (e.g., $C = \pi d$).
Some are described by a set of sequential steps and are called algorithms (e.g.,
the division algorithm).

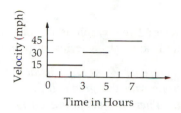

Fig. 4.3   Graph of velocity of a car.

Why bother with different labels for the same mathematical product? The major reason is that we are reminded to emphasize something different in our instruction. When we treat $C = \pi d$ as a theorem, we are focusing on proof. When we treat it as a formula (one kind of rule), we are emphasizing application in type or novel problem solving. Both aspects are important parts of mathematics instruction.

The final product of mathematics subsumes all those dealt with so far. A *mathematical model* refers to *a set of mathematical terms and statements that appears to be an idealized, but faithful, reflection of data and/or events in the physical world*. We emphasize "*appears to be*" since a model, by its ideal nature, cannot exactly match real world phenomena. Often a product of mathematics (such as a formula, a graph, a number system, or even a collection of points and lines) is called a mathematical model of a particular phenomenon.

Much of the mathematics taught in junior and senior high classes would be more meaningful to students if the concept of a mathematical model were introduced. Consider the two situations that follow and ways in which each offers the teacher an opportunity to help students sense the relevance and power of mathematics.

In an eighth-grade class, Jack Wiseguy raises his hand and offers the following contribution: "My father says $1 + 1$ isn't always equal to 2. Put one drop of water together with another drop of water. You get one drop of water." Jack may be showing off, but he's also posing a legitimate question. How would you respond?

Jack Wiseguy might be nonplussed if you showed him the following demonstration. Add 1 cup of water to 1 cup of alcohol. (You get *less* than 2 cups of liquid.) Here is an example of a mathematical model, the natural numbers, which behave as we'd like them to when we apply them to some physical objects but not to others. It would be difficult to explain all that to Jack, but this would be an excellent opportunity to have the class try to find other examples in the physical world where only certain kinds of numbers are used. A good "homework" assignment is the direction to write down the kind and size of numbers on cans in the cupboard, signs on the street, appliances in the kitchen, and so on. The possibilities for the next day's lesson are limitless.

In the next situation, a graph (Figure 4.3) has been flashed on the overhead projector screen in a ninth-grade class.

The teacher has described this graph as the picture of the velocity of a car traveling for eight hours and now asks a series of questions.

"What do the steps represent? What happens at the end of the third hour? There's something wrong with this graph. It doesn't quite match what happens in a moving car. Where are the points on the graph where these discrepancies show up?"

This teacher's set of questions suggests an entree to the topic of mathematical models, the idealized situation which here distorts reality badly if we're concerned with acceleration. Yet if average velocity over a time period is our only concern, then the graph isn't a bad picture of the data. Whenever we abstract from a physical situation, distortion must occur. If the distortions are too great, then the chosen mathematical model will not be a faithful predictor of the selected real-world events and must be rejected. The teacher has an opportunity to give students an illustration of the choices that must be made and, in this case, a practical rationale for doing so.

The consideration of mathematical models leads us to the second aspect of mathematics you were asked about in the Introductory Activity: How do mathematicians invent mathematics? What are their working activities?

4.3 PROCESS ASPECTS OF MATHEMATICS

Remember, "mathematics is also a verb." Deductive processes associated with actions such as assuming, computing, hypothesizing, and proving were referred to in the previous section. But so were inductive processes implied by actions like testing, conjecturing, and generalizing. Were these listed in the chart you formulated in Section 4.1? Which did you omit? If you included all the above, you have a head start on the work of Chapter 5, where we will consider the objectives of mathematics instruction.

However, we also portrayed mathematicians as those who sometimes idealized physical situations by *abstracting* and *symbolizing* both objects and relationships among objects—two more processes of mathematics. The language of mathematics has been a powerful, historic asset to developments in knowledge. Consider the classical Greek version of

$$a^2 + 2ab + b^2 = (a + b)(a + b)$$

Since the symbols in the above statement had not yet been devised, the Greeks could not easily handle problems involving the square of a binomial. Yet they used this relationship by operating with the dissection and rearrangement of square and rectangular shapes (Eves, 1963; Kline, 1972). Figure 4.4 illustrates one way they may have depicted the dissection of the square region with sides of length $(a + b)$ into the sum of four regions, a square with edge a, a square with edge b, and two rectangles, each with edges a and b. Imagine attempting to solve complicated equations by such methods. Yet they did. But, it is also

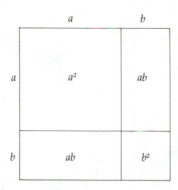

Fig. 4.4 The dissection of $(a + b)^2$.

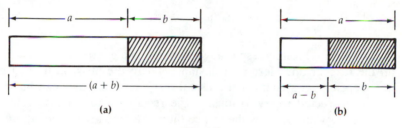

Fig. 4.5

understandable why some apparently simple areas of mathematics were delayed by the lack of the symbolic tools that many ninth-grade algebra students now manipulate with relative ease.

The Greek use of regions is not just a historical curiosity, but also an excellent way to introduce some of the algebraic formulas we teach. Have students use cutout square and rectangular shapes and attempt to generate different ways of picturing the same algebraic phrase. You will have to define $(a + b)$ as the placing of two strips of differing lengths next to each other, while $(a - b)$, where a is longer than b, is shown by overlapping the strips (see Figures 4.5a and 4.5b).

Next, demonstrate to them the product of two quantities as a rectangular region whose dimensions are the two factors, as in Figure 4.4. Students will easily obtain the usual equivalent for $a(b + c)$, but will find that transforming $a^2 - b^2$ requires more ingenuity (see Figure 4.6). Remind them that while you (and perhaps some of them) used algebraic tools to obtain the equivalent results, the Greeks obtained these by testing and merely using their agreed-upon assumptions. They used a result if it appeared to be helpful or simpler. Your students may obtain results that the Greeks chose to ignore. For example, $a^2 - b^2 = (a - b)^2 + 2 \cdot b(a - b)$. Of course, this expression can be transformed into the typical $(a + b)(a - b)$ by dividing by the common factor $(a - b)$. Would you expect the average ninth grader to understand that transformation? Reconsider the

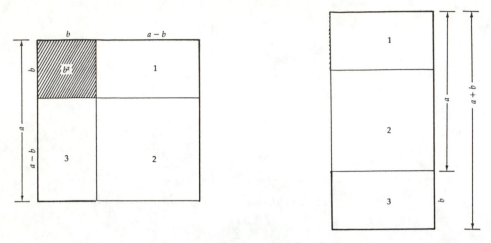

Fig. 4.6 The dissection of $a^2 - b^2$.

research results on reasoning, especially reasoning in algebra, from Chapter 3. So what can the teacher do? Here is an instance where the physical transformation of cut-out shapes helps students get a useful result in a way they can understand. They can be instructed to try to form single rectangles or squares, rather than L-shaped figures, whenever possible, since then only one area needs to be represented.

The history of mathematics contains other illustrations of the ways mathematicians used the processes of mathematics—sometimes to solve long-standing real world problems. Consider the work of the third century B.C. Greek mathematician, Eratosthenes. Eratosthenes worked on the problem of measuring the circumference of the earth. His fame is due to his creative use of data and the very simplicity of the processes he applied to solve this problem.

Eratosthenes was the director of the library at Alexandria and, as such, collected data he later used to obtain his final measure. He knew that at noon on the day we know as the summer solstice, the rays of the sun were reflected from the water in a deep well near Syene (now Aswan). At this time when the sun casts no shadow, it is at its zenith. Eratosthenes had learned the following relationships, all of which he used:

1. When a heavenly body, such as the sun, is at its zenith, a line joining that body to an observer passes through the center of the earth.

2. The rays of light coming from such a distant source appear to be parallel.

3. At noon, the sun is located directly over the observer's meridian of longitude.

Eratosthenes reasoned that if he knew the measure of angle C (see Figure 4.7) and the distance from Syene to Alexandria, then he could use a simple proportion to find the circumference of the earth. (By this time, the use of 360 degrees as the measure of a complete revolution was standard among astronomers.)

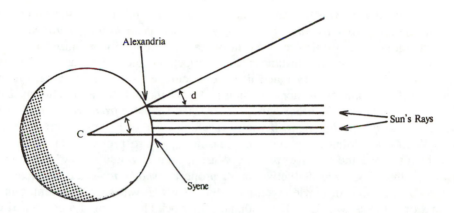

Fig. 4.7   Diagram for estimating circumference of earth.

Eratosthenes used an estimate of 5,000 *stadia*, or about 500 miles, as the distance from Syene to Alexandria. Now all he needed was the measure of angle C, an angle at the center of the earth. Yes, he knew, as geometry students learn, that the measure of angle d would be equal to that of angle C. Historians (see Boyer, 1968; Smith, 1925) are not sure how the measure of angle d was obtained. Perhaps Eratosthenes calculated the measure of d by measuring the length of the shadow of a pillar of known height—the shadow method of triangulation often taught to junior high students. His estimate for angle d was about $7°12'$. The rest was easy. He solved the problem by using the reasoning illustrated by the proportion

$$7°12' : 360° = 5000 : x$$

Eratosthenes thus obtained a circumference of 250,000 *stadia*. This is equivalent to a diameter of 7,850 miles, only 50 miles less than the polar diameter used today.

Did you notice the use of observing, collecting data, and reducing data to a minimal set in the work of Eratosthenes? Just as surely, he used agreed-upon assumptions and deduced his various estimates by calculation. Why were we careful to say he used the "reasoning illustrated by the proportion ... "? Remember, symbolism so natural to us was not available at the time of Eratosthenes. The history of the contribution of Eratosthenes is a valuable way to introduce students to the study of circles, the central angle, the measure of arcs, and more.

Apparently, Eratosthenes used both inductive and deductive processes in his measurement of the earth's circumference. Induction or deduction—which kind of thinking did Sherlock Holmes use? From the clues he found, he arrived at conclusions as to the killer, motive, and method. When Watson asked Holmes how he reached his conclusions, Holmes would reply, "Deduction, Watson, pure deduction." Was it pure *deduction*, or did Holmes actual use *induction*? Stop here and formulate an operational definition of inductive thinking and of deductive thinking. We'll warn you that the terms are frequently misused in the literature. If you said *inductive reasoning proceeds from the particular to the general*, you are correct. Inductive reasoning must be in operation when we generalize (arrive at conclusions) from specific instances. So Sherlock Holmes often used inductive reasoning. He behaved very much like the researcher who collects data, orders and classifies it, and then mentally "jumps from" the data to a conclusion. *Deductive reasoning*, on the other hand, *occurs when we move from an accepted generalization to specific instances.* If you're recalling some of Holmes' conversations with Watson as Holmes explained his reasoning, you're probably remembering that he also used the "If A were true, Watson, then B would follow" argument. Thus, Holmes also used deductive, more properly *hypothetico-deductive*, reasoning. Sir Arthur Conan Doyle invented a detective who was surely reasoning in a formal operational way. Like Eratosthenes, Sherlock Holmes used a combination of inductive and deductive reasoning—never *pure deduction*. You'll be helping your students learn through illustrations of both kinds of reasoning.

Inductive reasoning is an excellent way to help students see for themselves some of the rules and concepts of mathematics. Sometimes we call it *looking for patterns*. However, inductive reasoning must be treated with care. In the transcript of Ms. Pauli's lesson, several excellent tactics are employed, but she makes at least one serious error. Identify both the positive approaches she used and the error. Ms. Pauli is trying to have her junior high students "see" a pattern—in this case, a rule for multiplying two decimals.

"Class, as I write each example on the board, raise your hand if you know the answer."

1. $2/10 \times 3/10 = ?$

2. $5/10 \times 4/10 = ?$

3. $7/10 \times 6/10 = ?$

Ms Pauli quickly got answers of 6/100, 20/100, and 42/100. Next she wrote the following examples on the board and asked the class to compare these with the first three examples.

4. $.2 \times .3 = ?$

5. $.5 \times .4 = ?$

6. $.7 \times .6 = ?$

"Cindy, do you have an idea?"

"I know the answers. They're the same as before."

"What do others think? Is she right? Why?"

(Many hands wave agreement. Joe says that all Ms. Pauli did was change the fractions in the first three examples into a decimal form.)

"That's very good. Now try the next three examples."

  7. .9 × .2 =?

  8. .8 × .8 =?

  9. .3 × .5 =?

After checking the answers, Bob says that he has found a shortcut.

"I just multiplied the whole numbers, 9 × 2 in example 7, to get 18. Then I counted to the left for two decimal places."

"Class, let's test Bob's rule. Does it work for example 8? 9?

(All agree Bob's rule works for these examples.)

"Good. Let's test it on examples 4, 5, and 6."

(The class takes more time over example 4, but finally all agree that Bob's rule works for these three examples, too.)

"Now, class, all of you use Bob's rule on examples 1 and 4 from page 17 in your text. If it works there, we've proved that Bob's rule is correct."

Did you notice the sequence in which Ms. Pauli presented the examples? She wanted her students to observe data, classify that into a pattern based on previous knowledge, and be able to apply that pattern. Look at the examples again and try to identify the characteristics which seem to be positive aspects of pattern constructing.

Where is the error? Ms. Pauli's class did obtain a generalization from these instances but they didn't *prove* it. Nor will they prove it by further tests on other instances. Further positive tests will simply improve the *probability* that Bob's rule is the desired one. *Inductive reasoning never results in proof.* Could Ms. Pauli have *proved* Bob's rule? Yes, quite easily, if she had merely let Bob defend his rule. He might have argued that it followed from the earlier multiplication examples and the rewriting of a fraction with a denominator of 100 as a decimal. Bob may have used different words, but if his message was a paraphrase of that explanation then he would be using deductive methods of proof. Should eighth-graders bother with proof at all? Yes, whenever possible, for the essence of mathematics is lost without it, but teachers should encourage informal arguments and avoid formalistic rigor.

In this case, there is another flaw in Ms. Pauli's lesson. The conceptual pattern that is at the basis of the multiplication of decimals was captured more clearly by Cindy and Joe who saw that fractions with denominators of 10 or 100 were simply other forms of decimals. By seeming to emphasize Bob's shortcut, instead of Cindy and Joe's pattern, Ms. Pauli may be asking for trouble. Bob's shortcut may represent a misconception—a superficial pattern based on these limited examples. If he were asked to give the answer to $.3 \times .06$, perhaps he would apply his rule blindly and get a result of .18. Ms. Pauli must be sure that neither Bob, nor any of the other students, has invented a simple rule that is not based on meaningful mathematics. Careful questioning and gradually differentiated examples are always part of a lesson that includes finding patterns. The students will invent their own strategies. The teacher has to help them check on these strategies and connect them to earlier concepts and rules.

What can we do when the students just haven't enough mathematical background to even informally defend a generalization? Notice how Mr. Cain handles the finale in his seventh-grade laboratory lesson on π.

The students have measured the circumference of various cans with string and the diameter with metric rulers. All groups have found C/d to the hundredths place on their calculators.

"The group leaders should come to the board and fill in the data table."

After all have completed recording their results, Mr. Cain and the class begin to talk about the pattern they see in the resulting computation.

Mr. Cain: *"We noticed that all groups obtained a result of about 3.14. Why do you think there were some differences in the hundredths place?"*

Mark: *"It was hard to use the string and sometimes we were careless."*

Rosie: *"Some of the cans had rough spots on the top. Maybe those bumps caused trouble?"*

Mr. Cain: *"That's very good! Measurement inaccuracies are always with us. In fact, even high-powered scientific tools have measurement inaccuracies. Measurement is never exact. So we don't prove anything by using measurement, but we do use measurement to test ideas. As a matter of fact, your data seems to show that C/d is always a little more than 3. Would measuring more cans, bigger and smaller ones, prove that?"*

Johnny: *"No, but I bet we'd get the same thing."*

Mr. Cain: *"Aah, you're saying it seems very convincing! You're right. More data are what the scientist would need to test that pattern. But the mathematician always wants to prove rules. Do you know that centuries ago mathematicians did prove that, for every circle, C/d is always exactly the same number? They used an argument you'll study in high school. They also found* *out that the number they obtained was different from the ones we get when we measure objects. So later mathematicians gave that number a new name. They called it π (pronounced "pi"), a letter of the Greek alphabet. But they did want to measure circular objects, just as we do. Think of the circular shapes found in sports alone—the markings on the basketball court, the cross-sections of baseballs and golf balls, and the outline of an archery target. So we use an approximation of a number we can measure with, a number you obtained in your lab, 3.14. Sometimes we'll use 22/7 as an approximation of π. That's sometimes easier to work with, but it's still only an estimate. Now let's see how to use this famous number."*

Mr. Cain will have to return to these ideas often, because the concept of π is difficult to grasp. Why didn't he introduce the label *irrational*? Did you notice that he never stressed the difference between the physical models of the circle in the can shapes and the mathematical model that they represent? He'll have to be alert in follow-up lessons for the appearance of a common misconception, that 22/7 actually equals π. Since 22/7 is approximately equal to 3.142, some mathematics students believe that a computer program in which 22 is divided by 7 will result in the decimal expansion of π. "But π is irrational!" we hear you cry. Mr. Cain and his senior high colleagues have a lot of spiraling to do in helping students understand this concept.

Now look back at the instructional model that appears at the beginning of this chapter. The shaded "Structure of Mathematics" box is connected to that called "Intellectual Development of Students." To what extent might Mr. Cain's choices be explained in terms of this link in the model? What match is there between Ms. Pauli's choice of mathematics processes and the probable intellectual development of her students? As you interact with these and later illustrations in the text, look for goodness of fit of these two aspects of the model to what you have learned.

Unlike inductive reasoning, deductive reasoning *is* the method of proof, but it has its own constraints, which are important facets of this mathematical process. Mr. Greenberg's explanation of a^0 to his senior high class contains a subtle error which clouds a major process used by mathematicians. See if you can find it.

(The class had used the rules for $a^m \times a^n = a^{m+n}$ and $a^m/a^n = a^{m-n}$ where $m > n$ and where m and n are natural numbers.)

Mr. Greenberg: *"If $a \neq 0$, then $a^6/a^6 = 1$ since any nonzero quantity divided by itself is 1. But using our rule for division of like bases, $a^6/a^6 = a^{6-6} = a^0$. So, since quantities equal to the same quantity are equal to each other, $a^0 = 1$."*

Have you found Mr. Greenberg's error? That's right—he ignored one part of the assumption for using the division rule. He missed a great opportunity to illustrate the way mathematicians alter assumptions and construct definitions so that rules may be extended. Here m is equal to n and a zero exponent will result from application of the division rule. Hence the mathematician makes a *tentative* assumption that m and n may be whole numbers with $m \geq n$ in the case of the division law. Then, the mathematician checks to see if that assumption will lead to contradictions. In this case, no contradiction was found so the next step, formally defining $a^0 = 1$ if $a \neq 0$, was taken. Finally, it is proved that the extended laws hold under the new definition.

In all three of the previous illustrations both products and processes of mathematics were inextricably related. You must have found this when you developed your chart of processes and products. In the next section we synthesize these two aspects of mathematics in a single schematic, a diagrammatic representation of our thought model of the nature of mathematics.

4.4 A MODEL OF THE NATURE OF MATHEMATICS

By this point in the text, you've read about mathematical models and physical models of mathematical entities. You've also been repeatedly directed to study the instructional model that appears at the beginning of every chapter. Of course, the actual model doesn't appear on paper, but its representation does. The thought model, which we call an instructional model, exists in the mind and thus cannot be accurately captured by any representation. However, we've found that the selected representation stimulates an understanding of the complex processes of instruction. Every representation, or physical model of a thought model, has a similar reason for its construction—to clarify, to simplify, and to suggest novel relationships. The schematic thought model shown in Figure 4.8 is a synthesis of the process/product views of mathematics in relation to the physical world and the idea world. Study it carefully.

Each of the lines and shapes in the schema is there to convey an aspect of the thought model of mathematics. For example, we drew a solid line rather than a dashed line between the space representing the idea world and that representing the physical world. We wanted to emphasize the nature of mathematical concepts as inventions, constructs, "creations" of the idea world. At the same time the motivation for mathematical development often begins in the physical world and the models of mathematics are used constantly to solve real-world problems. Hence the physical world appears in the schema, but note that the space assigned to it is much smaller than that assigned to the idea world.

There are two places in this model where inductive and deductive reasoning are in operation. Notice the curved arrows between the physical world and the idea world. The arrows are curved toward one another to suggest a cyclic movement in and out of the two worlds.

There's also a branch connecting the inducing/deducing clusters in the idea world. What does this signify? Think of the times you've grappled with a tough mathematical proof. What were your working and thinking procedures? Did you test (perhaps with numbers?) some special cases, make a conjecture, test again, formulate a hypothesis, and try deducing the required result? If you came up

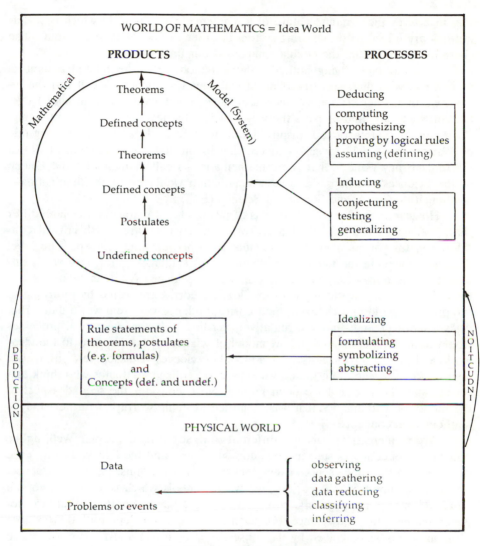

Fig. 4.8   A model of mathematics.

against a stone wall and hadn't yet thrown in the towel, you probably stopped, did some more testing and conjecturing, and so on. Implicit in that problem-solving effort was the seesaw use of induction and deduction; but in this instance, the specifics on which you used inductive reasoning were mathematical concepts or statements—inventions of the idea world.

Don't be concerned if you find some places in the schema which just don't convey an accurate picture of the corresponding thought model. You are experiencing first-hand the impossibility of a one-to-one correspondence between thought model and physical model. One problem that we struggled with was a way to convey the dynamic nature of a mathematical system, in which new definitions are added to the existing system in order to deduce new theorems. The chain of arrows within the circular shape was our final result.

One way of studying both the thought model and the related schema is by contrast with the sister discipline of mathematics, science. Recall that the inventions of mathematics have been used to communicate scientific knowledge, to represent data, and to pave the way to scientific development by simplifying, clarifying, and, in particular, inspiring new hypotheses. Read the fascinating tale of Watson and Crick's decision to use the double helix as a thought model of DNA. Is it any wonder that some mathematicians call mathematics the Queen of the Sciences? Perhaps the double appellation would be more illuminating—Mathematics, Queen and Servant of Science (E. T. Bell, 1951).

However, there are some aspects of this model of mathematics which differ sharply from any model of science. Two, in particular, are worth critical consideration for you as a mathematics teacher—theorem and concept. The label *theorem* appears in the model of mathematics. A similar-sounding, but vastly different, label, *theory*, appears in any model of science. Whereas theorems are proved in the idea world by deductive logic, theories are tested by returning to the physical world and checking their correspondence with real-world data. Theories are *not* proved; they are tentatively verified. What mathematical processes would have to be eliminated in any model of science? What happens to the idea-world and physical-world notions in a model of science? If these questions disturb your confidence, then join the crowd. There are college graduates who think that science has "laws" that have been proved. Next, consider the second aspect of the model of mathematics that was identified as being worthy of further study—mathematical concepts.

Are mathematical concepts different from scientific concepts? Well, unlike other kinds of concepts such as cow, dog, glass, ant, and the like, you cannot see or subject to the other senses exemplars of triangles, points, pi, or congruence. We write numbers, don't we? No, we write symbols which some prefer to call *numerals*, names for numbers. Now you have the key to another difference between mathematics and science. For scientific concepts include *both* those whose exemplars can be perceived by the senses, such as insect and flower, and those whose exemplars cannot be perceived by the senses, such as atom and gravity. As in the case of mathematics, these latter concepts are taught by using physical models or representations of the concepts. Now you should be a little closer to an understanding of some of the differences and some of the similarities between mathematics and science. You should also be starting to sense the enormous possibilities for helping students learn mathematics through the vehicle of science.

4.5 INSTRUCTION AND THE DYNAMIC NATURE OF MATHEMATICS

In a summary of recent research on mathematics teaching and learning, Romberg and Carpenter (1986) decried the kind of instruction that portrays mathematics as a static discipline, a body of information to be mastered. They emphasized the need to teach mathematical processes and the interrelationship of these to the invention of mathematical products. Other researchers (Thompson, 1985) have been studying the relationship between mathematics teachers' beliefs about the discipline of mathematics and the kind of instruction they design. If you were taught to look for patterns, to examine strategies, or to engage in different approaches to a problem, you were being taught something about the dynamic nature of mathematics. Your teachers were, in all probability, designing lessons that illustrated *their* beliefs about mathematics. In the introductory section of this chapter, we asked you to reflect on your beliefs. Subsequent sections of this chapter have included illustrations from the history of mathematics and from the classrooms of reflective teachers against which to test those beliefs. You'll need to continue to reflect on your beliefs about the discipline of mathematics as you engage in the life-long study of teaching. In this section, we consider some further illustrative strategies and principles that highlight the dynamic nature of mathematics.

From the Products Aspect

Although the concepts and assumptions which form the basis for every mathematical system are inventions of the human mind, they are not the thoughtless gibberish which might be assembled by a robot. There is a rationale behind each such product of mathematics. Sometimes that rationale takes the form of a motivating force, a need in the physical world, or a desire for a simpler way of handling a chore. Sometimes the rationale has its roots in history, in common usage, or in the etymology of a word. At other times, the rationale for teaching a particular concept at this time and in this way may be explained in terms of its sensible match to the previous learnings of your students. In the illustrations which follow, one or more of these views of rationale are detailed.

A trigonometry lesson   The teaching of trigonometric functions usually occurs at two distinct levels of complexity. In elementary algebra, the student may be introduced to the trigonometry of the right triangle in a unit on indirect measurement. In a later algebra or trigonometry course, the trigonometric functions, their graphs, and the trigonometric identities are all considered in depth. At each point in this instructional spiral, the problem of the introduction to the topic differs.

A promising approach to the introduction of right triangle trigonometry begins with a measurement lab. Provide each student with a metric ruler and a grid on which has been drawn a known angle, say 40°. Have the students measure the legs of right triangle BP_1A_1 and record the data in the table below the grid (see Figure 4.9).

Then they should use a calculator to get the ratio shown in the last column to the nearest hundredth. Allow the students to check each other's work for accuracy and encourage them to look for a pattern. Here is a case where your

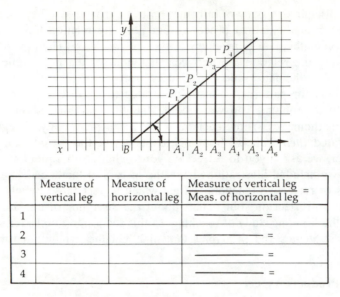

	Measure of vertical leg	Measure of horizontal leg	$\dfrac{\text{Measure of vertical leg}}{\text{Meas. of horizontal leg}} =$
1			——————— =
2			——————— =
3			——————— =
4			——————— =

Fig. 4.9   Worksheet for tangent lab.

preparation can help or hinder the students' progress. Carelessly chosen placement of P_1, P_2, P_3, and P_4 may result in avoidable measurement obstacles. A word to the wise is sufficient! Plan ahead and always dry-run the lab material before you use it in class.

Once the class has agreed on the apparent pattern, they can be helped to justify its presence from a consideration of similar triangles. Now the problem posed by A_5 and A_6 makes sense. Have the students measure BA_5 and BA_6 and find the length of the corresponding vertical leg without drawing or measurements. With more questioning, the rationale for the usefulness of this ratio is apparent. It's also clear that a ratio this useful needs a name, and now the label *tangent* can be associated with this defined ratio. The students will agree that an acute angle other than 40° would result in a different numerical ratio. All the teacher needs is to superimpose a 50° angle on the grid and use the same length BA_1 for the first right triangle. The rationale for always using the name of the angle, as in "tangent θ," has been provided. The provision of a table of values to circumvent repeated measurement and the substitution of the usual "opposite leg" and "adjacent leg" for "vertical" and "horizontal" to allow for triangles in varied positions is a natural development.

Notice how the label *tangent* appeared relatively late in this introduction, and *sine* and *cosine* were deliberately ignored. It is best to continue to ignore them until the students have become masters at the varied uses of tangent. The sine and cosine can be introduced together and without many of the above preliminaries.

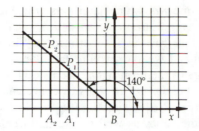

Fig. 4.10 Obtuse angle sheet for lab.

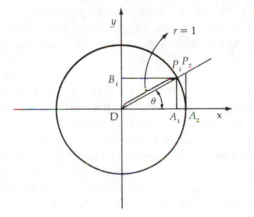

Fig. 4.11 Unit circle diagram.

If you are not careful, a presentation like the previous one can be convincing evidence that the trigonometric ratios only make sense with acute angles. This problem can be avoided if you challenge the students to measure the lengths of the vertical and horizontal components from points of the terminal side of an obtuse angle (as in Figure 4.10). The rewording of the definition to tan $\theta = y/x$ seems reasonable now, and the extension of that definition to any angle, θ, is an easy next step.

You are also a stone's throw from providing a rationale for the labels assigned to the first three trigonometric functions. If we place a unit circle on the grid so that its center is at the origin, we need measure only one length for each ratio (Figure 4.11). Notice that $\overline{P_2A_2}$ is a segment of a tangent to the circle and the length P_2A_2 is equal to the ratio called tan θ. Find a segment whose length represents the ratio called sine θ. Yes, $\overline{P_1A_1}$ is one example, but does the geometric orientation of this segment have anything to do with the label?

In this case, a meaningful label got garbled in its translation from one language to another. The Hindus called the function *ardhajya*, meaning half-chord. (Check Figure 4.11 again for the reasonableness of this label.) An abbreviated version of *ardhajya* became *jya*, which later was transliterated into three Arabic characters, *jyb*. However, European translators read *jyb* as *jayb*, Arabic for "pocket" or "gulf," and thus gave us the Latin term "sinus." (If you ply yourself with decongestants in humid weather, you're familiar with those pockets called "sinuses.") The etymology of the term *cosine* seems dull by comparison. Cosine is just a shortened version of *complementi sinus* or complement of sine—an obvious choice since $\cos \theta = DA_1 = P_1B_1 = \sin(90 - \theta)$.

The history of mathematics as well as the hierarchical nature of its products is a gold mine of these connecting links, which illuminate the mathematics you are teaching. In some cases, careful analysis of concepts and principles will help provide you with ties which must be embedded in your instruction. In many instances, a search into the multiple sources available to mathematics teachers will be necessary. If you are one of the lucky ones who has studied the history of mathematics, you have a head start on using this type of instructional resource.

A lesson in introductory algebra   Why is the product of two negative numbers positive? If you were to survey algebra teachers on the number of times this question is asked, you would hear a resounding, "Too often!" One of the most straightforward ways to approach the topic of multiplication of directed numbers, and thus emphasize the way definitions are constructed, is through a careful developmental lesson in which pattern-analysis is stressed.

First, the teacher must establish that it is reasonable to expect the multiplication of two positives to be positive. Students typically readily agree to this. Then the teacher needs to emphasize that since these directed numbers represent both quantity and direction, that mathematicians had to define multiplication, but wanted to construct a definition that wouldn't conflict with other mathematical patterns. Then, let students look for the patterns as they answer the following questions written, one-by-one in a carefully sequenced way on the board.

Mr. Ramirez writes

$$\begin{array}{r} {}^{+}10 \\ \times\, {}^{+}5 \\ \hline \end{array}$$

"By our agreed-on definition, the product must be what?"

Then, next to that:

$$\begin{array}{r} {}^{+}10 \qquad {}^{+}10 \\ \times\, {}^{+}5 \quad\; \times\, {}^{+}4 \\ \hline \end{array}$$

"Be watching for patterns. Don't answer too soon. What is the product?"

Mr. Ramirez continues in this fashion, getting products, but waiting for more and more students to indicate that they see one or more patterns.

He is careful to write the positive sign in every case. After the fourth example, he asks students for all the patterns they think he is using to write the examples. They notice that the multiplicand is the constant $^+10$, that the multiplier is decreasing by one each time and that the product is decreasing by ten each time. Finally, the array looks like this:

Find the products

$$
\begin{array}{cccccc}
^+10 & ^+10 & ^+10 & ^+10 & ^+10 & ^+10 \\
\times\,^+5 & \times\,^+4 & \times\,^+3 & \times\,^+2 & \times\,^+1 & \times \\
\hline
^+50 & ^+40 & ^+30 & ^+20 & ^+10 &
\end{array}
$$

"What do you think I will write next?"

Mr. Ramirez gets the response of zero for the multiplier and then reinforces the meaning of constructing definitions for this new set of numbers.

"Now we haven't defined multiplication for zero times a signed number, but what should the product be if the pattern of the products is to be maintained?"

After all agree that zero is the only number that will maintain the pattern, Mr. Ramirez emphasizes that, in general, zero times any signed number is zero, by definition—a definition that keeps intact patterns such as this one. The next step is to extend the three patterns with the help of the class. The entire sequence now looks like this

$$
\begin{array}{ccccccc}
^+10 & ^+10 & ^+10 & ^+10 & ^+10 & ^+10 & ^+10 \\
\times\,^+5 & \times\,^+4 & \times\,^+3 & \times\,^+2 & \times\,^+1 & \times\,0 & \times\,^-1 \\
\hline
^+50 & ^+40 & ^+30 & ^+20 & ^+10 & 0 &
\end{array}
$$

"Now we haven't defined the product of a negative and a positive, but if the pattern of the products is to hold, what must the missing product be?"

Concrete operational students can reason inductively and, given enough instances and careful attention to all of the patterns, will respond with the answer $^-10$. For practice in extending the pattern, the teacher should continue the sequence of questions for three or four more examples. This helps to reinforce the new definition. Next, Mr. Ramirez needs to introduce the need for the commutative property. Students will generally agree that it would be convenient if this property held for multiplication of these signed numbers. It's important for them to realize that mathematicians think about convenience and ways to construct simpler rules or ways to adapt an existing rule so it holds for more situations.

After some oral practice on multiplication restricted to two positives or to a positive and a negative, Mr. Ramierz is ready to use a similar technique to lead the students to the construction of the definition of the product of two negative numbers. The sequence might be built up, with questions very similar to those used earlier and the instruction to again look for all patterns.

Find the products

$$
\begin{array}{cccccccc}
{}^-10 & {}^-10 & {}^-10 & {}^-10 & {}^-10 & {}^-10 & {}^-10 & {}^-10 \\
\times\,{}^+5 & \times\,{}^+4 & \times\,{}^+3 & \times\,{}^+2 & \times\,{}^+1 & \times\ \ 0 & \times\,{}^-1 & \times \\
\hline
{}^-50 & {}^-40 & {}^-30 & {}^-20 & {}^-10 & 0 & ? &
\end{array}
$$

Again the zero product question can be asked. Mr. Ramirez emphasizes the horizontal patterns that the students have identified and asks the question:

What number must take the place of the ? for the pattern of products to be maintained?"

Now that the students have confidence in the power of patterns, most, if not all, students agree that $^+10$ is the needed replacement. Further extension of the sequence of examples again helps to reinforce the pattern and allows the students, or the teacher, to verbalize this definition, that the product of two negative numbers is a positive number.

This particular classroom-tested presentation is effective in helping students to construct the needed definitions and is an excellent way to make real one of the products of mathematics—the definition—and the very dynamic way in which those definitions might have been constructed by mathematicians.

From the Process Aspect

You've surely noticed that even though the previous section was labeled "From the Products Aspect," there were processes of mathematics both implicitly and explicitly specified in most of the illustrations. As you found from the very beginning of this chapter, the two are considered separately only for the purpose of focusing more thoroughly on one aspect at a time.

Generalizing was required in the introduction to tangent and in the introductory algebra lesson described earlier, as well as in several of the classroom illustrations of prior sections. You will find that this process is indispensable in all problem solving, whether in mathematics or in everyday life. However, there are dangers inherent in generalizing—dangers which you must help students recognize and compensate for. The most obvious danger is *generalizing from insufficient data.*

An algebra lesson   Consider an exercise based on a generalization obtained from a powerful mathematical product, Pascal's triangle.

$$1$$
$$1\ 1$$
$$1\ 2\ 1$$
$$1\ 3\ 3\ 1$$
$$1\ 4\ 6\ 4\ 1$$
$$1\ 5\ 10\ 10\ 5\ 1$$

Ask the student to add the numbers in each row of Pascal's triangle.

$$1 \qquad = 1$$
$$1+1 \qquad = 2$$
$$1+2+1 \qquad = 4$$
$$1+3+3+1 \ = 8$$
$$1+4+6+4+1= 16$$

Then ask them to find, without adding, the sum of the numbers in the 15th row, the 24th row, the nth row. Next challenge them to continue the following number pattern and compare results with that obtained in summing the numbers in the rows of Pascal's triangle.

$$11^1 = 11 \quad \text{and} \quad 1+1 \quad = 2$$
$$11^2 = 121 \quad \text{and} \quad 1+2+1 \ = 4$$
$$11^3 = 1331 \quad \text{and} \quad 1+3+3+1= 8$$
$$11^4 =$$

This apparent generalization eventually fails. It is important that the students are not told ahead of time that, in this case, the pattern will break down. A few examples like this mixed in with others where generalizing does yield a valid result will suffice to warn the students that care must be taken in the use of data.

The same illustration pinpoints the second danger in the use of generalization. When students fail to verify a presumed generalization, they fall into the trap of abusing this inductive process. Results must be checked against more data and, in mathematics, proved by deductive processes. Stop right here and test yourself. In the first example, what generalization did you obtain for the nth row? (See exercise B in Section 4.8, where a method of proof is considered. Work out a proof and check your argument against that of a classmate.) Then return to the second example and compare the data from this exercise with that from the first. Try to pinpoint the arithmetic behind the lack of a continuous, common pattern.

A lesson in networks   Just as the search for generalizations is an aid to problem solving, so the process labeled *idealizing* in the model of mathematics represents

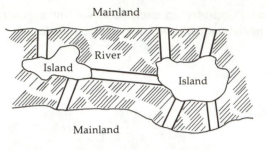

Fig. 4.12 Königsberg bridge diagram.

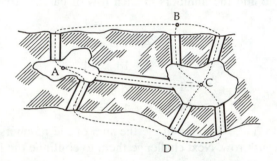

Fig. 4.13 Modelling the Königsberg problem.

ways to simplify a sometimes unwieldy problem. The solution of a well-known problem, called the Königsberg bridge problem, is a good example of idealizing in action.

In the eighteenth century strollers in the German university town of Königsberg walked along the shores of the Preger River and over the seven bridges which connected two islands to each other and to the mainland (see Figure 4.12).

The problem which one of these strollers is said to have posed was in the form of a question: "How can you take a walk so that you cross each of our seven bridges exactly once?" The problem was eventually solved by Leonhard Euler, who idealized the situation in the following manner. The bridges will be drawn as line segments; the islands and shore, as points of intersection (see Figure 4.13). Try to solve the problem yourself before reading further.

In the process, Euler invented networks, an aspect of that branch of mathematics called topology. Euler's analysis of networks led him to characterize points of intersection as either "odd" or "even vertices." *A* is an odd vertex since 3 arcs intersect at *A*. There are no even vertices in the Königsberg bridge network. He found that the number of odd vertices is limited to two or less if the network is to be traveled without retracing any arcs. So Euler's answer was, "It can't be done!" Euler's use of idealizing processes eliminated extraneous data which had only confused others who attempted to solve the problem. Idealizing sometimes results in graphs, equations, and geometric shapes. In your teaching of mathematics, you have many opportunities to point out the wisdom of some choices and the blind alleys resulting from others. For more teaching ideas on the subject of networks, see Graph theory: Euler's rich legacy by Copes, Sloyer, Stark & Sacco published in 1987 by Janson Publications, Inc., Providence, RI.

A geometry lesson   Generalizing is a valuable tool of the scientist, as is idealizing, but the processes most characteristic of the mathematician are those which result in a mathematical system. Somehow a study of Euclid's geometry only reveals part of the picture. Until students get their own hands dirty in the task of constructing an axiomatic chain, they have only partially learned these basic deductive processes. An exercise within the grasp of geometry students who have studied the family of parallelograms and learned how to deduce the properties of each member of the family centers around a quadrilateral called a "kite." A kite is defined as a quadrilateral with two pairs of congruent adjacent sides. $ABCD$ is one example. The students are asked to deduce the properties of a kite and state these as theorems and corollaries. They may define special kites. For example, a "right" kite could be defined as kite with a right angle included by a pair of congruent sides, as in $MNOP$. Of course, it could also be defined in other ways. Here is another opportunity for student discussion of alternative choices for definitions and the usefulness of each. Most important, the students have to work at the deduction process. Unlike the typical sequence of theorems involving the parallelogram family, this sequence is not familiar to students. They have no preconceived notions of the form of theorems further down in the chain. They actually have to deduce these from the definitions on which they've agreed. This kind of thinking actually takes more than one 40 or 45 minute lesson. The teacher can start the class on the work, but would be well advised to design a strategy in which small groups begin to work on the chain of theorems in class. Reports could be given after two or three days of work on the project outside of class. The kite exercise can do much to dispel the mystique of axiomatic thinking (Farrell, 1970).

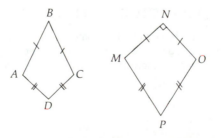

There are multiple examples in professional journals which can be used by the teacher to help students grasp more fully the nature of mathematics. How do you decide which ideas to use? That depends on the objectives you have set for your lesson. It now becomes clear that setting these objectives must depend both on the intellectual development of your students and on the nature of mathematics. As you interact with the material in the next chapter, keep checking your ideas with the theory and research on adolescent reasoning and the model of mathematics presented in this chapter.

4.6 SUMMARY AND SELF-CHECK

In this chapter we opened with a question: Mathematics—Invented or Discovered? and asked you to make an initial response and to test that response against the ideas and evidence presented in later sections. The processes and products of mathematics were explored by considering the known history surrounding several notable mathematical developments. The final synthesis of process and product into a model of mathematics crystallized the invented nature of mathematics by drawing attention to the nature of the theorems and the concepts of mathematics.

Throughout this chapter, you have been asked to interact with classroom illustrations of teachers attending to this model or distorting it. The power and weaknesses of generalization and the various ways to provide a rationale in mathematics were captured in their application to specific junior and senior high mathematics content.

Now you should be able to:

1. Operationally define each of the processes and products in the model of mathematics.

2. Explain physical world/idea world relationships and induction/deduction loops in the model of mathematics.

3. Identify errors of omissions or commission, in communicating the nature of mathematics during either a "live" or a "taped" lesson and give reasons for your judgments.

4. Provide rationale of differing kinds for selected content in junior/senior high mathematics.

4.7 SIMULATION/PRACTICE ACTIVITIES

A. Each of the objects listed in column 1 is sometimes used as a physical model of the mathematical concepts in column 2. In what way(s) do each of these physical models communicate and fail to communicate the mathematical concept?

Column 1	Column 2
a) baseball	sphere
b) point of pin	point
c) jet-stream of an airplane	curve
d) flashlight reflector	paraboloid
e) edge of a table	straight line segment
f) wall of a room	plane

B. In this chapter, we have emphasized that inductive processes do not result in proof. Yet the process called *mathematical induction* is used to prove some generalizations. Explain this apparent anomaly. Be sure to defend the use of the term *induction* in this connection.

C. Although contemporary mathematics texts use *axiom* and *postulate* as equally good synonyms for the mathematical assumptions which form the basis of deductive chains, Euclid characterized certain statements as axioms and others as postulates. Identify some examples of each, according to Euclid. Try to explain his rationale for using two different terms and contemporary mathematicians' rationale for disregarding this distinction. (Hint: An excellent source is Heath's *Euclid's Elements*, Vol. 1. Dover Publications, New York, 1956.)

D. Consult one of the sources on the history of mathematics and look up the mathematical contribution and the personal history of one or more of the following: Abel, George Boole, Galois, Sophie Germain, Hypatia, Sonya Kovalevskaya, Emmy Noether.

E. Refer to the Resource File modular assignment in the Appendix. This is an excellent time to begin collecting ideas in one area of that assignment. As you read, or hear of, ways to include in your instruction illustrations communicating the process/products of mathematics, excerpt the key features (sketches, historical notes, instructional ties) and begin filing these on individual sheets or 5×8 cards in the appropriate file folder. Ask your instructor to check your classification scheme and your use of it. Extend your file gradually to each subject you will teach. Continue collecting ideas from experienced teachers, as well as from professional journals and texts (see Chapters 9, 10, and 11 for other recommended sources).

F. Each of the following illustrations was drawn from actual classroom observations of student teachers. Each student in their classes is expressing honest confusion. If the teacher were unable or unwilling to unveil the apparent mystery, these students would have evidence that mathematics is unreasonable, illogical, or at best, incomprehensible. Assume the role of teacher in each of the five illustrations and formulate a response both mathematically accurate and consistent with the view that mathematics is a meaningful product of the human mind.

1. Mrs. Wampole has explained the rule for multiplying radicals to her ninth-grade algebra students. The sample example she presented is:

$$2\sqrt{2} \times 3\sqrt{5} = 6\sqrt{10}$$

Mike reacted in confusion: "But those are unlike radicands, and before you said we couldn't add or subtract the numbers in front of unlike radicands. How come we can multiply them?"

2. Mr. Tessema is reading the answers to a set of exercises dealing with the multiplication of algebraic fractions. He reads: "The answer to example 21 is $2(x - 2)/3(x + 5)$."

Lita: "I have a question: I wrote $(2x - 4)/(3x + 15)$ because you're always saying: 'Leave the answer in simplest form.' But *you* didn't."

3. Ms. Sutliffe's intermediate algebra class has been studying systems of equations. As a result of classwork on the system

$$3x + 4y = 18$$
$$2x - y = 1$$

Joanne says that system is equivalent to the system

$$x = 2$$
$$y = 3$$

Hye Joo disagrees: "How can that be? $x = 2$ is not equivalent to either $3x + 4y = 18$ or $2x - y = 1$." Who is right? How should Ms. Sutliffe respond?

4. Paul, a tenth-grader, asks if all circles are similar. What is your answer? Are all parabolas similar? Ellipses? Why or why not?

5. Connie, irritated with teacher insistence on symbolism, argues that $f(x) = x^2 + 3$ means exactly the same thing as $y = x^2 + 3$ so why bother with the symbol $f(x)$? Is she right? Why or why not?

G. Complete the checklist (adapted from Erb, 1971) provided here and share your results with those of other preservice or inservice teachers of mathematics.

Profile of a Mathematics Teacher

This checklist has been designed to help you reflect on the beliefs you hold as a prospective or present teacher of mathematics. For each statement, indicate whether you strongly agree (SA), agree (A), disagree (D), or strongly disagree (SD).

1. The textbook is based on mathematical fact and should not be questioned by students.

2. There is little justification for teaching structural concepts (e.g. group, set,...) at the junior high school level.

3. Collecting numerical data and formulating related problems should be part of a student's experience in mathematics.

4. School mathematics should be more a set of abstract ideas than a collection of practical skills.

5. It is important that students memorize textbook definitions of mathematical terms.

6. Since much of mathematics is accumulative, a student should master a concept before proceeding to the next concept.

7. The principal aim of mathematics teaching is to develop an understanding of the logical structure of mathematics.

8. Since mathematics is an exact science, students should be discouraged from guessing or estimating answers.

9. Mathematics classes should discuss how mathematicians develop mathematical concepts.

10. A teacher should frequently use real world problems to introduce fundamental mathematical ideas.

11. Students should have the opportunity for experimentation and original thought.

12. Constant drill is a good way for students to master mathematics.

SUGGESTIONS FOR FURTHER STUDY

Abbott, E. A. (1952). *Flatland, 6th ed. revised*. New York: Dover Publications.

The subtitle of this book is *A Romance of Many Dimensions*. The reader is first taken on a journey into a world of two dimensions where all of the inhabitants are some sort of geometric shape. However, these inhabitants move, communicate and seem to have feelings. The adventurer is then transported to Lineland and finally, to Spaceland. This book has been enjoyed by mathematics students and those interested in science fiction. It is an excellent way for students and teachers to explore Euclidean and non-Euclidean geometry, as well as concepts of relativity.

Bell, M. S. (1972). *Mathematical uses and models in our everyday world* ("Studies in Mathematics," Vol. XX). Standford, Calif.: School Mathematics Study Group.

This valuable paperback is aimed at providing the teacher with everyday examples of applications of mathematics accessible to those with little mathematical background. Bell has achieved his purpose in a noteworthy manner. This is not a book of readings nor a dissertation on mechanics, rocketry, or computer science, but carefully selected sets of problems, questions, and tasks. The range of situations is vast—from questions dealing with automobile safety, drug abuse, the dieting fads and so on. The approach to all problems is in the context of the concept of a mathematical model. Chapter 1 is highly recommended reading for further examples of simple, everyday uses of mathematical models. The entire volume is recommended as a source to be used repeatedly by the teacher of junior/senior high mathematics.

Crouse, R. J., & Sloyer, C. W. (1987). *Mathematical questions from the classroom (Part I and II)*. Providence, RI: Janson Publications, Inc.

The authors address the kind of student question that puzzles many teachers. They provide thoughtful explanations with mathematical background and also include idea articles related to many of the topics. The material is organized by junior/senior high course and topic within course. This is an excellent resource book for all mathematics teachers' personal professional library.

Grinstein, L. S. and Campbell, P. J. (Eds.). (1987). *Women of mathematics: A biobibliographic sourcebook*. New York: Greenwood Press.

This well-written sourcebook contains short biographies of 43 women mathematicians, brief and readable accounts of their contributions to mathematics, and an annotated reference list for each person. Mathematicians included in this volume range from Hypatia, the Alexandrian, to the contemporary Minna Rees. The appendices of the text include summary tables of the mathematicians in chronological order, as well as in terms of their education and fields of expertise. There is also a substantive list of references for each of the women cited in the text. This sourcebook should be on every mathematics teacher's reference shelf.

National Council of Teachers of Mathematics. (1969). *Historical topics for the mathematics classroom. (31st Yearbook)*. Washington, D.C.: NCTM.

This yearbook should be the property of every mathematics teacher. For example, if tomorrow's lesson includes an introduction to radian measure, check the index for background material. In a three-page article entitled "Angular Measure," the origin of the term, the development of its use, and a contrast with degree measure are outlined. These brief articles, called "Capsules," contain a wealth of historical information as well as some applications of mathematics.

Perl, T. (1978). *Math equals: Biographies of women mathematicians + related activities*. Reading, MA: Addison-Wesley.

Perl has written short biographical accounts of ten women mathematicians from Hypatia to Emmy Noether. Each biography is highly readable and followed by student-oriented summaries of the contributions of the mathematician, as well as by interesting exercises. These include puzzles, cryptograms and paper-folding activities. Perl ends this excellent teaching aid with a brief description of contemporary issues affecting the entry of women into the serious study of mathematics, a list of such women and more teaching ideas. An answer key to questions is included.

Petit, J. P. (1985). *The adventures of Archibald Higgins: Here's looking at Euclid (and not looking at Euclid)*. translated by Ian Stewart. Providence, RI: Janson Publishing Co.

This adult comic book introduces differences between Euclidean and non-Euclidean geometry to curious readers. The story line carried by Archibald, the elegant Sophie and the cast of pelicans, snails and demons is characterized by puns and clever imagery. This is suggested as a reading for bright students after they have cut their teeth on *Flatland*.

Polya, G. (1954). *Induction and analogy in mathematics*. Princeton, N.J.: Princeton University Press.

The title of Polya's book might be a subhead from the section on the processes of mathematics in this chapter. An extension of an earlier book, *How to Solve It*, and the first volume of *Mathematics and Plausible Reasoning*, this entire book is recommended. Illustrations of generalization, specialization, and analogy will delight the teacher who seeks ways to spark student attention. Polya includes sections on the use of induction and examines the process of mathematical induction. Although the problems posed are more directly related to the content of senior-high mathematics than junior-high, all 7–12 mathematics teachers will find Polya's work on the processes of mathematics an invaluable reference. Readers should appreciate the section titled "Solution to Problems."

Sawyer, W. W. (1964). *Vision in elementary mathematics*. Baltimore, MD: Penguin Books.

Don't be misled by the adjective "elementary" in the title. The author is referring to pre-college mathematics. This delightful paperback contains numerous visual, concrete ways to present concepts in pre-algebra and algebra. You will find pictures very much like the geometric region dissections used by the Greeks, as well as dynamic cartoon figures modelling an equation.

Wilder, R. (1968). *Evolution of mathematics concepts: an elementary study*. New York: John Wiley and Sons.

This little book will be of particular interest to the teacher of mathematics, for it emphasizes the cultural forces that affected the timing of major mathematical developments. Moreover, Wilder's emphasis throughout on the evolution of number helps to avoid mathematical complexities and eases the reader into a fascinating exposition.

The first chapter is required reading for those who need to delve further into the invented/discovered question. The entire volume may be read with profit for illustrations of the rationale for certain mathematical conventions, the creative decisions made by mathematicians and the ways in which real world needs affected the production of mathematics.

CHAPTER FIVE

INSTRUCTIONAL OBJECTIVES

Targets of Instruction

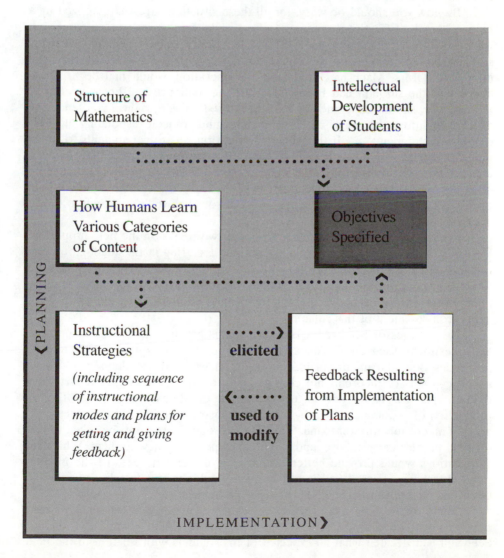

The comedian leaves the stage as the guffaws and cheers finally die down. Will he be asked back? Was he effective? The surgeon slowly and grimly leaves the operating theater. She must find a way to tell Mr. Mack that his wife died on the table. Will the surgeon be sued for malpractice? Was she incompetent? Professor Seedwell lectures to over two hundred students on the properties of a field. His voice is clear and his articulation good. Printed notes that accompany the lecture are well organized and easily adapted to incorporating additional material from the lecture. As the class ends, some students can be heard griping about his cold, impersonal style. "He never even looks at us." Does this necessarily mean that Professor Seedwell is incompetent?

By now you should be wary, for all these situations are characterized by a hidden agenda. Effectiveness seems to be tied to some result or outcome, but what outcome? If Professor Seedwell had lectured in such a fashion that many students left with smiles on their faces, would his lecture have necessarily been effective? If Mrs. Mack had lived after the operation, would that be firm evidence that the surgeon had been skillful? If the audience had been quiet after the last joke, should the comedian have been fired? You're right if you tended to avoid straightforward yes or no answers and found yourself responding in terms of, "It would depend... ." If the lecturer's intention was to get students to smile, then he and the comedian have both been effective to the extent that their audiences were left with happy grins on their faces. However, we all expect more of Professor Seedwell. His students are supposed to learn something about field properties. Let's look, in some detail, at Professor Seedwell's approach to teaching this topic.

Professor Seedwell had decided to spend two weeks on the field properties. He directed his graduate assistants to continue lecturing in the small-group sections so that more theorems could be proved for the students. No questions were to be directed at the students, and no time was to be provided for questioning by them. Is this choice of modes appropriate? If your response is no, then you agree with our assessment of this situation.

Next Professor Seedwell asked each of his graduate assistants to propose test questions based on the material related to the concept of a field and its properties. Joe Martin formulated questions in which the students would have to write proofs of theorems not considered in any of the classes, but Art Cary thought that was unfair and instead proposed questions that required the reproduction of proofs presented by one of the instructors. Sally Beers's questions were of an entirely different kind. She proposed that the students be asked to test for field properties given a set and two binary operations new to them. Which set of questions would provide better evidence of the effectiveness of the instruction? If you lean toward Sally's test but you wouldn't want to take it under the described circumstances, you'll have lots of company.

There ought to be a connection between instruction and testing. That connection might be characterized as "knowing where you're going." If Professor Seedwell had decided what he expected of his students with relation to the field properties, he might have proposed different uses of small-group time and then he should have been able to be quite clear about the kinds of evidence needed from a test.

Where are we going? How will we know when and if we get there? What are the objectives? The position of the shaded "Objectives Specified" box as an output based on analysis of the content of mathematics and analysis of the intellectual development of the students is a reminder that these two aspects of planning are precursors to defining "where we are going." In the activity that follows, be alert to the effects on choice of objective, of the type of mathematics content being studied and the probable intellectual developmental level of the students.

5.1 INTRODUCTORY ACTIVITY

Where are we going, and how will we know when we get there?

In order to perform this activity, you need to observe a junior high or senior high mathematics class.

A. Before the class, ask the teacher *only* the topic(s) to be developed in the class. While observing the class, take notes on specifics in the following areas:

 1. What do you infer that the students are expected to be able to *do* as a result of instruction? Cite evidence, verbal and nonverbal observables, on which you base your inferences.

 2. At what point in the lesson did you become aware of these possible objectives?

 3. What did the students say and/or do that seemed to illustrate that they knew what was expected of them?

 4. When and how did the teacher get feedback as to the extent to which the inferred objectives were met?

 5. Cite any verbal and/or nonverbal cues that might indicate student confusion about the objectives.

B. After the observation, ask the teacher to tell you the intended objectives. Share your observations and attempt to clarify areas of confusion.

C. Compare the results of your observation with results of at least two other classmates who observed different classes in your subject field. In classes where objectives seemed to be clear to both you and the students, which of the following characteristics were present?

 1. The teacher verbally related past learning to today's lesson.

 2. The teacher specifically told and/or showed students what they were expected to recall, how they were to apply a rule/principle, for what specific problem types they would be responsible.

 3. The teacher introduced each new concept and successive skill by tying these to earlier concepts and skills.

4. At times in the lesson the teacher attempted to get specific feedback on student achievement thus far, and the teacher gave oral feedback to the class relating to progress.

5. Instead of telling students only that they must "understand," the teacher followed up with expressions like "be able to give new examples of this concept" or "be able to use a formula to solve type problems."

If you were able to find examples of observables supporting each of the preceding, you have identified a class where teacher and students know where they are going and when they have arrived. If, on the other hand, the students began asking questions such as "What are we doing?" "What good is this anyway?" or "Why do I have to write all this?" then these are cues that the students were not tuned in on the objectives and, as a result, may have missed important developments in the lesson.

Your observations in this activity should be convincing evidence of the importance of having clear objectives and communicating these objectives to the students. Before you work through the next section of this chapter, try writing what seem to be suitable objectives for the class you observed. Be sure they are expressed clearly enough to communicate to students exactly what is expected of them after the lesson. As you interact with the reading in Section 5.2, modify your objectives as needed to make them consistent with the criteria you will learn to apply to such statements.

5.2 INSTRUCTIONAL OBJECTIVES VERSUS OTHER KINDS OF GOAL STATEMENTS

What are instructional objectives? In Chapter 2, you learned about diverse feedback strategies—ways to get and give feedback on progress toward objectives. In all those illustrations, who were the subjects of the teacher's feedback strategies? The students. Then the instructional objectives must be phrased in terms of *student* performance, not in terms of *teacher* performance. Remember Professor Seedwell? If he intended to lecture in an organized fashion, he apparently accomplished that goal. But he could have accomplished that goal in an empty lecture hall! There is no way to use that kind of teacher performance as a measure of *student* learning. But Professor Seedwell's graduate assistants were concerned about student learning and were still at odds over the nature of the test they should give. Suppose they had been told that the students were expected to "understand the field properties." Would that have helped? You're on the right track if you're still dissatisfied with this statement of an "objective." The verb *understand* is too broad in its scope to be helpful to either the students in the class or the instructors as a clue to what the test should demand. On the other hand, if the students were expected to be able to "test any set under two binary operations for the presence of the field properties and to justify their results," then the character of the test questions becomes much clearer. Notice that student performance in this case is described in terms of *observable behavior*.

Stop and check your understanding by studying the four statements of possible "objectives" below. Which of these represent clear statements of instructional objectives that could be used as a guide toward planning of instructional and feedback strategies? Which are defective, and why?

1. The teacher will illustrate the use of the four function calculator by a demonstration on a model calculator on the overhead projector.

2. The students will observe a teacher demonstration of the use of the four function calculator.

3. The students will understand how to key a calculator in computations involving order of operations.

4. The students will write the result of any calculation with any set of three to five numbers where order of operations must be treated, given the use of a calculator.

If you characterized the first statement as defective because it describes *teacher* behavior rather than *student* behavior, you have correctly focused on the first critical feature of instructional objectives. The last three statements are all written in terms of the student, so these seem to pass that test. Did you quickly reject statement 3 for its use of the word *understand* as a description of performance? Just as in the illustrative example, *understand* has too broad a range of meanings to be useful as an indicator of performance. Statements 2 and 4 should look good by comparison. Now put each of them to the dual test of feedback and content. How could a teacher get feedback on whether the students were able to perform the described task, and is performance of each task evidence that the students have learned calculator-related skills? Now statement 2 should seem less promising. On the one hand, there is some obvious difficulty in assessing whether students are "observing." If all students are looking at the teacher during the demonstration, are they "observing"? On the other hand, even if we could agree on specific feedback cues that would assess observing, there is a lack of match between observing in this case, and appropriate outcomes of a calculator demonstration. Observing is not one of the important terminal outcomes of a calculator lesson. Can you think of content areas where specific observing skills *would* be important terminal outcomes? If your ideas tend to cluster in the areas of biology, chemistry, earth science and the like, you're probably reflecting your own experience as a junior/senior high student. If you can't think of any in mathematics, it's time to refer back to the "Process" section of Chapter 4. For now, let's examine the fourth statement more closely. It is *specific*, is in terms of *student performance*, and does include *necessary conditions* under which the student must perform. Does the word "any" disturb you? It needn't. The teacher can sample the student's ability by selecting a variety of examples. If the sample is small or ill-conceived (such as $2 \times 3 + 5$), the teacher may infer erroneously that the student has met this objective. Effective sampling procedures are an important aspect of feedback collection and evaluation. You've already been alerted to sampling problems with respect to feedback collection and use in Chapter 2. You'll be reading an approach to sampling for evaluation purposes in Chapter 8.

By now you should be able to write your own operational definition of an instructional objective. Take a minute and try it. Check your definition against the nonexamples represented by the first three statements of "objectives" as well as the example illustrated by the final calculator statement. Now match your definition against the one we have devised. An *instructional objective is a statement that describes a desired student outcome of instruction in terms of observable performance under given conditions*. If your definition contained most of the above features, then you're off to a fine start. Why did we include the modifier *observable* before *performance*? The answer resides in the need to get feedback. You've got it. Feedback can only be obtained by observing what students do, write, or say.

As a first check on your understanding of the definition, react to each of the following statements written by Mr. Jackson. He was planning to teach a unit on areas of various special quadrilaterals to his seventh-grade class. The following statements were some of those that he wrote as objectives for various lessons within the unit.

1. The student will be able to state the formulas for the area of a rectangle, a general parallelogram, a square, and a trapezoid, given either the label or a diagram of each quadrilateral.

2. The student will discover that the area of a parallelogram can be obtained from the area of a rectangle by a paper-cutting laboratory.

3. Given diagrams of various quadrilaterals and appropriate dimensions, the student will be able to state the area of the quadrilateral.

4. Given word problems involving physical regions in the shape of a quadrilateral, the student will write the matching area formula that could be used to solve the problem.

5. The student will appreciate the varied parallelogram shapes used in design and construction.

6. The student will understand that *area* means a "covering" of an enclosed shape.

7. The student will construct a square or a rectangle, given a compass and straightedge.

Which of Mr. Jackson's objectives satisfy all the criteria specified in the operational definition? You should have listed statements 1, 3, 4, and 7. If you rejected statements 5 and 6 on the basis of the nonobservable verbs (*appreciate* and *understand*), you were absolutely correct. Statement 2 may have seemed less of a problem since the students will be performing in a paper-cutting laboratory. But how will Mr. Jackson know they have "discovered" anything? Statement 2 fails to meet the criterion of observable performance, but it does describe a desirable teaching mode aimed at meaningful learning of an area formula. If you are somewhat uncomfortable about eliminating statements 2, 5, and 6, you agree with Mr. Jackson and the authors that attention to underlying concepts (as in 2 and 6) and to attitudes toward mathematics (as in 5) are vitally important overall goals of instruction. Try rewriting those three statements so that they do

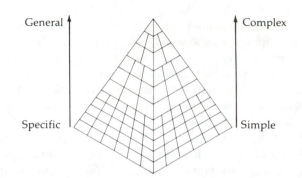

General ↑   ↑ Complex

Specific   Simple

Fig. 5.1   Model of a hierarchy.

satisfy the definition. Then check your efforts against ours as we consider various classes of objectives in the next section.

5.3 DOMAINS OF INSTRUCTIONAL OBJECTIVES

A cursory examination of Mr. Jackson's "objectives" makes it clear that he was concerned about learning in distinct areas of emphasis and at various levels of significance within some of those areas. The name given to the three major areas of emphasis into which all instructional objectives may be classified is *domain*. The *cognitive domain deals with recall or recognition of knowledge and the development of intellectual abilities and skills.* Most of Mr. Jackson's statements dealt with this domain, as will most of your objectives. However, remember that Mr. Jackson did try to write an objective aimed at attitude. *Changes in interest, attitudes, values and the development of appreciation belong to the affective domain.* The third domain, the *psychomotor domain, refers to the manipulative or motor-skill areas.* Did Mr. Jackson's objectives include any in this domain? Yes, statement 7 was an objective from the psychomotor domain. All of these domains should be considered sources of potential objectives.

Within each of these domains, there have been attempts to devise categorization systems called taxonomies. The purposes of such taxonomies are to make more explicit the varied levels of instructional objectives, to improve testing and research efforts, and to clarify communication among professionals in education. Why was the term *taxonomy* selected as the label for these systems of classification? You probably remember the biological taxonomy used in junior and senior high science classes wherein all living things are classified into categories such as kingdom, phylum, class, order, family, genus, and species. So a taxonomy is a set of standard classifications, and these categories are related in a hierarchical fashion. Figure 5.1 depicts a thought model of a hierarchy. At the base of the pyramid are the simple bits of knowledge. As one proceeds upward, ideas become increasingly complex. Similarly, one might think of the base as representative of the specifics of a field while the apex represents the generalizations. Since generalizations are built from specifics and since complex knowledge depends on simple units related in various ways, each layer of the hierarchy subsumes lower layers. Does the concept of hierarchy remind you of the nested stages model of Piagetian theory? You should be alert for correspondences between Piagetian theory and kinds of objectives as we build our taxonomies of instructional objectives.

Although all three domains are sources of potential objectives, taxonomies in two of the domains, the cognitive and the affective, are particularly useful tools for the secondary school mathematics teacher. Since most of your work will deal with cognition, we will start with a classification of objectives in this domain.

The Cognitive Domain

The most widely used taxonomy of cognitive objectives is that devised by Benjamin Bloom and colleagues (1956). Bloom's taxonomy contains six major levels, or classes. We will use a version of Bloom's taxonomy as illustrated in Table 5.1.

Table 5.1
Cognitive Taxonomy

Level	Descriptive label	Description of level
Above III	Evaluation	Judgments about the *value* of material and methods for given purposes.
	Synthesis	Putting together parts so as to form a whole pattern or structure of ideas not clearly there before.
	Analysis	Breaking down of material into its parts so that the relationships among ideas are made explicit.
III	Novel application	The selection and use of a learned rule, concept, method in a situation *novel* to the student.
II	Comprehension	The use of a specific rule, concept, method in a situation *typical* to those used in class.
I	Knowledge	The recall of material with little or no alteration required.

It is important to keep in mind that a taxonomy is a hierarchy. Therefore, a level II objective implies that command of related level I behaviors is assumed. For example, if a student is expected to be able to use the formula for the area of a square in computing areas given the length of a side of a square, that student is implicitly expected to be able to recall the formula for the area of a square. However, the reverse does not hold. If a teacher plans lessons only on level I, then luck alone will be responsible for student learning of the level II *use* of recalled material.

Before we get too involved with all this background, let's look at some specific examples. If Mr. Jackson had written at least one objective at each level of the taxonomy, his list might have included some of the following.

The student will be able to:

Level I	State the formulas for the area of a square, a rectangle, a trapezoid, and a general parallelogram, given the name of the shape.
Level II	Compute the area of a square, a rectangle, a trapezoid, or a general parallelogram, given appropriate lengths.
Level III	Compute the area of an irregular figure that can be dissected into three or more of the special quadrilaterals.
Levels above III:	
(Analysis)	List the facts, the relevant relationships, and the irrelevant information contained in a word problem different from those used in class.
(Synthesis)	Write a word problem that includes the use of at least three of the four area rules in the unit.
(Evaluation)	Write an assessment of the advantages and disadvantages of two different solutions to a word problem, where accuracy and economy are desired criteria.

Study each of the preceding objectives and the descriptions of the corresponding taxonomic levels. Why is the third objective considered a *novel* application? Note that the final three objectives also contain elements of *novelty*. When you are attempting to identify the level of a particular objective, this element of *novelty to the learner* is a crucial characteristic that separates levels I and II from all other levels. The first question to ask of yourself then, is "Is the student expected to perform a task that has some element of novelty?" A negative response leads you to the next question: "Can the objective be satisfied by recall alone?" An affirmative response leads to the identification of level I as the correct one for the objective (see Figure 5.2). For most classroom purposes, it is sufficient for beginning teachers to be able to distinguish among levels I, II, III, and above III. Table 5.1 gives descriptions of the subdivisions above III for clarification only.

Sometimes the idea of novelty is mistakenly equated with the notion of complexity. The ability to use 15 rules in a long calculus problem is still level II behavior *if* the problem is a typical one, whereas the ability to select the correct rule, however simple, in a situation new to the student is level III behavior. An example of such a situation is illustrated here.

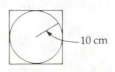

Find the area of the circumscribed square in the diagram.

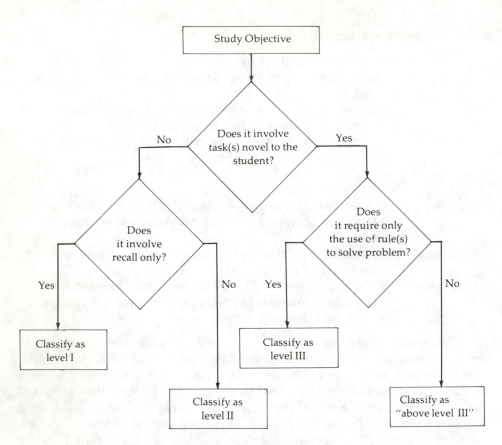

Fig. 5.2   Classification flowchart for cognitive domain.

Notice that the student must realize that the radius is one-half the length of a side of the square—a step that requires a mental restructuring of the diagram! This is a level III task. A second flow chart (Figure 5.3) schematizes this aspect of problem solving that distinguishes level III and above tasks from the lower levels of the taxonomy.

The "search" component of the flowchart may cause a person to think for a matter of seconds, minutes, or days. In any case, the objective represented by the problem is at or above level III. On the other hand, even though students cannot solve a type problem because they have forgotten needed formulas or are applying rules in an incorrect manner, the objective that is represented by the type problem is still a level II objective.

Examples and explanations are important ingredients in developing understanding, but there's no substitute for experience. Now it's time for you to check your own ability to classify objectives. Study each of the following objectives written by Ms. Bonner for her eleventh-grade unit on trigonometry and classify each at one of the *four major* taxonomic levels described in Table 5.1.

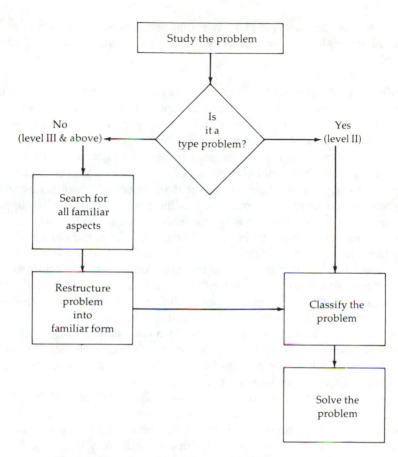

Fig. 5.3 Flowchart of level II versus level III and above behavior.

The student will be able to:

1. Calculate missing side lengths or angle measures in right triangle problems, by means of the six trigonometric functions, given a table of trigonometric values.

2. State the formulas for the law of sines and the law of cosines.

3. Verify that two unfamiliar trigonometric expressions are or are not identical by substituting appropriate formulas in the sequence taught in class.

4. Solve a trigonometric equation of first or second degree for a set of angle measures, within a given range, given a table of trigonometric values.

5. Explain the effect on the trigonometric functions if they are redefined for (x', y') on some nonrectangular grid.

6. Calculate a missing bearing in a navigation problem by application of oblique triangle and right triangle trigonometric formulas, given a table of trigonometric values.

Notice that Ms. Bonner took the same shortcut Mr. Jackson used in the last set of objectives. Since all objectives are in terms of student performance, both teachers wrote "The student will be able to:" only once before the entire set of objectives. As a matter of fact, some teachers omit that phrase entirely since it is understood to be present. Did you perhaps want to reject some of Ms. Bonner's statements as instructional objectives because verbs such as *calculate*, *verify*, *solve*, or *derive* suggest mental activity rather than observable performance? If so, you've been interacting carefully with the reading thus far. But we also slipped in some others like these earlier. Go back to Mr. Jackson's second set and note that some of his statements *seem* to be characterized by the same defect. If you're thinking that these objectives are perfectly clear and that to say otherwise is to make mountains out of molehills, we agree with you. Some instructors and curriculum writers would prefer to insert "in writing" or "orally" in each of the above statements. Whenever there is any ambiguity, we recommend this. However, as a general rule of thumb, highly specific, content-related verbs that are typically understood to imply observable performance may be used without any additional modifying phase. By the way, Ms. Bonner's third statement would have been less acceptable if it had ended after the word *identical*. If you're not sure why, talk this over with a classmate or your instructor.

Be sure that you have written down your classification of each of Ms. Bonner's objectives before you read further. We classified objective 2 as the only objective at level I. It is the only one of the six statements where recall *alone* is sufficient to meet the objective. Granted, some students may forget the formulas and, recalling the derivation techniques, may reconstruct the derivation in order to obtain the formulas. Although these students might be performing at level II, Ms. Bonner, as most eleventh-grade teachers, desired the eventual memorization of these formulas and intended this as a level I objective. If you classified most of her other objectives as level II, you are catching the idea. We classified objectives 1, 3, 4, and 6 as level II objectives and objective 5 as above level III. As written, each of the four level II objectives refers to the solution of *typical* problems for this unit. Even in the case of verification of identities, Ms. Bonner should have taught a series of strategies which the student is expected to use. If you classified objective 5 as level III, rather than above III, don't be overly concerned. You correctly identified the element of novelty. However, we see that objective as requiring *more than* the application of rules to a novel task. It also entails contrasting and comparing of the old with the new and thus we would more specifically classify this objective as at the analysis level. For further practice on this kind of task, see the Simulation/Practice Activities in Section 5.5.

Now you're ready to start on the first written component of each lesson plan—the stated instructional objectives. We asked you to test yourself on this

Table 5.2
A Sample List of Performance Verbs

add	describe	hypothesize	list	solve
calculate	design	identify	multiply	state
cite	diagram	induce	plan	subtract
contrast	divide	infer	plot	translate
criticize	evaluate	interpret	predict	verify
deduce	explain	interpolate	propose	write
defend	extrapolate	justify	prove	
derive	graph	label	select	

earlier by rewriting Mr. Jackson's defective statements from Section 5.2. Two of these statements 2 and 6, were cognitive, so it's appropriate to consider those now. Compare your versions with those of the authors.

> Substitute 2. *The students will write a generalization for computing the area of a parallelogram in terms of its base and its altitude after completing a paper-cutting laboratory and tabulating the data obtained by all students in the lab group.*

> Substitute 6. *The students will compute the area of unfamiliar shapes using the results of "covering" the regions with smaller cutout shapes of given area.*

If your versions differ substantially from the above and you are not clear as to their suitability, check with other classmates and/or your instructor. Like most beginners, you may encounter initial difficulty in selecting performance verbs that accurately convey your intentions. Thus we have prepared a sample list of those verbs that have proved particularly useful in your subject matter field (see Table 5.2). Use it to the extent it proves helpful, but don't assume that including one verb from this list *guarantees* a well-structured objective.

The Affective Domain

Remember Mr. Jackson's defective objective that was rejected because it included the nonobservable verb *appreciate*? Mr. Jackson attempted to include an objective in the affective domain (feelings, attitudes, and values) that would help students to relate mathematical concepts to physical world applications. He was struggling to communicate in a domain studied and classified by Krathwohl, Bloom and Masia (1964) who constructed a taxonomy of five levels—commonly called "Krathwohl's taxonomy." We use a version of this taxonomy that includes a modification of the second and third levels of Krathwohl's taxonomy. See Table 5.3 for a description of these three levels.

As in the taxonomy of cognitive objectives, this taxonomy is also a hierarchy. At the lowest level, the student may, for example, merely sit quietly in a

Table 5.3
Affective Taxonomy

Level	Descriptive label	Description of level
III	Valuing	Commitment to a value shown by consistent and stable response to objects, people, phenomena, etc.
II	Responding	Voluntary participation in activities, or selection of one activity out of several.
I	Complying	Passive acceptance of role assigned by teacher. No overt avoidance of activity.

condition of apparent listening during a lecture, rather than chatting with neighbors, doing homework, or reading *Popular Mechanics*. When question/answer begins, those students who volunteer are exhibiting behavior beyond level I. But the teacher must refrain from the immediate assumption that these students are interested in the subject. They may only be interested in being "on stage" momentarily. As you may have guessed, it is relatively easy to write objectives at levels I and II and far more difficult both to write a level III objective and to have it attained by many students. Yet there is little point in being a mathematics teacher, in the opinion of the authors, if you do not work toward motivation based on the acceptance of some of the values inherent in or related to the subject matter. Let's see what Mr. Jackson might have written if he had wanted at least one objective at each of the three levels of this taxonomy. Recall he was teaching seventh-graders a unit on area.

Level I	Participates in the lab-group role assigned by the teacher.
Level II	Attempts an optional challenge problem on areas of regular polygons.
Level III	Volunteers illustrative examples from nonassigned outside sources during a class discussion on the application of geometry to the real world.

As you compare each of the above objectives with the description of the matching taxonomic level, you will probably realize that levels II and III cannot be attained with any certainty if the teacher "motivates" tasks by either the threat or promise of a grade. In these cases, students may merely be complying with instructions—thus behaving at level I. The students may, in fact, be interested in the lab activity, but obedient participation gives the teacher no feedback as to this interest. The word "voluntarily" or a synonymous word or phrase will be found in a level II objective. However, a major distinction between level II and level III is that in a level II objective the teacher has defined the choice(s) to which the student can *respond*. Notice that in Mr. Jackson's level II objective, he will have to devise a challenge problem and state the free choice aspect of completing it. However, in his level III objective the reference to "nonassigned outside sources" suggests that students would have to voluntarily do some investigating and have formed some judgment as to the value of applications, rather than responding to a specific task posed by Mr. Jackson. Over the course of the entire two-week unit, Mr. Jackson would be looking for repeated instances of similar commitment before he could feel any confidence in the attainment of level III objectives by any one student.

This simplied affective taxonomy should be represented by some objectives in the total set written by each teacher as a new unit is planned. Ms. Bonner included these in the set she wrote for the trigonometry unit. Study each statement carefully and classify each at one of the three taxonomic levels of the affective domain.

1. Voluntarily attempt one or more of the problems in set C each time these are identified as free-choice challenge examples.

2. Volunteer to put homework derivations on the board.

3. Do all assigned homework neatly.

4. Work quietly at task when assigned group work on identities.

5. On his or her own initiative, investigate library resource materials on surveying equipment after a classroom demonstration of the equipment.

6. Raise questions in physics class about the mathematical contributions to physics of men such as Kepler, Galileo, and Newton.

We classified objectives 3 and 4 as level I, objectives 1 and 2 as level II, and objectives 5 and 6 as level III. The major difference between the level II and level III objectives seems to be evidence of student-initiated interest over time. It is surely true that objectives at level III have little chance of success unless the teacher has consistently worked toward this level of performance. It is also true that objectives in this domain necessitate matching assessment forms. We will be developing this area in Chapter 8.

You're almost ready to begin writing your own affective objectives. Check your first attempt, the revision of Mr. Jackson's defective objective 5, with our version.

Substitute 5. *The student will elect to do an outside project that illustrates the role of parallelograms in design.*

Have you observed the intrinsic connections between the cognitive and the affective domain? For instance, the student who is able to meet the above objective will, at the same time, be exhibiting behavior at level II in the cognitive domain. You will observe similar overlap in other objectives in both of these domains. However, where the intended emphasis is on the development of feelings, attitudes, or values rather than on recalling, comprehending, or applying intellectual skills, the objective is classified as affective.

In the not-so-distant past, affective objectives were rarely included in curriculum materials. It was hoped that the intrinsic overlap of cognitive with affective domains would somehow become actualized. Yet we have generations of mathematics students who have passed geometry but are vocal about their dislike of that subject—solid evidence that there's something wrong with that hope. Notice that we said "passed geometry," not have "become skillful proof-constructors." There definitely is an intrinsic overlap of the cognitive and affective domains and when one domain is ignored, the other suffers. The work on beliefs about mathematics referred to in Chapter 4 has shown us that when students believe that mathematics is mysterious, a collection of unreasonable rules with no apparent real world connections, they tend to approach the subject with little confidence and increasing amounts of frustration. If your students have acquired such attitudes because of their previous experiences in mathematics classes, you will have to incorporate many activities that are open-ended, illustrate the importance of trial and error approaches in problem-solving, and emphasize the human decisions that are a part of mathematics. In addition to the ideas in Chapter 4, see especially the illustrations and sources in Chapters 9, 10 and 11 for specific activities to use in this way.

"All right," we hear you say, "attitudes are important; and I do want my students to like mathematics, or at least not to dislike it. But why does a mathematics teacher need to include psychomotor objectives?" Read on, and see.

The Psychomotor Domain

Check out the label given to this third major category of human learning capabilities. Note that *psycho* conveys the notion that motor (muscle) learning is intertwined with mind, soul, and spirit. Earlier we called attention to the interconnections among the cognitive and affective aspects of learning and stressed that it was largely a matter of the major emphasis of a given objective that allowed classification into one domain versus another. So it is with targeting instruction on manipulative skills important to mathematics. These kinds of objectives *do* require specific and intentional efforts on the part of teachers. Teachers must choose to select those to be included as important goals of the course and must then design special strategies to promote their attainment. Novice teachers are prone to assume that this category of objectives is inappropriate for the junior and senior high mathematics classroom. One might be tempted to agree with them after observing groups of eighth-graders wielding little more complicated equipment than paper and pencil for days on end, or tenth-graders passively watching a teacher write out a proof on the chalkboard. However, by this time you should be disabused of the notion that teaching modes that systematically exclude laboratory activities are a desirable match to either the intellectual development of your students or the nature of the content. Measuring activities, paper-folding laboratories, and model building have as much to contribute to the learning of mathematics as the more often seen protractor and compass. But surely the *use* of such devices needs no special attention. Observe an eighth-grade class where students are supposed to be applying compass-use skills to produce copies of elaborate designs. Walk around and tabulate the number of students holding the compass in the center of the palm, placing the pencil at an awkward height, unable to adjust the compass to match a desired radius, unable to draw a complete circle, and other evidences of the *absence* of psychomotor skills. Then believe the evidence instead of the pious hopes of teachers and curriculum guides, and take the first step toward heading off such disasters in groups you will teach. That first step is specifying objectives in the psychomotor domain. The time to begin is now.

We have constructed a few sample objectives—some with deficiencies—to help you get started. Read each carefully. Then decide whether or not each (1) contains a specific performance verb, (2) communicates clearly, (3) places primary emphasis on coordinated muscle movements, and (4) makes obvious the materials and equipment that would be made available to the learner. (It is our experience that one could write "given access to all required equipment and materials" after almost every objective in this domain. This seems senseless to us so we *assume* that phrase is understood to be part of each objective *unless* there is some good reason to state more specific limitations on these conditions for performance.)

1. Measure rectilinear shapes with a metric ruler to within ±.5 mm.

2. Describe how to operate a hand-held calculator to obtain sums, differences, products, and quotients of integers.

3. Adjust a georule to illustrate geometrically shaped letters of the alphabet.

4. Fold wax paper according to instructions to obtain models of the parabola, the hyperbola, and the ellipse.

5. Prepare a working model of Watt's linkage, given a set of precut and prepunched links and all other required materials.

6. Manipulate a set of cutout rectangular and square shapes to illustrate equivalent algebraic expressions.

Now let's see how closely your analysis of these sample objectives agrees with ours. We consider measuring shapes, describing procedures, adjusting a georule, folding wax paper, preparing a model, and manipulating shapes to be specific performances, and we think that each of the six statements communicates clearly. However, did you pick out the fact that *describe* in objective 2 emphasizes the cognitive aspects of learning and does *not* call for a demonstration of the indicated motor skills? We certainly hope so, for there is a world of difference between talking about manipulative skills and actually performing them, though comprehension is often a helpful prerequisite to motor learning. Perhaps this very thought occurred to you when you considered objective 6. It did to us when we wrote it. Why did we state conditions for objective 5 and not the others? We simply wanted to delimit the expectations by ruling out the measuring of suitable length links and the positioning of joints in appropriate locations as being part of this particular objective. Does objective 4 seem to represent a motor skill that definitely does not require specific instruction? We have observed college mathematics majors bungling these folding instructions. But don't take our word for it. Just observe and believe.

You should now be ready to try constructing a few objectives on your own. Think in terms of the manipulative skills associated with the use of devices such as tangram shapes, geo-d-stix, compass, string models, geoboard, transit, graduated cylinders, stop watch, and pan balance. Then write at least three objectives relevant to a subject you expect to teach and submit them to a critique by your instructor or a classmate.

In the cases of the cognitive and affective domains we concerned ourselves with classifying objectives at a variety of levels within each domain. However, we will *not* deal with a taxonomy within the psychomotor domain. Why? Isn't there any such thing? Yes, there is a taxonomy for this domain, but it appears much more relevant to the elementary school age group or physical education content than to secondary school mathematics instruction.

5.4 SUMMARY AND SELF-CHECK

Instructional objectives can be considered analogous to route directions written on a road map. Without these the teacher can easily fall into the trap of jousting at every windmill sighted along the way. The route map must be well designed so that an equally trained professional, another teacher of the same subject, would agree on the nature of specific behaviors represented by the objectives. We emphasized the need for clear communication of ideas without excessive verbiage. Recall how the later objectives did not contain the commonly assumed phrase, "The student will be able to:" nor conditions that ought to be obvious to any other trained teacher. You may find it difficult to write both clearly and succinctly. If it comes to a choice, there is no argument. Clarity should win out.

Throughout this chapter, you were provided illustrations of objectives in each of three domains—the cognitive, the affective, and the psychomotor. Three criteria to be used in writing instructional objectives of any kind were stressed and categorizations within the cognitive and affective domains were described and illustrated.

At this time, you should be able to:

1. Operationally define instructional objective, cognitive domain, affective domain, and psychomotor domain.

2. Operationally define each of the levels in the cognitive and affective domains.

3. Identify given statements as either meeting or failing to meet all criteria for an instructional objective and give reasons for your decisions.

4. Classify given instructional objectives according to domain and according to level for those in the cognitive and affective categories.

5. Write instructional objectives for each level of the cognitive and affective domains.

6. Write instructional objectives in the psychomotor domain.

The exercises in the next section are designed to provide you with some further experience in identifying, classifying, and writing instructional objectives. Skills developed in these areas will give you a head start in designing lesson plans and in constructing appropriate assessment measures—both everyday tasks of the classroom teacher.

5.5 SIMULATION/PRACTICE ACTIVITIES

A. Below are ten statements purported to be instructional objectives. Assume that each is of educational value to its subject matter area. React to each *only* in terms of whether or not it satisfies all three criteria for instructional objectives. Use an X to indicate your judgment.

	No	Uncertain	Yes
1. Identify the primes smaller than 100.	____	____	____
2. Know the Pythagorean theorem.	____	____	____
3. Derive the formula for the law of cosines.	____	____	____
4. Appreciate the symmetry forms in physical objects.	____	____	____
5. Explain the "delta process" used in obtaining the first derivative.	____	____	____
6. Factor the difference of two squares, given that each square is a monomial.	____	____	____
7. Graph any function of the form $y = ax + b, a \neq 0$.	____	____	____
8. Draw a diagram and write the "Given" and "To Prove" from any "If, then" statement in plane geometry.	____	____	____
9. Understand the nature of a circular argument.	____	____	____
10. List four ways to prove triangles congruent.	____	____	____

If you checked any of the above "no," revise those statements so that you would check each "yes." Then compare all your responses with those of two other students. Discuss differences in judgment, attempt to arrive at a consensus, and then ask your instructor for feedback on your efforts.

B. The statements below are instructional objectives based on junior/senior high school mathematics content. Classify *each* according to domain (cognitive, affective, or psychomotor) and then by level for those within the cognitive and affective domains.

   1. Measure an angle to the nearest degree, given a protractor (Math 7).

   2. Generalize a nth term relationship given the first six terms of a numerical sequence (Algebra).

   3. Define parallelogram, rhombus, and square (Geometry).

   4. Raise questions in social studies class about the reasoning heard in television political debates and the instances of circular reasoning, reasoning from a converse, and so on studied in geometry class (Geometry).

   5. Solve an equation of the form $ax^2 + bx + c = 0$, $a \neq 0$ by means of the quadratic formula, for roots in radical form (Algebra).

   6. Select mathematics-related reading material when given "free" reading time in English class (any level).

   7. Write at least two inferences based on the line graph of a set of data (Math 8).

   8. Move "spiro" gears to trace a polar curve (Algebra).

   9. State the domain and range of a function given a graph of the function (Algebra).

   10. Write a one-paragraph "story" in which mathematical concepts are used, given a topic sentence such as "I dreamed I was a point in a non-Euclidean plane" (Geometry).

C. Choose a topic from the subject matter of junior/senior high mathematics. Check textbooks and syllabi to ensure that the selected topic would be one developed over at least a two-week period. Study student exercises and resource materials related to the topic. Then write 10 instructional objectives in the cognitive domain that would be appropriate for this topic and the anticipated students. At least 5 of the objectives should be at level II. Include at least 1 at level III and at least 1 above level III.

D. Use the topic selected by you in exercise C to write at least *five* instructional objectives in the affective domain. Include some at level II and at least one at level III.

E. Use the topic selected by you in exercise C or choose another topic and write at least *three* instructional objectives in the psychomotor domain.

SUGGESTIONS FOR FURTHER STUDY

Mager, R. F. (1968). *Developing attitude toward learning*. Belmont, CA: Fearon Publishers.

In chapters 1–5 Mager emphasizes the importance of the affective domain for learning any school subject. Mager uses an easy-to-read interactive style to illustrate what he calls "approach behaviors" indicative of positive attitudes. Attention is also given to interrelationships with the cognitive domain, and readers are directed to reflect upon the development of their own system of values.

Mager, R. F. (1962). *Preparing instructional objectives*. Belmont, CA: Fearon Publishers.

This brief paperback provides a simple introduction to writing objectives. Most novice teachers can complete the book, which is written in programmed format, in a little over an hour's time. The explanations are brief; the examples, clear. Feedback is immediate and those who catch on quickly are directed to skip repetitive materials.

Sund, R. & Picard, A. (1972). *Behavioral objectives and evaluational measures: science and mathematics*. Columbus, OH: Charles E. Merrill.

Behavioral objectives and their use in designing evaluation measures are viewed within the framework of a systems analysis approach to instruction. The authors include a rationale for the use of behavioral objectives, provide clear instructions for writing such objectives (including numerous examples from both mathematics and science), and relate these to the taxonomies of both the cognitive and affective domains. The use of objectives in curriculum design comes in for some attention but much more emphasis is placed on their use in developing evaluation measures.

CHAPTER SIX

THE LEARNING OF MATHEMATICS

Stepping Stones to Planning

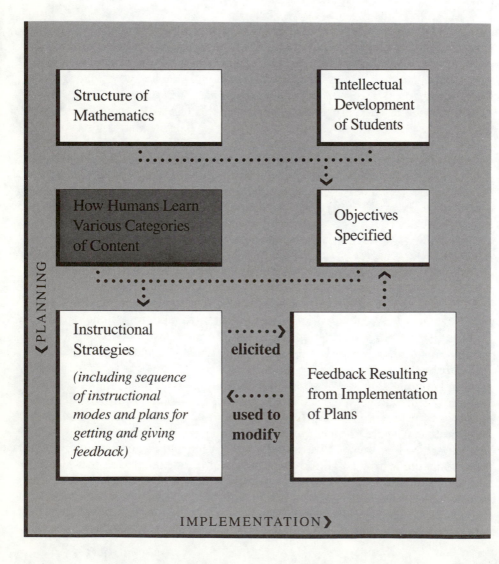

We have come a long way in our study of systematic instruction. Together we explored the modes used by teachers and the feedback strategies associated with those modes. We sought an answer to the question: "What are the intellectual capabilities of the typical junior/senior high student?" and to the equally important query: "What is mathematics?" Armed with this background, we considered the nature of instructional objectives. Now we have mapped out where we are going, with whom, and for what purpose. But how do we get there? Instructional modes surely are part of that answer, but modes need to be chosen, sequenced, and implemented on a dual basis—the choice of specified objectives and the evidence illuminating the ways learning takes place.

How do humans learn various categories of mathematics? That question should look familiar. Of course, you've been in a position to see it each time you begin a new chapter of this text. Notice the place of this component in the instructional model and be alert to the interconnections to lesson planning that will be foreshadowed in this chapter. Wait a minute. Haven't we already studied learning? Didn't the work of cognitive developmental psychologists, particularly Piaget, provide us with all the evidence we need as to how learning takes place? You're making a common mistake if these are your thoughts, but you're not completely out in left field. Piaget studied the ways in which intellectual structures develop—the spontaneous development of knowledge as opposed to learning attributed to instruction. We have already stressed that his data and his theoretical constructs are invaluable inputs in our choice of objectives and in the eventual design of instructional strategies. We have also learned about the common reasoning strategies of students in certain areas of mathematics, as well as something about individual difference characteristics affecting reasoning. The focus was on the students in Chapter 3—what they bring to the mathematics classroom. Now we need to examine the content again, from the perspective of research on learning that results from intentional attempts to change behavior.

Let's be sure we're on the same wavelength when we use the term *learning*. We concur with the definition used by most contemporary psychologists that *learning is a change in human attitudes, cognitions, or psychomotor skills that is not due simply to the process of growth*. The definition excludes a change in human capabilities, such as increase in the size of the muscles, but includes specific eye-hand coordination abilities. Moreover, if learning is a *change*, then it is necessary for teachers to get feedback on the student's capability *before* instruction as well as *after* instruction. Have you had the experience of sitting through a college calculus course where at times you were bored by the repetition of concepts you had learned in high school? Were there perhaps other times in the same course when you were lost by an all-too-brief treatment of a content idea to which you had been exposed in high school but which you had never really learned? What accounts for such selective learning and remembering? Why is it that we seem to learn some ideas so thoroughly that they are easily recalled while there are others that we never could understand? Even stranger, why are there ideas we thought we had indelibly learned but can no longer recall? Remembering, like learning, becomes a mental process of more than passing interest.

Memorizing is the bane of most students. Yet probably every teacher of yours emphasized memory to some degree. (Too much, perhaps?) "SOHCAH-TOA," chorused the class. Was this one of your memory crutches?

$$\text{sine } \theta = \frac{\text{opposite}}{\text{hypotenuse}} \quad \text{SOH}$$

$$\cos \theta = \frac{\text{adjacent}}{\text{hypotenuse}} \quad \text{CAH}$$

$$\tan \theta = \frac{\text{opposite}}{\text{adjacent}} \quad \text{TOA}$$

"SOHCAHTOA" is an example of a mnemonic, a mental trigger to assist the memorizer. The student who successfully applies the mnemonic is able to state the three definitions above. Any human capable of imitating the verbalisms in the above statements and able to recall statements of this length can be taught the mnemonic and the related sentences. Animal learning is limited in this respect. The use of symbols of all kinds to represent ideas makes human learning far more complex than some psychologists once believed.

Experiments with pigeons, laboratory rats, and even higher animals have intrigued psychologists for years. Early attempts to equate human learning with animal learning led Thorndike, a psychologist, to write a methodology text (1921), in which he promoted the teaching of 100 addition facts as separate bits of unrelated material. Teachers were warned that $3 + 2 = 5$ and $2 + 3 = 5$ were separate bonds, each of which needed distinct instruction and practice. Although Thorndike was interested in relevance and problem solving, his followers applied his approach to instruction in extreme ways and drill and practice became the only instructional event in most mathematics classrooms. Little wonder that educational psychology left a bad taste in the mouths of some teachers. Where was the meaning? Were there not relationships among parts? Which terms needed to be memorized? Which might be deduced, or even reconstructed when and as needed? Names and labels must surely be learned differently from concepts, skills, problem solving, proof constructing and the like. What are those differences? These are some of the questions we address in this chapter. We begin by engaging you in an activity that further explores the intricacies of memory and its relationship to understanding.

6.1 INTRODUCTORY ACTIVITY

You will need to enlist the aid of two or three acquaintances to serve as subjects for this activity. Seek out mathematics majors who are *not* presently in this course and have not taken it previously.

A. Provide each volunteer with a quiet place to study a typed copy of the list of words below. At the end of one minute ask the subject to look up from the list and recite the words *in order*. Stop the person at the first error and provide another minute of study time. Allow five such study periods of one minute duration each and record the number of correct words (in sequence) achieved by the student at the end of each study period.

List of words

math	proofs	incurred	she
her	wrath	all	a
seeking	instructions	as	teacher's
could	do	student	constructions
defined	locus	but	path
always	young	without	of
bright			

B. Using the same volunteer(s), substitute for the list of words a typed copy of the limerick below. Repeat five similar trials and keep comparable records of the results.

Limerick

A bright young student of math
always defined locus as path.
She could do all constructions
without seeking instructions,
but her proofs incurred teacher's wrath.

C. Compare the data you collected with that of at least five to seven of your classmates. Does a clear pattern emerge? If so, how do you account for the fact that one ordering (sequencing) of the same words was easier to learn than the other? Was there any factor other than sequencing that could also have made a difference in the ease of initial learning? Discuss your thoughts on these matters with classmates and your instructor and remain alert to further inputs in the sections that follow.

D. Design a simple way to check up on comparative retention of the list versus the limerick. We suggest allowing at least seven days to elapse between the initial learning and the remembering (retention) trials.

6.2 MEANINGFUL LEARNING

What made the limerick easier to learn than the same words in scrambled order? Doubtless your discussions generated ideas such as meaning, rhyme, and rhythm as likely causes of the observed results. If you further proposed that *meaning* was the most important factor, then your thinking is attuned to what has been clearly demonstrated both by researchers (Ausubel, 1979; Brownell, 1935; Bruner, 1960; Dienes, 1960) and effective teachers (see the many articles authored by teachers in the journals of the National Council of Teachers of Mathematics). Further, meaning of the material has been shown to be the prime factor associated with retention (remembering) of subject matter over time. Even the most cursory reflection on the nature and extent of the subject matter you are preparing to

Rote ◄───► Meaningful

Fig. 6.1   Rote/meaningful learning continuum.

teach underscores the need to give careful attention to the central task of ensuring meaningful learning. Unlike computers, the human intellect is *not* capable of storing or retrieving large amounts of discrete bits of information.

Although meaningful learning and instructional strategies that promote the meaningful learning of mathematics have been the subject of writings and studies by many mathematics educators and psychologists (e.g. Ausubel, 1979; Brownell, 1935; Bruner, 1960; Colburn, 1830/1912/1970; Dewey, 1910; Dienes, 1960; Wertheimer, 1945/1959), David Ausubel is known for making a substantial contribution to our understanding of the psychological character of meaningful learning. Writing in an era when many mathematics and science curricula projects were designed to reflect the structure of their disciplines, Ausubel clarified loose notions of what might make mathematics content meaningful to students. In the paragraphs that follow, we adapt Ausubel's ideas to the teaching of secondary school mathematics.

The term *learning* has already been defined in the introductory section and we urge you to review that definition at this point. Now let's see if we can nail down the key components of that all-important idea of *meaningful*. Meaningful to whom? The learner, of course. Recall that the directions for the Introductory Activity specified the use of mathematics majors. The words *locus, construction,* and *proof* all have special meanings to one trained in this subject field and these in turn facilitate comprehension of the whole idea of the poem. Persons who do not attach subject-specific meanings to these key words might learn to recite the limerick perfectly given sufficient time, but would respond differently to indepth questioning about the student's plight as described in this poem. Thus, new content becomes *meaningful* to the extent that it is *substantively (nonarbitrarily) related to ideas already existing in the cognitive structure of the learner* (Ausubel, 1968). This definition stands in clear contrast to that of *rote* learning wherein the *new content is arbitrarily (nonsubstantively) related to the existing cognitive structure of the learner*. If we imagine a continuum ranging from pure rote to highly meaningful learning, the task of memorizing the scrambled word list would be placed near, but not at, the rote (no-sense or nonsense) pole (see Figure 6.1).

As an independent information bit, each *familiar* word did relate to existing cognitive structure. However, the list did not represent a meaningful whole. Had the scrambled list consisted of nonsense syllables (XTU, KLMA, DTTIZ), then we would clearly place the task *at* the rote pole. On the other hand, a competent mathematics teacher learning the limerick would be performing a task near the highly meaningful end of the continuum.

Consider a very real learning problem that occurs in all too many tenth-grade geometry classes each fall. Students are confronted with the task of learning a host of postulates and definitions, the names of numerous shapes, and relationships among them. Do these constitute *potentially meaningful content*? Of course they do. No one would argue against the importance of the understanding of the axiomatic structure of geometry. Recall, however, that the crucial point is to make new content meaningful *to the learner*. What already exists in the cognitive structure of these tenth-grade students to which the new material can be substantively related? Are concepts such as point, ray, segment, betweenness, and union already there in a stable form? If not, and time isn't taken to establish such prerequisites, students face a horrendous task of rote learning in this unit. Yes, much depends on what was meaningfully learned and retained as a result of junior high mathematics courses.

By this time you have undoubtedly surmised that we believe that meaningful learning and retention depend primarily upon the *way* the learning occurs. Our constant reminders to you to interact with the material, to compare answers with those of other classmates, and to hypothesize and then check out your hypotheses are all specific learning strategies that are supportive of meaningful learning. In the post-Sputnik era of curriculum reform, some teachers and some curriculum writers behaved as if all learning processes could be categorized as one of two types: reception learning or discovery learning. Indeed, some went one step further and equated reception learning with rote learning and discovery learning with meaningful learning.

We've already explored the difference between meaningful and rote learning. But to what do reception and discovery learning refer? The term *reception* might remind you of a telephone receiver, a receptionist, a receipt. Thus, *reception learning* occurs when *the entire content of the intended learning is presented to the learner in its final form and the learner incorporates the content into his or her cognitive structure*. If the new content becomes substantively related to ideas already present in the individual's cognitive structure, then meaningful reception learning has occurred. If this condition is not met, then *rote reception learning* would be the appropriate descriptor.

Which modes would you identify as potentially promising ways of promoting reception learning? If you chose lecture as a potential way to promote reception learning, your judgment is in accord with ours. However, if you believe that lecture could not be employed to promote discovery learning, you doubtless have an erroneous concept of discovery learning. In contrast to reception learning, in *discovery learning the learner must generate the desired content end-product or construct a missing interrelationship*. As in the case of reception learning, discovery learning may be *either* meaningful or rote, depending upon the kind of relationship (arbitrary or substantive) established between the new and previously learned content.

It is true that a lecture aimed at student discovery would be carefully structured to pose a problem and highlight conjecture and would not fill in all the gaps for the student. If you've already decided that a mixture of lecture with question/answer, laboratory, or some other mode would be even more successful in promoting meaningful learning of either type than lecture alone, you're absolutely correct. Furthermore, while lecture might be used to promote either reception or discovery learning, the use of the laboratory mode is not a guarantee of the coexistence of discovery learning, although it should be. A frequent abuse of the laboratory mode in junior/senior high mathematics classes is to tell the students what results they will obtain *before* they have begun to perform any of the manipulations. Imagine how that kind of teacher behavior affects meaningful learning. How are those students likely to view the process aspects of the nature of mathematics? Does that mean that the teacher stands back and lets the students fumble away at their own pace? Not likely. *Pure* discovery learning is almost never a viable approach. We agree with Ausubel that there simply isn't enough time to have students rediscover all they need to learn.

Furthermore, secondary school mathematics students do not yet possess the background knowledge, intellectual skills, and sometimes even the laboratory techniques required to learn without guidance from teacher and text. In fact, the discovery learning recommended by many teachers and scholars is more correctly called *guided* discovery learning. The teacher sets the scene, cues judiciously, and carefully structures the sequence of events so that the students need not reinvent the wheel. This kind of guided discovery has received much attention from Jerome S. Bruner (1960, 1966), a Harvard psychologist, whose research in school learning has resulted in both scholarly treatises on the nature of learning and essays to teachers on the nature of "going beyond the given."

However, ensuring that learning will be meaningful is not as easy as it sounds. Remember all those *potentially* meaningful postulates we mentioned earlier? Making content meaningful to the learner is a two-edged sword. The teacher must consider characteristics of the content as well as the match between the new content and the student's existing mental structure. We already learned that mathematical content could be classified in diverse ways—by process and product; by concept, postulate, and theorem. To what extent do these differences in content affect learning? What ways exist for categorizing various types of learning tasks and what conditions facilitate the learning of each type of task? These are the considerations to which we next direct our attention.

6.3 CATEGORIES OF HUMAN LEARNING

Unlike the early twentieth-century learning theorists, Robert Gagné rejected the notion of classifying all learning into a single category. Instead he added to and modified the theories of Thorndike and Skinner and selected aspects of the theory proposed by the Gestalt school of psychology. Moreover, he did all this in the context of school learning. Not only did he continuously conduct experiments with human subjects, but much of his data were collected in existing classrooms as opposed to the carefully controlled and contrived environment of a pseudoclass in a college laboratory. As a result, his inferences make practical instructional sense and are translatable into instructional strategies. In the following sections, we summarize two of Gagné's major contributions on which we base instructional strategy design to be considered in Chapter 7.

Learning Types

Gagné (1970) classified all human learning into eight major types, which are related in hierarchical fashion (Figure 6.2). In Gagné's later writings (Gagné, 1977, 1979; Gagné & Briggs, 1979), he collapsed the eight types into four larger categories and added a fifth human capability, attitudes. We have chosen to retain eight categories but in slightly modified form, since our experience and that of our students is that this hierarchy provides a helpful analysis of learning related to the cognitive and psychomotor domains. We will need to look elsewhere for background on learning in the affective domain. The hierarchy depicted in Figure 6.2, like the others you have studied, contains categories ranging from simple to complex, with each successive layer depending upon and subsuming those directly under it. However, unlike either the nested stages model or the taxonomies of instructional objectives, Gagné's hierarchy of learning types contains a branch midway up. This indicates that type 5 learning may depend just on related type 2 and type 1 learning. Branching of diverse kinds is prevalent throughout the learning of any subject. For example, learning to divide natural numbers may depend on first learning to subtract them *or* on first learning to multiply them. This concept of prerequisites *necessary* to future learning is the second of Gagné's contributions which we will study and relate to mathematics learning.

For the time being, we need to pay closer attention to the levels in Gagné's hierarchy. What does he mean by "concept"? Does his meaning agree with what we learned in Chapter 4? Would rule include the idea represented by such statements as the commutative principle for addition or the square root algorithm? The answer to these last two questions is a resounding yes. And although you will be primarily concerned with the learning of discriminations and the types dependent on these, the hierarchical nature of learning makes it imperative to have at least an acquaintance with all eight types of learning.

Signal learning   Gagné was not the first to distinguish between signal learning and stimulus-response learning. Probably the most commonly known experiments in signal learning are those of Pavlov, whose dog learned to salivate in response to the signal of a buzzer. The shell-shock symptoms demonstrated by war-weary soldiers on hearing a car backfire or firecrackers explode is another example of signal learning. The buzzer or the noise of the backfire serve as signals (conditioned stimuli) in these illustrations and the response of the learner—salivating in the case of the dog and fear symptoms in the case of the soldier—are conditioned responses of a reflexive, emotional nature. Notice that a general attitude, in this case fear related to a stimulus, is learned as the result of conditioning.

Stimulus-response learning   In stimulus-response learning we move toward more differentiated responses. Now the signal, or stimulus, must be connected with the response and the response itself is a *specific* terminal behavior that provides satisfaction to the learner. The training of animals and, indeed, the shaping

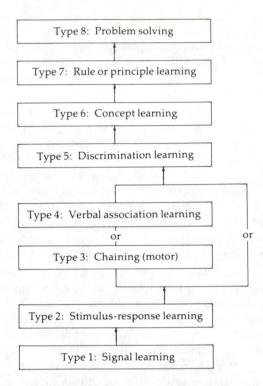

Fig. 6.2   Hierarchy of learning types.

of human behavior to respond in specific ways to verbal or nonverbal cues are good examples of these $S \rightarrow R$ (stimulus-response) connections. Some aspects of classroom management (for example, lab groups being taught to cease talking when the lights momentarily are switched off-then-on) are applications of stimulus-response learning. There have been entire texts written on the subject of behavior modification that deal with this kind of learning. Suffice it to say that (1) the correct response must result in some reinforcement—perhaps praise, a reward, or a success experience; (2) the reinforcement must occur fairly close in time to the response; and (3) the stimulus must be repeated often with partially correct responses being identified and positively treated. As you interact with Chapter 12, look for cues such as "use Grandma's Rule" and "be consistent." These are specific applications of $S \rightarrow R$ learning to classroom control. "You mean learning theory is practical?" You bet it is.

Chaining   Learning to swim requires a whole series of coordinated responses— each subunit being a $S \rightarrow R$ connection. The movement of arms and legs and the breathing behavior must all be appropriately linked, or *chained* together. So chaining is the name given to the type of learning represented by these nonverbal sequences.

Think back to the behavior described by the sample instructional objectives in Chapter 5. In which cases did the objectives clearly refer to the learning type Gagné has called "chaining"? If you fumbled over the answer to that question, you'd better go back and reread Section 5.3 with special attention to the psychomotor domain. Yes, psychomotor objectives all require that the student chain together individual $S \rightarrow R$ units. (1) These units must be well learned and (2) then integrated in the correct sequence. (3) Again, immediate reinforcement of the final response and repetition of the entire chain and pieces of it in close time succession are conditions required in order that chaining may occur. In the example given, learning to swim, the reinforcement for most people is success, an example of an intrinsic or internal reward. Some novices mistakenly believe that only extrinsic rewards (such as prizes, verbal praise, or grades) are satisfying to the learner. Initially, it is true that the struggling student may need the satisfaction of an external reward. However, if some internal reward does not gradually replace the external one, the learning has less chance of permanence.

Verbal association learning Gagné's type 4 learning encompasses much the same bonding of stimulus and response as that described by chaining. However, in this case, the response is a verbalism. Naming geometric shapes, labeling constants such as π, even the memorizing of verbal information such as "the square root of 2 is approximately equal to 1.41" are instances of the learning called verbal association. All the conditions required to assure the learning of motor chains are also required here. Of course, the stimulus situation now includes a drawing, an object, or a printed expression and an initial repetition of the desired response by the teacher. The teacher may also include cues, such as the mnemonic "SOHCAHTOA," that must be learned and then recalled to assist the learner in obtaining the desired longer verbal response. As you remember from the Introductory Activity, long verbal chains are easily forgotten unless they are learned in a meaningful context. Verbal association learning in mathematics includes fewer long verbal chains than social studies or even science, but it is complicated by a written and spoken language of symbols and groups of symbols.

Discrimination learning Closely related to this last illustration of verbal association learning is the learning of discriminations, Gagné's type 5. The ability to perceive the differences in shape between { } and ( ) may follow the learning of the respective verbalisms "set-braces" and "parentheses," but is a prerequisite if the student is to correctly distinguish one printed mark from the other. Similarly, the ability to perceive the *distinctive* features of objects observed, sounds heard, materials touched, foods tasted, and odors smelled are all examples of discrimination learning. Even intelligent adults are sometimes tricked by ignoring one perceptual change or overemphasizing another. How many smart chefs know this and slice all sandwiches on the diagonal? The sandwiches look bigger. The importance of discrimination learning to the learning of concepts cannot be underestimated. Some students never learn the *essential* features of a class of objects and are at a loss when novel examples are proposed. Geometry teachers have experienced this phenomenon when diagrams involve overlapping triangles or shapes turned in an unusual orientation. Thus, the most important condition needed to promote discrimination learning is the presentation of diverse exemplars of the feature to be learned. Perceptual problems are often the source of difficulty at this level of learning—a difficulty that blocks progress at the levels above.

Concept learning   Concept learning is the basic coin of the realm in areas usually described by words such as *thinking*, *understanding*, and *problem solving*. In Chapter 4 several kinds of concepts were used as examples—triangles, a defined concept; point, an undefined concept; greater than, a relational concept. An operational definition of *concept* was provided. Do you remember the use of the term, *classification* in the definition of concept? Classification, as used by Piaget, by logicians, and by all scientists, is the key to the conditions under which a concept is learned.

Suppose Mr. Mapes had written a definition of a triangle on the board and had drilled on the oral recitation of the label and definition? Would his sixth-grade students be likely to have learned the concept of triangle? If not, what could they be credited with learning? If you said they probably learned the *name of the concept* and a verbal association describing that name, you're in agreement with what experience has taught us. Suppose the students had been tenth-graders? Would it have made a difference? Yes, *if* they had already had concrete referents to attach to the presented verbalisms; otherwise, no. In general, the conditions for concept learning include (1) the availability of prior prerequisite discrimination and/or verbal association learning and (2) the presentation of gradually differentiated examples and non-examples. In the case of the concepts of mathematics, the examples and non-examples take the form of physical models or the names of prior concepts. For example, 2, 3, 5, 7, and 11 might be given as examples of primes with 4, 9, 15, and 16 labeled as non-examples. Sometimes an analogy is used to exemplify a mathematical concept. "$2x$ and $5y$ are illustrations of *unlike* terms. It's as if you have two apples and five oranges."

Whatever method the teacher uses to establish the conditions for learning, the evidence that a concept has been learned is *not* the recitation of a definition, nor is it any other feedback that might signify nothing more than accurate recall, such as responding correctly to examples used by the teacher during instruction. However, if the student responds correctly to examples not used in instruction and can produce novel examples when asked, then the teacher has obtained positive feedback on concept learning. *Concept learning*, then, is demonstrated by *the ability to generalize beyond the instances used in the learning situation and beyond the physical similarities present in some instances*. For example, a student who has learned the concept *triangle* will not be misled whether shown the intricacies of the geodesic dome at the United States Pavilion in Expo '67 or the lacy web constructed by a spider. Thus learning of concepts frees the student from total reliance on the physical world and makes it possible for rules and principles to be meaningfully learned.

Rule/principle learning   Rules and principles, the heart of mathematics, depend on concept learning. Why? Let's look at an example of rule learning. The formula for finding the area of a triangle might be memorized without any prior learning but the formula itself is only a *statement of a rule* just as the label "triangle" is the *name of a concept*. What is a rule? Identify the learning you would desire with respect to the given area formula. If you'd expect the ability to *use* the formula in a variety of situations, you've captured the essence of rule learning. Now to use the formula, Esther (one of your eighth-grade students) would need to have learned the concepts of triangle, area, equals, base, height, and one-half. She would also have to know how to multiply (another rule!) and finally would have to use all those concepts and in this case, an earlier rule, in the proper sequence and manner. *Rule learning*, then, is *the capability to respond to a class of situations with a class of performances where the situations and performances are related by a chain of concepts*. The rule itself is a chain of concepts. In this instance, given a variety of problems whose solutions require that the area of a triangular region be found, Esther will have to be able to classify each problem situation correctly, apply transformations as needed, and compute the area of the appropriate region. Such problem types might include triangular shapes drawn in atypical orientations and the instruction: Find the area of each region. Esther would have to identify the dimensions needed, measure these and perform the calculation correctly. If a deeper understanding of the rule were desired, the problem types might be real world situations such as the tile problem in Chapter 3. In such problems, the words "area" and "triangle" are often not mentioned, but the application of these concepts would be apparent if Esther had learned these concepts and the rule for finding the area of a triangle in a meaningful way. In all of these cases, it is impossible to tell what she might be thinking, but if the final performance results in the solution of the problems, then it is inferred that the rule has been learned.

Notice that her ability to state the formula is not even mentioned. However, you would probably want Esther to be able to state the formula to avoid constant searching for this repeatedly used tool. That's fine, but that's a verbal association that must be learned differently and tested separately. Just don't make the mistake of assuming that instant recall of the formula guarantees the ability to use that rule. Furthermore, don't assume that success, given the base and height lengths as the only lengths indicated on a diagram, will be repeated if the teacher labels the length of a median or of a noncorresponding base. Are you getting the idea? Your instructional objectives with regard to any rule may range from low-level and restricted use to complex and widely generalizable use. If, however, there is to be any subsequent problem solving (type 8), the rule that has been learned must be of the latter class.

What conditions must be present so that widely generalizable rule learning may take place? As in the example given: (1) The concepts that are to be chained must be separately mastered first. (2) The teacher must clearly let the students know what kind of terminal performance is expected. (Esther should be told that she'll be asked to find areas given triangular shapes and any necessary measuring instruments *if* that is what her teacher has decided.) (3) Verbal cues, concrete examples, or a carefully structured exercise can be used to (a) help students recall essential concepts and to (b) encapsulate the structure or main idea of the rule. (4) The use of the rule should be demonstrated in the format desired by the teacher. (5) Finally, the students must be asked to demonstrate the rule in *diverse* situations. If they can demonstrate its use successfully, they have learned the rule. Retaining it is another matter. In a later section in this chapter, we consider retention and transfer of learning.

Problem solving   Rules, no matter how complex the situation they encompass, are useful only if the problem can be characterized as belonging to a particular kind. However, throughout much of our in- and out-of-school life, the questions that intrigue us most are not typical problems. They belong instead to Gagné's type 8 learning, problem solving. Gagné is referring here to the moves toward the solution of *novel* problems—that is, problems *novel* to the student. (You should be reminded of the cognitive taxonomy.) Since the student cannot classify the problem as a typical one, search behavior continues until the problem is solved or at least restructured. Search behavior includes defining the problem, formulating hypotheses, verifying these, or altering hypotheses and then verifying the modifications. At this point we part company with Gagné, for he seems to imply that learning does not take place if the problem is not solved. We assert that thoughtful strategies engaged in by a student faced with problems like the mind-boggler below are behaviors characteristic of type 8, whether or not the problem is solved.

> Prove that if the lengths of two angle bisector segments (segment from the vertex of the bisected angle to the intersection of the angle bisector with the opposite side) of a triangle are equal, then the triangle is isosceles.

The modifier *thoughtful* eliminates erratic trial and error attempts or blind algorithmic tactics. The student who has engaged in problem solving may have been successful in intermediate stages. Some approaches may have been rejected after testing them. Additional data may have been deduced. The problem is definitely restructured, even if it has not yet been solved.

Emphasis on problem-solving strategies for all students has been identified as a major instructional objective by the National Council of Teachers of Mathematics in major reports, such as the *Agenda for Action* (1980). The characteristics of successful problem solvers have been studied extensively (See the summary provided by Suydam (1980), but interest in how problem-solving is learned is not new. Gestalt psychologists, such as Duncker (1945), gave examples of the

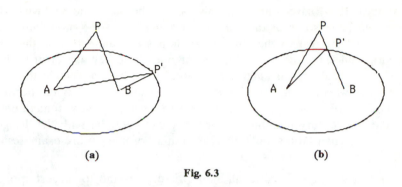

(a)   (b)

Fig. 6.3

restructuring done by successful problem-solvers. Consider the following problem:

A and B are foci of an ellipse. Show that for any point P outside the ellipse, $PA + PB > P'A + P'B$, where P' is any point on the ellipse.

A successful problem-solver, after studying the problem, would search for rules related to the ellipse and relationships involving distance. Since the locus definition of an ellipse provides information on distances from a point on the ellipse to the two foci, the problem-solver might restructure the problem by choosing the point, P', so that it is on $\overline{PB}$ (Figure 6.3b). Then, by writing a relationship involving the sum of the lengths of the sides of a triangle, and using the parts of segment $\overline{PB}$, the initially difficult problem is solved.

These two illustrative problems are good examples of the kinds of content that students must be engaged in if they are to learn problem solving strategies. Students who persist in trying different approaches on each problem, even when these do not result in final solution of the problem, are learning about problem-solving processes. What conditions enhance the occurrence of this kind of learning?

(1) The problem must be a problem to the learner—that is, the learner must conceive of the problem as posing a difficulty, an obstacle. Many so-called problems posed by teachers are considered simplistic questions by the students.

(2) The student must have a clearly defined goal whose attainment is desired. Unless the student understands the nature of the problem and is motivated to try to solve it, there will be no learning of problem-solving processes.

(3) The relevant prerequisite rules and concepts must be recalled by the learner. If these were learned previously in meaningful ways and retained in long-term memory, then the student already possesses the knowledge needed to work on the problem. Suppose the student just hasn't been instructed in one or more relevant rules? Isn't it a hopeless task to expect that student to work toward solution of the problem? Although it may seem that the obvious answer to that question is yes, some educators (e.g. John Dewey, 1910;

Fremont, 1969) have found that this can be the best time to have a student stop and learn some of the needed prerequisites. If the problem or project is of great interest to the student, an impasse could motivate that student to stop and learn the needed, relevant rules. The key aspect of such problems is that students are highly motivated to solve them. Think of real-world examples where such behavior is not at all surprising. Contemporary renovators of old homes sometimes have to stop and learn fundamentals of nineteenth century plumbing before they can continue with the design of a colonial kitchen. You should be able to think of many more examples of this kind of behavior.

(4) Cues to help the learner recall appropriate rules and to suggest approaches to the hypothesizing, testing, and modifying processes are assets to problem solving. However, if the cues become a step-by-step exposition of a solution, then the student is off the mental hook and has lost out on this most important aspect of mathematics teaching. The student must be given time to fumble, to explore unpromising paths, to make mistakes. Indeed, in the final condition we emphasize this aspect of student performance.

(5) The instructor must stress the nature of the task and carefully distinguish expectations here from those in rule learning. It is *not* the case that a shortcut, algorithm, or formula is the important output. The objectives here are to seek sensible strategies, to develop systematic ways of checking conjectures, to be open-minded about both possible solutions and potential routes to a solution. Subsequent to work on the problem, an examination of the profitable and unprofitable approaches is in order to further clarify the potential of this new strategy.

Terms like *hypothesizing* and *systematic approaches* were used in this text in an earlier chapter. Remember the floating bodies problem and the approaches of the formal versus the concrete operational student in Chapter 3? Piaget's data clearly illustrate the effect of intellectual development on the nature of problem-solving abilities. In particular, more guidance and cues would be required if the concrete operational student were facing a problem having multiple potential factors. What are some other possible differences? Compare your ideas with those of a classmate.

Attitudes   Attitudes were given prominence in Chapter 5 when we considered objectives in the Affective Domain. It should be fairly clear that behaviors associated with Level I of that domain may represent nothing more than compliance with classroom regulations. When we think of attitudes specifically related to mathematics, we are talking about objectives that correspond to Levels II, III, or III+ of the Affective Domain. Each of those domains is associated with a degree of student choice and actions based on that choice. Thus, our definition of attitude is taken from Gagné and Briggs (1979). An attitude is *an internal state*

which affects an individual's choice of action toward some object, person, or event.
Attitudes are usually described in terms of positive or negative tendencies.

In the previous sections, we have alluded to attitudes or dispositions some-times being learned along with a reflex action or a chain of responses. Some researchers, notably Skinner (1968), have suggested that attitudes of liking for a topic area might be learned by following the work in that topic area by some rewarding activity. The theory is based on the idea that the student who likes the subsequent activity (the reinforcer) will eventually acquire a liking for the prior activity, work in the topic area. Some classroom teachers have tried to apply this theory with rewards of candy for completion of arithmetic exercises. They reported that although the students wanted to complete the exercises in order to receive the candy that subsequent measures of student attitudes toward arith-metic were not more positive. It seems that the reinforcer (the external reward) must be connected to the prior content work in some substantive mathematical way. In general, it is assumed that success in completing mathematics work, es-pecially problems that have been characterized as challenging, might lead to a positive attitude toward similar problem work. In this case, success acts as an internal reward and thus, is intimately connected to the mathematical activity. If you know an exception to this principle, you are beginning to identify the tenu-ous nature of research on the learning of attitudes. What is success? When are certain mathematical activities perceived as challenging, but not frustratingly dif-ficult? Is the student more concerned about gaining a certain grade than reach-ing the goal of completing the mathematical activity? These are just some of the questions related to the learning of attitudes.

Bandura's work on human modeling (1969) provides some hope for be-ing more specific about the conditions that foster the learning of attitudes. The importance of role models or *significant others* has already been mentioned in Chapter 3 with respect to forces affecting gender-differences in achievement or persistence in mathematics coursework. Many of these same issues are relevant to the participation of various ethnic groups in elective mathematics courses or mathematics-related careers (See Matthews, 1984). According to Gagné and Briggs (1979), the essential conditions for learning attitudes, using human model-ing, include the following. (1) The learner must already identify with, or respect, the human model and (2) the learner must already have learned any cognitive skills related to the attitude being fostered. For example, it is difficult to learn a positive attitude toward proof-constructing activities if the learner doesn't pos-sess the prerequisite rules and concepts for doing a proof and has not learned what is meant by a deductive argument.The next set of conditions all refer to actions by the human model. (3) The model must demonstrate (or describe) the desirable behavior and (4) show some overt sign of satisfaction with some outcome of the behavior. In the case of proof-constructing, if the teacher had already gained respect from the students, she or he could demonstrate the tenta-tive, problem-solving nature of proof-constructing by trying different routes, iden-tifying unsuccessful strategies, showing pleasure at new ideas and "neat" routes to proof. Students regularly identify the importance of this kind of role model in their decision to take another mathematics course and in the emergence of their positive attitudes toward the subject (CASDA, 1985–1986).

Study the section on problem solving again for cues to the connections between the affective domain and this aspect of the cognitive domain. In fact, the importance of cultivating a positive attitude, or disposition toward problem solving has been repeatedly stressed by those who study and write about problem solving in mathematics (see especially Krulik, 1980; Polya, 1962; Schoenfeld, 1979; Silver, 1985). Throughout the description of the conditions necessary for learning problem solving are suggestions and warnings about the importance of the milieu of the classroom. One way of describing that milieu is in terms of four freedoms: (1) freedom to make a mistake, (2) freedom to think for oneself, (3) freedom to ask a question and (4) freedom to choose methods of solution (Fremont, 1969).

6.4 TASK ANALYSIS

One of the most striking characteristics of the subject matter of mathematics is its hierarchical nature. Small wonder that Gagné's emphasis on prerequisites has been found to be especially useful in mathematics instruction. An outgrowth of Gagné's analysis of learning types led to the development of a technique called *task analysis*. Very simply, Gagné recognized the fact that instructional objectives at the concept, rule, and problem-solving levels depend upon the attainment of subbehaviors and then the integration of these. He devised a method by which complex objectives can be analyzed for instructional purposes—a method which consists of asking the following question: "What *must* the student be able to do in order to meet the terminal objective?" Suppose the terminal, or major, objective is the following:

> *Solve a quadratic equation of the form $ax^2 + bx + c = 0$ where a, b, c are real numbers, $a \neq 0$ and $ax^2 + bx + c$ can be factored over the rationals.*

A task analysis might result in the partial learning hierarchy depicted in Figure 6.4. Such hierarchies must be read from the top down. Each of the prerequisite objectives (2a, b, and c) must be mastered by the student if the terminal objective is to be met. Since all three are *necessary* prerequisites, they are joined by a three-way branch. These must be integrated in some fashion before objective 1 can be met so a single arrow connects the branch to the terminal objective. Why are these prerequisites on the same level? Surely a student might meet objective 2a before meeting objective 2c? That's true, but the task analysis is intended to illustrate *necessary dependence* and none of these three prerequisites depend on one another. Thus, task analysis helps the teacher identify the range of choices open for the sequencing of instruction. However, a task analysis does not depict the sequence in which a student must *use* these three skills in order to master the terminal objective. In this instance, the student must learn to use 2a, 2c, and 2b in that order—another cue that the whole is more than the sum of its parts in learning.

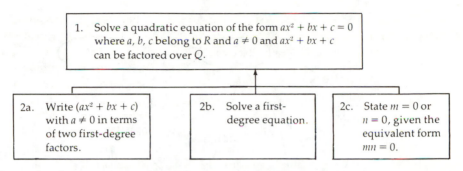

Fig. 6.4 A partial learning hierarchy.

Let's see if you have the idea. Below we've listed five additional objectives which are prerequisite to those in Figure 6.4. Read each carefully and sketch out the extended learning hierarchy by asking of each upper-level objective the task analysis question: "What *must* the student be able to do in order to perform this complex task?"

1. Transform first-degree equations into equivalent forms by the addition and/or multiplication property of equality.

2. State that "or" is equivalent to union.

3. State that $0 \cdot c = 0$ and $c \cdot 0 = 0$ where $c \in R$.

4. Factor any second-degree polynomial into prime factors over Q.

5. List the members of a solution set by using the relationship that "or" is equivalent to union.

We recommend the writing of the essence of all nine objectives on cards and arranging them on a flat surface, such as the floor. Then test each one by asking the task analysis question and checking carefully the lower objectives. Our response to this exercise can be found in the Simulation/Practice Activities, where we ask you to go one step further with this partial hierarchy.

Our student teachers have found that task analysis of the objectives in a unit they are to teach is an excellent way for them to identify the prerequisites for each objective, the content links among objectives, and appropriate ways to assess learning.

6.5 CONCEPT MAPPING

Most learners don't think about subject matter in tight, sequential chains, such as that portrayed by learning hierarchies. They more often associate concepts with one another or link them in terms of some relationship. For example, after instruction in beginning number theory in seventh grade, a student's representation of the concepts that are associated might take the form shown in Figure 6.5. Concept-terms that are connected are associated by some relationship. The fact that some curved arrows have no stated relationship simply indicates that

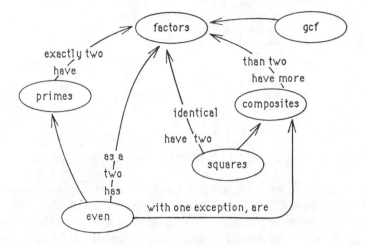

Fig. 6.5   Concept map.

the student couldn't verbalize the association. Notice the problem this student had with the concept EVEN. Figure 6.5 is one example of a concept map, a diagram that students construct to try to picture how they mentally link concepts. Although several researchers (Geeslin, 1973; McDonald,1982; Shavelson, 1974) have used forms of concept maps, the work of Novak and Gowin (1984) is particularly helpful. Novak and Gowin used concept maps to help identify student misconceptions. One way of proceeding is to give a class a group of concept labels, 8–10 at most. Then ask them to choose the concept they think is most important and write that term in a balloon in the center of their paper. Then, tell them to select other concepts that seem to be associated with the first one, enclose them in balloons and connect the ones they relate together. The first two or three might be done together. After all labels have been considered, help the students to go back and decide what the relationship is that led them to connect pairs of concepts. The emphasis is on the relationship constructed by the *students* between pairs of concepts, rather than on some ideal relationship the teacher has constructed. Concept maps constructed in this way can be an important graph of the students' mental representations of the content. Misconceptions or absence of important associations can be identified. O'Connell (1984) used this technique with sixth grade science students. The sixth grade science teachers found that the concept maps created at the end of instruction corresponded to the results of the individual students on classroom achievement tests. It's probably no surprise to learn that the concept maps of formal students differ significantly from those of concrete students (McDonald, 1982).

   We've found that concept mapping is another excellent way for teachers to analyze the mathematical structure of a unit—this time focusing on concepts and the associations between them. In Chapter 7, concept maps are referred to as an approach to long-range planning.

6.6 ADVANCE ORGANIZERS

It should be obvious from the word *advance* that an advance organizer comes prior to something else and from the word *organizer* that it is designed to facilitate putting things together in a meaningful way. Thus the term itself tells when an advance organizer occurs in an instructional sequence and sheds light on its overall purpose. David Ausubel (1963, 1968), the cognitive psychologist who originated this idea, has identified the attributes essential to this concept. First, *the advance organizer must present relevant content ideas that are of a higher order of abstraction, generality, and inclusiveness than the new material to follow.* Advance organizers typically take the form of broad concepts, rules/principles, thought models, theories, or conceptual schemes (themes) which subsume the more detailed knowledge to be learned next. Thus it becomes clear that teachers must have command of the structure of the subject matter, as presented in Chapter 4, if advance organizers are to be used in instruction. For example, the thought model of "group" could be taught as an advance organizer for related subsumed concepts/rules such as set, binary operation, closure, Abelian or commutative group, associative property, and permutation group.

Second, *the advance organizer must be presented in terms of what is already known by the learner.* In other words, the teacher must find out what relevant knowledge the learners possess and then use it to teach the generalization(s) that will serve as the advance organizer. For example, assume that the teacher finds out that the students already know (either from life experience or from previous instruction) that the order of operations makes a difference in some computations and activities (as in subtraction of natural numbers or in putting on one's socks and shoes). The teacher can then use these ideas as prerequisites to build comprehension of the desired generalization (group), which in turn will subsume the related facts, operational definitions, concepts, and rules/principles to be learned in the new work.

You should be starting to get the idea of what an advance organizer is. Now let's consider a few potentially confusing non-examples—that is, what an advance organizer *is not*. Many mathematics texts begin each chapter with a short introductory or overview section that consists of anywhere from one paragraph to several pages of writing. Often the one- or two-paragraph variety is really a summary of the main ideas to be treated in the chapter. These overviews almost always fail to meet *either* of the essential criteria for an advance organizer since (1) the ideas presented in capsule form are at the same level of abstraction as the content to follow and (2) little or no provision has been made to use the existing knowledge of the reader to teach the ideas summarized in such an introductory section. Similarly, several pages of introductory material tracing the historical development of a major mathematical idea may stimulate the interest of some students but fail to qualify as an advance organizer on the basis of one or both essential criteria. On the other hand, the history of mathematics, as well as the conceptual themes of mathematics, can be used to structure advance organizers.

How did we tackle the problem of providing you with advance organizers? We elected to use our model of instruction as a unifying (conceptual) theme throughout this text, beginning with the "To The Student" section. Our plan was to use this overarching idea to subsume all the main ideas and information in this book. Thus, both the diagrammatic representation of this thought model, and relevant written material appear at the start of each chapter. Then common background of the reader (both from real-life experiences and from preceding chapters) was used to teach meaningfully a new aspect of the model which in turn would constitute ideational scaffolding for the contents of subsequent chapter sections. To the extent that we were successful, each introductory section should have provided you with anchoring ideas and bridged the gap between what you already knew and what you needed to know in order to learn the tasks at hand. Did our attempts work in your case? Feedback from past students has been very encouraging and therefore we continue to use this technique.

Why are advance organizers important? One of their major functions is to facilitate the initial learning of new material so that it is of the meaningful variety (as opposed to rote). There is a growing body of research evidence that the degree of meaningfulness of newly learned material correlates positively with both remembering and the ability to use that material in applicable situations. Since both remembering (retention) and future applied use (transfer) are major goals of education, any device with potential for promoting their achievement merits our careful attention and best efforts.

Think back to previously learned material that might help you structure effective advance organizers. We have already called your attention to the contributions of Gagné as they apply to this task. Now consider the research of Piaget summarized in Chapter 3. What comes to mind first? Most people think of the nature of the concrete operational student and cite the need to include many concrete referents in an advance organizer. This is good thinking, as far as it goes, but it does not go far enough. Can you identify yet another application of Piaget's work to making effective use of advance organizers? If not, turn back to the nested stages model in Chapter 3 (Figure 3.5) and focus your attention on the thought modes available to formal operational students when they are working with content for which they do not have a base of concrete experiences. Always remember that in the long run all is lost if the initial learning is meaningless (rote) to the learner.

6.7 RETENTION, TRANSFER AND PRACTICE

We have already seen that humans are ill-equipped to behave like walking computers. People are just not capable of storing huge numbers of isolated information bits to be retrieved instantly upon demand. It is also true that much of what our students will need to know in their adult life 10 to 50 years hence is not now in the storehouse of human knowledge. Thus, formal schooling must educate the young to *transfer* learning—to develop both the *ability to perform new tasks at about the same level of difficulty as previously learned ones (lateral transfer) and also perform those of more complex difficulty by using the base of past learnings (vertical transfer)*. Students who have learned the lengths of any pair of corresponding altitudes, medians, or angle bisector segments of similar triangles are proportional to the lengths of any pair of corresponding sides should give evidence of lateral transfer by making like predictions for the ratios of the lengths of corresponding diagonals, altitudes, and the like in the case of similar parallelograms. Further, we look for evidence of vertical transfer from students who, having mastered the algebraic solution of a set of two first-degree equations in two variables, later encounter problems involving three first-degree equations in three variables. How can we as teachers ensure that the maximum amount of transfer takes place? We can make certain that those factors known to promote transfer are accounted for in planning and implementing lessons.

Transfer, going beyond present learning, obviously depends upon a student's ability to *remember* or *recall previous learning (retention)*. As noted earlier, there is firm evidence to support the assertion that the most important factor in promoting retention is the degree of meaningfulness of the initial learning to the student.

The work of Gagné, Ausubel, as well as Bruner, Dienes and the Gestalt psychologists have helped us to understand the importance of meaningfulness. More recently, information-processing psychologists have concentrated on the way learners encode knowledge, the nature and capacity of memory and the ways knowledge is retrieved from memory.

Retention

According to information-processing theorists (Resnick & Ford, 1981), when we pay attention to environmental stimuli (e.g. music, teacher's questions and explanations, a silent movie), sensory input is registered and will be lost within one second unless we make an attempt to encode the information (perhaps in symbolic, pictorial, or verbal form). The encoded information is temporarily stored in short term, or working, memory which has a limited capacity. If we now have some reason to reflect on the encoded information and can relate it to other information in our attempts to remember it, the knowledge will be transferred to long term memory, where it will be retained until there is a need to retrieve it (Figure 6.6).

The process schematized in Figure 6.6 is often compared to the workings of a computer. Working memory is thought of as one memory storage area where all processes and data essential for the completion of a task are stored. Another storage area, but one of vast capacity, is labeled long-term memory. Computer-users are often frustrated when the message,"Out of Memory. Cannot Undo this Procedure," flashes on the screen. Like working memory, certain amounts of memory are reserved so that procedures can be completed. The "Load" command is analogous to a mental search in long term memory and the attempt to

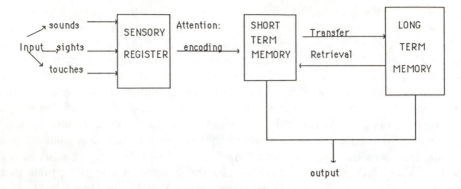

Fig. 6.6 Information processing model.

retrieve needed information for use in working memory. Unless some meaningful clusters have been generated by the learner, the search may be fruitless, as it might be if a data file were scrambled.

Larkin (1977) used the construct of "chunking" to explain how learners seem to process information. For example, a better student might chunk a cluster of area formulas, not by trying to memorize the symbolic, or verbal, rule statements, but by storing the process by which one shape can be dissected and transformed into another. Then, when the formula for the area of a trapezoid is needed, such a student may retrieve the process and quickly, dissect the trapezoid into two triangles, or a rectangle and two triangles. Information-processing theorists suggest that retention depends on the ability to invent chunks that can subsume, or be subsumed, by new chunks.

It is important to realize that this view of memory means that all learners chunk somehow. However, some learners do so in ways that are not efficient and sometimes not directly related to the structure of the subject. These chunks often represent superficial patterns invented by students. Refer back to Chapter 3 for specific examples of error patterns or trivial generalizations that some students construct. Unfortunately, some teachers mistakenly offer students superficial patterns (e.g. a rhymed rule for division of fractions) to help them remember a mathematical generalization. In the short run, this strategy is successful. In the long run, it is not only unsuccessful, but can lead to a learned error pattern on the part of the students. Figure 6.7 graphically illustrates how long term retention of such material might be affected when teaching promotes nonsense learning. Frightening, isn't it? Yet, the research findings related to adolescent reasoning and learning and the analysis of the structure of mathematics should help you design instructional strategies that will help to avoid the situation depicted in Figure 6.7.

There are also other measures you can take to promote retention. The hierarchical structure of the subject matter makes it possible to help students think in ways that will facilitate retention and retrieval. Students can be taught the value

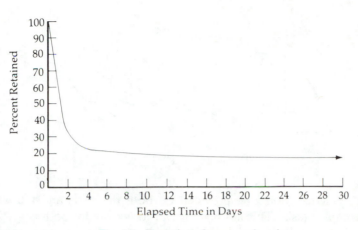

Fig. 6.7 Retention of nonsense learning.

of recalling the picture of the basic sine or cosine curve whenever questions concerning the amplitude, frequency, or value of $f(x)$ for $(a\sin bx)$, $(e\cos dx)$, or even $(a\sin bx + e\cos dx)$ are encountered. A few experiences are usually sufficient to convince students that one can use the pictorial model to reconstruct curves such as $f(x) = (1/2)\cos 2x$. Demonstrating the degree of utility of an understanding of these basic trigonometric functions also helps establish both the intent to remember and the students' confidence that they will be able to remember, two additional factors that promote retention. Skillful teachers have learned to stress the relatively small number of thought models that need to be mastered in order to give one command over the many principles and in turn, the even more numerous concepts that constitute the product aspect of mathematics. Of course, such instruction must be coupled with strategies aimed at getting and using feedback if it is to produce the desired effect.

Practice

What is the role of practice (drill) in promoting the retention so essential to transfer? Surely the time-honored tradition of drilling students on newly learned content must contribute heavily to later recall? Not necessarily. In fact, there is good evidence (Resnick & Ford, 1981) that practice *per se* has little effect on retention! The desired positive effects of practice can be enhanced by attending to four factors.

First, drill sessions should be kept short and spaced out over time. Massed sessions in which students "plug in" numbers for a, b, and c in a dozen or more Pythagorean theorem type problems are neither efficient nor effective. The equivalent amount of time divided into five- or ten-minute practice sessions distributed throughout a two-week period would yield higher returns for the time invested.

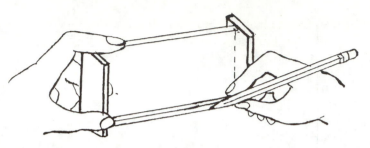

Fig. 6.8   MIRA practice.

Second, practice should be provided on both the parts and the whole in the case of complex tasks. This has been found to be true for both cognitive and psychomotor learning. For example, it is important to devote some portions of practice to each of the separate subtasks of completing a histogram from a set of raw data. These might include: deciding on the range of the groups to be plotted on the horizontal axis, getting the frequency counts for each group, scaling the axes, graphing data points, and drawing the bars to complete the histogram. It is also necessary to allow sufficient time to practice performing all of these parts within the total problem complex. Similarly, students need practice in the psychomotor task of drawing MIRA lines, locating reflected images and moving the MIRA to correspond to visual feedback (Figure 6.8) and in performing each manipulation as part of the total integrated technique. Notice that the MIRA must be held vertically so that the drawing edge is on the paper and the student must practice drawing the MIRA line against that drawing edge. Next, the student has to move so that he or she is looking into the MIRA and then move the MIRA, as needed, until the desired image is reflected in the MIRA. One caution! In the case of motor skills, the sequence of part-whole practice needs particular attention. Motor skill learning is enhanced when the whole skill is practiced first, followed by practice on each subskill and, finally, by practice on the subskills as part of an integrated whole (known as the whole→part→whole approach). In the example of the MIRA, the student might begin by "playing" with the MIRA and noticing its apparent effect as it is slid or turned on a cartoon face. Then the student needs to practice locating specific images of specific points on a diagram, identifying images when the MIRA is placed in specified locations, and finally using all these skills together in locating lines of reflection under given conditions.

Even in the cognitive domain, it has been found effective to begin with practice on a simplified whole, then practice on gradually more complex applications of the parts, and finally practice on the integrated whole. Thus, the teacher might begin by using logarithms to the base two and contriving examples in which all numbers were powers of two. The students are able to calculate $(128 \times 32^3)/64$ very quickly from a table and appreciate the calculation shortcut. After sufficient practice on the total process, the students have ideational scaffolding on which to hang the learning associated with parts in the usual logarithm to the base ten problems. Sound like an advance organizer? It is.

Third, practice is more effective when it is structured within a framework that the student would consider meaningful—such as real-world applications. For instance, students who have demonstrated success in finding the ratio from two pieces of data can be given a ten-speed bicycle and asked to find the ratio of the number of revolutions of pedals to the number of revolutions of the rear wheel for each shift position. It is clear that while the initial instruction may emphasize the solution of type problems (level II—cognitive taxonomy), retention depends partly on practice which places the student in a novel situation (level III—cognitive taxonomy).

Last, but perhaps so logically obvious that we tend to forget it, practice must *actively* involve the learners. This does not imply that students must be engaged in some sort of obvious and vigorous physical activity. It does mean that repetitious and boring drill which encourages students to take a mental vacation must be avoided. How can anyone profit from a cognitive learning activity if the mind is not attending to the task at hand and if there is little effort or intent to learn? Because of past unpleasant experiences, just the use of the label *drill* is enough to turn off many students. Thus, we have learned not to use the word with junior/senior high school students. Remember the example of using the ten-speed bicycle to extend practice so as to include applications in context? Doesn't it at the same time include drill on the computation of ratio and on the way to obtain like quantities for substitution in a ratio expression? It certainly does, and students do become mentally active in working out these solutions.

Transfer

If we are able to design instruction to maximize retention, the task of promoting transfer is 90 percent accomplished! What constitutes the final 10 percent? One of the most important conditions for promoting transfer is to make sure students know that they will be expected to apply their learning to novel situations. Equally important is that the students have learning experiences related to that objective. Such learning experiences should include ways to help students *verbalize the methods* of problem solution, in the case of the cognitive domain, or *comprehend the theory* that underlies each motor skill to be learned, in the case of the psychomotor domain. Yes, understanding the reasons for performing a manipulation in a certain way does promote transfer of that skill to other relevant situations—another reminder that the three domains of human learning are not like watertight compartments.

Above all, *never* think or behave as if transfer is automatic. Prior to the beginning of the twentieth century the human brain was commonly considered analogous to a muscle. One could certainly develop the biceps by repeated lifting of a blacksmith's hammer, and this increased the capability of that set of muscles to move any other heavy object. Thus, it seemed logical that exercising the memory portion of the brain by memorizing lengthy Latin poems ought to facilitate the memorization of mathematical formulas. However, countless research studies (See Rosskopf, 1953 and Shulman, 1970 for summary) performed from 1890 through the present day continue to provide evidence that refutes this notion. Muscle tissue does *not* equal nerve tissue! Analyzing the standard proofs in geometry does not automatically help students cope with data analysis in physics or vice versa. It may not even help students become better proof-doers in the case of novel exercises. Transfer must be specifically taught if it is to be caught.

6.8 SUMMARY AND SELF-CHECK

Learning is an activity we engage in throughout our lives, but we seldom stop to reflect on how we learn. However, successful teaching depends on thoughtful reflection and study. So we chose to begin with the learning of a jumble of words and then a limerick as a way to clarify some characteristics of meaningful learning. Discovery learning, learning hierarchies, learning types, concept maps, and the role of an advance organizer were described and applied to the learning of mathematics. The pervasive threads of retention, drill (practice), and transfer were treated by considering an information processing model.

You should be able to:

1. Operationally define learning, meaningful learning, rote learning, discovery learning, reception learning, Gagné's learning types, task analysis, learning hierarchy, advance organizer, and concept maps.

2. State the conditions for learning *each* of the types of learning.

3. Construct a learning hierarchy in your subject field.

4. Identify concepts (defined, undefined, relational) and rules/principles by an analysis of syllabi, course outlines, or textbooks in your teaching field.

5. Evaluate the extent to which textbook presentations use advance organizers and justify your decision.

6. Construct a concept map for a unit in your subject field.

7. Assess the extent to which feedback in a "live," "canned," or simulated classroom scene would justify inferences that a concept or a rule had been learned.

8. Given a "live" or video lesson, cite episodes where the teacher appears to be aiming at retention and transfer. Justify your choices.

9. Given a "live" or video lesson in which practice is occurring, characterize the practice as either rote or meaningful and justify your decision.

10. Design practice sets for a specific rule/principle that have potential for retention or transfer.

The exercises that follow are designed to test your ability to meet the preceding objectives and to extend your acquaintance with related writings in this area. We encourage thoughtful consideration of as many of these activities as possible.

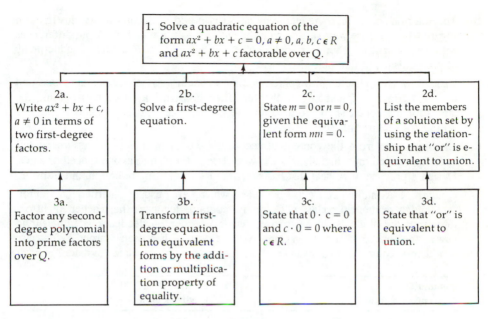

Fig. 6.9

6.9 SIMULATION/PRACTICE ACTIVITIES

A. Obtain a state or local syllabus or course outline for a subject you are likely to teach. Read through the first two major units and make separate lists of concepts (defined, undefined, and relational) and rules/principles that are referred to as learning outcomes. Be sure to include those concepts prerequisite to each rule you list whether or not these were specifically identified in the syllabus. Compare your results with those of another classmate.

B. Obtain a copy of two contemporary texts that are used in secondary mathematics classes. Read the first few pages of several chapters and decide on the extent to which the authors have written advance organizers. Justify your decisions.

C. In each of the articles below, the authors have focused on problems associated with the learning of mathematics. Choose any *two* of these and prepare a written review of two or three paragraphs. Include in your review a summary of the writer's chief ideas and a consideration of the match among those ideas and the positions taken by the authors of this text.

1. Bruner, J. S. (1960). "On learning mathematics." *Mathematics Teacher*, **53**, 610–619.

2. Brownell, W. A. (1987). "Meaning and skill—Maintaining the balance." *Arithmetic Teacher*, **34** (8), 18–25. (Originally published in 1956).

3. Dienes, Z. (1963). "On the learning of mathematics." *Arithmetic Teacher*, **10**, 115–126.

4. Garofalo, J. (1987). "Metacognition and school mathematics." *Arithmetic Teacher*, **34** (9), 22–23.

D. The solution to the learning hierarchy question posed in Section 6.4 is illustrated in Figure 6.9. Compare your version with the authors' solution and check out differences with your instructor. Then task analyze objective 3a and construct a learning hierarchy of prerequisites to that objective alone.

E. Read through a chapter in a contemporary secondary school mathematics text and list 8–10 concepts found in that chapter. Then construct a concept map using the labels for the concepts. Try to describe the way the concepts are related by phrases on the connecting linkages.

F. Choose a rule from the content of secondary school mathematics. Assume it has been introduced meaningfully. Now, a week later, you plan to assign spaced practice. Design a practice worksheet that has potential for optimizing retention and transfer.

G. Column 1 contains concepts or rules which are usually learned in junior/ senior high mathematics classes. Column 2 contains feedback the teacher might obtain from the students. In each case, decide whether the feedback is *sufficient* to assure the teacher that the matching concept or rule has been learned. What else would you require in each instance of inadequate or inappropriate feedback?

Column 1 Concepts and Rules	Column 2 Feedback obtained
1. Commutative property for addition	1. States that "$a + b = b + a$."
2. Prime number	2. Labels 2, 3, 5, 7 as primes and 4, 6, 8 as "nonprimes," when asked for examples and nonexamples of primes.
3. $A = \pi r^2$	3. Finds area of a circle given the radius.
4. Typical percent problems, involving use of $p = rb$.	4. Finds the percent if given the rate and the base.
5. Parallelogram	5. Chooses only (d) when asked to select shapes which are parallelograms

6. Bilateral symmetry	6. Draws the lines of reflection shown:

SUGGESTIONS FOR FURTHER STUDY

Bruner, J.S. (1960). *The process of education*. Cambridge, MA: Harvard University Press.

This little book has become a classic reference on the curriculum reform movement of the 1950s and 1960s. Bruner illustrates the ways in which the teaching of the structure of the subject matter will facilitate retention and transfer. The examples are often from secondary school science and mathematics and Bruner's style of presentation makes the text highly readable.

Davis, R. B. (1984). *Learning mathematics: The cognitive science approach in mathematics education*. Norwood, NJ: Ablex.

Davis presents examples of error patterns drawn from research on mathematical learning. His analysis of student misconceptions provides excellent insight into probable information processing strategies of students from elementary school to high school. We believe that the reading would be particularly valuable to the inservice teacher who can match the reports of children's thinking patterns to his or her classroom experience.

Fehr, H. (Ed.). (1953). *The learning of mathematics* (21st Yearbook). Washington, DC: National Council of Teachers of Mathematics.

This yearbook is a source of excellent illustrations of the special learning problems of mathematics. We recommend, especially Chapter 1, "Theories of Learning Related to the Field of Mathematics" by Howard Fehr, Chapter 7, "Transfer of Training" by Myron Rosskopf, and Chapter 8, "Problem-Solving in Mathematics" by Kenneth Henderson and Robert Pingry.

Shulman, L. S. (1970). "Psychology and mathematics education," In E. G. Begle (Ed.), *Mathematics education: The sixty-ninth yearbook of the National Society for the Study of Education* (Part 1). (pp. 23–71). Chicago, IL: University of Chicago Press.

Shulman summarizes aspects of the work of Gagné, Ausubel, Dienes, Bruner and Piaget. His work is an excellent follow up to the ideas on meaningful learning, discovery learning, retention and transfer presented in this chapter.

Wertheimer, M. (1959). *Productive thinking*. Enl. ed. New York: Harper.

In this classic written by the father of Gestalt psychology, the reader is taken into the classroom to observe students' responses to novel problems in geometry. The blind grinding-out behavior of one student is contrasted with the insightful tactics of another. Of particular interest is the chapter in which the problem-solving process is dissected from the moment of presentation to that of solution. This is a book worth reading in its entirety.

CHAPTER SEVEN

DESIGN OF INSTRUCTIONAL STRATEGIES

The Game Plan

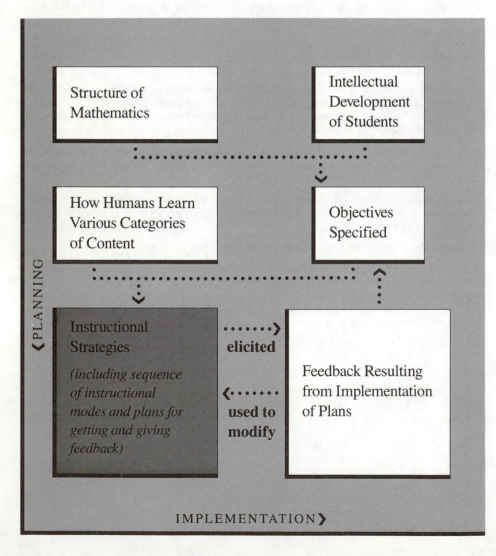

"Tom, I'm really glad you were assigned to do your student teaching with me this semester. You have asked many meaningful questions during your first few days of observing my classes. I have noticed you assisting individuals during class and working with students who come in after school for extra help. I know you are anxious to start teaching a class section on your own, and I have decided that the second-period geometry class would be best for your initial assignment. They are a typical sort of group, and geometry is your strongest area. Let's see. Today is Thursday and we'll be finishing the congruence topic tomorrow. Monday would be a good day for you to take over. Bring me a proposed lesson plan tomorrow; we'll look it over together; and I'll see what suggestions I can make. Then you will have the weekend to polish things up and be ready for a solid start on Monday."

You are Tom (or Thomasina). Being an excellent student, you have thoroughly learned the material presented in the first six chapters of this text. You have learned to analyze the nature of mathematics and couple this with knowledge of the intellectual development of students in order to specify objectives that are clearly stated, accurately representative of the content, and attainable by the intended learners. You understand some of the major findings of cognitive psychologists with respect to human learning and can identify uses and abuses of nine main teaching modes. And not only are you alert to the need to give and get feedback during lessons, but you also can design a variety of ways to provide for this all-important aspect of instruction. What else could you possibly need in order to whip that first lesson plan into good shape?

Note the shaded box in the instructional model on the opening page of this chapter and recall that this is the same box we directed attention to at the start of Chapter 1. At that time we concentrated on commonly employed instructional modes and said very little about the design of instructional strategies—the overall theme of that part of the model. At that point in time we had developed neither the prerequisites nor the need for detailed attention to the task of strategy design. Now you have *both* background and need. Efforts to plan effective lessons will be stymied until you are able to synthesize instructional strategies based on all you have learned thus far.

But what is an instructional strategy? We define an *instructional strategy* as *a sequence of instructional modes designed to promote the attainment of a particular type of objective.* Think in terms of the notion of patterns. It is neither necessary nor productive to think of teaching each bit of subject matter as an entirely novel task. Just as we can categorize many items of content as concepts, we can also construct an overall instructional strategy pattern to teach concepts. Likewise, we can design appropriate overall strategies for teaching other kinds of outcomes such as principles/rules. The introductory activity that follows is intended to provide some initial experience in the critical matter of strategy design.

7.1 INTRODUCTORY ACTIVITY

Planning is a Bloom level III–VI activity.

This activity is based on the use of the ruler lab described in Section 2.2 of Chapter 2. If you've forgotten the details, take time to refresh your memory now. The activity refers to a quiz situation faced by mathematics majors who, like you, had studied the ideas incorporated in Chapters 1–6. The students participated in the ruler lab and then wrote their responses to a follow-up quiz question. The question and one student's response are reproduced below.

> Assume you are teaching a lesson incorporating the ruler lab to a ninth-grade mathematics class in which most of the students have been assessed as concrete operational. Write two objectives that would be appropriate for this class. Then list a sequence of modes that would be likely to achieve your stated objectives and that would incorporate the ruler lab.
>
> **Mary's answer**
>
> *Objectives:*
>
> 1. Choose a graphic way to display the data and justify the decision.
> 2. Extrapolate the coordinates of the next three points on the basis of the graph.
>
> *Modes used in sequence:*
>
> 1. Divide Ss into groups and have them perform the ruler lab.
> 2. With total group watching, T has small groups record cumulative data on the board.
> 3. T lectures on feedback T observed.
> 4. T lectures on "best" way to graph this data and Q/A Ss as to reason it is "best" way.

After studying the above response, react to:

1. the aspects of Mary's answer that were consistent with what you have studied thus far,
2. the match between the strategy and the stated objectives,
3. the match between the type of Ss and the modes, and
4. the sequence of modes and choice of modes.

   a) Look for omissions.

   b) Identify places where students, rather than the teacher, should be at the focal point.

Check Simulation/Practice Activity A for a response we judged more adequate, *after* you have interacted with the preceding exercise.

7.2 DAILY PLANNING BASED ON THE INSTRUCTIONAL MODEL

How can plans be designed so as to attend to all aspects of the instructional model? How much should be written? What written format is helpful to the beginner? We have found that detailed written plans organized to correspond to key components of the model are invariably excellent bases for the beginning teacher. Such plans do not guarantee success, but their absence correlates highly

Topic _____   Date _____
Class/Period _____

Instructional Objectives: Routines:

1 CONTENT ITEM	2 SPECIAL MATERIAL, EQUIPMENT	3 INSTRUCTIONAL STRATEGIES	4 FEEDBACK STRATEGIES		5 TIME EST.
			GET	GIVE	

Fig. 7.1 Daily plan format.

with failure. In other words, they are necessary, but not sufficient, conditions for teaching effective lessons.

What format is amenable to the organized planning we have been emphasizing? We have found that the one depicted in Figure 7.1 not only accounts for all aspects of the model, but also has proved workable in the hands of both novices and experienced teachers. Analyze the lesson plan format in Figure 7.1 and note the categories explicitly represented in the outline. Some items, such as date, topic, and class period, are simply identifiers for the teacher or visitors. The routine box is included so that announcements, attendance notes, and other such items might be recorded. However, the remainder of the headings should make sense as a synthesis of modes, feedback, objectives, and characteristics of students and of content. Most novices find that the spacing in Figure 7.1 is inadequate in certain areas. You should adjust the spacing to fit your needs. Under *content item* are listed the labels of the concepts, the rule statements, the rule use ideas, and so on, in the sequence in which you expect to introduce these. Across from each content item in column 3 would be a description of the sequence of modes designed to achieve the stated objective(s) with respect to that content item. If materials other than standard chalk and chalkboard are to be used, these are listed opposite the related strategy in column 2. In addition, we added two columns labeled *feedback strategies* to give particular emphasis to the need to plan ways to *get* feedback as well as ways to *give* feedback. Be careful. These columns are not meant to be diaries of what happened, nor fond hopes as to what students might say. They should contain the strategies you have chosen in order to elicit feedback at critical times and to give certain kinds of feedback during the lesson. Finally, column 5 should contain your time estimates for a strategy aimed at a particular objective. After the lesson has been taught, these estimates should be checked against actual times to assure more realistic planning of time use in the future.

Skeletons may provide helpful clues to the trained archeologist, but beginners need to study the human body in the flesh before graduating to the inference-making of the science of archeology. In like manner, the teacher-to-be needs to analyze completed lesson plans before attempting to construct plans. In the subsections that follow, we have included some sample plans that deal with differing kinds of content. Study each of these plans carefully and look for patterns.

Planning to Teach Concepts and Vocabulary

The plan that follows (Figure 7.2) was designed for a seventh grade class that had previously been taught lessons on the concepts of even and odd numbers. In this context, they had learned that an even number is divisible by two, or may be rewritten in factored form, as 2 times some other factor.

We recommend that you study the plan before continuing with the reading in this section. In your first reading of the plan, read the objectives and just the first three columns so that you can get a sense of the sequence and emphasis of the instructional strategies. Study the lab sheet (Figure 7.3) to be sure that the student hands-on activity is clear. It also helps to reflect on their possible strategies as you build equally tall columns using all six, seven, or eight checkers. (Pennies will do if you don't have checkers handy.) Stop now and turn to Figure 7.2.

You should assume that this plan is, at least, a second draft attempt on the part of a student teacher. The cooperating teacher would have checked objectives, the match of strategies to objectives, the sequence, and the time estimates. Notice the time ranges indicated at several points in the plan. If the maximum times are used throughout, 47 minutes will be consumed. But the class is scheduled for 40 minutes. What implication does that possibility pose with respect to the need to give directions on the puzzle handout near the end of the period? No, you can't keep students beyond the assigned class time. Suppose that the minimum times are used. You should have obtained a sum less than 40 and, if this were your plan, you should be worried about what might happen in that leftover time. If you don't plan an activity for all parts of the class period, you can be sure that students will innovatively use the time in ways you might prefer to consign to oblivion. This plan badly needs an *elastic clause*—an instructional strategy that can be inserted into the lesson at the teacher's discretion as a response to feedback. The nature of the elastic clause will determine its position in the plan, but we recommend that it be inserted somewhere in the plan rather than "tacked on" at the end. Do you see why? The old reward and punishment

Topic: *Concepts of Prime and Composite*
Class/Period: *Math 7, Period 3*

Date: *October 4, (Wednesday)*

Instructional Objectives:
1. Operationally define prime and composite in terms of checker piles.
2. Define prime and composite in terms of factors.
3. Characterize natural numbers, not used in today's class, either prime or composite, and justify the characterization.
4. Give examples of prime or composite numbers different from those used in lab.
5. Use the words "prime" and "composite" in written and oral work.

Routines:
1. Take attendance, via seating chart.
2. Collect late work from Mary and Alf.

CONTENT ITEMS	SPECIAL MATERIAL	INSTRUCTIONAL STRATEGIES	FEEDBACK STRATEGIES		TIME EST.
			GIVE	GET	
Recall of concepts: even, odd, factor and principle of divisibility		T has each student count off and tells them to remember their number names. Tells Ss to stand and remain standing as "name" is called. T calls: "2, 8, 12, 6, 4,..." Asks Ss who think they know the rule to raise their hands. T elicits operational def. of even and why. T then asks for description of names of the seated Ss to get def. of odd. T uses Q/A to elicit recall of concept of factor and principle of divisibility	T waits. T asks for more hands T takes ans; asks other Ss if they agree.	T praises Ss with hands up T confirms	5 min.
Number patterns history and informing Ss of outcomes		T reminds Ss of past lectures on interest of Greeks in number patterns and how they used pebbles to make shapes. So 3 was a triangular number; 4, a square number. T tells Ss that today they will do a lab to discover some other number characteristics first noticed by the Greeks			1 min.

Fig. 7.2 Sample concept and vocabulary plan.

CONTENT ITEMS	SPECIAL MATERIAL	INSTRUCTIONAL STRATEGIES	FEEDBACK STRATEGIES		TIME EST.
			GIVE	GET	
	lab sheets, demo set of checkers, OH lab sheet, Boxes of checkers	T has Ss pass out lab sheets and tells all to fill in heading. T gives lab instructions: a. Ss will work in pairs as yesterday b. Each pair to get box of checkers c. Lab—to model task T will demo, to talk about patterns they find, and to record results and patterns on sheet. d. Collection, use and return of materials. T asks S to read headings on lab sheet. "We'll work together on 6. We'll need to do this systematically. We can make one pile of checkers using all the checkers." T demos and records 1 under "pile" heading and 6 under "number of checkers" heading on OH lab sheet. T tells Ss to copy these data on the same place on their sheets. T asks if all 6 checkers can be used to make two equally tall piles. T demos and records data on OH lab sheet and tells Ss to copy on their sheets. Then continues Q for 3 equally tall piles, 4, 5, and 6. T gives signal for preassigned pairs to begin lab.	T scans papers of a few. T takes ans. from one S; takes straw poll. Spreads Q	T corrects as needed T or S confirms by demo.	5–7 min.
Number patterns		Pairs of Ss work on lab. T gives time signal, reminds pairs who are finished to look over data for patterns and to discuss their ideas with each other.	T tours & asks Qs on procedures and results T cks. data on sheets	S to check ea. other's strategies & results T praises progress	10–15 min.

Primes Composites checker piles Primes Composites factor Exclusion of 1	T—Q different pairs for data to fill in on OH lab sheet. T elicits patterns from as many pairs as possible; notes common patterns and, if not elicited, directs Ss' attention to differences in "amount" and kind of data for numbers such as 13, 7, 2 vs. 15, 8, 6. If needed, uses contingency Q and repeats checker demo to highlight differences. T elicits "checker" def. of these number groups; asks for other numbers that fit one or the other group. If no S has yet described these in terms of factors, T elicits definition of these in terms of factors. T emphasizes the unique role of the number 1.	T sees if Ss agree Some straw polls. T calls on diverse Ss	T confirms T writes patterns on board Has S confirm	10 min.
Vocab. prime composite	T says and writes: *prime number* over set of examples and *composite number* over another set of examples as T asks: "What kind of a number is 3? 7? 9? 2? 14?...? T directs Ss to copy labels and examples on their lab sheets.	T checks sample papers. T spreads Q.	T gives non-verbal+signal. T corrects as needed	3 min.
generalizing to other cases	If no S has named a number greater than those on the lab sheet, T asks whether 27 (32,41,...) are prime or composite. Tells Ss to write ans. and reasons on back of lab sheet.	T tours and Q Ss.	Has Ss demo with checkers.	3 min.
Look ahead Puzzle sheets	T hands out primes puzzle sheet to begin now and complete by tomorrow.	T tours		0–3 min.

Fig. 7.2 (Continued)

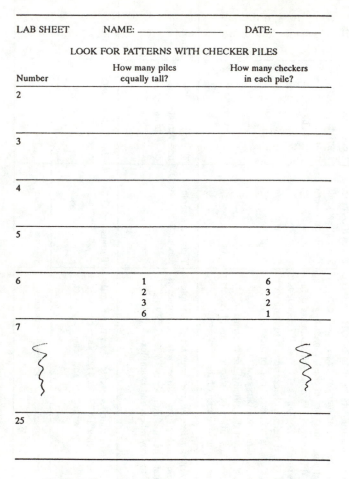

LAB SHEET	NAME: _____	DATE: _____
LOOK FOR PATTERNS WITH CHECKER PILES		
Number	How many piles equally tall?	How many checkers in each pile?
2		
3		
4		
5		
6	1 2 3 6	6 3 2 1
7		
25		

Fig. 7.3   Part of lab sheet on primes and composites.

aura rears its ugly head if the elastic clause comes over as "You've done so well, you can do some more of these."

Suppose that questions on the rationale for the concept labels were inserted prior to distributing the puzzle sheets. The students could be asked to volunteer other ways the words "prime" and "composite" are used and to try to relate these to the mathematical use. Others could check the class dictionary for the dictionary definition and the etymology of both words. Finally, the teacher could add some historical background. For example the Pythagoreans were said to consider 10 a perfect number since there were equal numbers of primes and composites before it—exactly 4 (Boyer, 1968, p. 62). This elastic clause would help students realize that labels are invented and used to name concepts by humans for a reason. They would also learn that the processes of observing, classifying and generalizing used in the lab sometimes lead to results with enduring uses and sometimes, to results that seem to have more aesthetic, than practical, value.

This sample plan deals with the concepts, prime and composite, and their concept labels (i.e., vocabulary). Which objectives are related to the concepts? Which, to the vocabulary? Analyze the instructional strategies column for strategies matching the conditions for concept learning outlined in Section 6.3 of Chapter 6. Where are the examples and the non-examples? Notice that, in this case, the contrasting kinds of checker piles are meant to dichotomize the collection of numbers into examples of primes and non-examples of primes, the composites. Conversely, the non-examples of the composites are the primes. The subject matter of this lesson lends itself to this approach. Such is not always the case and then the teacher must take care to include contrasting, but potentially confusing non-examples to help students sort out essential versus non-essential attributes of the target concept(s).

Why did the teacher demonstrate with the number 6, rather than with the smallest number on the lab sheet, 2? Remember, most of these seventh graders are likely to be concrete operational and, thus, are not aware of the range of possibilities, of the possible differences between 2 columns of 3 checkers and 3 columns of 2 checkers, of the importance of recording the single column or columns with one checker each, and most important, of the need to record data systematically in order to expedite the pattern-finding.

Teachers who have used these three dimensional models in this lab with systematic recording of data on a lab sheet have found that most students isolate the examples of the primes from the examples of the composites. If that doesn't happen in this class, the teacher has a backup strategy. Did you notice that the teacher doesn't expect to get the typical definition of primes and composites immediately? A checker definition is quite acceptable! In fact, the cooperating teacher, Mrs. Lopez, advised this student teacher not to ignore the checker definition if some student first described the two groups of numbers in terms of their factors. In her experience, some students needed to return mentally to the checker piles and she had found it was helpful to maintain the connection between that physical model and the mathematical concept. Moreover, Mrs. Lopez had another good reason; a checker lab would be used later in the week to develop the concepts of common factor and greatest common factor.

If you followed our instructions and didn't read the feedback strategies columns, now is the time to return to Figure 7.2 and analyze those strategies in terms of the instructional strategies opposite them. When and how does the teacher plan to get feedback on the extent to which students' thinking is starting to focus on the essential attributes of the concepts? Developmental Q/A, used in conjunction with demo and lab modes, certainly is the key to this crucial aspect. Will it work? Yes, *if* the teacher implements it well. That's why novice teachers are well advised to write out the exact wording of key questions, check them out with the cooperating teacher in advance, and prepare contingency questions in case responses to the first planned questions are not along the desired lines.

Many beginning teachers have found it useful to prepare three-by-five cards listing key questions and to carry these into class as a supplement to the lesson plan sheet(s). Experience will gradually reduce the need for specific written teacher cues but, as a beginner, use as much detail as needed to make the plan work for you in your classroom.

When does the teacher plan to get feedback on whether today's objectives for these concepts have been met? That's right! The best evidence of this would be the tour during the generalizing to other cases part of the plan. At this time, the teacher has a chance to observe individual students respond to examples and non-examples not used in class and try to extend the physical modeling activity to numbers for which they do not have enough checkers.

You should have been able to identify connections among the conditions for learning a concept and the instructional strategies outlined in this plan. However, the specific instructional strategies in this plan can readily be generalized to an instructional strategy pattern common to all plans designed to teach concepts. Study the pattern outlined below; note its relationship to Gagné's conditions for learning a concept; and identify the specific strategies in the prime and composites plan that illustrate the generalizations in the pattern.

Instructional Strategy Pattern for Concepts

Provide differentiated examples and non-examples in sequence; sometimes model by analogy; get essential and non-essential characteristics identified; elicit operational definition; elicit generalization of the concept to a variety of specific instances not previously used.

If some of the strategies in the sample plan seem to be "extra," you may have correctly excluded those that are aimed at the teaching of vocabulary. Objective 5 referred to the learning of verbal associations, important goals of mathematics instruction that are often interwoven with the teaching of concepts. It is important to notice that these labels were one of the last items attended to in the plan. There is an old adage, "Don't name the baby before it's born," that is worth applying to most concept and vocabulary lessons. An unfamiliar label for which the student has no concrete referents is meaningless if introduced early and can sometimes lead to a negative attitude on the part of the students. "Mantissa? What's that? Oh, who cares. More big-word math."

Even more mysterious to students is the premature introduction of the unique vocabulary of mathematics known as symbols. A geometry teacher developed the concept of congruence by matching a variety of congruent shapes through physical slides, flips and turns and trying to match relevant non-examples, such as similar figures or those with exactly one congruent angle, arc or segment. After saying and writing the word "congruent" to describe the appropriate shapes, the teacher introduced the symbol $\cong$, wrote it on the board and alluded to its separate symbolic parts, the equal sign and the similarity sign and their relevance to the new concept of congruence. Then the teacher reinforced that the symbol $\cong$ is verbalized as "is congruent to" and is used in statements such as $\triangle ABC \cong \triangle DEF$. Next this teacher insisted that the students write the correct symbolic statements as they answered a set of practice exercises and that they correctly state the verbalization of the symbols when responding to questions on the exercises. Immediate feedback given by the teacher who toured during supervised practice corrected any sloppy or incorrect written symbols.

Symbols appear in formulas such as $V = lwh$; as names of concepts, such as π; and as signifiers of operations, such as Σ. Some listeners have characterized mathematics lessons as lessons in a "foreign" language. Imagine the plight of students not proficient in this language if their teachers were to conduct lessons almost entirely in mathematical language. Thus, it is important to pay close attention to the generalized instructional strategy pattern for vocabulary that follows and match it against the specific illustrations provided thus far.

Instructional Strategy Pattern for Vocabulary

Show object (or exemplify idea); then pronounce name and spell or write it on board; have students do likewise; repeat (practice); give name and elicit statement of idea or description of object; have students use in context.

The two instructional strategy patterns outlined in this section are standards against which concept and/or vocabulary plans can be checked. They are also guidelines both novices and experienced teachers have found useful in constructing their own concept and vocabulary plans. However, important as the strategy patterns are, they are ineffective unless used in conjunction with the other components of the instructional model. Note that the choice of modes, laboratory and demonstration in particular, was heavily concrete. That kind of choice agrees with the Piagetian implications you studied earlier, just as the particular set of objectives reflects the structure of mathematics at a level suitable for seventh-graders. What else is contained in the single plan? There is an attempt to produce an overall mix of guided discovery with reception learning, and *if* the teacher implements this plan effectively, the result promises to be meaningful learning. Elements of an advance organizer appear in the "Number patterns in history and informing Ss of outcomes" section of the plan. The opening set of strategies should help the students to recall relevant, prior concepts and to focus on the spatial arrangement of the even (odd) numbered students. Moreover, as we'll read in a later section, this activity also has the potential to get attention on the lesson at the start of class.

Have you wondered why dashed lines are used to separate strategies from one another? Lines are useful at the planning stage to help us check our own thinking and are very helpful during actual implementation as an assist to keeping track of where we are in the lesson. However, solid lines would tend to convey more separation among lesson segments than is intended. Dashed lines are meant to imply the need for the kind of connections that will enable the lesson to flow smoothly. Are such connections provided in the sample plan? Go back and read the end of each strategy and the beginning of the next and identify the connections. Are they explicit? What could the teacher say or do so that students will comprehend the connections? Be sure to satisfy yourself on this important concern before continuing. Perhaps you are thinking that sequencing decisions can either enhance the building of connections or make the task all but impossible. We agree! Try mentally rearranging the strategies on any lesson plan and then analyze the resulting effects. Sometimes you will find equally (or perhaps more) productive ways to structure the lesson. In other cases bizarre results will show up fast.

There certainly is a lot more to this business of planning lessons than is obvious to the casual observer. And just think—we have considered only concept and vocabulary instruction thus far. Does the task seem overwhelming when you realize that coping with plans aimed at rules, novel problem solving, proofs, and psychomotor skills lie ahead, and that many lessons will involve combinations of these? Don't let yourself be discouraged. The situation is not nearly as momentous as it may seem at this point. What you learn about concept and vocabulary plans will serve as the base for all these other types of plans. Thus, the next task is to apply that and add some new ideas that have special relevance to various other types of target outcomes. Since mathematics is said to be a rule-governed subject, we consider planning for principle (rule) learning in the next section.

Planning for Rules/Principles

There are several major types of rules that are found repeatedly in mathematics lessons: formulas and algorithms, translation between everyday language and mathematical language, type problems solved by algebraic methods and rules for writing synthetic proofs. All have the common characteristics found in rule-learning, but each possesses unique characteristics that must be considered by the mathematics teacher.

Formulas and algorithms   The rule lesson found in this section is intended to help students learn the rule, $C = \pi d$. It was based on the effective implementation of a prior day's lesson on the concept of π. In that lesson, the students were involved in a measurement lab in which they measured the distance around (circumference or perimeter) and the distance across (diameter or diagonal) the tops of containers that were either cylindrical or rectangular solids. At the end of the lab, the students agreed that for cylindrical shapes, C/d was approximately equal to three. The teacher provided the label, π, for the ratio of circumference to diameter and confirmed that the ratio was a constant, a special number. Then the teacher briefly gave the students some historical background and suggested uses of the ratio.

Part 2: Group 7 in Ms. Mason's class handed in the lab
    sheet below. The leader, Jerry Batt, complained
    that some joker had erased part of their work. Help
    Jerry by filling in the blanks.

Object	Circumference	Diameter	C/d
Soup can	24. _____ cm	8.2 cm	3.0
Jug	___ . 0 cm	10.0 cm	3.1
Half dollar	_____ . _____ cm	4.0 cm	3.1
Disc (large)	620.0 cm	____ cm	3.1

Fig. 7.4

The π plan ended with a reference to Handout 2 to be completed by the
students for use in class the following day. One question from Handout 2 is
reproduced in Figure 7.4

The plan that follows (Figure 7.5) is that designed by the same student
teacher for the second day of instruction with this seventh-grade class. Study it
carefully for the earmarks of rule learning from Section 6.3 of Chapter 6. Once
again, we recommend that you interrupt your reading of the text material to
study the rule plan. Then check out your ideas with the comments and questions
that follow in the text. This time the student teacher designed an elastic clause
based on the two starred objectives in the plan. The elastic clause may be saved
for another day for many reasons. These seventh-graders may be weak in basic
calculation skills and become bogged down in computations, or they may be very
bright and offer diverse explanations as to the nature of this mathematical model,
or they may ask about the existence of other patterns they observed with respect
to the exercises of Handout 2. As you might guess, the cooperating teacher was
shown a draft of the new handout, a list of the practice problems, and a complete
blow-by-blow exposition of the material to go in the students' notes.

However, the central issue here concerns the rule-learning objectives and
the strategies that are related to the conditions for rule learning. You should have
identified specific strategies which conform to the pattern below.

Instructional Strategy Pattern for Rules/Principles

Get students to recall/review prerequisites; indicate nature of expected terminal performance; cue (via questions, lab work, applications) students to find the pattern by
chaining concepts; get the rule stated (by students, if possible); provide a model of
correct performance; have students demonstrate instances of the rule in a variety of
situations. *Fix and maintain skills by spaced and varied drill.

Topic: Formula: $C = \pi d$

Class/Period: Math 7, Period 3

Date: November 8 (Tuesday)

Instructional Objectives:
1. State that $C = \pi d$ in symbols and words.
2. Compute the measure of either C or $d(r)$ given the measure of the other by applying $C = \pi d$ and using $\pi \approx 3.14$.
3. Express the measure of C in terms of $d(r)$ and π, or of $d(r)$ in terms of C and π.
*4. State that 22/7 is another estimate of π.
*5. Calculate as in #2 by using $\pi \approx 22/7$.

Routines:
1. Take attendance via seating chart as Ss enter.

CONTENT ITEM	SPECIAL MATERIAL OR EQUIPMENT	INSTRUCTIONAL STRATEGIES	FEEDBACK STRATEGIES		TIME EST.
			GET	GIVE	
C as a multiple of d d as a factor of C	Acetate copy of Part 2 on overhead projector (OH) with 1st two ans. written in	HWPM. As Ss enter, select diverse Ss to fill in acetate sheet. Tell others to ck. work and circle differences in pencil. Be ready to defend ans. or find error. Get attention of all on 1st and 2nd ans.	Tour and look for problems. Take poll. Q Ss for reason. Spread Q/A and poll selectively.	Praise all Ss for Mon. gp. work.	
		Q/A through other exs., helping Ss decide on correctness of ans.		T verifies errors and corrects ans.	5-7 min.
Where we're headed Rule: $C \approx 3.14 \times d$		T notes what Ss have been able to infer and states today's goal—to use pattern in systematic way. T uses dev. Q/A to elicit more general pattern. "Yesterday we agreed to use 3.14 as an estimate of C/d. So if d had been 1 cm, C would be about? cm? Suppose d were 2 cm? 3 cm? 4 cm? etc." T gives more exs. until most Ss have idea. T elicits $C \approx 3.14 \times d$ and writes this on board.	Spread Q/A and seek hands. Straw polls.	Write correct ans. on board in orderly pattern.	2 min.

Fig. 7.5

				Time
Rule: $C = \pi \times d$	T reminds Ss that 3.14 is only an estimate for C/d. T asks for exact value of C/d. T uses lecture and Q/A to have Ss treat π as they had been treating 3.14 above and gradually elicits $C = \pi \times d$. T lectures on nature of formula, use to ans. Qs such as those on Handout #2.	T spreads Q/A until almost all Ss are involved.	Write correct ans. on board under previous ans.	2 min.
Model problem 1 (notation $\pi\,d$ for $\pi \times d$ and rationale) Acetate #2	T reminds Ss to take notes as T and Ss work out model problem written on acetate. T introduces πd notation, asks Ss if they can guess why $\pi \times d$ might be confusing. T emphasizes the form desired at each step of the labeling, the change from $C =$ to $C \approx$; the use of ()() for "times."	T tours and scans several notebooks from time to time. Asks one S to react to another's ans.	Praises esp. good rationale.	3 min.
Practice Set Find C, given d Find C, given r Acetate # 3 Find d, given C	Ss to try some on their own in Supv. Pract. Selected Ss are sent to board to put good work on. Others are told to check work against ans. on board. If necessary, T stops classwork so all may Q/A procedure. If no particular problem, T encourages Ss to try "little stickler" ex. where r is given. Depending on progress, T assigns another with r given or immediately assigns "big problem," where C is given.	T circulates. T circulates and warns all to read given.	T indicates how all are doing, points out common errors, etc. T reads correct ans.	8-10 min.
Summary of d, C, r relationships	T emphasizes stating $C = \pi d$ in words, then has Ss repeat. Q/A for $d = 2r$, d in terms of C and π, C in terms of π and r. Ss to write major relationships in notes.	Ss to repeat aloud.		2 min.

Fig. 7.5 (Continued)

CONTENT ITEM	SPECIAL MATERIAL OR EQUIPMENT	INSTRUCTIONAL STRATEGIES	FEEDBACK STRATEGIES		TIME EST.
			GET	GIVE	
Mathematical model $C = \pi d$		T poses thought Qs *re* need of $C = \pi d$ when $C \approx 3.14 d$ seems to do.	T uses "wait" time, checks several resp.	Verbal praise for esp. good ans.	1-2 min.
Expressing C in terms of π and d		T notes that some exercises do not require use of 3.14 and Q/A, C in terms of π for $d = 4$ cm, 2 m, 3½ dm, etc., then d in terms of C and π.	Spreads Qs.	T writes ans. on board.	2-3 min.
Elastic clause: 22/7		T lectures on historical background as to estimates of π, gives Archimedes' values of π as between 3 10/71 and 3 1/7. Has Ss change to improper fraction and decimals. T states use of 22/7, rationale for this, and emphasizes $22/7 \neq \pi$. If time, T and Ss begin selected exs. using 22/7.		2 volunteer Ss give calculator result.	5-10 min.
Analysis of mixed ex.	Handout #3	Oral Q/A, e.g., "Must 3.14 be used?" "Which exs. ask for the value of r?" etc.	Fast diverse Q/A. T asks for defense from other Ss, straw polls.	T confirms.	3-4 min.
Applying formulae with variety of problems	Puzzle Sheet Attachment to Handout #3	Ss to do as much of puzzle as possible. The HW for Wed. is to bring in 4 cutout discs based on pattern on bottom of puzzle sheet. Tell Ss they will be used in a lab exercise investigating surface.	T circulates.	T may ask ind. Ss to help one another.	5 min.

Fig. 7.5   (Continued)

The key elements in the rule strategy pattern are prominent features in this or any other well-designed rule/principle plan. Notice, though, that one feature often merges with another. In this case, recall of prerequisites indicating the outcome, and cuing to find the pattern are encompassed by the strategies from HWPM (homework post-mortem) up to the beginning of model problem 1. Yet, "Where we're headed" is explicitly treated by the teacher as well as implicitly handled in HWPM and the sequence of developmental questions. Although the explicit consideration of a goal should be present in every plan, early in a rule lesson the students must be alerted to the specific terminal expectations of that lesson. Then their outlook during the eliciting of the rule is not cluttered by musings such as where we're headed, what I'll need to remember, whether two questions in a sequence are related or not. They know what to listen for and concentrate on. When the teacher later "provides a model of correct performance" as this designer of a plan proposed to do with model problem 1, the details of the teacher's expectations for the student should be crystal clear. Finally, no rule instruction is complete if a lesson does not contain a well-structured strategy aimed at *student* demonstration of learning. Too many novice teachers are trapped by lazy or confused students into doing "one more problem together" and thus demonstrating that the *teacher* has learned the rule. You were warned about this abuse of feedback in Chapter 2. Sometimes, it's true, the students are honestly confused because the teacher didn't initially clarify the expected student outcomes and/or has in the past immediately given practice examples far more complex than the model problem. Once again, we emphasize the need for gradually differentiated practice examples and for in-class decisions as to the number and kind of problems to be assigned, based on feedback. We hope you noticed that this plan included more than one written practice sequence as well as oral practice. That final five minutes of written practice is a *must*. Unless the teacher obtains positive feedback on a substantial part of these mixed exercises, there is no solid evidence of student capability on such tasks.

In every rule plan, the emphasis is on the rule, i.e. the use of the chained concepts. However, there is often a verbal association, in this case a string of symbols called a formula, to be learned along with the rule. Which objective(s) is (are) related to the learning of this verbal association? The teacher wrote Objective 1 to meet this goal. The related instructional strategies are much later in the plan. (If you have wondered why the sequence of objectives does not match the sequence of instructional strategies in this case, you are interacting with the written material in the way we hoped. In fact, many teachers write objectives as they think of them without regard to sequence. There is a choice here, but there obviously is considerably less choice when it comes to the sequencing of instructional strategies. If you would find it easier to have lists of objectives sequenced to correspond to instructional strategies, build this into your own plans.)

Why did we star the last sentence in the instructional strategy pattern? The star is meant to identify the long-range nature of this aspect of the strategy pattern. Intellectual skills, however effectively introduced, are maintained only by means of selective practice in later lessons. Since learning that is not retained over time is of little interest, we'll come back to this topic in a later section of this chapter.

Translation between everyday language and mathematical language   Translation skills are prerequisites for the solution of type problems so important in mathematics, science, and the applied fields, as well as for the solution of atypical problems from all areas of real life and the not-so-real puzzle problems. However, some mathematics teachers are unaware that many problems require two levels of translation skills and thus, these same teachers misinterpret student confusion as reading comprehension difficulty, lack of concentration or just plain lack of competence.

Compare the two problems that follow. Consider the steps students must take to solve each by means of equations.

1. The difference between two numbers is 24. Twice the smaller number is equal to the large number minus 14. Find the two numbers.

2. A bottle containing 40 cc of tincture of iodine (iodine crystals dissolved in alcohol) is labeled as having 2% concentration of iodine. However, each time the cap is removed some alcohol evaporates, and thus the concentration of iodine is altered from the medically prescribed percentage. How much alcohol would have to be evaporated in order to double the recommended concentration? To triple it?

The difficulty becomes obvious, doesn't it? The straightforward left-to-right translation that works so well for problem 1 doesn't seem to get us anywhere with problem 2. We call problems like problem 2 *situation problems*. Since the solving of meaningful situation problems is one of the most important objectives of mathematics instruction, strategies directed toward this end deserve our special attention. But, first, let's take a longer look at the kind of instruction needed to learn the first level of translation skills.

How does a student become a skillful translator? There are clearly some prerequisite vocabulary/symbol learnings. Words such as *difference, equal to, twice, minus,* and the like, as well as their related symbols, should have been mastered in previous lessons. Then translation from English to mathematical phrases and sentences and back might be taught as a number game.

The following number game model is one way to make translation highly concrete. The teacher asks a student to think of a number but not to reveal it, perform a set of specified set of operations on that number, and write the final result on paper. Then, the teacher writes the same result on the chalkboard. The teacher repeats the process with other students and continues to appear to read minds. Finally a set of plastic containers and a set of checkers is used to model one of the problems (see Figure 7.6). The teacher might also contrive a demonstration with colorfully drawn pictures on an acetate or simulate the

Direction	Teacher talk	Model
1. Think of a number	Since I don't know the number, let's assume that you put that many checkers in this box.	
2. Add 2	Place 2 checkers next to the box.	
3. Multiply by 4	That means 4 times your number and 4 times the 2 checkers or 4 boxes and 8 checkers.	
4. Subtract 4	Take away 4 checkers	
5. Divide by 4	That leaves one box and one checker.	
6. Subtract your original number	Take away the box. Your answer is 1.	

Fig. 7.6 Translation model.

mental action associated with various steps by moving cutout shapes on the overhead, on a felt board, or even by means of masking tape on a chalkboard.

Following lessons of this kind, students can be gradually introduced to translation exercises without the benefit of pictures or models. Now the teacher must be alert to evidence of reading deficiencies, special vocabulary problems (such as *exceeds*) and the need to teach word-for-word reading of mathematics.

Type problems solved by algebraic methods It should be clear from the introduction to the rule planning section that the teaching of type problems can be an important objective. Notice that we said: *"can be."* Unfortunately, the designation of type, or stereotype, problems has a negative connotation for both past students and mathematics educators who suffered through convoluted age problems or puzzlers such as digit problems. For many students, these represented uninteresting conundrums.

Moreover, even when interesting type problems are used, some teachers behave initially as though the students should be engaging in novel problem solving strategies. Yet, at the end of the lesson the students of these teachers learn that there is *one* strategy they should have "discovered" and *one* procedure they are expected to use with similar problems from now on. Even more unfortunate, the teacher has lost the opportunity to help students see the power of mathematics to classify important groups of problems that may then be treated in an algorithmic way. Thus, as with all instruction in rule learning, it is vital that the teacher let the students know the nature of the expected outcomes. In this case, the outcome is for the students to identify a problem as belonging to a certain type, a type of sufficient interest and usefulness that it recurs frequently in the real world.

It is equally important that the lesson begin with an interesting problem. Most students understand that motion relationships are important in many areas of life from the Olympics record-breakers to the car manufacturer. Thus, an attention-getter like the pigeon problem can create a positive mind-set toward the new topic.

> *Pigeon racing, a development of the use of homing pigeons in the ancient Olympic Games (776 B.C.–393 A.D.), originated in Belgium. The longest recorded flight was estimated to be 7000 miles flown in 55 days by a pigeon owned by the Duke of Wellington. The flight ended when the exhausted pigeon dropped dead one mile from its home loft in London, England, on June 1, 1845. What average velocity in mph was attained by this record breaking pigeon? (McWhirter & McWhirter, 1976)*

The pigeon problem contains a characteristic even more important than that of simply provoking curiosity. It makes sense. It is a *bona fide* motion problem to which even we non-pigeon-fanciers can relate. And that latter characteristic, the meaningfulness of the situation *to the student*, is the one most frequently ignored by textbook writers and thus by those teachers who rely solely on textbook problems.

Even though the pigeon problem contains extraneous information in terms of the question asked, the information is not extraneous in terms of real world events. As long as the students have learned the prerequisite relationships among distance, rate and time and know the conversion from days to hours, the final question can be solved by applying the distance formula. Students who follow the progress of their school track team, the results of the Indianapolis 500 or any of the other, multiple real world distance/time events will quickly see this problem as one of an important type. Notice that we haven't advised that a chart be set up. Although some teachers find charts indispensable, we recommend that charts be used sparingly, if at all. Too often, they are presented before the students have had the opportunity to study the problem, talk about its meaning and try their hand at solution strategies.

Problems that can be represented in terms of known formulas are situation problems, but the problem of translation is relatively simple. The student must first recognize that the problem situation is modeling some known formula and then study the problem for the quantities corresponding to the concepts in the formula. One important aid in studying the problem is the use of a diagram. For example, with motion problems, labeled arrow diagrams form a pictorial representation of the problem. Two important questions: What changed? and What remained the same? should then be asked. The answer to the second question points the way to the equation—perhaps "time going equals time returning." Then the distance formula is used as a tool to represent time going and time returning, rather than being directly used as in the pigeon problem.

Some type problems cannot be represented by a common formula. The alcohol evaporation problem given earlier is a good example of such a situation problem. In order to solve such a problem, the student must be able to apply translation skills at two levels of complexity. In the following paragraphs, we outline the idea concocted by Mrs. Armstrong, who was beginning to plan a lesson on an introduction to solution problems. Mrs. Armstrong kept in mind the two characteristics of situation type problems pointed out earlier.

1. The situation must be meaningful *to the student* and

2. The student must be alerted to the need for an initial strategy other than translation.

The first characteristic is the key to what should occur in the construction of the advance organizer and the follow-up development of this kind of rule. The situation must be made meaningful in a concrete way. The plan itself is not included, but you should be able to expand the development described below into an appropriate sequence of instructional and feedback strategies.

"I'll start with a demonstration that can be matched to a specific problem. I'd better start with a situation in which water is added; evaporating may befuddle their thinking," Mrs Armstrong mused.

After borrowing two 100 cc graduated beakers, two 10 cc graduated beakers, and a bottle of fluorescein dye from the chemistry teacher, she added drops of the dye to the 90 cc of water in one of the beakers until an intense color was present. She recorded the number of drops used and then observed the effect of adding 10 cc of water on the color. There was a perceptible change.

Mrs. Armstrong decided to do the final step of the demo in exactly the same way at the beginning of class and then question the students as to their observations. As a result of a last-minute brainstorm she decided to use all four beakers with the two 100 cc kind already containing identical amounts and intensity of the fluorescein solution, while the two 10 cc beakers would each contain 10 cc of water. When the students entered class, they would see the apparatus set up as in Figure 7.7.

The students in the front rows would be able to read aloud the total number of cc of liquid in each of the four beakers, but it would be up to the instructor to reveal the nature of the ingredients and the concentration of the solution in beakers A and C.

Mrs. Armstrong intended to pour the water in beaker B into the solution in beaker A but leave the other two beakers as is, so that students might have a ready reference as to the "before" situation. She knew she must obtain answers to two major questions: (1) What changed? and (2) What remained the same? She would have to use contingency questions to elicit the hidden constant—that is, the constant volume of the fluorescein dye in beaker A

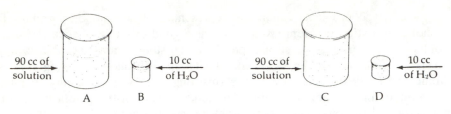

Fig. 7.7   Beakers set up for solutions demo.

both before and after the demonstration. Then she would help the students compose a list of varied practical situations where mixing of this kind might occur but where the desired final concentration would be known (in order to clarify where the class was headed).

If Mrs. Armstrong implements the above idea successfully, she should next provide students with a model problem. The model problem should be matched to the action illustrated by the demo (that is, one ingredient should be added to a mixture) although the unknown might differ. Then she will need to move gradually from the demo to the mathematical model in at least three steps (pictorial, English sentence, mathematical sentence). Mrs. Armstrong would probably cue students to help complete:

1. A labeled sketch of the situation in the case of the model problem with perhaps a "before" and "after" version.

2. An English sentence that describes what stays the same (for example, the cc of fluorescein dye "before" is the same as the cc of fluorescein dye "after").

3. The corresponding mathematical sentence with the appropriate designation of the unknown.

Notice the levels of translation that are provided for in this lesson outline. The situation and its dynamics are pictured and labeled. The importance of this kind of iconic representation of the problem is unparalleled in helping students identify the changing and unchanging quantities in the problem. Now the students must create an English sentence based on their analysis of the iconic representation. This step transforms the problem into a statement that can be translated from left to right with the first level of translation skills.

Although the new rule has been obtained at the equation-stating step, the students should still be asked to complete the problem and check the result in the statement of the problem as well as in the original equation. Moreover, as in all problem-solving instruction, it is vital that the teacher and the students review the process which led to this rule. Next comes student practice of the new rule, right? Yes, but it takes a relatively long time to completely work through even a small number of these problems. And leaving the bulk of them for homework is never a sound substitute for supervised practice. The answer is to assign several problems, direct the students to label the variable(s) and set up the equation for all examples, but to completely work through only one or two designated examples.

Mrs. Armstrong's approach might seem time-consuming and unnecessarily elaborate unless you've read the results of the National Assessment of Educational Progress administered in 1986. According to Brown, Carpenter, Kouba, Lindquist, Silver & Swafford (1988), the tested students lacked the conceptual knowledge needed for success in problem solving, application and reasoning questions. These authors emphasized that even though the content areas analyzed in this analysis were primarily arithmetic in nature, even the eleventh grade students did not demonstrate good results.

Our own classroom experience has convinced us that the rote application of a standard tabular arrangement can be presented quickly and will yield fairly high scores on a quiz given the next day on exactly the same kind of problems. However, if the teacher slips in investment problems, dry food mixture problems, and coin problems (all possessing the same structure as solution problems), the students will be lost and must be taught to memorize still more procedures for each of these "types." Mrs. Armstrong's initial investment of time will pay off dividends in meaningful learning and make her later attempts to transfer learning of this rule to all problems in the same family far more successful.

Rules for writing synthetic proofs   Why is proof-writing being considered under the heading "Strategies for Rules/Principles"? Did you classify proof constructing as problem solving rather than rule learning? If so, then you're correctly focusing on one of the important processes of mathematics. However, theorems involve products of mathematics as well as processes. The learning outcomes are a mixture of both rules and novel problem solving, of both process and product.

Almost every theorem serves a dual role: (1) to be applied in computational questions and (2) to be applied to deduce other theorems. For example, the inscribed angle theorem is used as a formula to find the measure of an inscribed angle given its intercepted arc. It is also the key theorem used to obtain a proof of other angle/arc measure theorems. Both of these related, but distinct, rules must be specifically provided for in instruction—from the advance organizer to the model problem to appropriate practice. That sounds simple enough but in reality it is far from simple. In particular, the rule-use of deducing other theorems adds the ingredient of the axiomatic process to the mixture.

Each and every theorem is capable of being deduced from prior concepts, postulates, and/or theorems. Certainly the overall major objective of secondary school geometry is to help students become capable proof constructors. But there are two stages in proof construction. The first, designated the *analysis* of the proof, is the process by which the student, through selective trial and error, conjecture, and testing, actually arrives at a solution to the deductive proof. The student's solution may or may not appear on paper. It may be symbolized by drawings and notes but, in any case, if questioned, the student would be able to outline the core of the solution. This analysis stage, *if left to the students*, is an example of Gagné's type 8, problem solving.

Synthetic proofs, on the other hand, are characterized by the systematic application of logical rules. The presentation of a synthetic proof by a student, usually written, must start with the hypotheses and then list new results deduced from the hypotheses and prior assumptions or theorems until the desired conclusion is reached. Each new assertion must be justified by a generalization that already exists in the axiomatic system. When asked to write a short, deductive proof, Juan wrote the following:

$AB \cong CD$ was given, as was D as the midpoint of C, therefore

$CE \cong DE$ from the definition of a midpoint.

Finally $AB \cong DE$ since segments congruent to the same segment are congruent to each other.

Whether paragraph style or column style is used, the requirement is the same. The written *synthesis* must repeatedly illustrate the logical relationship

$$p \text{ and } p \rightarrow q$$
$$\therefore q.$$

Thus, the prescribed character of the synthetic presentation is rule bound. Although the nature of this complex rule is constant, it is not a rule to be taught in a single lesson or two. Indeed, throughout the course, variations in synthetic arguments will occur (such as presentation of the indirect proof), and objectives, instructional strategies, and feedback strategies must be designed to account for these variations.

A single theorem, then, has the potential for yielding both a new numerical rule and a new axiomatic rule and, in the process of applying the latter, of involving the student in the problem solving of analysis and the rule learning of synthesis. Is it any wonder that mathematicians hailed Euclid as a mastermind and for centuries reviled any who criticized lapses in his work? Even the simplest part of the axiomatic system requires a thorough analysis of all these aspects of the content by the teacher if meaningful plans are to result.

But why should students be guided through the reconstruction of proofs that could be given to them as models for study? If the teacher and the class explore conjectures together (Textbooks should be closed! Students can seem like geometry wizards otherwise.), then the process has a purpose analogous to the presentation of type word problems. In the analysis stage, the teacher can help the class with key questions that they should ask when they try novel proofs. Guidelines and ways to test conjectures can be suggested.

Guideline 1: *If you think an auxiliary segment is needed, try to use points already in the diagram and draw as few segments as possible.*

Hans thinks: *"I need a central angle. I'll use radius $\overline{OC}$ and point A."*

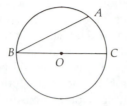

Guideline 2: *If you think a relationship exists, put in numbers and check it out.*

Royann thinks: *"I think $m\angle DCA = 2m\angle ACB$. I'll try $20°$ for $m\angle A$ and $70°$ for $m\angle B$, then $m\angle ACB = ...$"*

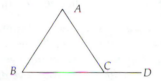

The teacher needs to characterize some hints as rules of thumb to be used with every proof of a certain type while others should be classified as more general cues to be tried when the proof cannot immediately be classified as to type. (Cues of the latter kind are sometimes called *heuristics*. We will be seeing more of them in the section on novel problem solving.) It's obvious that the teacher who shortcuts the analysis stage by forcing or giving certain answers is wasting everybody's time.

Occasionally teachers erroneously assume that the only thing that really counts is a two-column proof. In their enthusiasm, they omit the analysis stage entirely and immediately ask the following sequence of questions: "What is step 1? Why? What is step 2? Why? What is step 3?" and so on. The students soon tire of the guessing game and begin reading the answers from their texts. Synthesis without analysis is *nonsense* mathematics; but analysis can live without routine subsequent synthesis. When the reconstruction of the synthetic argument will provide needed practice in writing proofs or when it includes a novel element, then the *students* (Notice. We said "the students.") should reconstruct the argument with gradually decreasing teacher assistance as the course proceeds. As always, the teacher must let the students in on the objectives of this part of the lesson, help them identify novel aspects of the argument, and clarify the use to be made of both the product of the proof and the process of the proof.

Planning for Novel Problem Solving

Problem solving of the nontypical variety is really where it's at if you believe, as we do, that the ideal of education is to teach the students to think for themselves. In the section on theorems in geometry, we designated the analysis stage of proof constructing as problem solving if the analysis is the responsibility of the students rather than of the teacher and the proof in question is not being studied as a type problem. Similarly, in an algebra class, it would be a natural next step to move from the solution of type problems to the solution of diverse novel problems. However, in both cases, that shift of responsibility in student thinking has to be gradually fostered by the teacher. Thus, a teacher who wants to teach future problem-solving lessons should incorporate into rule lessons such behaviors as descriptions of the way the teacher has fumbled toward a solution, questions as to the advantages and disadvantages of various modes of attack, and hints as to ways to get feedback without recourse to the teacher.

Mr. Potter had been gradually moving his geometry class toward problem solving. He included all the above behaviors and, in addition, encouraged students to work in groups and to defend their work to one another. On the day of the first problem-solving lesson, here's what he told the class:

We're going to try a little different approach today. You're going to behave like working geometers—conjecturing, deducing, and assessing different approaches. I've prepared a handout containing five geometry problems, all of which can be proved in more than one way. I've divided you into groups and assigned two of the five exercises to each group. When I give the signal, the groups will move to their assigned locations and the group leader will take over. The leader must see that all directions are followed and should try to give all students in the group an opportunity to participate. The group should find as many different proofs for each of the two exercises as possible, should work each out and then discuss the advantages and disadvantages of each. Is one proof more rigorous, easier to follow...? Keep a record of your conclusions so that you can report on them when I ask you to stop the group work. Questions? [Two or three questions.] When I turn on the overhead projector, you will see the location where you are to sit and the exercises assigned to your group. The leader's name is starred [overhead projector turned on]. You may move into groups now.

Mr. Potter's success today will depend partly on his prior developmental work and partly on the nature of those geometry exercises. They must be above level III in the cognitive taxonomy with enough of the known so that the students can begin hypothesizing, and with the right mix of novelty to insure the blocking of "pat" solutions. Mr. Potter's quoted preamble would constitute his introduction to the activity. You should be able to identify the next instructional strategy he would like in his plan and the associated feedback strategies. That's right. Next would come small-group discussions with Mr. Potter touring, listening for conjectures, trying to get students to help one another, praising an insightful idea, and so on. Take a few minutes now and sketch out the rest of the plan with appropriate time estimates. Don't forget to write the instructional objectives. After you have produced an outline, check it for correspondence with the instructional strategy pattern presented next.

Instructional Strategy Pattern for Problem Solving

Present problem; may question students to elicit alternative approaches and will emphasize the desirability of a variety of search strategies; arrange for individual work or small-group discussion (in the collection of data, the analysis of data, the making and testing of conjectures); reassemble class; ask students to weigh the advantages and disadvantages of the proposals (including processes) that resulted from the group discussions or individual work.

This instructional strategy pattern included references to individual or group work. In fact, recent research on both problem solving and adolescent reasoning is supportive of *both* individual and group work, but for different purposes. One of the characteristics of the successful problem solver is persistence. Thus, it is important that the teacher structure some long-term project work dealing with problem solving so that students realize that many atypical problems require thinking time, time away from the problem and time reconsidering the problem from a different point of view. Here is where the individual project becomes a useful instructional mode. However, it is also clear from the work of researchers such as Schoenfeld (1979) in problem solving and Slavin (1980) in cooperative learning, that carefully structured small group (or pairs) discussions add another dimension to the learning of problem solving. The requirement to share tentative ideas and to talk out a sequence of strategies has great potential in generating a problem solving attitude. We remind you that small group work often follows a period of individual work on a problem or situation. Notice once again the importance of modes that are likely to enhance cognitive interaction, often through social interaction.

We've already emphasized the need for a gradual move toward instruction in problem solving. These prior teacher-led explanations of "thinking through a problem" need to be continued and expanded during problem-solving lessons. Reread the final step in the strategy pattern. That step includes class consideration of the *processes* used by small groups or individuals during work on the problem. It is analogous to the summarizing step prior to practice in lessons on type word problems, but the difference resides in the focus of the summary. In type problem work, the teacher's aim is to clarify the structure that is reflected in all similar problems and, therefore, the typical steps to solution. However, in novel problem-solving lessons, the aim of this summarizing step is to clarify the tactic(s) used in this case and to consider the pros and cons of a more general use for these specific processes. Over time, the teacher should help the class attain a list of such tactics that *may* illuminate a problem but are not guaranteed to produce a solution. Such tactics are labeled *heuristic strategies* or simply *heuristics*. *Heuristic* is a word derived from the Greek *heuriskein*, which translates roughly as "to find out." Of course, sometimes you *find out* that the particular heuristic you tried is of no help . We've compiled a list of potentially useful heuristics with some examples from the literature and our classroom experience. We recommend that you begin collecting additional examples of heuristics.

Heuristics

1. Use analogy or contrast. ("This series is behaving *like* the coefficients of Pascal's triangle. Let's try... .")

2. Change the scale (or frame of reference). (Shrink or stretch a shape.)

3. Use successive approximation; exploit errors (Guess, try, correct, guess again.)

4. Exploit symmetry. (Use a folded paper disc and the radial symmetry of the circle to prove that the perpendicular bisector of any chord passes through the center of a circle.)

A
B
Match A to B

5. Ask "What if such and such were *not* true?"

6. Change the exercise to a problem you can do. (Polya [1962] describes a use of this heuristic when demonstrating the solution of the problem: Given any triangle ABC, inscribe a square in $\triangle ABC$ so that one side of the square lies on $\overline{BC}$. Polya tells us to inscribe a small square, one vertex on $\overline{BA}$, and one side on $\overline{BC}$. He claims that the original problem has been solved. [Hint: Draw a line through P and parallel to $\overline{AC}$])

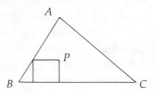

7. Look at the extremes. (In a computational situation, let the numbers get very tiny and very large.)

8. Focus attention on one part of the problem at a time.

9. Ask another student.

It's clear that some of these heuristics may not be useful tactics in the case of certain problems and students will need to be reminded that none of them guarantees success. A "guaranteed successful" stamp on a tactic is a sign that the tactic is really an algorithm and the problem, a type problem.

Are novel problems difficult to find? Not at all. There are numerous sources of novel problems, including professional journals, some curriculum projects, and texts devoted solely to them. But you do have to know what to look for. Here is a sampling of a few different kinds of novel problems.

1. Given a triangle ABC and any point P on $\overline{BC}$, draw a line through P so that triangle ABC will be divided into two regions equal in area. (A construction problem)

2. How can one get the greatest number of cars into a parking lot, permitting access and egress? If one needs to put in still more cars, how can we do it so as to minimize shuffling? (A real-world problem from *Goals for the Correlation of Elementary Science and Mathematics*, 1969.)

3. A teacher prepared a quiz on a stencil, but when she ran the stencil, part of one question did not show up on the copies. Complete the question in as many ways as possible and answer each such question:

    Q5   Let a, b and c represent the sides of a triangle and let $a + b = 7$, $a + c = 9$, and $b + c = 8$. Determine _____ (a reconstruction of an otherwise typical problem).

4. In the product $9 \cdot \text{HATBOX} = 4 \cdot \text{BOXHAT}$, find the 6-digit numbers HATBOX and BOXHAT. (A cryptoarithmetic example from *The Mathematics Student Journal*, November 1964).

5. Mr. Scott, his sister, his son, and his daughter are tennis players. The following facts refer to the people mentioned:

    a. The best player's twin and the worst player are of opposite sex.

    b. The best player and the worst player are the same age. *Which one of the four is the best player?* (from Summers [1968]. *New puzzles in logical deduction*. New York, Dover Publications, Inc.)

Novel problems, then, may belong to recreational mathematics (puzzles, riddles), advanced mathematics (more complex problems on the topic being studied), or applied mathematics (problems from the natural sciences or social sciences). There is a time when each of these kinds of problems serves an instructional purpose. We encourage you to begin collecting such problems in appropriate folders of your resource file. Be sure to organize *within* folders so that novel problems are separated from relevant type problems. You will find selected references to use as a starting point at the end of this chapter and additional references in Chapters 9, 10, and 11.

Planning for Psychomotor Learning

The next type of plan relevant to junior/senior high school teaching is that aimed at instruction in psychomotor skills, the kind of learning that was identified in Chapter 6 as *chaining*. These motor chains are also sometimes called *manipulative skills*. Be alert, future mathematics teachers, to a second meaning assigned to the term *manipulative skills* by some mathematics textbook writers. Often they equate calculation abilities with manipulative skills. We will *never* use the term *manipulation* in that sense.

Refer back to Section 5.3 for a sample of the kinds of psychomotor objectives that might be included in a mathematics teacher's plan. This is also a good time to refresh your memory as to the possible errors made by students drawing circles with compasses for the first time. Now assume that the teacher of a junior high class wants to design instructional strategies on the use of such compasses so as to avoid most of the gross student errors listed in Chapter 5. The teacher makes the following decisions:

1. All students must have identical sturdy compasses, sharpened pencils *not* in the compasses, pieces of cardboard, and looseleaf notebook paper.

2. The teacher will use a pair of demonstration compasses as much like the students' as possible rather than the large board compasses.

3. A demonstration will be performed on the lighted overhead stage or on a sheet taped to the board.

Why are each of the above decisions likely to promote the learning of these particular kinds of psychomotor skills? If either decision 1 or 2 isn't clear, then you've forgotten scenes from your own classroom days. The pencils jammed way up in the holder, the holes in desks, the cheap compasses that would not fix at a given radius, the board compasses whose use differed in major respects from the normal instrument (that is, if you could even manage to draw a circle with it)—all of these deterrents to learning need to be avoided. The value of decision 3 may be unclear if you've never experienced the use of the overhead projector's stage to *project* enlarged images of objects held above or on the stage. There is one problem with this decision. Can you guess what it is? Think of the images of a pencil lying on the stage, then a pencil held so it is vertical to the stage, and, finally, a pencil tilted at an acute angle to the stage. The image of that vertical pencil is a dot, if you can get your hand out of the way. So the teacher will have to practice with the compasses until a reasonably good image is obtained. An eraser on the tip of the sharp point will keep the stage from being scratched.

> **Instructional Strategy Pattern for Psychomotor Skills**
>
> Demonstrate (show how) one step at a time; have students perform each step immediately after the teacher shows each; watch students perform each step and get and give feedback; then show several steps put together; have students do several steps put together; have students practice to get closer approximations of correct performance; then have them practice to increase speed.

How did your draft compare? Did you identify steps such as the way to physically find the correct location for the pencil, the proper placement of the hands on the instrument, the positioning of the other hand on the paper, the proper starting position of the hand, the movement of the hand on the instrument during the drawing? The students would have to be told that the teacher had already performed the first step for them—the sharpening of pencils. Have you figured out why? Just envision 30 seventh-graders lined up at the single pencil sharpener. Chaos! (Since the students will be expected to sharpen their own pencils on other days, the teacher had better devise a routine to avoid a similar mob scene.) The feedback strategies and the use of feedback elicited can make or break this lesson. One of our student teachers was sufficiently concerned about feedback to prepare an audiotape to correspond to her planned demonstration. She found that this freed her to observe student progress more completely. An experienced teacher made a home videotape of the complete demonstration which he was able to show while he gave directions and toured systematically. Segments of the videotape were repeated whenever he observed a common error.

The use of the compasses to generate complex designs may be motivation for some students. Others may get "turned on" by an introduction to mechanical drawing and careers that use these skills. What did you use as a tieback to previous lessons and how did you elect to present a rationale for learning this skill? Pictures, architect's plans, pop art charts, and excerpts from the history of mathematics are possible instructional aids you might use to achieve both a tieback and a look ahead. You should now understand the need for yet *another* kind of material to add to your resource file.

Planning for Attitudes

Reread the definitions of levels I and II of the affective domain and take a second look at the two sample plans in this chapter. If all the planner was after were level I objectives (compliance), the careful instructions before laboratories and the tours during lab work and supervised practice should help to promote this level of affective objective. In addition, both plans indicate places where students may volunteer, perhaps to answer a question or to try a problem identified as "a little stickler." However, these are only first steps toward level II objectives. Both level II and level III affective objectives require attention over time and might not show up in isolated plans. However, over a period of several days, the teacher can include strategies likely to promote positive attitudes towards mathematics. For example, after the lesson on primes and composites, the teacher might suggest that interested students use their library time to find out some further historical background on number patterns that they might share with the class. The teacher might show the students one or two sources that are fun to read and could be borrowed from the teacher at the end of class. Adler's (1972) *Readings in Mathematics* is one possible source. Other students might enjoy the challenge of completing other puzzles related to primes and composites. See the *Aftermath* series or the *Activities for the Hundred Number Board* produced by Creative Publications (for catalogue information, see Chapter 11). In any case, it is important that the teacher follow up the suggestions, behave as if some Ss will have chosen to find out more or try the challenge problems, provide a way for them to share their work with the class and demonstrate the teacher's own enthusiasm for their work. At the same time, if this is to be a real choice, the teacher must not demonstrate negative attitudes toward those who did not choose to go further. Notice how these teacher behaviors and plans match the instructional strategy pattern given next.

Instructional Strategy Pattern for Attitudes

Provide opportunities for voluntary extension activities; facilitate by making initial activities relatively easy to choose; follow up soon after choice was offered and provide opportunity for Ss to share efforts with class; demonstrate enthusiasm for effort; and incorporate results into later lessons.

One of the misconceptions of beginning teachers is the assumption that their enthusiasm for mathematics is sufficient to generate enthusiasm for mathematics among students. Here is another case of a necessary but not sufficient condition. The teacher must, as you can see from the strategy pattern and the illustrations given here, plan strategies at regular intervals throughout the unit to foster positive attitudes toward mathematics. That means considerable homework on the part of the teacher to collect interesting, but not impossible, challenge problems, to identify library sources at the appropriate reading and interest levels, to prepare bulletin boards that pose questions, and so on. It's clear that this is another reason for storing a rich supply of ideas in your resource files.

7.3 PUTTING IT ALL TOGETHER

Just as single plans often contain a mix of concepts and rules, so psychomotor skills are frequently taught in conjunction with some rule. In other words, two or more of the instructional strategy patterns outlined earlier will typically be needed in a single lesson. The teacher must analyze the content to be taught and choose strategy patterns to match each content category. Our students have found it helpful to have all the basic strategy patterns in one place, so we have combined all into one table (Table 7.1) for easy reference.

Events of Instruction Revisited

In Chapter 2 we introduced you to the Events of Instruction in order to explore the feedback relationships implied in that sequence of occurrences. However, this same set of events should be considered a capsule treatment of daily, unit, and course plans. As you study the seven steps listed below, look for connections to planning strategies at *all* levels.

The Events of Instruction

1. Gaining and controlling attention.
2. Informing the student of expected outcomes.
3. Stimulating recall of prerequisites.
4. Presenting the new material.
5. Guiding the new learning.
6. Providing feedback.
7. Appraising performance.

Do events 2 and 3 sound familiar? They have been illustrated in each sample lesson plan and the strategy patterns for each kind of learning. Unit plans and course plans should also be designed in terms of the Events of Instruction. For example, initial lessons and initial units should be high in interest—"gaining and controlling attention"—and subsequent lessons and units dependent on earlier prerequisites can be planned to take less time—"stimulating recall of prerequisites." It should now be clear that the time spanned by each event varies widely. In a daily plan, "informing the student of expected outcomes" may be effectively done in less than two minutes, whereas "presenting the new material" might span 10 to 15 minutes, with part of that time taken up by "guiding the new learning." In the actual implementation of a plan, the events will usually flow smoothly into one another *IF the teacher is able to get the process started*. Gaining and controlling attention, thus, becomes an event of more than passing importance.

Gaining and controlling attention   Some authors refer to this event as motivating the students or "turning them on" to instruction. Whatever it's called, its presence is essential to meaningful learning. Experience convinces us that the teacher must *get attention on the lesson* within the first few minutes of the period—the sooner the better. We're not referring to commands to "Pay attention." The *repeated* occurrence of these are cues that the teacher has failed to get attention *on the lesson*. One of the easiest ways to "turn off kids" is to begin every class in the same way, to conduct routine homework postmortems without concern for feedback, to announce the topic in "big-word mathematics" prior to any concrete experiences.

Table 7.1
Instructional Strategy Patterns for Mathematics Content

Kinds of content outcomes	Examples	Instructional strategy patterns
Vocabulary	Labels of polygon, prime, limit and symbols such as i, $\triangle$	T shows object (or exemplifies idea); then pronounces name and spells on board; students do likewise, repeat (practice), give name; T elicits statement of idea or description of object; T has Ss use in context.
Concepts	Number, prime, greater than, point, locus	T shows differentiated examples and non-examples in sequence; gets essential and non-essential characteristics identified; elicits generalization of the concepts to a variety of specific instances not previously used.
Rules/principles	Square root algorithm, area problems, Congruence proof writing, $T.P. = -b/2a$	T gets Ss to recall/review prerequisites; indicates nature of expected terminal performance; cues (via questions, lab work, applications) Ss to find the pattern by chaining concepts; gets rule stated (by Ss if possible); has Ss demonstrate several instances of the rule in a variety of situations. *Fix and maintain skills by spaced and varied drill.
Novel problem solving	Analysis of novel proofs, puzzles, gambling problems	T presents problem; may Q/A Ss to elicit alternative approaches to solution; T emphasizes desirability of a variety of search strategies; individual work or small group discussions (data collecting, data analysis, making and testing conjectures); T asks Ss to weigh advantages and disadvantages of proposals (and processes) which arose from group discussions and/or individual work.
Psychomotor learning (manipulative skills)	Use of protractor, geoboard, clinometer	T demonstrates (shows how) one step at a time; has Ss do each step immediately after T shows each; T watches Ss perform each step and gets and gives feedback; then T shows several steps put together; has Ss do several steps put together, practice to get closer approximations of correct performance, then practice to increase speed.
Attitude learning	Challenge ex., historical research; search for relevant cartoons	T provides opportunities for voluntary extension activities; facilitates by making initial activities relatively easy to choose; follow up soon after choice was offered and provide opportunity for Ss to share efforts with class; demonstrate enthusiasm for effort; and incorporate results into later lessons.

What does get attention? We've provided you with several examples thus far—the most recent being the demonstrations in the sample concept/vocabulary plan and the use of the overhead to seek patterns in the sample rule plan. Notice that each illustration is highly interwoven with the subsequent strategies and so immediately highlights the lesson, while having potential for sustaining attention beyond the first few minutes of the class. These are the two necessary characteristics of the opening gambit: (1) to get attention focused *on the lesson* and (2) to keep attention focused on the lesson. Can you see why the opening joke by the comedian teacher is likely to get attention, but *not on the lesson*? Teachers who use this ploy often create a monster they can only handle with authoritarian reprimands—not a very promising start to a class, is it? However, sometimes even apparently content-related material does not get attention on the lesson. For example, a junior high teacher decided to teach set union and intersection by having the students place groups of jelly beans inside string loops. To his dismay, most student interest was focused on consumption of the jelly beans. Thus, the "on the lesson" aspect is critical, both as a preventive of undesired student behavior and, more important, as an initiator of learning. Once attention has been focused on the content, keeping attention should follow automatically. Right? It should, but it often doesn't! If the class begins with the presentation of a relevant problem dealing with teenage Olympic stars, the teacher is likely to get attention on the mathematics needed to solve the problem. However, if the problem is dropped and the mathematical rules are presented with no cross-references to the initial problem posed, the potential for keeping attention decreases rapidly.

What kinds of things do usually elicit student attention? The following categories have proved consistently useful:

1.   An unfamiliar, puzzling or unusual event or idea.

2.   A familiar object (circumstance) behaving in an unfamiliar way.

3.   Materials or activities with high sensory appeal (the use of color, sound, or touch, for example, or a combination of these).

4.   The use of materials or circumstances matched to the students' "here-and-now" interests.

5.   The use of materials or circumstances corresponding to applications in other school subjects or in the nonschool world, where these applications have potential for students' "here-and-now" interests.

In the preceding chapters, as well as in earlier sections of this one, each of these has been illustrated. The use of labels from soup cans to introduce the surface area of a cylinder is another example of a familiar object being used in an unfamiliar way and a material with sensory appeal. The fifth category is a corollary to the fourth one. However, the fifth category must be applied with discretion. For example, if none of the students take industrial arts, there's not much interest potential in an introductory problem based on that subject.

Similarly, income tax forms are rarely of any concern to the adolescent who will not fill out a real one for several years.

What *are* some major "here-and-now" interests of students? The following list contains a sample of interests obtained from the only reliable source, junior/senior high students themselves.

Students' here-and-now interests

Acceptance by peers	Computer games	Music	Ten-speed bikes
Acne	College admissions	Pets	Telephoning
Alcohol	Hobbies	Sex (opposite)	Tobacco
Automobiles	Money	Sports	Video games and
Body (*theirs*)	Movies		shows

Your own students will help you add to this list if you listen. Where can you find source materials related to these areas of interest? Check the local and school newspapers, *Popular Mechanics*, professional journals, and source books, plus all the many other resources identified in Chapters 9, 10, 11.

One final piece of advice before we leave the topic of daily lesson plans. Write post-mortem comments on each *immediately* after implementing them in an actual classroom situation. Revise time estimates, make notes on what worked particularly well, and earmark any section in need of repair while the experience is fresh in your mind. Our student teachers who have followed this practice report that it pays big dividends when they teach the same lessons to other classes of students. They have advised us to urge you to form this habit. Consider yourself urged.

7.4 LONG-RANGE PLANNING

As we have already seen, day-to-day planning is vital to success. But isn't long-range planning also a very important part of the teacher's task? It most certainly is if the daily lessons are to fit together into a meaningful whole. In fact, logic would seem to dictate blocking out plans for the entire year-long course first, next developing the more specific treatments to be given each of the major sequential subcomponents to fit within that overall frame of reference, and then finally working out the details of each daily lesson. Yet we are directing your attention to these levels of planning in the reverse sequence. Why? Our experience has been that novice teachers find long-range planning both a hopeless and meaningless task until they have first acquired some experience in designing and implementing daily lessons—another example of how learning most often follows psychological rather than logical principles.

Unit Planning

After a couple of weeks of experience with planning and implementing daily lessons, you should be ready to try your hand at the next step—blocking out plans for the next unit. By a *unit* we mean a *major topic that will occupy approximately*

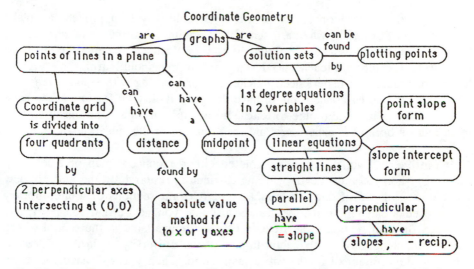

Fig. 7.8   Part of a concept map on coordinate geometry. *Permission granted by David Laiosa.

two to four weeks of instructional time. One full-year course is typically composed of a sequence of eight to twelve such units.

Recall the Resource File modular assignment we asked you to begin in Chapter 4. At that time we directed you to select one unit as a point of departure for building a file of teaching ideas that would serve as a base for future plans. Obviously, you need to fill other folders (as directed in that assignment) prior to starting plans for additional units because these materials will constitute the idea base for future instructional strategies. Also recall the Learning Hierarchy and the Concept Mapping assignments given in Chapter 6. These assignments provided experience in both (1) identifying major objectives expected of all students, or concepts to be learned by all and (2) analyzing the interdependent relationships among parts of a major topic. Since there is not time to teach all possible aspects of a unit topic, selectivity is essential. In addition, prerequisite concepts must be introduced prior to the point at which related principles/rules and their applications are taught.

Concept maps   If a novice teacher has already prepared either a learning hierarchy or a concept map for a unit, then much of the task of getting acquainted with the scope and emphasis of the unit has been done. Study Figure 7.8, a concept map prepared by a student teacher, David Laiosa, for a unit on coordinate geometry. It is clear that considerable thinking went into the arrangement and relationships pictured on this concept map. He found it a particularly valuable way to analyze the unit before he began to student teach. The concept map also served as a point of departure for David and his cooperating teacher. Now individual plans and the sequence of strategies within plans could be considered in the light of the concepts he had associated on the map.

We believe that concept maps are a valuable way to approach the planning of a unit, especially when a teacher is beginning a unit never taught before. However, until schools and school schedules are redesigned, it would be unrealistic to expect a full-time teacher to design concept maps and learning hierarchies for every unit. Some experienced teachers, after working with student teachers who have completed concept maps, have designed their own for units they have found particularly troublesome to teach. In our opinion, this is an excellent way to reflect on both your experience and the structure of the subject matter.

Unit outlines   If you have not completed either a concept map or a learning hierarchy, then you must begin by doing curriculum research on the unit. Review the course syllabus, if one is available, and relevant sections of contemporary books used as student texts. We do suggest that you go beyond the particular text used in your school. Other texts are typically available at the school where you are teaching, in the curriculum library of the university, or in the offices of the state department of mathematics instruction. Then you will have the same background as the designer of either a concept map or a learning hierarchy.

Next, you will need to prepare a *topic* outline, in which you build in a potential sequencing scheme. You consider the first such outline as a draft that should be modified as you rethink ideas and begin to consider relative emphasis of subtopics and ways to relate particular topics to one another. Word processing packages are particularly handy in this kind of endeavor.

The second stage in moving from a topic outline to a unit plan involves allocating the available time and listing some initial planning ideas. You will need to block out projected time allotments for parts of the outline. Next, you should begin to list (by descriptive title) potentially useful labs, demos, films, field trips, homework assignments, bulletin board ideas, and the like from your resource file. If the "cupboard is bare" for some topics, you will have to dig into the sources suggested in Chapters 9, 10 and 11 to fill these voids. Otherwise, the unit plan will *not* serve its intended purpose of providing an adequate base for more detailed day-to-day planning. Projecting time estimates is always a problem for the novice, and there is no use in pretending that there is any substitute for the experience of having taught the unit several times to varying groups of students. However, the problem must be faced squarely by every novice, and we can make suggestions that will alleviate the task to some extent. Attempt to identify topics that are either extensions or modifications of ideas previously presented. These, along with content ideas familiar to students as a result of extensive experience outside of school, can be assigned shorter instructional time than totally new work. Longer time periods should be planned for new ideas that will provide a base for more sophisticated notions to occur in future units.

Arrange the unit plan in three columns as shown in the partially completed sample of a unit plan on Systems of Equations for Ninth-Grade Algebra (Figure 7.9). Column 1 lists topics in the sequence determined by the teacher while column 2 contains the estimated number of instructional periods to be devoted

Unit 5: SYSTEMS OF EQUATIONS
NINTH-GRADE ALGEBRA

Topics	Time estimates in days	Learning activities
A. Algebraic solution of two first-degree equations		Bulletin Board—"Peanuts" problems (A-BB #1)
1. Addition/subtraction	3	Demo—box with red & blue marbles— problem situation (A-D #2)
2. Substitution	2	Demo—Dienes blocks in illus. $+,-$ (A-D #31) Problem cards HW from Sci. & Bell's *Everyday World* (A-P #3-10)
B. Graphic solution of two first-degree equations and inequalities		Bulletin board of Howard Johnson problem (B-BB #2) Lab with springs and weights (B-L #2)
1. Equalities	2	Demo with acetates (B-OH #1-5)
2. Inequalities	2	Problems from newspapers (B-C #3)
C. Solution of two second or one second- and one first-degree equation		
1. _____	___	Filmstrip on fishery work (C-F #3)
2. _____	___	

Fig. 7.9 Part of a unit plan.

to each topic. Column 3 contains the gold-mine entries, selected instructional resources from the teacher's resource file described in a phrase as well as by a coded entry. The phrase provides immediate information for the reader and the coded entry (for example, A-BB #1 for the first [Ath] folder of the unit, the first bulletin board item) shortens the retrieval time as the teacher moves from the unit plan to daily plans. (Computer-wise teachers will recognize the importance of filing as many of your resource ideas as possible on computer disks.) You should provide your cooperating teacher with copies of (1) the unit plan and (2) all the related resources identified in the learning activities column. Schedule a conference after your cooperating teacher has had time to review these materials but far enough in advance of the time when you must begin developing the first few daily plans of the unit. At least several days of lead time are desirable. Heed the advice given and ask questions to help in thinking through various possible approaches. Examine further learning activities which may be suggested, talk out potential problems which may arise, and discuss details which might be added or deleted, in case time requirements deviate from those projected. Having done all this, you are bound to feel much more confident in developing detailed day-to-day plans, and smooth transitions within the unit will be more easily achieved.

As in the case of daily lesson plans, notes to yourself written on the unit plan as implementation proceeds will prove valuable in future years.

We advocate treating the final topic outline as a guide and source of stimulation for your own thinking rather than as a requirement to be followed blindly. Experience convinces us that the final outline must make maximum sense to you, the teacher, if it is to serve as a frame of reference for daily lessons which will make sense to your students.

Course Planning

Speaking of years, 365 days does seem like a lot of time. But is it, in terms of how many full periods of 40 to 50 minutes are actually available for instruction? State regulations, school calendars, and administrators frequently refer to a 180± day school year. (This figure takes into account weekends, various holidays, and summer vacation periods when school is not in session.) Does this mean one should plan a course based on the assumption of 180 full periods available for instruction in new content? Not quite. Further time reductions must be planned to account for realities such as the half-days of school before major holidays, standardized tests that all of your eighth graders must take during your math class, public address system announcements that interrupt your class, assembly programs during class time, and mass illnesses during the winter flu season. Your own schedule of tests/quizzes and related activities will also deduct from time available for instruction in new content. It is reasonable to assume that 8 to 10 full-period tests and 25 to 35 quizzes (10 to 20 minutes each) will be given during the year. These are essential uses of instructional time, but is it really defensible to add fuel to this fire by routinely coupling a full-period review and a half-period post-mortem to each of the big tests? Review the recommendations in Chapter 2 and 8 aimed at minimizing these problems.

So much for the myth of the 180 day school year! We have found 140 periods a much more realistic target when planning a year-long course. Eight units would thus *average* about 17 full class periods each. Obviously some could take longer, but you would then have to compensate with less time for others in the long-range plans.

Course planning schema   Is a course plan, then, merely a list of unit plans designed to fit within a 140 day school year? There are basic flaws in that approach even when each individual unit has been thoughtfully designed. Yes, sequencing may be out of whack, interconnections may be ignored, and mindless redundancy may take the place of meaningful spiraling. There's only one way to avoid these disasters and that way begins with a thorough study of all available course materials. We recommend that you commit to paper the five to ten *major* instructional objectives of the course. If your list exceeds ten statements, you may be including some less important objectives or ignoring the dependency of one objective on another. When you're satisfied that your list emphasizes the core of the course

(Did you include processes as well as products of mathematics?), sketch in a simple learning hierarchy among just those five to ten major objectives. Don't worry if interconnections are rare. You may have identified several distinct and relatively independent terminal objectives. These statements, then, would become the uppermost objectives in a vast learning hierarchy. Next, match the topics, into which you had previously subdivided the course, with the objectives. If interconnections are missing here, go back to the drawing board. Finally, estimate the number of days to be assigned to each topic on the basis of (1) the relative contribution of each unit to the objectives, (2) the location of each unit in the sequence, and (3) the presumed range of student intellectual development. One teacher, Ms. Aronowitz, developed this kind of course outline for tenth-grade geometry. She wrote five major course objectives.

1. Construct a synthetic argument of a proof, given hypotheses from the major topic areas of plane geometry.

2. State generalizations in "If, then" form, given experiences reflecting a pattern.

3. Evaluate an argument (geometric or nongeometric) as to its match to deductive logic, its precision, and rigor.

4. Calculate measures (linear, angular, circular, area, volume) given data and relationships, diagrammatic or written, from which to obtain further data and/or rules.

5. Analyze the relationships between real-world phenomena and corresponding mathematical models from geometry.

Then she matched the five objectives to the eight unit areas into which she had previously divided the course (see Figure 7.10). Notice the subdivisions under "Lines, planes, angles" and "Congruence." Constructions are listed under both unit topics, and coordinate geometry under unit topic 1. Subdivisions still must be added to the remaining units. The first two units were further synthesized by the addition of topic sentences. The beginning of proof considerations will be the focus of unit 1—for example, distinctions between assumption and theorem and between a geometric proof and a rationalization based on many experiences. However, the writing of synthetic arguments will be left for unit 2. That's also depicted by the growing width *and* length of the arrow associated with objective 1. Why does that arrow stop short of topic 8? Ms. Aronowitz is following well-established practice in eliminating this topic from those in which students will have to be able to write proofs. In like manner, each of the other arrows representing objectives identified the units in which that objective will be given explicit attention. See if you can follow Ms. Aronowitz's thinking here. The curved arrows connecting unit topics are other indicators of sequence. However, these represent the axiomatic links inherent in the connected topics rather than strands or overarching themes. "Parallelism" and "Area of polygons" both contain essential prerequisites to the proofs of the basic similarity theorems in the

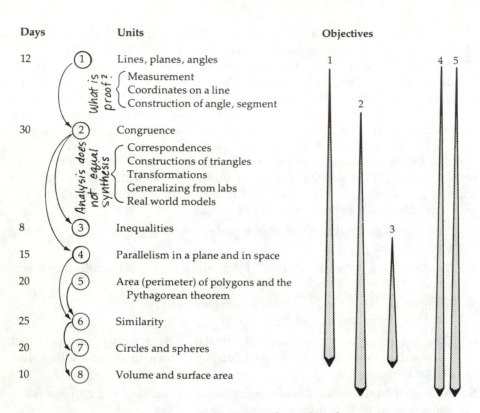

Fig. 7.10   A course planning schema for tenth grade geometry.

sequence being followed by Ms. Aronowitz so two curved arrows lead from unit topics 4 and 5 to topic 6. Each of the other curved links has a like reason for existing and, of course, multiple other links are possible. But this teacher envisioned these as the major hierarchical connections which she should emphasize. A thorough grasp of the subject matter of geometry is clearly essential.

Now turn to the time allotments for each unit. Why were some planned for as little as 8 days while others were given as much as 30 days? Ms. Aronowitz identified "congruence" as the initial key to proof—the time to involve students in many concrete experiences, to build on the concepts and principles introduced in unit 1, and to develop the writing of simple synthetic arguments. On the other hand, "inequalities" would be built on prerequisites from other courses. The novel aspect would be the introduction of the indirect method of proof that would then become a strand throughout successive units. Other time allotments were arrived at by this kind of balancing of sequence, prerequisites, extent of novelty, and nature of objectives. There is nothing sacrosanct about these figures. They represent the best thinking of this teacher. As always, feedback during instruction may result in some differences between the actual and estimated times.

Such information should be recorded and appropriate modifications made for future years. But any change must continue to reflect the conceptual framework designed by the teacher.

Now reflect on your own reactions to this particular overall course-planning guide. Does it provide a frame of reference for planning the sequence of the units it subsumes? Does it represent an accurate view of contemporary geometry and yet have high potential relevance for tenth-grade students? Are interrelationships among ideas within and across units clarified? We answered yes to all these questions after studying the fully completed schema. Further, we judged it to have excellent potential for its intended purpose. Does this mean that this specific schema is *the correct one* to use for a tenth-grade geometry course? No, we would make no such claim—only that it ought to be a highly usable one for the person who created the schema and could implement it effectively.

7.5 SUMMARY AND SELF-CHECK

In this synthesis of all the previous chapters, we presented strategy patterns for vocabulary, concept, rule/principle, novel problem-solving, psychomotor and attitude planning. Sample daily plans were analyzed both in terms of the related strategy patterns and the earlier work on objectives, modes, feedback, adolescent reasoning, research on human learning, and the structure of mathematics. In addition, the unique characteristics and problems of lessons involving vocabulary, type word problems, and proof were outlined. Then, the sequence of the *events of instruction* were reconsidered with particular emphasis on getting and keeping attention. Finally, we turned from daily planning to guidelines for constructing unit and course plans.

Now you should be able to:

1. Operationally define instructional strategy.

2. Describe in sequence, the major steps in the strategy patterns for vocabulary, concept, rule/principle, novel problem solving, psychomotor and attitude instruction.

3. Analyze a set of type word problems from an algebra course in terms of the level of translation skills required to solve them by means of equation(s).

4. Distinguish between the strategies essential for teaching type word problem solving and those essential for the teaching of novel problem solving and identify the bases for the differences.

5. Identify the kind and quantity of "foreign" mathematical language used by the teacher in a "live" or video-taped lesson.

6. Describe the use of 3–4 heuristics that might be useful in a novel problem solving lesson.

7. Write a daily plan for a lesson in your major teaching field which corresponds in format to the plan outline, and in structure to the strategy patterns

appropriate to the content, as well as to all components of the instructional model treated in the first six chapters.

8. Critique both a unit plan and a course plan for correspondence to the characteristics of sequence, time estimates, and use of resources.

9. Write a unit plan and a course plan that correspond to the sample outlines in this chapter *if you have taught*, and justify the choices of topic, sequence, and timing made.

10. Critique the opening five minutes in a "live" or canned lesson for its attention-getting and -keeping potential.

11. Design an "attention getter" for any given lesson and outline its projected use throughout the lesson.

The next section contains exercises related to some of these objectives and simultaneously provides additional samples of instructional activities.

7.6 SIMULATION/PRACTICE ACTIVITIES

A. The Introductory Activity of this chapter included a partially inadequate response to a quiz question. You were asked to critique that response. Now compare your judgments against Tony's more adequate response to the same question. Tony's two objectives were just rephrasings of those written by Mary, but here is his sequence of modes:

Tony's response to the sequence of modes portion of the question

1. Do a demo of the ruler lab with the assistance of two Ss.

2. Divide Ss into groups and have them perform the lab.

3. Have small groups record data on board.

4. Have Ss in small groups discuss optimum way(s) to display total class data.

5. Ask group leaders to report on consensus and use Q/A and lecture to reach a decision.

6. Have each S graph data.

After identifying the favorable characteristics of Tony's response, reread the objectives and compare his response with the objectives. What else would you add in order to match the instruction to the objectives?

B. Construct a lesson plan designed to introduce junior high or senior high mathematics students to one or more concept(s) and/or rule(s). Be sure to check your choice of topic with your instructor.

C. Write an **analysis** of the proof of an "original" theorem from high school geometry. Then write a **synthetic** proof of the same theorem in both paragraph and two-column format. Compare all three versions.

D. Consult sources of problem-solving material for problems that could be used for a lesson on novel problem solving at the junior high level, in an elementary algebra class, or a senior high geometry class. Two excellent references are:

Krulik, S. (Ed.). (1980). *Problem solving in school mathematics*. (1980 Yearbook). Reston, VA: National Council of Teachers of Mathematics.

and

Bushaw, D., Bell, M., Pollak, H.O., Thompson, M. & Usiskin, Z. (Eds.). (1980). *A sourcebook of applications of school mathematics*. Reston, VA: National Council of Teachers of Mathematics.

E.   Locate four articles in recent issues of *Mathematics Teacher* and *Arithmetic Teacher*, in which the authors suggest approaches to instruction on some secondary school concept or rule. Write reviews of all four articles. Be sure to give attention to the extent to which the suggested approaches seem to match the instructional strategy patterns in this chapter, correspond to the probable reasoning levels of the students, and emphasize the structure of the mathematics model.

F.   Design a problem suitable for initiating a novel problem-solving lesson based on the information below:

In Raleigh, N.C., rats have been found able to survive 2 1/2 to 6 times the normal killing dose of a commonly used rat poison. Apparently a genetic trait is involved. In Scotland about half the farms have rats, and 40 percent of them are resistant to this same poison. (*The New York Times*, October 17, 1971.)

G.   Outline way(s) in which each set of objects in column 2 might be used to *get* attention on the corresponding topic in column 1.

Column 1	*Column 2*
(A) Fractions—Grade 7	(a) Sections of colored egg cartons and pebbles
(B) Sine curve—Algebra 2	(b) Tuning fork and clarinet
(C) Motion problems—Algebra 1	(c) Toy car, inclined plane, stopwatch
(D) Alternate interior angles, given parallel lines—Geometry	(d) Periscope
(E) Slope—Algebra 1	(e) Videotape on local ski slopes
(F) Ratio—Grade 8	(f) Music box with gears showing

SUGGESTIONS FOR FURTHER STUDY

Fremont, H. (1969). *How to teach mathematics in secondary schools*. Philadelphia: Saunders.

We highly recommend Chapters 6–20 of this well-written text. These chapters are a rich source of ideas for getting and keeping attention as well as for introducing and developing concepts and rules in mathematics. Both experienced and novice secondary school mathematics teachers have found this book to be a gold mine that seems to be replenished on return visits. What higher praise is there?!

Lindquist, M. M. (Ed.) (1987). *Learning and teaching geometry, K–12* (1987 Yearbook). Reston, VA: National Council of Teachers of Mathematics.

This yearbook is particularly recommended for chapters that include examples of novel problem solving, emphasize visualization, or provide examples of the application of geometry to other fields. The chapter by M. A. Farrell, *Geometry for Secondary School Teachers*, includes a part of a lesson on the analysis of geometric constructions, as well as a thinking aloud excerpt during a proof-analysis lesson.

NCTM. (1970). *The teaching of secondary school mathematics*. Washington, DC: NCTM.

Several chapters of this yearbook are especially useful in the planning of lessons. Chapter 10, "Generalizations," and Chapter 11, "Skills," include specific problem material and suggestions for use in lessons. In Chapter 10 there are multiple connections to our earlier work on the processes of mathematics and an excellent section on the use of target tasks. Chapter 11 includes several examples of practice sets designed to promote retention and transfer. In addition, you are directed to the material in Chapters 12–15 in which planning ideas for arithmetic, algebra, and geometry are illustrated. Above all, don't miss the superior classroom tactics described in Chapter 16, "An Example of Planning for Low Achievers."

Polya, G. (1962). *Mathematical discovery* (Vol. 1). New York: John Wiley and Sons.

The subtitle of this book is "On understanding, learning, and teaching problem solving," and that subtitle tells it all. Yes, Polya is referring to *novel* problem solving, albeit of the purely mathematical variety, rather than the real-world correspondences. Polya emphasizes seeking patterns, making conjectures, and testing these systematically. You must become a problem solver yourself as you work through his insightful and challenging questions. A note to the less confident: Answers are provided!

Sawyer, W. W. (1964). *Vision in elementary mathematics*. Baltimore, MD: Penguin Books.

This valuable paperback has been suggested in earlier chapters. It is included again in this chapter for its illustrations of stages of translation—iconic, English language and symbolic applied to problems in pre-college mathematics.

Souviney, R. J. (1981). *Solving problems kids care about*. Santa Monica, CA: Goodyear Pub. Co.

Souviney extends the instructional strategies considered in our text and gives explicit instructions for using groups to work on problem solving. Included in the text are reproducible problem-starter sheets, and a complete analysis of each problem, the approaches the teacher might take and the solution. Problems titles include *Tooth Truths, Cow Thoughts, Hamburger Heaven, The Bicycle Dilemma* and others sure to provoke student interest.

CHAPTER EIGHT

EVALUATION OF INSTRUCTION

The Proof of the Pudding

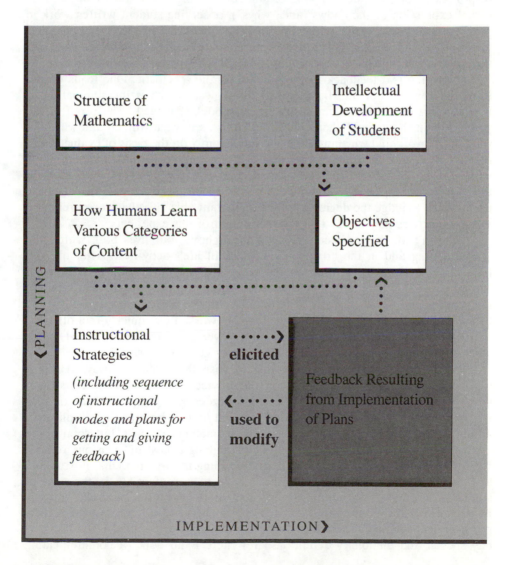

Structure of Mathematics

Intellectual Development of Students

How Humans Learn Various Categories of Content

Objectives Specified

PLANNING

Instructional Strategies

(including sequence of instructional modes and plans for getting and giving feedback)

elicited

used to modify

Feedback Resulting from Implementation of Plans

IMPLEMENTATION

Yes, we are again back to the feedback box portion of the instructional model! Our previous treatment of this aspect in Chapter 2 focused on the minute-to-minute and day-to-day concerns of instruction. The emphasis was on getting data on which to base immediate decisions such as whether to speed up, slow down, stop, provide more or varying examples, or present a concept in a different way. Similarly, we explored ways and means of providing learners with information on their progress toward attainment of the objectives set for today's lesson, last night's assignment, or yesterday's laboratory exercise. Much dependence was placed on quick and informal means to these ends—spreading oral responses among a wide sampling of students, taking straw votes (followed by verbal expression of the "hows" and "whys"), observing student written work in progress, and giving verbal praise for correct answers and productive approaches to problems. All of this background is prerequisite to the longer-range view and the more formal means of assessment to which we now turn our attention.

Note the two feedback loops depicted on the schematic. One leads to and from the key component "Instructional Strategies," which is the summation of the planning dimension of the instructional model. If indeed "The proof of the pudding is in the eating," then crucial decisions as to what worked and why, and what didn't work and why must be made intelligently on the basis of evaluation of results. Then and only then are we in a position to redesign instructional inputs with realistic hopes of improved success. Similarly, the other feedback loop to the "Objectives Specified" component points to the need for a firm data base upon which to judge the degree to which important objectives have been realized. Initial objectives may need to be revised in light of this experience.

Haven't all of you been evaluated throughout your lives both within the school setting and in the broader context of all life's activities? After all, you have spent a good bit of time on the receiving end during some 16 years of formal schooling. Shouldn't this experience equip you to deal with the topic on the sending end of the process? Without a doubt, you do bring some background to the task. Student teachers with whom we've worked can quickly reel off a list of ineffective techniques and practices. However, they are frequently at a loss when asked to provide the remedy: examples of good models.

Moreover, there is no sense trying to wish the problems away. Within a week to ten days of student teaching, the novice teacher typically constructs, administers, and scores one or two short quizzes. By the end of three or four weeks of student teaching, a full-period test will have to be prepared, duplicated, administered, and scored. These tasks are formidable enough, but soon come even tougher jobs—interpreting results and making a host of decisions regarding future instruction, mid-marking period warning reports, remedial instruction, and marking-period grades. All of these have to be defensible in the eyes of students, parents, school administrators, and, most important, yourself! You will hear claims that the test wasn't "objective." A parent who is an ex-teacher may question its "validity." These and other bits of jargon are abused in both everyday speech and dictionary definitions. Yet there is no hope of communicating feedback to students, parents, or administrators without some clear understanding of the language associated with the topic of evaluation. The next section provides you with the background for the understanding of several relevant terms. It is up to you to communicate that understanding to those who receive the results of evaluation.

8.1 EVALUATION VERSUS TESTING

Evaluation and *testing* are often used synonymously but, in fact, they refer to closely related but distinct processes. The root word *value* is clearly central to the concept of evaluation. Thus, by *evaluation* we mean *any process of making judgments against selected criteria as to the worth of things or ideas, based on relevant data.* Relevant data? That's where the notion of testing comes in. *Testing* will be used to label *any procedure designed to collect evidence that indicates degree of attainment of objectives.* Note that we do not limit testing to paper-and-pencil instruments and that the results of testing are not viewed as evaluations but rather as data upon which judgments (evaluations) will be based. For example, Jill's record shows percentage scores of 85, 99, 80, 76, and 92 on a set of written tests/quizzes over a ten- week period, but the 85 refers to a pretest given prior to instruction on the unit. As a result of that score, Jill was placed in the group of students who were to work on individualized learning activity packages. All of the remaining scores were attained on quizzes or tests administered after certain periods of instruction. How should her teacher evaluate these data for purposes of deciding her report card grade? If your response is, "I can't tell because you still haven't told me all of the criteria against which to judge these data," you are catching a good part of the idea.

Jill's first test was given for purposes of *diagnostic evaluation. Diagnostic evaluation* is *characterized by one of two purposes: (1) to place a student at the proper instructional starting point or (2) to find out the causes of instructional defects that have been isolated during instruction.* So Jill's score on the pretest would not properly be included in the data her teacher is evaluating for purposes of reporting a grade. Jill's teacher had administered the second type of diagnostic quiz to a group in the class who had been making repeated errors on three of the rules in the unit. By including diverse examples at varied levels of rule application, the teacher had tried to pinpoint the *causes* of the errors. Should these scores be included in the report card evaluation? Absolutely not! However, each of Jill's other scores will be included in some fashion (more on that in the next section!) in the final evaluation. Thus, all of these test scores will serve the purpose of *summative evaluation, the use of data to make judgments as to the extent to which instructional objectives have been achieved by the students.* All final course exams fall in the category of testing solely for the purpose of summative evaluation. Regardless of error patterns now identified by the teacher, instruction is over and these data cannot be used to affect the instruction of that group of students (see Figure 8.1). Such data can and should be used to plan instruction for future students in this course. A third kind of evaluation, *formative evaluation*, is regularly

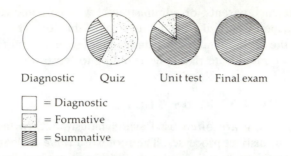

Diagnostic   Quiz   Unit test   Final exam

☐ = Diagnostic
▨ = Formative
▧ = Summative

Fig. 8.1   Relative emphasis on the three kinds of evaluation in various types of tests.

used in systematic instruction. The chief purpose of *formative evaluation* is *to assess the extent to which progress is being made on the instructional objectives and to identify those objectives that need further instructional attention.* Note that data from a short quiz serves two purposes: summative and formative evaluation. So does data from a unit test, but the emphasis from such data is now primarily on summative evaluation. The circle graphs in Figure 8.1 depict this changed evaluative emphasis as one moves from quiz to unit test to final exam. (The sectors in these graphs should not be interpreted as exact matches to the evaluation emphasis in any particular test/quiz. They should be thought of as representing a ball-park figure.) Notice the small sectors designated as diagnostic evaluation in both the quiz and unit test circle graphs. Although these kinds of tests are not *constructed* so as to discover causes of known errors, data from them sometimes yield this kind of information. You will be making judgments based on data gathered for all three types of evaluation. Knowing the what, when, and why of the process is a paramount aspect of those judgments.

Objective vs. Subjective and Reliable vs. Valid

Another commonly expressed concern is to what extent the data gathered on the written tests were objective as opposed to subjective. *Objective* literally means that *no judgment entered into the process.* We take the position that no quiz or test could possibly meet this definition! Why? Didn't someone have to *decide* (judge) such matters as (1) which questions to include, (2) how to phrase the questions, (3) the answer or range of acceptable responses, (4) the credit value of each item, and (5) the time limit for responding to the test? Thus we will not speak of objective tests or of objective test items. It seems more honest to refer to *objectively scored test items* as *those that would be scored identically by anyone using the same answer key.* Similarly, *subjectively scored test items are those that are constructed to allow judgment of the rater to enter into the scoring process.* A word of caution is in order at this point. Do not automatically equate "objectively scored" with "good" testing technique nor "subjectively scored" with "poor" testing technique. The nature of the subject matter at stake and the particular kinds of objectives being assessed help determine which approach makes the most sense.

But don't objectively scored items lead to increased test reliability? Generally. However, let's not fall into the trap of confusing reliability with validity. *Reliability is the extent to which a test yields repeatable results* (tells a consistent story) whereas *validity is the extent to which a test measures what it is supposed to measure* (tells the truth). Assume that a manufacturer inadvertently produced a batch of metric rulers 11 cm long which were each calibrated into 100 equal segments labeled mm and 10 equal segments marked cm. Skillful students using these devices would get consistent (reliable) but incorrect (invalid) measurements! Obviously we want both valid *and* reliable tests so that the data they produce can be trusted as a base for educational decision making. Fortunately for us, it turns out that highly valid tests typically turn out to yield respectable reliability. (Warning: the reverse is *not* true!) How does one insure validity? Obtaining a close match of well-structured test items to carefully specified objectives is the best way to achieve content validity. It is with this last task in mind that we direct your attention to the Introductory Activity that follows.

8.2 INTRODUCTORY ACTIVITY

Step right up and take a chance!

Test taking shouldn't resemble a carnival game of chance but, sadly, it sometimes does. Very often, this is due to poorly constructed test items. This activity places you in the role of a critic of a set of such test items. Assume that clear directions on the recording of responses have been given but that each item in the following set is defective in some way—for example, might be incorrectly answered by capable students or might be correctly answered by poor students who guess well. For each item, identify the defect(s) and rewrite the item so as to eliminate the problem(s).

Selected items from a Math 8 test

Completion

1. A line segment joining two points on a circle is _____ .

2. _____ circles are those with the same _____ and unequal _____ .

Multiple choice

11. The area of a triangle with a base of 4 and an altitude to the base of 2 is
    (1) 16   (2) 2   (3) 4   (4) 8

12. A polygon with all sides congruent is called

    (1) equiangular   (2) equilateral
    (3) regular   (4) a square

True-false

16. π is equal to 3.14.

17. Certain line segments containing the center of a circle sometimes divide a circle into two semicircles.

After you have completed your analysis of these items, compare your corrected versions with those produced by another student. Then check on your thinking as you interact with the material in the next section.

8.3 ASSESSMENT OF COGNITIVE OBJECTIVES

The first objectives you will encounter in assessment situations in student teaching will be those belonging to the cognitive domain. For better or worse, this kind of outcome is what schools emphasize above all others. Further, the means of assessing these are often limited almost exclusively to paper-and-pencil instruments called quizzes and tests. This doesn't need to be the case, since there are several other ways to gather evidence of achievement of this kind of objective. More importantly, this shouldn't be the case if processes of mathematics, other than procedural knowledge, are to be emphasized. Furthermore, it shouldn't be the case if the teacher wishes to collect the kind of data in either diagnostic or formative evaluation that represents the best promise for improving instruction. If the collected data includes information on students' strategies, error patterns, or the rationale for the application of a procedure, the teacher will have specific evidence on which to individualize instruction and to improve instruction for the larger group. Thus, although we devote considerable attention to paper-and-pencil tests as an ongoing and important part of assessment, we first turn our attention to the more qualitative types of assessment, represented by tasks other than paper-and-pencil tests.

Assessment Other Than by Paper-and-Pencil Tests

Ability to communicate mathematics by constructing and translating physical, visual, and symbolic representations is one of the processes emphasized in Chapter 4 of this text. This same ability has been emphasized more recently on a national level by the writers of the *Curriculum and Evaluation Standards for School Mathematics* (1987). This ability is just one example of the kind of competency that might be assessed by tasks other than paper-and-pencil. Data for assessment of this particular ability might be obtained by systematic observation of groups of students working on a problem solving task with manipulatives or by sampling their audiotaped explanations of a representation they have built. Data could be recorded in a simple anecdotal report for each student with such reports stored in a computer file. Anecdotal reports are just that—comments about observed student behavior—with the date and lesson type or objectives recorded. Recall the checkers lab that was used in the sample lesson plan on the concepts of prime and composite in Chapter 7. Teacher observation of student work with the checkers might later lead to comments, such as the following:

Barry seemed to have great trouble in moving from the checkers problem to the generalizations. He continued to build checker piles for each number in the list even though his partner suggested shortcuts.

or

Eileen generalized very fast. After she had built checker piles for the first three numbers, she told her partner she was going to complete the rest of the sheet and just check later by building the piles.

It should be obvious that these students stood out because of the quality of their behavior. The teacher cannot expect to collect sufficient data to write anecdotal records for each student in class after a single lesson. However, over time, the entire class should be sampled and data recorded. Gross judgments of student progress could be recorded in a grade book type format, by symbols such as $+\sqrt{}$ or $-\sqrt{}$. This kind of data collection can be completed more quickly than the anecdotal reports, but does not provide the teacher with specifics for later use in diagnosis and future instruction. A combination of assessment types should be considered when evaluating complex behaviors.

Oral reports of library research can be presented and assessed on a written critique sheet. It is important to let the students know, ahead of time, the criteria on which they will be assessed and to share the written critique with them after the oral reports have been completed. The criteria in this case might include: evidence of thoroughness of the library study, and organization and clarity of the oral report. Similarly, written reports on take-home labs and in-class projects can be assigned and analyzed for evidence of learning. Moreover, don't the actual products produced in laboratory work and bulletin board design sessions yield relevant data? Also consider the potential use of anecdotal records made by the teacher as students participate in question/answer, small-group discussion, inter-active computer sessions, supervised practice, and laboratory work.

In Chapter 1, a list of topics suitable for a research paper in mathematics was provided. In Chapter 5, one of the objectives found in Section 5.6, Exercise B, referred to the writing of a "story" using mathematical concepts correctly, given a topic sentence such as "I dreamed I was a point in a non-Euclidean plane." These types of written work provide data that are rich in potential for assessing progress toward higher level cognitive objectives. Again the teacher must be sure neither to ignore the extent to which grammar and spelling are correct, nor to allow these two components to overshadow the correct use of mathematical relationships. Illustrative examples of other non-paper-and-pencil tasks were provided in Chapter 1. For further help on ways of deriving assessment data from such tasks, see the Suggestions for Further Study at the end of this chapter.

Types of Paper-and-Pencil Items

In the following section, we consider each of five types of short response items and the essay, or long response, item-type. In each case a set of clear directions to students must be our first concern, since we have to be sure that the answers reflect an understanding of the content being tested rather than the students' skill in guessing the nature of the task. Ambiguous directions not only promote undesirable guessing, but also frequently confound the teacher's work when the completed tests are being scored. Yet one of the major advantages of short response items is supposed to be ease and speed of scoring. Therefore, we will begin our consideration of each item-type by providing you with good models of directions. We suggest that you type each model direction on a separate card for inclusion in your resource file. Second, we will list a set of sample items, but these will be a mixed bag of acceptable and defective items that you will be asked to analyze with the help of some cues. Advantages and disadvantages inherent in the item-type under consideration will be treated next. Finally, some "rules of thumb" to follow when constructing the item-type will be suggested.

True-false   Most test construction experts classify this item-type as one of the most abused. Let's see why as we analyze the sample items that follow. (Remember to type the model directions on a card for your resource file.)

Directions: Circle "T" if the statement is true. Circle "F" if the statement is false.

1.   The altitudes of a triangle meet in an interior point, called the orthocenter.   1.   T   F

2. π is equal to 3.14.   2.   T   F

3.   The lowest common multiple of 5 and 12 is 60.   3.   T   F

What answers would you accept for these? The point where the altitudes meet *is* called "orthocenter." However, it is not an interior point in the case of the right triangle or the obtuse triangle. How, then, would you interpret the instructional implications of a response of "false"? Would you infer that (1) the student knows about the varying location of that intersection point or (2) the student believes that the name of that point is something other than "orthocenter"? Also consider how to interpret a response of "true" to example 2. Would this mean the respondent knows that the value given is correct to the nearest hundredth, or that the respondent thinks that 3.14 is the exact numerical value of pi? The problem of interpretation of true-false results is further complicated by the fact that the probability of guessing the correct response for each item is 50 percent.

There are other problems, too. Try writing a number of statements that are unequivocally true or false, and you will soon discover that your efforts fall into one or both of two categories. The items either test *only* recall of specific facts and/or contain key words that act as clues to the correct responses. Test-wise students have learned that words such as *may, generally, usually, sometimes,* and *probably* correlate with true statements while *never, none, always,* and *all* usually indicate false statements about mathematics.

Is there *any* advantage to be claimed for using this type of test item? The one most frequently cited is that many items can be answered in a short time, thus increasing the sampling of knowledge. However, this feature quickly loses its attractiveness in view of the fact that what is typically sampled is simple recall of factual information. In our view, the true-false item-type is better suited for review/discussion purposes than it is for testing use. Thus, no rules of thumb for constructing this type are included.

Modified true-false   This item-type is sometimes considered an improvement over true-false items, since the student must do more than circle T or F. How much better is this item-type for sampling student achievement? Consider the set of items that follows.

Directions: Circle "T" if the statement is true. If the statement is false, fill in the blank with the word or number that would make the statement true when substituted for the underlined term.

1.   The value of the 6 in 635 is two times the value of the 3.   1.   T _____

2.   Trapezoids are parallelograms.   2.   T _____

3.   As x increases from $3\pi/2$ to 2π radians, sine x increases.   3.   T _____

Item 1 is a good example of this type of item. The underlined word identifies a frequent misconception with respect to place value and the statement clearly calls for the substitution of the correct value. Now contrast this with the second example. Start listing the range of literally correct responses that could be made by the students who have been taught that trapezoids are not parallelograms. How would you interpret responses such as "polygons," "simple closed curves," "four-sided," "interesting," and "important"? Another kind of problem is built into the third example. Did you spot the fact that it really describes a two-tailed situation? Obviously, the value of sine x is likely to either increase or decrease (a constant value is an unlikely guess), thus making this item a true-false type in disguise! This example would be much improved by amending it to read" ... increases from -1 to 0."

Good modified true-false items are not easy to construct, even when aimed at lower levels of the cognitive taxonomy. Another limitation inherent in modified true-false is student lack of experience with this type of item. For this reason we suggest using modified true-false items on homework or worksheets prior to using them on tests. Students have to be taught that no credit will be given for (1) substitutions of equally correct terms in true statements or (2) simply writing *false* after incorrect statements.

Two advantages of the modified true-false over straight true-false can be claimed. The guessing factor is reduced substantially from 50 percent if the items are well structured and if approximately half of the statements are false. Also, it is more nearly possible to construct items that measure learning at levels II and III of the cognitive taxonomy. You may find this advantage to be more theoretical than practical because many teachers find such items difficult to construct.

Rules of thumb for constructing modified true-false items include:

1. Construct "true" statements that are absolutely correct.

2. Use approximately the same number of true as false statements.

3. Underscore a word that limits the range of substitutions in false statements.

4. Avoid where possible the use of specific determiners.

5. Avoid negative statements.

6. Keep all true and false statements approximately the same length.

Completion or fill-in-the-blank   This item-type often brings out unsuspected creativity in students, much to the teacher's chagrin. Try your own hand at the items in the sample set.

Directions: Read the sentences below and determine the word(s) or number(s) that would have to be substituted for the blank to make each sentence complete and correct. Then write these words or numbers in the correspondingly numbered blanks on the right.

1. The man who wrote *The Elements* was _____(1)_____ .   1. _____

2. Lines which intersect a circle in exactly one point are called _____(2)_____ .   2. _____

3. The _____(3)_____ of a number, N, is the exponent indicating the _____(4)_____ to which it is necessary to raise a given _____(5)_____ to produce N.   3. _____   4. _____   5. _____

6. The positive value of $\tan(\arccos \sqrt{2}/2)$ is _____(6)_____ .   6. _____

Do you want to demoralize a class and start a near riot? A surefire way to accomplish both is to include items such as 1 and 3 on a quiz. Then go into class the next day and tell the students you marked their plausible, but non-keyed, answers as incorrect because they were not "what I wanted." Students who completed item 1 with an appropriate descriptor of the man's age, occupation, nationality, or mental ability cannot reasonably be marked wrong, since the question does not specify that his name is the desired response. Note how examples 2 and 6 avoid this common error that shows up even in many published texts and workbooks! Can you guess the process that generates such monsters as that illustrated by item 3? Typically such ill-conceived guessing games result from teachers "lifting" a sentence (out of context) from the textbook and compounding the felony by replacing several key words with blanks. Fortunately this type of gross error is becoming rare in published textbook and workbook examples, but watch out for it in exercise material you assign. Yes, a serious limitation of the fill-in-the-blank item-type is the difficulty of constructing unambiguous items. You will also find it difficult to write items of this type that go beyond level II of the cognitive taxonomy—another serious limitation.

Is this type of item ever useful? Some kinds of mathematics content, such as recalling concept labels and formulas and solving type problems, do lend themselves to this format. In fact, many mathematics tests contain a number of items such as item 6 in order to test ability to respond accurately to basic rules and principles. However, consider the limited interpretive value of knowing *only* the answer a student arrived at and not seeing steps in the student's work that led to the response. Thus, during the early stages of formative evaluation, it makes sense to use completion for single-step computational problems and to test multi-step problems by other means. Subsequently, mathematics teachers may wish to include some slightly more complicated examples as completion items, especially those where many of the steps are based on skills learned much earlier. An item like the one that follows, worth two credits with no partial credit allowed, falls into this category for intermediate algebra students.

7.   Solve for x : $2^{x+5} = 8$. $x =$ _____?_____   7.   _____

At a later stage of formative evaluation, the teacher may not be seeking feedback on process errors, but instead may be emphasizing accuracy via this item-type with its "all or nothing" credit format. Mathematics teachers would be well advised to combine this valid emphasis on accuracy with an equal (or greater) emphasis on process that must be achieved by means of other item-types.

Some useful rules of thumb follow:

1.   Use only *one* blank per item.

2.   Type a question mark on the blank within the item to avoid Ss writing the response there rather than on the numbered blank at the right.

3.   Put all blanks at the end of the sentence.

4.   Make all blanks the same length.

5.   Be sure the statement clearly delimits the range of potential responses (e.g. include degree of specificity of numerical answers).

6.   Avoid the temptation to copy out-of-context sentences from texts and then substitute a blank for a key term within the sentence.

7.   In the case of computational problems, restrict use to the single-step type during the early stages of formative evaluation.

Multiple choice   This type of short response item is *the* one most favored by professional test writers. They find that well-structured multiple-choice items can more effectively assess many of the lower level outcomes often measured by other short response items. Additionally, this item-type can also measure a variety of objectives at levels III and above of the cognitive domain. As is the case with all other item-types, good items require careful attention to construction details. However, the inherent advantages of multiple-choice items over the types considered so far make for higher payoff in terms of time invested. Now check out each of the following examples for structural soundness and make mental note of any changes you might propose.

Directions: Write in the blank provided the capital letter preceding the expression that best completes *each* statement or answers each question.

1. The sequence $3, 6, 12, \ldots, 3(2)^{n-1}, \ldots$ is an example of a(n)
    A. arithmetic progression
    B. finite sequence
    C. geometric progression
    D. harmonic progression   1. _____

2. In triangle ABC, if $m\angle A = 30°$, $a = 15$ and $b = 12$, then triangle ABC must be
    A. acute
    B. isosceles
    C. obtuse
    D. right   2. _____

3. If the set of points represented by $\{(x,y) \mid |x| = 3\}$ is translated two units to the right, the new set is represented by $\{(x,y) \mid$
    A. $|x + 2| = 3\}$
    B. $|x - 2| = 3\}$
    C. $|x| = 5\}$
    D. $|x| = 1\}$ 3. _____

4. Rhombi
    A. have unequal sides
    B. have area equal to the product of the diagonals
    C. belong to the class of parallelograms
    D. can be separated by one diagonal into two scalene
        triangles   4. _____

5. If in triangle ABC, $m\angle B = 60°$ and $AB > AC$, then which relationship must be true?
    A. $m\angle C > m\angle A$
    B. $m\angle C < m\angle A$
    C. $m\angle C = m\angle A$
    D. $m\angle C < m\angle B$
    E. $m\angle C = m\angle B$ 5. _____

Did you spot one weak alternative among the four supplied in item 1? Finite sequence is a poor distractor, because it clearly limits the number of terms. A sound item always includes only plausible alternatives (distractors) plus one correct response (keyed answer) among the alternatives. The net effect of one poor distractor in a list of four alternatives is to increase the guessing factor from 25 percent to $33\frac{1}{3}$ percent. Note that none of the other sample items suffer from this type of error. In fact, you may have wondered if item 5 would be considered to be superior on this account since it contains five plausible alternatives. The five-alternative type does reduce the guessing factor 5 percent (from 25 percent to 20 percent) but the trade-off is both (1) the difficulty of finding that extra distractor and (2) increased reading time, thus reducing the number of questions students can answer in the time available. For these reasons test experts usually recommend use of the four-alternative type. You must have noticed that item 4 looks different from the others because the alternatives are all long in comparison to the one-word stem of the question—just the opposite of what is considered sound structure. Each of the other sample items contains a stem that is either a clear question or a completion-type statement followed by shorter alternatives parallel to each other in construction. This practice makes the task more explicit to students—always a desirable feature of a test.

Are there any other limitations in addition to the care needed in item construction? Yes. Multiple-choice items emphasize recognition of the correct response. Thus this item-type is a weak match for objectives that specify outcomes such as *recall* or *synthesizing* an original response. We must use other means of assessment to match these objectives.

Obvious advantages inherent in use of multiple choice include the sampling of many objectives in a short time, speed and ease of scoring, and reduction of the guessing factor to 25 percent. But don't overlook additional good features that may not be so obvious. The fact that a student has been attracted to a particular distractor has diagnostic value and also tells the teacher something about the functioning of the questions included in the test. Both of these desirable features are explored in detail in a later section on item analysis. Items 3 and 5 illustrate the potential of assessing level III and above objectives with multiple-choice questions.

Rules of thumb to follow in constructing multiple-choice questions include these:

1. Write the stem so that it presents a single, specific problem in either question or completion statement form.

2. If the stem incorporates an exception, emphasize it by solid caps and underscoring (<u>EXCEPT</u>).

3. Include in the stem all words that would otherwise be common to all alternative phrases.

4. Make the alternatives as brief as possible and in no case any longer than the stem.

5. Keep alternatives within an item parallel in form and grammatically consistent with the stem.

6. Use distractors that are plausible and incorporate typical errors and misconceptions.

7. Sequence alternatives in alphabetical or numerical order.

8. Place alternatives in a vertical column, not in a horizontal row.

Matching   In our view, this is really a special case of multiple choice. Two columns are presented, and the task is to match items from one column with items from the other column. Multiple stems are to be matched with multiple alternatives. Thus you should apply what you just learned about multiple choice as you analyze the examples that follow.

1.   Directions: On the line to the right of each quantity in Column B, write the letter of the phrase in Column A that most closely corresponds.

Column A	Column B	
A. $A = s^2$	1. rectangle	1. _____
B. $A = h/2(b + b')$	2. regular n-gon	2. _____
C. $A = bh/2$	3. rhombus	3. _____
D. $A = lw$	4. square	4. _____
E. $A = (b/2)(h/2)$	5. trapezoid	5. _____
F. $A = ap/2$	6. triangle	6. _____
G. $A = ap$		
H. $A = dd'/2$		

2.   Directions: On the line to the right of each expression in Column B, write the letter of the expression in Column A that fits it. Each expression in Column A may be used *only ONCE*.

Column A	Column B	
A. $y = 4x + 3$	1. circle	1. _____
B. parabola	2. $y^2 + 4x^2 = 3$	2. _____
C. $y^2 + x^2 = 3$	3. conic	3. _____
D. ellipse	4. first-degree equation	4. _____
E. $y^2 - 4x^2 = 3$	5. $y = 4x^2 + 3$	5. _____

No doubt you have surmised that one of these two examples is intended as an illustration of correct performance, while the other suffers from several defects. How many defects did you spot in example 2? Did you catch on to the fact that the use of short and equal columns guarantees that achievement of three correct matches will assure the fourth match (since each Column A expression can be used only once)? If the directions hadn't included this restriction, the teacher would have even a bigger mess to contend with. Conic is correctly associated with all but one of the expressions in Column A! Note that example 1 avoids these kinds of problems in a number of ways. Recommended practice was followed in that (1) unequal length columns were used, (2) the shorter column lists five to seven items, and (3) the longer column includes a maximum of ten alternatives. Yes, it is difficult to construct items that meet these criteria, and that is an important limitation of matching questions This limitation becomes even more severe when you attempt to avoid the problem of multiple combinations of matches illustrated by example 2. Homogeneity of the type of expression within each column is the best way to eliminate this particular difficulty. For instance, Column A could be limited to characteristics of various geometric shapes with Column B listing the names of those shapes. But doesn't this process then restrict matching questions to the assessment of fairly low-level objectives? Yes, it frequently does just that—another limitation of this item type.

Aside from quick and easy scoring, it is difficult to conceive of other advantages of matching questions. Even the advantage of quick and easy scoring pales in view of the fact that other types of short-response items will accomplish that and more. No doubt this explains why matching questions are rarely used by professional testmakers.

Rules of thumb for matching questions include the following:

1. Include, in the directions, the basis for matching and state whether or not responses may be used more than once (if either is needed for clarity).

2. Place the briefer expressions in the right-hand column (easy to scan) and in alphabetical or numeric order.

3. Use unequal length columns with a range of five to seven items in the shorter, right-hand column and seven to ten in the longer, left-hand column.

4. Make the material within each list homogeneous. For example:

Column A	*Column B*
Achievements	Names of persons
Events	Dates
Definitions	Concept names
Graphs	Equations
Concepts or rules	Symbols or formulas
Geometric shapes	Classification categories

Long response   This item-type is also often referred to as essay, although some teachers use the term *essay* to indicate that the response desired is in the form of one or more paragraphs. Long-response items of various kinds are needed in order to test important objectives that are difficult or impossible to assess by means of short-response items. They are also required in order to get feedback on students' ability to function at the highest levels of the cognitive domain. Just as is the case with all other item-types, considerable care in construction is essential if such questions are to serve their intended purposes. Study the following examples and decide if each is likely to achieve its purpose.

1.   a.   Solve for tan θ to the *nearest tenth*:

$$2\tan^2\theta - 5\tan\theta + 1 = 0 \qquad \text{(Show all work.)}$$

b.   How many different *acute* angles are there that satisfy the equation in part a? Justify your answer.

2. Given: $\angle A \cong \angle B$, $\angle C \cong \angle COD$ in the figure $ABOC$.

    Prove: $\angle OEA$ is a right angle.

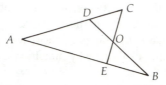

3. Show that the equation $x^2 + xy + y^2 = 3$ represents an ellipse.

4. Solve the system of equations graphically and indicate the solution set.

$$3x + 4y = 5$$
$$x - 8y = 4$$

5. Can you explain why we need three different measures of central tendency (mean, median, and mode)?

6. Write an essay on the importance of geometry to everyday life.

7. Black Bart guided his drag racer through the standing one-quarter mile strip in 5.95 seconds. However, Wonderful Willie beat him by .025 seconds. How much faster was the average acceleration of Willie's car in ft/sec^2? Show all work.

8. Two separate streams of lava have flowed down a mountainside and are slowly approaching a fence. The first gets closer and closer to the fence but never goes beyond. The second moves closer and closer to the fence, and, at last, flows one-eighth inch beyond. Could the fence be described as the limit of either flow? Of both? Explain.

9. Write out the "multiplication" table for the integers 0, 1, 2 under addition, mod 3. Compare this table with the table of rotations of an equilateral triangle. In what way(s) are they similar, different?

Would you have a difficult time grading responses to item 6? We would! This question as stated is so broad as to provide for a virtually limitless range of student responses. The item could be vastly improved by indicating a narrower frame of reference that would focus responses more directly on a cluster of specific objectives the teacher wishes to assess. Unless you can list the main points or key ideas that should be included in a complete and accurate answer, the question requires reworking. Otherwise that item will have very low reliability. Did you spot the error in item 5, or is it so simple a fault that you overlooked it? The answer to that question as phrased is a simple yes or no (another true-false item in disguise). Eliminating the first two words and replacing the question mark with a period would repair the item quite well. Care in item construction is needed in order to overcome the two big potential limitations of long-response items—low validity and low reliability.

The other seven examples are intended to illustrate well-constructed items that assess objectives that cannot be assessed by short-response items. Outcomes that have to do with abilities such as solving equations, writing proofs, applying a rule in a slightly novel way, constructing graphs, analyzing the structure of mathematics, and using logic, evidence, and basic assumptions to justify answers all require long responses if the assessment means are to match objectives. But why not cast item 7 into a completion or multiple-choice format? The cue here is in the direction to "show all work." The long-response format of this question allows the teacher to find out more than just who was able to obtain the correct numerical answer and to assign partial credit to responses that indicate varying degrees of comprehension.

Rules of thumb for constructing/scoring long-response items include:

1. Use long-response questions to assess *only* those outcomes that cannot be satisfactorily measured by short-response item-types.

2. Limit the scope so that the task is clear and the time required to respond is reasonable in terms of both credit and time to be allotted to each question.

3. Prepare a key that includes all major points of information, ideas, and steps that should appear in correct and complete responses. Be sure that the part of the response involving major principles and/or concepts is assigned more credit than simple computation aspects.

4. Plan the credit distribution within each question (in terms of guideline 3) **prior to** administering the test.

5. Do *not* use "optional" questions. (Otherwise, not all students have taken the same test.)

Credit Assignment for Items

"How much does this count?" the student asks. If you are ready to ask the same question, then you are probably hampered by experience as a test-taker in which the tests seemed to consist of only one or two item-types. In general, it is common practice to assign one credit for recall items and two credits for short-response items that do not simply involve recall. Although it seems reasonable to assign more than two credits to short-response items that involve multiple processes, there is a problem with this. The inability to give partial credit since no work is to be shown puts a heavy burden on complete accuracy, or lucky guessing in the case of all but completion items. Thus, we would recommend that short-response items be consistently scored 1 credit for recall only and 2 credits for items beyond recall. Obviously, we would also recommend that when complex processes are to be tested, the teacher include some other item-types that can be scored with credit related to recall, other credit to choice of correct process or to concepts and correct use of principles, and still other credit for accuracy in computation.

Storage and Retrieval of Test Items

Busy teachers need a system that allows for quick location and retrieval of a large number of test items. Contemporary computer systems are especially useful as a management tool for this purpose. The particular microcomputer and software available to you will differentially affect some of the data input procedures. However, regardless of system, you will want to begin storing potential items (with keyed answer and credit assigned) using the guidelines presented in this section. Retrieval will be facilitated if each item can be coded by item-type, mathematics topic and subtopic, domain assessed and taxonomic level for all but psychomotor domain. After an item has been used on a quiz or test, it would be important to add codes for the difficulty level and discrimination index of the item, characteristics treated later in this chapter.

Don't wait until you begin teaching to start writing items. As you find apparently useful items in any course you are likely to teach, create appropriate files and begin to store items. Don't overlook the possibilities of creating an item based on a cartoon in which mathematical concepts are embedded. For example, analyze the logical principle behind Mom's warning in *Family Circus*, "If you don't clean your room, then you can't go out to play." A relevant item might contain the question: "Did Mom promise that her son can go out to play if he *does* clean his room? Justify your answer." If your computer system includes access to a scanner, maps, pictures and the like could also be stored for use with items for class work, homework, as well as for testing purposes. Warning! Some test bank software includes a set of items that cannot be modified, as well as information on credit distribution for long-response items. Before you purchase software of this type, be sure that you are able to modify the original set of items as desired. What do you do if you don't have access to a computer? Write items on index cards and code these.

The Unit Test

Within a week you will be completing instruction in a major unit in probability. Feedback obtained during group problem-solving sessions, supervised practice, lab work, and on the results of a few short quizzes is convincing evidence of the class progress to date. But can they put it all together? It's time to draft the BIG ONE!

Designing the unit test Unfortunately, some unit tests are patchwork quilts of earlier quiz or textbook questions with no apparent parallel to instructional emphasis or sequence. If you've been victimized by such unit tests, you probably learned to play the game of school in order to reap the rewards of second-guessing the teacher. However, a comprehensive assessment of objectives ought not to be a capricious collection of items, but a thoughtful, integrated part of instruction. That can only happen as a result of thorough planning.

UNIT ON PROBABILITY

	Objectives by Cognitive Level			
Units of Content	I	II	III	Above III
Basic probability concepts				
Multistage events				
Independent and dependent events				
Permutations and combinations				
Bernoulli Experiments				
Binomial Theorem				

Fig. 8.2   A partially completed table of specifications.

What are you assessing? It should be the extent to which the students can meet the objectives of the unit. If your instruction was directed toward the mastery of objectives at levels I and II of the cognitive domain, then your *test results* should *report whether students did or didn't achieve each objective (criterion-referenced testing)*. If you included low-level objectives that all or most students should master as well as higher-level objectives that fewer students might attain, you would be more likely to report *test results in terms of each student's relative position in the group (norm-referenced testing)*. Each of these types of testing is characterized by specific test construction principles. Since the secondary school teacher's test more often is modeled after norm-referenced instruments, we have chosen to examine testing from that vantage point. In either case, test planning begins with the consideration of the selected objectives.

Mr. Zidonis, an eleventh-grade teacher, began his test planning by completing the margins of what is called a *table of specifications*. He listed major content topics of the unit in the horizontal margin and the taxonomic levels of the cognitive objectives in the vertical margin (see Figure 8.2).

Why not list each cognitive objective? Just imagine the size of the resulting table! Such a table of specifications would become an unmanageable monster rather than a guide to test design. Mr. Zidonis apparently included all levels of the cognitive taxonomy in his instruction, and he intends to sample the effectiveness of that instruction at each level. But levels of the affective domain and objectives in the psychomotor domain are not included. Did he ignore these domains in his instruction? Definitely not, but he chose to assess them by means of long-term projects and anecdotal records during lab work rather than as part of the unit test. (Other ways of assessing objectives in these domains are treated in later sections of this chapter.) Decisions! Decisions! There's no getting around it. The decisions that result in the completed margins of the table of specifications have already framed in the future test. But the professional testmaker wouldn't stop there. Next, each box of the table would be filled in with a decimal

UNIT ON PROBABILITY

| Units of Content | Objectives by Cognitive Level | | | | |
	I	II	III	Above III	Credit
Basic probability concepts	3	$1, 6, 17^3$		10^3	12
Multistage events	12	$4, 11^3$	13^3		10
Independent and dependent events	7	$2, 14^3$	15^3		10
Permutations and combinations		$9, 16^3,$ $19^3, 20a^5$	$20b^5$		18
Bernoulli Experiments		5, 8	21^{10}		14
Binomial Theorem				$18^3, 22^{10}$	13
Credit Totals	6	34	21	16	77

Fig. 8.3   A completed table of specifications.

representing the instructional emphasis given the topic and the matching objectives. "You must be kidding!" Well, *they* aren't, but then their purpose and skills differ from those of the beginning teacher. Your next step is considerably different. You begin selecting and/or generating items.

You already know quite a bit about the need to match items to objectives, the pitfalls inherent in some kinds of items, the advantages of others, the scoring of varied types of items. Where do you begin? The suggestions that follow have been found useful by both novice and experienced classroom teachers.

Even if you do work on a computer system, experienced teachers have found it useful to begin with two pencilled starter sheets. One sheet contains a table of specifications, similar to the one created by Mr. Zidonis. As you create an item or choose one from your resource file, you give each a temporary number and write that number in the appropriate cell of the table of specifications. You also pencil in the credit for that item as a superscript. Thus, the 14^3 in the second column and third row of Figure 8.3 represents the fourteenth item selected so far and the assignment of 3 credits to that item.

The second starter sheet is typically divided by a horizontal line into two sections—the top section for material that could probably be tested as short-response items and the bottom section for that more adapted to long-response items. Many teachers also divide the top section into columns for item-types they would like to include on the test. Then, you need to quickly scan the text material, your lesson plans, quiz sheets, homework assignments and other handouts for particular concepts and rules and the relative emphasis on processes and products of mathematics. As you do this, pencil in a key word or phrase in the appropriate section on your second starter sheet. Now you have an additional guide for the item-types you need.

Next, comes the writing, searching and re-writing process. As the entries begin to fill the matrix, stop and "eyeball" both the number of items in each box and the percent of the total credit thus far assigned to each box. You may need to begin writing items in different areas of content and for neglected levels of objectives. The test emphasis represented by credit assignment may need adjusting if the test emphasis is to match the instructional emphasis. A pencil with an eraser will come in handy!

When, in your judgment, the completed matrix seems satisfactory, prepare a typed copy of the entire test. It is generally good practice to start with all short-response items. They should be clustered by type, with each type preceded by appropriate directions for that type and with credit for each item in that section indicated. Now is the time to cut and paste from your resource file, the standard directions that were provided earlier in this chapter. The long-response items follow next and there are no hard and fast rules for sequence here. Again, be sure that credit for each item is indicated. Obviously, this means that the temporary numbers assigned the items in the preparation stage may need to be changed. Before you do this, examine the short-response items in each group. In particular, write down the letters designating the correct responses for the sequence of multiple-choice items. Does there appear to be a built-in pattern? If so, don't change the choices. (Remember, these should be kept in numerical or alphabetical order!) Instead rearrange the sequence of the items to eliminate the apparent pattern. Also consider the adjacent items within each cluster of items. The answer to question 4 should not "give away" the answer to question 5.

Finally, before you leave the keyboard, add headings for the test, with a space for the student's name, and numbered spaces in a column at the right of each short-response item. (Why might reading specialists approve of the answer spaces in a right margin, rather than a left margin?) Now, print a draft of your test and take it yourself. When this caution is ignored, the powerful word processing imp has a way of deleting important parts of questions to be found during the test by a smart student, or not at all by confused students.

Did you notice that Mr. Zidonis's completed table of specifications indicates a test that (1) loads almost equally on all units of content with a to-be-expected heavy loading on Permutations and Combinations, (2) provides minimal rewards for straight recall, and (3) gives equal and heavy weighting to level II and to levels III and above III combined. This picture of the test would satisfy Mr. Zidonis if it matched closely the objectives and instructional emphasis of the unit. The total credits don't add up to 100! There is no reason, other than superstition, to suppose that it should. What sense would there be in juggling credits to obtain this magic number? This might destroy the match of test-to-objectives emphasis he had worked hard to achieve. It would be far better to use a conversion table or calculator to translate raw scores into percentages if that is desirable in terms of local custom or school policy.

As you work on varied stages of test preparation, be sure to share your attempts with your cooperating teacher. Modifications based on thoughtful experience will simplify your job.

To review or not to review?   Since you decided, on the basis of positive feedback, that the time for a comprehensive test had arrived, the students must be "ready" for the test. So why review? If your feedback sampling has been adequate, the answer is that typical review days are often a waste of valuable instructional time. Remember those mythical 180 days and the ways the total gets reduced? Suppose your feedback sampling was spotty. In that case the chances are that a review day will become a hurried and ineffective attempt to repair several weeks of instruction.

Don't students need some guidance in how to study for a test? Yes, and they also need information on the parameters of the test you have designed. After all, you made selective decisions as to the scope of the objectives to be tested. You may have decided to extend the test over two class periods or to include laboratory work as well as paper-and-pencil items. These decisions should not be secrets. The students should know what will be expected of them and the nature of the testing conditions.

At least four to five days prior to the test date, announce the scheduled test. If your instruction has consistently been based on the spiraling of objectives, your class will profit from a structured working session where you help them highlight major concepts. That condition is not to be passed over lightly. You must teach students how to approach a mixed collection of content topics—no easy task, since most textbooks encourage students to expect that all items in the same section will deal with the same task. Furthermore, well-managed supervised practice may have given students the false impression that they are ready to "ace" a test. What a surprise when the teacher refuses to answer questions during the test! Test preparation throughout the unit should include some simulated test sessions where no teacher or student-to-student help is given. This kind of preparation cannot be left until the day before the unit test, or it is doomed to failure. However, a summing up of all earlier practice sessions, a planned review work session focusing on areas the teacher has diagnosed as needing special attention, and a summary lecture in which the teacher outlines the format of the test, its scope and any special conditions are not only desirable, but necessary. Watch out for poorly planned review sessions that depend heavily on student-initiated questions. This frequently degenerates into a "fishing expedition" as students cast about blindly trying to locate specific items that are to appear on the test. Some characteristics of pretest work sessions that teachers and students have found successful include:

1. Short periods of supervised practice interspersed with student demonstrations, board work, or quick recall Q/A.
2. Carefully sequenced sets of written questions, where the concepts, rules, and problems most in need of review are placed first in the set, where there are

more questions than can be completed in class, and where separate answer keys are distributed at the end of the session to those who wish to complete the set.

3. Tactics that allow more capable students to assist the teacher or to spend this time on a project of their choice.

Some teachers use review games very successfully. Others warn that games in which chance dictates the order and kind of question to be answered may entrap the class into experiencing a pleasurable today and a painful tomorrow when test questions fail to match game questions.

Administration of the test Because testing periods that are badly managed lead to control problems, the basic routines for administering a test are outlined in Section 12.3 under "Effective and Efficient Handling of Routines." You may wish to look ahead at that short section right now. In that section, we allude to the problem of student cheating. Why do some students cheat? You know, from your own experience, that external pressures of varying kinds tempt even some bright, but tense, students to engage in dishonest practices. We know of no magic way to eliminate the very real pressures of college admissions, parental expectations, peer mores, and the like. There are, however, some specific suggestions that have proved useful in (1) convincing students that their chances of "getting away with it" are minimal and (2) demonstrating that built-in self-administered penalties are likely to result for culprits.

Copying from an adjacent classmate is probably the simplest and most frequently used tactic of cheaters, and even the most vigilant teacher may fail to spot occurrences in a crowded classroom. In Section 12.5, "A Pound of Cure," we describe a classroom where the teacher suspects copying has occurred during a test. Three courses of follow-up behavior are outlined, and you are asked to react to the relative effectiveness of each. Take the time to read ahead in that brief section now. Of course, we'd all prefer to avoid discipline problems so that a "pound of cure" wouldn't be needed. We'd recommend as an "ounce of prevention" in test administration that the first unit test be prepared in two parallel forms and distributed to the class in accordance with the directions in Section 12.5. There are several ways to concoct question papers that look alike when one glances over a shoulder. You might (1) scramble the order of the choices for each multiple-choice question (as suggested in Section 12.5), (2) reorder individual questions within each cluster of items, (3) include items that are open-ended and require a variety of responses, and (4) alter the details of explanations students are to give in the open-response items. Be sure to read the details of distributing papers, proctoring, scoring, and returning papers in Section 12.5. If you have more than one class section taking a test on the unit, you will have to construct parallel forms unless you are willing to give an automatic handicap to the first class. If you have a single section taking the test, must you always construct parallel forms? Those teachers who have used unannounced parallel forms for the first unit test find that only sporadic subsequent use is necessary. The students are now never sure whether their neighbor's test is the same form as theirs. An effective preventive? You bet it is!

How can a teacher prevent the successful use of "crib" notes? The best defense against crib notes is the construction of test items that cannot be answered solely on the basis of any kind of notes. Questions above level II are guaranteed to frustrate the student who is depending on hidden notes. The next level of defense is constant vigilance on the part of the teacher and adherence to the routines recommended in Section 12.3.

Remember, the whole point of constructing a test is to sample what students have learned about the unit, not to assess their eyesight. You should be basing future instruction on the analysis of these results. If the results are a mixed bag of half-truths, who suffers most? The successful cheater now may be tempted to cheat even more on the next unit test.

Assessing test results   Before any student's paper is scored, a key should be prepared for each form of the test. The form of the key depends on the form of the test, but it should be constructed with efficiency of scoring built in. If the students have been instructed to write answers or the capital letter of the keyed choice in a space in the right margin, the teacher's key can be constructed by correctly filling in all spaces on a copy of the test. It also helps to write the total possible credit for each cluster of items in the right margin of the key at the end of each cluster. With the key beside a student's paper, the teacher can locate and mark errors and begin the recording of credit obtained by that student. Figure 8.4 illustrates a portion of such a key, one student's responses to the first two sets of short-response items and the teacher's scoring notations thus far.

Since Sam received 16 credits for his responses to the multiple-choice items, he must have correctly answered items 4–9. Notice how the teacher lined up the key on top of Sam's paper so that corresponding responses could be quickly checked, marked only the wrong responses, and indicated the credit accumulated for each section of the test above the slash line and the total credit accumulated thus far below the slash line.

It is good policy to score all short-response answers on each paper before addressing student efforts on open-ended questions. However, it is not good policy to score all open-ended responses on one paper before going on. Do you see why? Let's assume that the Locus test included two items in which students were asked to write proofs. Even though your prepared key would include the optimum responses to each question, together with the credit to be assigned to varied portions of a response, you would find enough variability among responses to make judgments about scoring difficult. After carefully reading and assessing Sam's response to the first proof, you will compound the problem of keeping the scoring reliable if you now move on to a different item on Sam's paper. That makes sense, doesn't it? What makes even more sense is the advantage gained

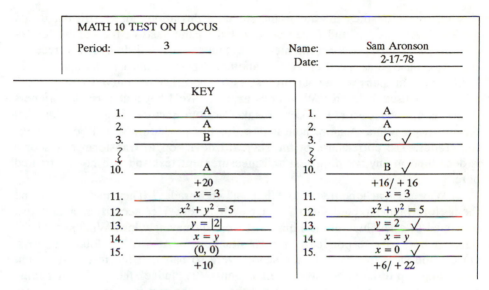

Fig. 8.4   A partially scored unit test.

in scoring efficiency. By the time the fifth student's response to the same essay item has been read, particular scoring decisions begin to repeat and thus can be made more easily.

At last all papers are scored and you are ready to record the grades in your grade book (computer-based, where available). An additional step may be needed at this point in the case of schools that require the reporting of letter grades. Remember, the raw scores represent *data* that will be used in *evaluating* student achievement. Whether raw scores alone are reported, or whether you need to report letter grade plus raw score or percentage plus raw score, you must make a judgment as to the meaning of the reported grade. Follow the suggestions of department head or cooperating teacher if it is necessary to translate raw scores into letter grades. In the absence of clear written or unwritten guidance as to the quantitative and qualitative match of raw scores to letter grades, we recommend that you determine a cutoff score to represent the lower limit of the D's. This is a judgment based on the total possible credit assigned to the test and the nature of the content topics and objectives it was designed to sample. If you haven't already done so, arrange the papers in rank order and write all total scores in order in a vertical array. A consideration of clusters of scores will help you make further decisions about cutoff scores in the case of A, B, C, and D papers.

Notice that we haven't suggested "curving" the grades! Why not? What does "curving" the grades mean? Every one of you is familiar enough with statistics to know that "curve" in this case relates to the normal curve. If the population being tested is normally distributed—an assumption hard to defend with class-size groups—then the mean and standard deviation can be calculated and grades of A, B, C, D, and E can be awarded on the basis of the number of deviations of a raw score from the mean. That means that a little over 2 percent of the class must be assigned an A, but another 2 percent must be assigned an E. Is that what happens when your professors tell you they've "curved" the grades? We'd bet it usually doesn't. What does happen? We'd bet that variable numbers of points are added to raw scores to make the total picture congruent with what the professor wants. A more honest term for this procedure would be "fudging" the grades. The correct use of the standard deviation to transform raw scores is described in any standard test and measurement text and will not be treated here.

Why do teachers resort to "fudging" the grades? They may have found themselves in the predicament faced by Mrs. Rely. Her scores on a unit test consisted of a few high grades, but most were dismayingly low. What should she do? Teachers have responded to similar situations in *each* of the following ways: (1) tell the class that most of the scores were so bad that the test won't count and a makeup test will be given to all students, (2) "fudge" the grades by adding an increment to the low scores, (3) tell the class the test is over, the scores are in the grade book, and that's all there is to it, or (4) carefully analyze details of test results to identify the possible source of poor student achievement and then share this information and the decisions based on it with the class. Which of these approaches is likely to increase student confidence in the evaluation process and the teacher? To us, the fourth choice is the only reasonable alternative, particularly if the teacher has followed earlier suggestions on test preparation. But after carefully constructing the test and accurately scoring all the papers, what is left to analyze? That's exactly what we need to consider next.

Item analysis   Even the trained and experienced test constructors at the Educational Testing Service (ETS) regularly reject items after analyzing the scores of a sample population. Why would they reject well-written items that match the objectives in terms of *logical* analysis? *Logical* does not equal *psychological* here any more than it does in the areas of intellectual development and human learning. Students may "read into" an item a meaning not intended by the teacher. If this happens in a random way, the teacher might well discount it. But if a number of students misread an item in exactly the same way, the item needs to be studied for the source of the error. Suppose a number of high-scoring students got a particular item wrong, while a similar number of low-scoring students got the same item correct? You'd check that item very carefully. Would you be suspicious of an item's wording on the basis of the score of one student? Two students? More than half the class? How do you decide? Here we are guided by the professional test constructor who uses, among other things, two indices: item difficulty and item discrimination.

The usual unit test (unless all the unit objectives are to be mastered by all students) is designed to differentiate the more capable students from the less capable. The teacher intends to include items of varying degrees of difficulty. Is that what happened? It's easy to ascertain. The *item difficulty* (or *difficulty index*) is defined as the *percentage of the class who succeeded on that item*. The computation of the difficulty index for two different scoring cases is illustrated in examples 1 and 2 below.

Example 1:   Item 7 is a multiple-choice item worth one credit. No partial credit was given. Twenty-four students in a class of 36 students answered item 7 correctly.

$$D_f = \frac{Ns}{T} = \frac{24}{36} \approx .67 \quad \text{or} \quad 67\%$$

(D_f = difficulty index; Ns = number of successful students; T = total number of students taking the test.)

Example 2:   Item 20 is worth 10 credits, but partial credit was given. In the same class of 36 students, some students received 10 credits; some 8 credits; some 5 credits; and so on. The sum of the credit obtained by the entire class on the item was 183 credits.

$$D_f = \frac{\Sigma_c}{T \times I_c} = \frac{183}{36 \times 10} = \frac{183}{360} \approx .51 \quad \text{or} \quad 51\%$$

(Σ_c = sum of the credits and I_c = credit for the item.)

The two items in examples 1 and 2 would be considered moderately difficult. In general, you should expect the difficulty index of many items to range between 60 percent and 70 percent. It is often appropriate for a teacher-made test to include a number of items with higher or lower indices. The teacher is the final judge of this, and that judgment depends in part on the original objectives set for the unit. In any case, test designers would recommend a long, hard look at items where $D_f \geq 90\%$ or $D_f \leq 30\%$. Notice the apparent anomaly. Professional test constructors call this index *item difficulty*, even though the higher percents represent easier items. As you read further, remember a D_f of 92 percent represents a very easy item for that group of students, while a D_f of 21 percent represents an item to which few students were able to respond successfully.

We also have need of another kind of index to help with analysis of items. Why? What else might we want to know? Study the information given in example 3 and try to identify one further area of potential concern.

Example 3:   Item 7 described in example 1 was successfully answered by 6 of the 12 students in the top third of the class, by 8 of the middle group of 12, and by 10 of the 12 lowest scoring students.

What did you infer from the data in example 3? If you red-flagged the scoring results of the highest and lowest students on this item, you're on the right track. A test is supposed to differentiate those who have met the instructional objectives from those who haven't. Yet in this case half of the top scorers, the "haves," got the item wrong while more than three-fourths of the low scorers, the "have nots," got the item right. Why did this happen? The wording of the stem may be at fault, or the nature of the distractors may suggest erroneous information to the brighter student. So even though this item seemed to be acceptable from the point of view of item difficulty ($D_f \approx 67$ percent), it is providing false information as to the "haves" versus the "have nots." The data provided in example 3 is that used in determining the second index, *item discrimination*. In example 4, we illustrate the computation of item discrimination for the item referred to in examples 1 and 3.

Example 4:   In a class of 36, $1/3 \times 36 = 12$. Therefore, there are 12 highest scorers (H) and 12 lowest scorers (L) on the total test.

$$D_c = H_s - L_s = 6 - 10 = -4$$

(D_c = discrimination index; H_s =number of H students who successfully answered this item; L_s =number of L students who successfully answered this item.)

The negative number is an immediate signal that this item is discriminating in the reverse direction from that desired. The use of the top third and bottom third of the class is a modification of the 27 percent used by professional testwriters—a modification that works fairly well for a class size of 20 or more. If the class size is less than 20, the top and bottom halves of the class should be used with the middle scorer ignored in the case of an odd number. How is the discrimination index computed for an open-ended item worth partial credit. In example 5, we illustrate the computation for item 20 referred to in example 2.

Example 5:   Students could obtain 1 to 10 credits on item 20. The H group (12 students) in this class of 36 accumulated 96 credits, while the L group (12 students) accumulated 36 credits.

$$D_c = (H_\Sigma - L_\Sigma)/I_c = (96 - 36)/10 = 60/10 = 6.$$

(H_Σ = sum of credits obtained by H group; L_Σ =sum of the credits obtained by the L group; I_c =total possible credit value of the item, as before.)

Notice that the formula has been adjusted in example 5 to obtain, as before, an integer. In the case of item 20, where item difficulty was 52 percent, this positive discrimination index of 6 characterizes this item as discriminating in favor of the top scorers. On the basis of these two indices, item 20 appears to be doing the job it was designed to accomplish.

Although both discrimination and difficulty indices can be obtained from a computer program, most of the commercially prepared programs are not adapted to small class sizes. It is an easy matter to check a program available to you with the calculation rules provided here for several special cases. Be sure to check such a program for the kind of data entry it can handle. For example, in the case of multiple-choice items, it is useful to enter the actual distractor (O for omitted response and S for correct choice) and not just a code for success and failure. Do you see why? Remember, this analysis of items has two functions: (1) the improvement of future tests and (2) the diagnosis of individual student errors. Figure 8.5 depicts a completed set of data from a test in Mrs. Bowden's class. Each student's complete set of data was entered and then the entire set was sorted in order from highest to lowest total score. Without a computer, the papers would have been arranged in appropriate order first. The column headed N_s or Σ_c contains the number of students who succeeded on the short-response items (N_s) or the total number of points obtained by the class for the long-response items (Σ_c). The difficulty index and the discrimination index head each of the next columns. Six students got example 2 correct. Therefore, $D_f = 6/26 \approx .23 = 23\%$. Item 2 has a discrimination index of 4 since $H_s - L_s = 4 - 0 = 4$. Now it's time to check your understanding of the two indices. First, check Mrs. Bowden's figures where given. Then complete the rest of the table. You'll find our results in Simulation Exercise D.

Does the work Mrs. Bowden must have done after the test seem like "closing the barn door *after* the horse has wandered away"? It will be just that if she files the analysis sheets neatly in a file drawer and does nothing further with them. But she had much more in mind. Think back to the test post-mortem suggestions of Chapter 2. *Before* Mrs. Bowden returns these tests, she will have completed the item analysis in order to (1) identify error patterns and (2) identify students who need individual help or a differentiated follow-up assignment. The test post-mortem will be planned on the basis of this information and structured according to suggestions given in Section 2.3, Chapter 2. If Mrs. Bowden has isolated some "poor" items, identified items that many students got wrong or omitted, or identified items in which one distractor was chosen above others, she can share that information with the entire class. As a result, her questions can focus on these distractors and items. There's nothing more deadly than a test post-mortem in which the teacher or a student recites each and every answer and tells why it's correct, item by item. The "haves" are bored by the repetition, and the "have nots" are discouraged. Often the "have nots" had some reason for making an error and they are likely to repeat the same error if the limitations of that reason are never explored. However, if Mrs. Bowden structures her lesson by drawing attention to the data from particular items, the entire class can be meaningfully absorbed in questioning the results. Consider the ways the data from item 5 might be analyzed.

Fig. 8.5   A partially completed item analysis sheet.

Item statistics (S_{s26} / Item #):

Item #	N_s or Σ_c	D_f %	D_c
1	14	54	7
2	6	23	4
3	4	15	—
4	15	—	—
5	7	—	—

Student response and score matrix:

Student	1	2	3	4	5	30a(7)	30b(3)	Total (50) raw score	Group
Rob	O	A		E	B	0	0	24	L
Tod	E	C	E	E	E	1	0	24	L
Milly	E	B	E	O	B	2	0	24	L
Walt	O	O	O	O	C	2	0	25	L
Rachel	D	O	E		B	4	0	26	L
Sara	O	A	A	B	B	5	0	28	L
Jack		O	E	B	B	4	0	28	L
Mike	D	A	E	B	O	4	0	29	L
Debby		O	D	D	O	6	0	30	
Shelly	O	O	D	C	B	6	0	30	
Alice		E	C	C	B	6	0	32	
Karen	C	B	A		B	4	2	32	
Barb	A	O	D	D		4	1	33	
Barry	A	E	D		O	6	1	34	
Ted			C	A		5	2	36	
Tom	A	E	O	D	B	5	3	37	
Mary				B	B	6	2	38	
Dee		B	A			6	2	39	
Jo			A	B	B	4	2	40	H
Mitzi		E	C		B	7	3	40	H
Saul		B	A	C		7	2	42	H
Ann		E	C	B		7	3	42	H
Maud		E				7	3	46	H
Sue			C		B	7	3	48	H
Bob						6	3	49	H
Fran						7	3	50	H

Bottom-section totals:

	N_s or Σ_c	D_f %	D_c
30a(7)	128	—	—
30b(3)	35	—	—

Item 5.   If f and y are the measures, in feet and yards respectively, of a given distance, find k in $f = ky$.

A.   1/12   B.   1/3   C.   1   D.   3   E.   12

Data from the Test

Choices	A	B	C	D*	E	Omit
# of Ss	1	13	1	7	1	3

Question/answer and straw poll techniques can be used to get students thinking about *why* half of the class members were misled by distractor B while so few selected A, C, or E. Mrs. Bowden might also profitably explore the reasons for the three omitted answers. Such an analysis not only has attention-getting and -keeping potential, but helps to convince the students that the test and the test post-mortem are parts of instruction. Mrs. Bowden may subsequently decide that the multiple-choice format is not the best way to test this objective. If she wants to avoid reinventing the wheel each year, she'll record that kind of change when she adds information on these test items to her test bank file.

8.4 ASSESSMENT OF AFFECTIVE OBJECTIVES

Complying, choosing to participate, exhibiting stable and consistent attitudes— these were the three levels of the affective domain described in Chapter 5. How does the teacher evaluate such objectives? There are two chief types of assessment that teachers have found useful: (1) self-evaluation forms (that is, student response forms intended to reflect their beliefs, attitudes, opinions) and (2) observation instruments.

Student self-evaluations that are honestly completed represent a student's *perceptions* of likes, dislikes, ability, and beliefs. It is well to keep in mind that how a person perceives he or she will behave is frequently inconsistent with actual behavior. Yet, taken as a whole, the direction and intensity of likes and dislikes are a key to attitudes and so, to behavior. Students are sometimes asked to react to a collection of statements by checking or circling a numeral representing the extent to which one of two polar words represents their attitude. Such a scale consisting of polar descriptors listed in two columns is called a *semantic differential*. The scale depicted in Figure 8.6 requires the student to identify an overall attitude toward mathematics.

A scale such as this is easily constructed. All you do is list polar words or phrases characterizing the extremes of the attitude being assessed in two columns. One caution! All the verbal cues that tend in the same attitudinal direction should *not* be listed in the same column. For example, "Valuable to Me" and "Valuable to Society" are listed in opposite columns in Figure 8.6. This construction feature will tend to identify the careless reader who circles numerals without reading each pair of descriptors. If students have had no experience with a semantic differential, the teacher will have to spend some time on the meanings associated with the numerals. Typically, one extreme end will represent strong

I THINK MATHEMATICS IS . . .

Simple	1	2	3	4	5	Complex
Easy to learn	1	2	3	4	5	Difficult to learn
Boring	1	2	3	4	5	Interesting
Impractical	1	2	3	4	5	Practical
For everyone	1	2	3	4	5	For scholars only
About real things	1	2	3	4	5	About theories
Valuable to society	1	2	3	4	5	Worthless to society
Worthless to me	1	2	3	4	5	Valuable to me
Related to biology	1	2	3	4	5	Unrelated to biology
Related to physics	1	2	3	4	5	Unrelated to physics
Unrelated to art	1	2	3	4	5	Related to art

Fig. 8.6   Sample semantic differential scale.

agreement and the other extreme end, strong disagreement. Some teachers prefer to keep these ideas before the students by placing a + over one end of the scale and a − over the opposite end. Middle school teachers may be well-advised to use cartoon faces with a wide smile at one end of the scale and an extreme frown at the other. Why are the students directed *not* to put their names on the response sheet? Anonymous responses are more likely to be honest, especially when attitudes perceived as undesirable from the teacher's point of view could be revealed. Student teachers have used this type of scale early in their teaching experience to assess student attitudes toward algebra and geometry as well as toward the broader area of mathematics in general. The results can be helpful to the teacher. For example, if most of the students' responses indicate little or no correlation between mathematics and biology, the mathematics teacher can begin to work cooperatively with the biology teacher to emphasize such interconnections as the kinds of symmetry exhibited by living things or the surface area versus volume relationships so important to cell size and function. A readministration of the scale at the end of the course is a way of assessing changes in attitude. But don't expect a *massive* shift in attitude despite your concentrated efforts! Experience and research results (Kulm, 1980) indicate that attitudes are not easily changed and are sometimes held despite controverting data. Witness the long and continuing struggle against racial prejudice.

It is not easy for the teacher to identify unintentional affective instruction without systematic feedback from the students. One way of obtaining such feedback is by means of a short teacher-constructed inventory that focuses on what the teacher hoped was included in instruction. These instructional features, often in the form of questions, might be rated on a three-point scale (agree, disagree, or uncertain) or on a five-point scale (Corcoran & Gibb, 1961). Such scales are fashioned after that developed by Likert and are thus called Likert-type scales. Figure 8.7 illustrates one such scale.

Scales such as this one can be modified by providing a "comments" space after each item. For instance, a student who circles 1 or 2 on item A might then

Answer each of the following questions by circling one of the numerals after each question.

	Definitely Not	I Don't Think So	I Can't Decide	I Think So	Definitely Yes
A. Do you understand most of the mathematics in the unit just completed?	1	2	3	4	5
B. Do you see any way to apply the content in this unit to real-life situations?	1	2	3	4	5
C. Were the homework assignments usually too long?	1	2	3	4	5
D. Were the homework assignments usually interesting?	1	2	3	4	5
E. Was the mathematics presented in a way which interested you?	1	2	3	4	5
F. Do you think too much was expect of you in this unit?	1	2	3	4	5
G. Would you like to study further on this topic?	1	2	3	4	5

Fig. 8.7 Sample Likert-type scale.

list areas or topics that seemed most difficult. Notice the use of the pronoun *you*. It is important to emphasize that each student should reflect personal reactions rather than what "a lot of kids say." It's strange how "a lot of kids" boils down to two or three individuals when all students have a chance to express themselves without fear of peer pressure. On the other side of the coin, it's well to avoid the pronoun *I*. Item F, for example, was designed to avoid this problem. The reader often reacts differently to the same item if phrased: "Do you think I expected too much of you?" Should this kind of inventory be administered immediately after the students have been given test grades? Can you imagine the effect on responses of the student who was coasting along and got a failing grade in this test? Generally, such inventories prove most useful if administered after the students have taken the test, but before the test grades are reported. Could the inventory be administered on the test day after the students have handed in the completed test. If *all* students have the five to eight minutes needed to complete the inventory, this is an effective use of time. Otherwise, it can be administered at the beginning of the next class. In any event, inventories should not be completed by some students on one day and by others at another time, and *never* ask students to complete these outside of class time. In both cases, responses are more likely to reflect peer group comments than individual perceptions, although forms taken out of class may just disappear—to be found in the cafeteria, on the school bus, or tucked in a library book. A carefully thought-out inventory that is administered with due regard for these cautions is more apt to be taken seriously by the students, especially if feedback is shared with them later. Be warned; overkill can destroy the impact! An inventory administered after *every* test becomes a routine.

Another type of student self-evaluation of attitudes involves the writing of open-ended essays. The students may be asked to write an essay on the topic

"What Mathematics Means to Me" or to expand on a topic sentence or question, such as: "A mathematician, like a painter or a poet, is a maker of patterns." Again students need to be told why the teacher is asking them to write these essays and what use will be made of them. Feedback on areas of major agreement and disagreement should be shared with the class. This particular device has enormous possibilities for identifying and affecting attitudes as to the nature of mathematics. (Remember the "invented versus discovery" question raised in Chapter 4?)

Essay statements might be used in structured small-group discussions or expanded on by the teacher, who could present data from the history of mathematics or about the nature of mathematical processes and products. The teacher who has specified objectives dealing with attitudes about the structure of mathematics can use phrases from those objectives as topics, topic sentences, or questions. The essay device used in this way becomes a powerful technique for getting feedback and for using that feedback in subsequent instruction. This is another instance in which the cognitive domain is closely meshed with the affective domain. An essay on the real-life applicability of mathematics may disclose strong biases based on erroneous or completely missing information.

The second of the assessment types listed at the beginning of this section, observation, does input individual data. Systematic observation shares with the essay technique the ability to focus on higher-level affective objectives. Moreover, observation has an advantage over all types of student self-analysis because actual behavior, rather than perceptions as to likely behavior, can be identified and recorded. The form shown in Figure 8.8 was designed by a teacher who had specified seven affective objectives to be aimed at during a lab-oriented approach to a unit on similarity. Observation must be conducted on a scheduled basis so that no students are inadvertently ignored. Hours after the event, selective recall takes over and much relevant data is lost.

8.5 ASSESSMENT OF PSYCHOMOTOR OBJECTIVES

A quick review of the psychomotor objectives listed in Section 5.3 of Chapter 5 will convince you that there is *one* valid way of assessing such objectives: systematic observation. The teacher must observe each individual perform the motor skill. An observational recording sheet analogous to that illustrated in Section 8.4 can be constructed for this purpose. Then the teacher can set up a lab practicum test in such a way that small numbers of students perform a task at lab stations with the teacher observing and recording behavior while the rest of the students work at pencil-and-paper tasks at their seats.

8.6 REPORT CARDS AND FINAL GRADES

Scores on paper-and-pencil tests of cognitive objectives are by far the most commonly used ingredient in arriving at report card grades. Such grades, which are intended to represent student achievement over a marking period or entire

Students

Behavior	Paul	Barry	Lisa	Allan	→
1. Works cooperatively with other students.					
2. Treats equipment with care.					
3. Tries some of the "extra" challenge problems.					
4. Volunteers to add real-life pictures, clippings, etc., to display on similarity.					
5. Works extensively on labs when given a choice between these and free time.					
6. Asks for reference books on surveying, art or photography.					
7. Chooses to do a science-related project.					

Fig. 8.8   A sample observation record form.

course, are indicators of summative evaluation. Shouldn't degree of attainment of affective and psychomotor objectives also be incorporated into such grades? That depends partly on the overall objectives of the course and partly on the definition of the report card grade used by a particular school. As a student teacher or a teacher starting out in a new school, be sure to check both written policy and unwritten tradition on these matters with the cooperating teacher or department head. Also find out if class participation and work on out-of-class projects is to be quantified and, if so, how. Suppose some diagnostic quizzes were given solely to determine the future course of instruction. Clearly these should be omitted from the calculation of a composite score. Were the unit tests designed to assess units of varied importance? If so, these scores cannot be treated as if each unit was of equal worth. Figure 8.9 depicts part of a page from Mr. Means's grade book. Since Mr. Means has recorded raw scores, he may simply obtain the sum of the raw scores of all quizzes and tests, except that given on October 31. (We hope you noticed that.) For the four weeks, depicted here, he would obtain 141 for K. Abrams. If a percentage grade is to be reported, that would be calculated by dividing each student's total by 150. Notice the difference in total possible scores on the congruence test and the inequality test. If Mr. Means averaged 88 and 35 (K. Abrams's scores), K. Abrams would be assessed as achieving 62 percent of the work on these two units. If K. Abrams is as alert as her actual

GEOMETRY—PERIOD 4 CLASS

Week 6

	10/10-10/14					10/17-10/21					10/24-10/28					10/31-11/4				
	M	T	W	Th	F	M	T	W	Th	F	M	T	W	Th	F	M	T	W	Th	F
1. Abrams, K.	8				88					10					35	15				
2. Anthony, R.	7				78					6					30	15				
3. Butler, A.	10				85					9					38	18				
23. Zeh, T.	2				55					5					25	10				

Column labels (vertical): Quiz—Congruence (10); Test—Congruence (90); Quiz—Inequalities (40); Test—Inequalities (40); Diag. quiz—Parallels (20)

Fig. 8.9   Sample entries from a grade book.

cumulative score on these two tests $(123/130 \approx 95\%)$ indicates, she'd be complaining loud and clear! And she should! What if Mr. Means had converted individual raw scores into percentages, a common practice, and then averaged all unit tests? Would the students have been treated fairly? Let's see what happens to K. Abrams. She'd receive 98 percent $(88/90)$ on the first test and 88 percent $(35/40)$ on the second. Her average on the two would be 93 percent. A fluke? Well, teachers-to-be, you know how to find out. Is

$$[(a/b) + (c/d)] \div 2 = [(a + c)/(b + d)]?$$

You'd be amazed at the number of teachers who behave as if they are! Of course, all this concern for conversions that maintain the initial emphasis of instruction and related assessment is based on the assumption that the teacher took this into consideration in planning and test construction. Moreover, if Mr. Means had identified ambiguous items after item analysis—items which substantially altered final test scores—and did nothing to indicate the lesser degree of validity of that test, then all bets are off.

Mr. Means has a number of other decisions to make. He also required a construction/design project of each student. How should this assessment count? Whenever psychomotor objectives are part of instruction, their assessment should be part of evaluation. In most cases, the report card grade referred to as *achievement* includes assessment of all instructional objectives. Once more the teacher has to make a policy decision. How much shall performance on these related psychomotor tasks count? The answer, as always, is based on the overall set of objectives and the emphasis of instruction.

In addition, several students volunteered to construct a large demonstration model after engaging in the required construction design project. If Mr. Means's school reporting system includes a space for "effort" or "attitude," he has a specific way to report such results. As in all other school reporting systems, the operational definition of "effort" must be gleaned from faculty handbooks and tradition. The particular interpretation placed on that definition by Mr. Means, as with any teacher, should be communicated to the students early in the year. This category of reporting is perhaps the most abused in the evaluation process. It is not unheard of for Mike to receive an A in the achievement column for algebra and a 1 (inadequate effort) in the effort column for that subject. Discerning parents will rightly question that teacher's understanding of evaluation and the objectives of instruction. Mike will undoubtedly continue sliding through algebra class when he can meet the objectives set by the teacher at the A-level without half trying. In the same class, Eileen received an E in achievement and a 5 (top of the scale) in effort. Do you see any reason for a parent-teacher-guidance counselor conference before sending such a report home? Considerable care is always called for in reporting affective assessments.

There are no easy answers to the questions posed here. However, it is important to keep three principles in mind:

1. Report card grades always represent a *value* judgment. (Don't let the use of numbers fool you or anyone else into believing they are objective results.)

2. Decisions as to weighting of varied projects, quizzes, tests, activities, and so on, must reflect instructional emphasis. (The die is cast after you report results on the first project—perhaps during construction of the first test.)

3. Overall principles guiding the decisions you've made must be shared with the students as early in the game as possible. (Past experience may cause them to mistrust assessment.)

The last principle is not as easy as it sounds. A good practice is to introduce the students to the teacher's task in marking report cards. Have each student keep a record of his or her individual scores and let each use a calculator during a class period to compute composite quiz and test scores according to the principles you've decided to follow. Marvin who had a string of 8s on seven of nine 10-credit quizzes and a pair of 2s begins to see what those low scores do to a composite score. You can explain how projects, laboratory work, and the like are included and then have each student submit (1) the individual computations, (2) the final grade deserved (in his or her judgment), and (3) the reasons why that grade is deserved. Teachers who use the above practice are often pleasantly surprised by the students' discerning judgment. The success of the venture depends largely on the respect the teacher has engendered thus far in evaluation and the realization that while the final *judgment (evaluation)* is the teacher's responsibility, any new data will be studied carefully before that decision is made.

8.7 SUMMARY AND SELF-CHECK

Repeatedly throughout this text, the importance of feedback getting, giving, and using has been emphasized. In this chapter, the formal feedback process known as evaluation was explored. The reader was introduced to a variety of assessment techniques, including the observational scale and the student checklist, for each of the domains. For the cognitive domain, special attention was given to the advantages and disadvantages of various types of paper-and-pencil test items. The classroom test process was outlined from table of specifications through to the reporting of grades.

In focusing on evaluation, we are once again emphasizing the need to continually and systematically assess your teaching. All the popularity contests may be ignored if the "most pleasing" teacher never achieves the objectives of instruction.

After interacting with the material in this chapter, you should be able to:

1. Operationally define evaluation, testing, formative, summative and diagnostic evaluation, objectively scored items, subjectively scored items, norm-referenced testing, and criterion-referenced testing, reliability and validity.

2. Identify the common defects in test items and revise such items in accordance with the rules of thumb in this chapter.

3. Construct test items that match specified objectives and correspond to the rules of thumb in this chapter.

4. Critique a completed table of specifications for match of items to the indicators in each margin, given a copy of the corresponding test.

5. Construct a table of specifications given a unit test.

6. Complete an item analysis sheet (including the calculation of item discrimination and item difficulty), given a set of scored test papers.

7. Critique individual test items, identify error patterns, and outline the major components to be included in a test post-mortem, given a copy of the test, the corresponding table of specifications, and the completed item analysis sheet.

8. Convert a set of raw scores into letter grades and justify your evaluation decisions.

9. Design an inventory checklist or observational scale to assess given attitudinal objectives.

10. Design an observational scale to assess given psychomotor objectives.

Check your own mastery of these objectives as you respond to the exercises that follow. Both student teaching and regular contractual teaching will offer repeated opportunities to further develop your evaluation skills.

8.8 SIMULATION/PRACTICE ACTIVITIES

A. Each of the following questions is defective in some respect. Identify the defect and revise the question so as to correspond to the rules of thumb in this chapter.

Group 1: Completion items

1. A _____(1)_____ is a parallelogram with one right angle.

      1. _____

2. The length of a side of a square is 5 inches. Its area is _____(2)_____ .

      2. _____

3. A parallelepiped with rectangle faces is called a(an) _____(3)_____ _____(3)_____ .

      3. _____

Group 2: Multiple-choice

4. How many faces does a cube have?

    A. 6   B. 8   C. 4   D. 5

      4. _____

5. The product of two reflections is

    A. odd   C. rotation

    B. reflection   D. translation

      5. _____

6. If the discriminant of a quadratic equation is equal to 9, then the roots are

    A. imaginary   C. real and equal

    B. larger than 3   D. real and unequal

      6. _____

B. Refer to the Learning Hierarchy Modular assignment in the Appendix. For each objective included in your response to that assignment, construct a matching assessment item.

C. In a student teacher's table of specifications, items 3, 10, and 12 were listed under level III of the cognitive domain. The cooperating teacher agreed with the classification of item 12 but questioned the designation of the other two items as level III. Help the student teacher reclassify items 3 and 10 and justify your decisions in terms of the criteria for each appropriate level of the taxonomy. *(No log table was given to students.) (What format defect needs to be corrected in item 12?)

3. If the number 0.00000084 is expressed in the form 8.4×10^a, what is the value of a?

      3. _____

10. Express in simplest form: $\dfrac{(b/a) - (a/b)}{(1/b) - (1/a)}$

      10. _____

12. If $\log_{10} 2 = 0.3010$, then $\log_{10} 5 =$

    A. 2.5×0.3010 D. $1 - 0.3010$

    B. $0.3010/2.5$ E. none of these

    C. $2.5 = 0.3010$

      12. _____

D. In Section 1.3 you were asked to compute the values of the indices missing from Mrs. Bowden's Item Analysis sheet. The correct results are listed here.

Item #	$D_f(\%)$	D_c
3	15	3
4	58	3
5	27	5
30a	70	4
30b	45	7

With this information, the data on choices from the Item Analysis sheet, and the items themselves, Mrs. Bowden can now decide whether particular items need restructuring before storing them in her test file and whether certain error patterns provide an answer to learning problems. Item 5 has already been subjected to this kind of analysis. For items 3 and 4, reproduced here:

a) Identify distractors that contributed little or nothing to the item and rewrite these.

b) Analyze the major error patterns and conjecture the probable learning problem that led to those errors. Suggest way(s) of remediating this learning problem.

3. If $x(x - y) = 0$ and if y does not equal zero, which of the following is true?

   A. $x = 0$

   B. Either $x = 0$ or $x = y$

   C. $x = y$

   D. $x^2 = y$

   E. Both $x = 0$ and $x - y = 0$

4. The town of Mason lies on Eagle Lake. The town of Canton is west of Mason. Sinclair is east of Canton but west of Mason. Dexter is east of Richmond but west of Sinclair and Canton. Which town is farthest west?

   A. Mason

   B. Dexter

   C. Canton

   D. Sinclair

   E. Richmond

E. On a unit test with a total possible raw score of 105, the following raw scores were obtained for a class of 31 students. Assume no problems with defective test items or test administration.

105–1	87–1	80–2	71–1
101–2	86–1	76–3	69–1
100–1	84–2	75–1	68–1
92–2	83–3	74–1	59–1
91–1	82–1	73–1	57–1
90–1	81–1	72–1	

Your school has a fixed scale to be used when assigning letter grades to test scores. Raw scores must first be converted to percentages.

Scale	Percentages
A:	100–91
B:	90–83
C:	82–71
D:	70–65
E:	Below 65

1. Assign letter grades to the above set of scores by using this fixed scale.

2. Find the median score (the score above or below which one-half of all scores lie). Assume that the median score should be assigned a C and assign letter grades to other scores based on "natural" clusters.

3. Contrast the results of these two methods of assigning letter grades. On what assumptions are each of these methods based? What are the advantages and disadvantages of each?

SUGGESTIONS FOR FURTHER STUDY

Braswell, J. S. (1976). *Mathematics tests available in the United States*, (enl.) Washington, D.C.: NCTM.

This pamphlet lists tests by author, grade level (primarily K–14), and forms. It includes information on availability of norms, the name and address of the publisher and reference location in the *Mental Measurements Yearbook*.

Bureau of Mathematics Education. (1986). *Guide for rating Regents examinations in mathematics*. Albany, NY: The State Education Department.

Don't be put off by the apparently New York state–restricted scope of this source! In fact, the writers included a range of typical test items, both short response and essay , that are part of the baseline testing of every mathematics teacher. Guidelines for assigning credit to the essay questions and sample student responses with corrections and rationale were included in the source. Our only major quarrel with the guide is the stance on credit associated with proofs in symbolic logic. Otherwise, we recommend this source as a starting point to learn about scoring questions based on a reasonable set of guidelines.

Carpenter, T. P., Coburn, T. G., Reys, R. E., & Wilson, J. W. (1978). *Results from the first mathematics assessment of the National Assessment of Educational Progress*. Reston, VA: National Council of Teachers of Mathematics.

Carpenter, T. P., Corbin, M. K., Kepner, H. S., Lindquist, M. M., & Reys, R. E. (1981). *Results from the second mathematics assessment of the National Assessment of Educational Progress*. Reston, VA: National Council of Teachers of Mathematics.

These two sources contain a wealth of test items, data and analysis of data in major areas of the curriculum and, in the case of the second assessment, in the areas of attitudes, achievement of minorities and sex-related differences in mathematics achievement.

Sund, R. B., & Picard, A. J. (1972). *Behavioral objectives and educational measures: science and mathematics*. Columbus, Ohio: Charles E. Merrill.

We encourage you to use this text as a source of sample test items and assessment tasks in the cognitive domain and of various assessment techniques for objectives in the affective and psychomotor domains. For some unknown reason, the authors chose not to highlight the psychomotor domain, but careful readers will find illustrative assessment items hidden in observational record sheets, such as that found on page 119.

Suydam, M. N. (1974). *Evaluation in the mathematics classroom*. Columbus, OH: ERIC SMEAC.

We especially recommend Suydam's book for additional information on various evaluation procedures, including interviews, scales, observations and inventories. She particularly emphasized widening the scope of evaluation to include data on how a student gets an answer. In addition, she included information on standardized tests and a list of selected references with annotations.

Wilson, J. (1971). "Evaluation of learning in secondary school mathematics." In B. S. Bloom, J. T. Hastings & G. F. Madaus (Eds.), *Handbook on formative and summative evaluation of student learning* (pp. 643–696). New York: McGraw-Hill Book Co.

Wilson included examples from the National Longitudinal Study of Mathematical Abilities to illustrate ways to assess cognitive objectives and affective objectives. Although the taxonomy referred to by Wilson is not identical to the one explained in Chapter 5 of this text, the assessment items, especially those at the higher cognitive levels and those in the affective domain, are worth examining as models.

Wilson, N. (1970). *Objective tests and mathematical learning*, Hawthorn, Victoria: Australian Council for Educational Research.

No, the author of this text doesn't really believe that some tests are objective and others subjective. The title refers to ways to increase objectivity from item construction to scoring. The reader will find that the topics presented in this little paperback supplement those handled in Chapter 8 by Farrell and Farmer. Highlights include a host of diverse item types, two sample diagnostic tests, attention to sampling and assignment of letter grades, and a transcript of the conversation of a group of teachers constructing a common test. The reader will notice that the cognitive taxonomy is sliced somewhat differently from that used by your text and that the discrimination index is computed as a decimal. However, these minor differences should cause no problems in view of the wealth of helpful material contained therein.

CHAPTER NINE

PERSPECTIVES OF MATHEMATICS EDUCATION

Learning From the Past

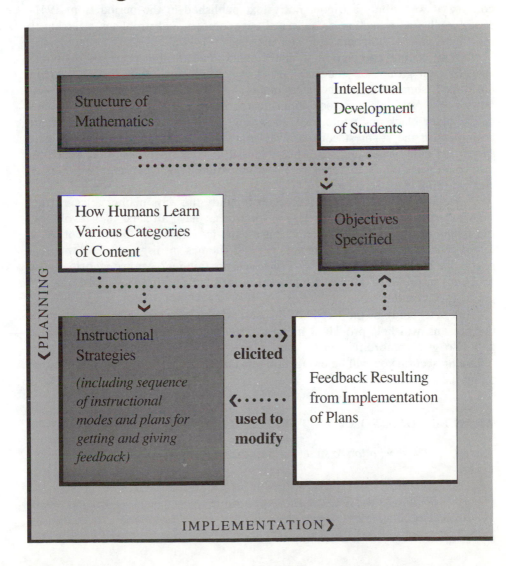

By this time you have learned that the instructional model on the facing page of each chapter depicts a dynamic interaction of multiple perspectives to be considered when you plan and later implement lessons. We have focused on **how** instructional objectives can be attained and much less on **what** texts, course materials and syllabi might be used to attain objectives. After all, a teacher's first concern is with appropriate instruction. Furthermore, don't text writers consider these same perspectives when they prepare materials? Well, they should, but all too often, they are influenced by other forces, such as parental cries for more emphasis on calculation skills or press reports on the need for technological applications. In fact, choice of topics has even been determined by needs of a country at war. Study a trigonometry text published in the period from 1941–1945; you'll find a section on spherical trigonometry and problems referring to the flight paths of bombers or fighter planes.

Why should contemporary mathematics teachers be aware of textbooks used by past groups of students? Aren't our newest materials the most highly developed, somewhat like the latest model car? Well, like the latest model car, our newest materials may look sophisticated in appearance compared to many of the older black and white texts. However, the latest model car's light frame crumples on the slightest contact. Was something important sacrificed to gain speed and ease of handling? Is it possible that the text materials of the past contain some gems that a contemporary teacher would delight in using? We think so and we think you will agree!

We also believe that it is important to study the ways mathematics instruction and curriculum have evolved, the forces that have affected their evolution, the issues that have been concerns of mathematics educators. Our students have found that some new "bandwagons" are old themes in disguise. Why was that particular bandwagon abandoned? What were its failures? Are we ignoring those problems again and dooming the present movement to failure? We can only begin to touch on these matters in this chapter.

A brief study of the trends of the past, which have culminated in issues of the present, will help provide a frame of reference for the contemporary scene and also give some direction to your own search for worthwhile ideas. In the following section you will be engaged in an activity designed to start you thinking along these lines.

9.1 INTRODUCTORY ACTIVITY

Those who fail to study the past are condemned to repeat it.

For this activity, you and a partner will need to obtain four texts. These should include:

1. the Milne *Algebra* text or any other algebra text from the first 20 years of the twentieth century,

2. an algebra text published during 1930–1940,

3. the School Mathematics Study Group *Algebra* texts—Books 1 and 2 (or any other algebra text of the immediate "post-Sputnik Curricular Reform Era" suggested by your instructor), and

4. an algebra text published in the last five years.

Each person should analyze *two* of the texts. Study the contents of the two texts you selected for answers to the following questions:

1. Which text(s) use(s) vocabulary such as *commutative, associative, identity property*? What differences in symbolism are found? (Check for set symbolism and symbols used to illustrate square root, ratio.)

2. Which text(s) use(s) the axiomatic process to explain results or deduce new properties? (How, for example, is the product of two negatives explained?)

3. What real-life areas are used in the problem material? Which text(s), if any, use situations meaningful to the teenager?

4. Check through the exercise sets. Are these chiefly routine practice or is any novelty included?

5. Review the context of the "word" or verbal problems in each text. Are the activities stereotyped by gender, or are both males and females portrayed in the same kinds of activities? More generally, does the problem-context portray algebra as a subject that **humans** apply?

After you've responded to all five questions, compare results with that obtained by your partner. Using the text from the immediate post-Sputnik period, try to identify those characteristics that might be aspects of "new math." Most parents believe that new math replaced an "old math." What, if anything, seems to have been replaced?

If you've found that parts of the older texts are still very contemporary and that even the newest versions seem to be barely removed from the over 20-year-old SMSG text (or parallel one you analyzed), then you're beginning to be properly skeptical about curricular bandwagons. Four texts hardly constitute an exhaustive sample, but they *are* a beginning in our search for data. As you read the following section, rethink your responses to this activity in the light of *events* that occurred in the time periods outlined.

9.2 FROM THE THREE R'S TO THE STANDARDS

In the sections that follow, we briefly outline the history of mathematics education from colonial America to the present. (See Jones & Coxford [1970] for a detailed treatment up to 1970). Our emphasis is on forces and issues affecting what was taught,to whom, why, and how.

Although colonial America began to place some emphasis on the importance of formal education in the middle of the seventeenth century, mathematics was a stepchild that was rarely, if ever, mentioned. Massachusetts, for example, passed two education laws during the seventeenth century. The law of 1642 mandated instruction in reading and the catechism, as well as apprenticeship in a trade, while the law of 1647 required that each town of 50 families provide an elementary school teacher and each town of 100 families provide a Latin grammar school. Reading, but not mathematics, was required for admission to the Latin grammar school. These Latin grammar schools were modeled on those of England. The typical seven-year course included *no* specific attention to mathematics, history, or the natural sciences. Instead the students read the classics in Latin and presumably learned to speak Latin. Both accomplishments were considered useful in a variety of occupations and required for admission to college.

At what point was some kind of mathematics also required for admission to college? Arithmetic was made an entrance requirement at Yale in 1745, at Princeton in 1760, and at Harvard in 1807. In 1820 Harvard became the first college to require algebra of its entering students. If these constituted the entrance requirements, then what mathematics was offered by the colleges? By the middle of the eighteenth century a program at Yale included arithmetic, algebra, trigonometry, and surveying. Some institutions included astronomy with mathematics; some added a course in geometry. A fraction of a percent of the population attended college and only a few more enrolled in the preparatory schools. Thus, elementary and secondary mathematics instruction, as we know it, was nonexistent. Add to this the dependence on Europe for texts. The first mathematics text written and published in the United States was Isaac Greenwood's *Arithmetick, Vulgar and Decimal*, printed in Boston in 1729. Greenwood was a professor of mathematics at Harvard from 1728–1738. His text was probably used in his college classes, but college students were not laboring over exactly the same calculation problems as contemporary primary-school children. Arithmetic texts were constructed to cover the waterfront from early work with vulgar (common) fractions to complicated applications to trade and commerce. Thus, it is obvious that the adolescent and the pre-adolescent in eighteenth-century America had little acquaintance with the mathematics you will be teaching.

When did that situation change and why? More states enacted laws requiring towns to establish schools and the Latin grammar school gave way first to academies and later to the English high school. Arithmetic, algebra, and geometry began appearing in the offerings of these schools. By mid-nineteenth century, Horace Mann had started America on the road to free public education, which was to alter the character of the schools, increase the need for teachers, and raise unending questions as to the kind of instruction needed by this vast and diverse citizenry. None of this happened overnight. At the beginning of the twentieth century, men such as Joseph Mayer Rice, a pediatrician with an interest in education, wrote articles deploring the state of the schools, the plight of illiterate child laborers, and the lack of concern over the education of the increasing number of non-English-speaking immigrant children. Even compulsory education laws did not dramatically increase the number of students who went to high school. Children simply continued to attend the grade school or rural one-room school until they reached the legal "leaving" age.

For all practical purposes, the bulk of our heritage in mathematics curriculum and instruction can be found by reviewing the texts, reports, and history of the nineteenth and twentieth centuries. This is what we propose to outline as we seek answers to the questions: Where have we been? Where are we now? And where are we headed?

From the Three R's

The early colonial records of instruction in simple arithmetic portray a classroom scene in which pupils painstakingly copied exercises from the master's text or a slate. Later instruction followed a rule-recitation method. Without explanation, the teacher would recite or write the rule; the students were expected to commit it to memory and apply it to one or two typical exercises. This mechanistic approach to the teaching of arithmetic was also applied to algebra and geometry through much of the nineteenth century (Some would add, even today in some classrooms!) despite the early, well-founded criticism of Warren Colburn. Colburn's 1830 lecture entitled "Teaching of Arithmetic" is a classic with applicability today. His exhortations to teachers to use practical examples, to guide the student through the process rather than provide solutions to be memorized, and to analyze the student's thinking processes are just as important today as they were in 1830.

Yet the history of the teaching of mathematics continued to be sprinkled with reformers' complaints about mindless drill, dull classroom teaching, and little transfer of learning. Recall the references in Chapter 6 to treating the mind as if it were a muscle and to subdividing content into tiny bits. Despite such emphasis on the "basics," testing of draftees in World War I identified a shocking portion of the citizenry who were deficient in the three R's of reading, [w]riting, and [a]rithmetic.

The history of the period between the two world wars is a period of conflicts over ways to improve mathematics education. Many of these were related to the research on how students learn mathematics and have been alluded to in Chapter 6. Thorndike's texts on arithmetic and algebra were published in the 1920s and these, as well as his lectures to future teachers, had a lasting influence on pedagogy, especially with respect to drill and practice. Proponents of Thorndike's psychology often applied his theories in extreme ways so that instruction in arithmetic and algebra consisted of drill routines. Others misapplied Dewey's philosophy that students should construct their own knowledge and learn mathematics as needed for projects of interest to them. These opponents of boring drill and practice went to the extreme of teaching mathematics **only if it happened to be needed** in a project chosen by the students. As a result, little mathematics was taught in their classrooms. Two major psychological groups railed at both of these excesses. Brownell, the leader of one group, studied the achievement of students who learned arithmetic under the drill theory and under the incidental theory, and found both severely wanting. He emphasized the need for a theory of instruction that he called the meaning theory. You will find his work to be as current today as it was when written in 1935. Gestalt psychologists, who fled to America from Nazi Germany, began lecturing in American universities. Their construct of a structured whole (gestalt) and their emphasis on the role of insight appealed to mathematics teachers who were dismayed at the static teaching of mathematics that had developed in too many classrooms and beleaguered by the animosity towards mathematics that seemed to be so popular among all levels of citizenry. Reeve (1936) documented this distressing situation in his chapter, "Attacks on mathematics and how to meet them," in the Eleventh Yearbook of the National Council of Teachers of Mathematics.

Yet, even at the beginning of World War II, Admiral Rickover (1960), among others, roundly criticized the teaching of mathematics and science. Not only were large numbers of recruits deficient in basic skills, but that segment of the population who had been educated in high-school and even college mathematics was generally incapable of applying what they had learned in the various technological fields important to the war effort. Other critics deplored the outdated nature of school mathematics content.

The situation described in the preceding section appalled a good many people, but it was not news to many mathematics educators. For decades, journal articles, lectures at professional meetings, and committee activity of organizations such as the National Council of Teachers of Mathematics (NCTM) and the Mathematical Association of America (MAA) had identified the shortcomings of the system and recommended changes. The relatively few changes that did occur took place in an extraordinarily leisurely fashion. In the long run, change would only occur when implemented by teachers, and most teachers were not educated for change. Did World War II act as a catalyst? Not really. It took a Russian spaceship called Sputnik to jolt the nation.

The Curriculum Revolution

In the Cold War era of the late 1950s, an advance like Sputnik I frightened the nation into pushing for massive strides in science and mathematics education. The National Defense Education Act (NDEA) of 1958 made it possible for agencies such as the National Science Foundation (NSF) to distribute large sums of money to implement changes in curriculum. The number of curriculum-writing projects mushroomed and the scope of their activities increased tremendously. Institutes, both summer and academic year, were designed to update the content background of tens of thousands of teachers. Demonstration classes, often involving talented high-school students, were incorporated into some of these institutes. Mathematicians from both industry and universities figured heavily in all projects. Mathematics educators and mathematics classroom teachers were involved on a somewhat less critical basis. Above all, the content was to be updated. And it was!

Plane Euclidean geometry texts at last corrected some of the problems inherent in Euclid's treament—the erroneous characterization of axioms as "self-evident truths," the use of superposition in proof, failure to deal with betweenness, and so on. An attempt was made to treat algebra on an axiomatic basis rather than merely as generalized arithmetic. Topics from probability, abstract algebra, and even analysis found their way into precollege mathematics. Language, both symbolic and nonsymbolic, was given special attention. Precision and correctness were to be characteristics of such language from the earliest years. As a result, the symbolism associated with set operations appeared in texts since set was to be treated as a unifying theme. (Instead, it often appeared to be another attempt to mystify the common folk.)

These content characteristics, along with the introduction of topics such as number bases other than ten, unfortunately became known as the "new math." Some parents (and some teachers) thought that *everything* unfamiliar to them must be newly invented mathematics. Labels such as *commutative*, that had appeared in the report of the Committee of Ten in 1895 (Bidwell & Clason, 1970, p. 135) and in algebra texts of the pre-Sputnik era, were assumed to be recent additions to mathematical language. No matter that mathematicians reacted against this misconception. They explained that the arbitrary nature of axioms had been established with the work of Bolyai, Lobachevsky, and Riemann more than 100 years ago and that the basic ideas of probability dated back to at least the seventeenth-century work of Pascal. Few listened. Wasn't the subject called "new"? Some of it certainly looked new. In its anxiety to catch up with Russia, the nation accepted the superficial novelty and never understood the intended real novelty. According to later studies (NACOME, 1975), most elementary teachers added the symbolism and language to their lessons, but not the meaningful patterns of mathematics. There's also evidence (Fey, 1979) that suggests that many secondary mathematics classrooms reflected a similar concern for "grinding out" the products of mathematics with little or no concern for the processes. Too many teachers of mathematics, like the rest of the nation, just didn't understand the goals of this revolution and were unable to implement the new curriculum projects effectively.

The picture as of 1970 was not a success story, but neither was it a complete failure. For the first time texts contained "better" mathematics and reflected a clearer picture of the nature of mathematics (Howson, Keitel, & Kilpatrick, 1981). Curriculum writers, realizing the needs of teachers, began adding tests, background reading for the teacher, masters from which acetates or multiple copies could be made, texts on varied reading levels, and a wide variety of extratext resources. Mathematics educators, such as W. W. Sawyer, Robert Davis, Ernest Ranucci, and Max Sobel, wrote articles and lectured to teachers on creative ideas and meaningful approaches to mathematics. Mathematician Zoltan Dienes took Piagetian theory into the mathematics classroom. Even Morris Kline, a constant critic of the curriculum projects of the 1960s, spurred others to begin to interweave applications into mathematics texts. Thus, in addition to the potential resource ideas in curriculum projects, writers/teachers developed a wealth of curricular resource ideas in articles written for professional journals, in softbound "idea" books and in the yearbooks of the National Council of Teachers of Mathematics.

Curriculum projects   By 1970, 32 American curriculum projects in mathematics and 49 international mathematics-related projects had developed sufficiently to be outlined in the *Seventh Report of the International Clearinghouse on Science and Curricular Developments* (Lockhard, 1976). Of these, we have selected seven as representative of the diverse curricular trends of the time.

The University of Illinois Committee on School Mathematics (UICSM) predated Sputnik, for it was initiated in 1951 under the leadership of Max Beberman. In an attempt to improve the mathematics taught to the college bound, UICSM writers and teachers attempted to produce high-school texts that would reflect the structure of mathematics as a unified whole rather than as disembodied branches. One of the then-novel aspects of text presentation was the incorporation of a guided discovery approach to the concepts and principles of mathematics. In order to train teachers in the modes of instruction deemed critical to the project, summer and academic year institutes for teachers included courses in mathematics and pedagogy, as well as demonstration classes. High-school texts, examinations for some of the units, self-instructional texts, and teacher-training films were produced by the project staff.

After 1963, a group of University of Illinois staff headed by David Paige initiated what was called the University of Illinois Arithmetic Project. The emphasis of this project was toward the students at the other end of the achievement and motivation continuum. The project staff were concerned about the low achieving, inner city youngsters who were trapped in a frustrating cycle of repetitious, low level arithmetic courses. These teenagers who were in middle school or junior high school by virtue of social promotion were poor readers, had experienced repeated failure in mathematics classes and had generally poor attitudes toward school, in general, and mathematics, in particular. Two sets of texts, one set of four books entitled *Stretchers and Shrinkers* and another set of four entitled *Motion Geometry*, were tested successfully in inner city schools. To students the cartoons and story-line approach of *Stretchers and Shrinkers* were immediately appealing. The characters in the story were teenagers of various racial backgrounds who were working in a real-life stretching and shrinking factory. *Motion Geometry* placed concepts in a transformation geometry context, with plenty of hands-on flipping, sliding and turning of cutout shapes. The books were created as modules that could be inserted into existing courses wherever the teacher found it helpful. Teacher's guides that included additional tests made these curricular materials especially useful for the classroom teacher.

The School Mathematics Study Group (SMSG), organized in March 1958 at Yale University, is probably the best-known project of the curriculum revolution. Under the leadership of E. G. Begle, professor of mathematics, SMSG produced texts and teacher's guides for kindergarten through twelfth grade. Like UICSM, SMSG writers worked at incorporating precise language and careful logical deduction into the texts. However, SMSG texts (especially the 9–12 texts) reflect the presentation of mathematics via thoughtful exposition rather than guided discovery. In addition to a set of core texts for each grade, SMSG produced alternate texts for various courses (such as *Geometry with Coordinates* as well as *Geometry* for grade ten), programmed texts, enrichment texts for teachers and/or students, teacher training texts, reports of research, and summaries of a longitudinal study of achievement. By 1970, 229 items were listed under the SMSG title. These included reprints of classics in mathematics and Spanish translations of many of its texts. With its emphasis on the structure of mathematics, SMSG's first secondary school texts were designed for the college-bound student and that student had to be a good reader! Subsequently, alternate prealgebra texts were written at a slightly lower reading level. Where were the concrete examples, the practical illustrations? They were few and far between.

The Madison Project was initiated in 1957 as a supplementary mathematics program with stress on creative learning experiences. Based at Syracuse University, Syracuse, New York, and then at Webster College, St. Louis, Missouri, the writers and teachers produced supplementary texts and teacher's guides for grades 4–9 on topics in algebra, coordinate geometry, science applications, and even matrix algebra. In addition, project staff produced teacher-training films portraying actual classroom lessons. One of the most novel aspects of the Madison Project is the set of "Shoebox" packages for physical experiments. The impact of Piagetian theory is reflected in the nature of these laboratory exercises.

The School Mathematics Project (SMP) organized in 1961 in Southampton, England, is of particular interest to American mathematics teachers. Student texts and teacher's guides for courses at three levels were developed and used by over 100,000 students ages 11–18 in Great Britain. SMP texts A–H and X, Y, and Z reflect a spirit of guided discovery, the spiraling of concepts, and a wealth of concrete beginnings (labs, visualization, real situations). Practical examples are used to stimulate curiosity and to provide a firm base for abstract concepts. The advanced SMP texts, Books 1–4, present sophisticated mathematics with its applications to science. In addition to these texts, Activity-Investigation cards were designed to supplement the work of Books A–H at three levels—remedial, mainstream, and enrichment.

The Secondary School Mathematics Curriculum Improvement Study (SSMCIS), 1965, was developed by Howard Fehr of Columbia University. SSMCIS texts contain a secondary school (grades 7–12) course appropriate for the talented mathematics student. Emphasis is on the axiomatic structure of mathematics and the group concept is utilized as a unifying theme. Not only is the instructional treatment of topics at a sophisticated level, but the topics themselves include many usually taught at the post-secondary level.

The final project outlined here is the Comprehensive School Mathematics Program (CSMP) begun by Burt Kaufman in 1965. The purpose of CSMP was to implement the major recommendations of the 1963 Cambridge Conference. Individualization of the K–12 mathematics curriculum and presentation of sound mathematical content are the two priorities of CSMP staff. As a result, mathematicians are important contributors to text materials. In the first decade of its work, CSMP developed a set of texts for highly verbal, well-motivated secondary school students and activity packages using a variety of media for elementary school children. Since all instructional materials incorporate considerable independent student work, the teacher must operate on a consultative, supportive basis.

As we approach the last decade of this century, CSMP continues to be an active curriculum development project. The elementary project materials have become more fully developed and have undergone extensive evaluation. Inservice materials have been developed for key teachers who are expected to train other teachers in their district in the philosophy and use of the materials. The secondary materials have primarily been used for the mathematics education of talented students. The materials are commercially available, as is a standardized test of Novel Problem Solving based on the elementary project materials.

Did you notice the diversity as well as the commonality in the seven projects just described? There was continual emphasis on "good" mathematics—correct, precise, and up-to-date. There was also much emphasis on the college-bound student with an occasional interlude in favor of the slow learner, and then a swing to the talented student. Some projects seem to be constructed on the assumption that the college-bound student is a good reader and needs little in the way of concrete underpinnings while a few others, especially the University of Illinois Arithmetic Project, the Madison Project and the School Mathematics Project, lean heavily on labs, visual illustrations, real-life examples, and the like.

Recall that the impetus for the curriculum revolution was the space race that began with Sputnik. The emphasis of most of the curriculum projects produced in the decade following Sputnik clearly reflects attention to educating future mathematicians, engineers, and scientists. Yet by the middle of the same decade, the attention of the American public was diverted from the space race to riots in the cities and school desegregation issues. Consequently, the limelight began to shift to the low achiever and the disadvantaged student. Federal funds were no longer available for any and all curriculum projects. The American taxpayer began demanding that schools be held accountable for teaching *all* the students.

The Reaction

There are more chapters to the story of the reaction than can be told in a few short paragraphs. Of most importance to you are four curricular trends that were affected by the reaction against excessive symbolism, lack of real-world relevance of mathematics, and excessive formalism.

First, the *continued* low level of achievement in computation (Many writers acted as if pre-Sputnik children were whiz kids in addition!) received national attention. As a result, projects that promoted the *basic skills* were "in." By the late 1970s, programmed texts, tape and slide kits, and criterion-referenced instructional packages were finding their way into most junior high schools and some senior high school classes. A *few* of these basic skills kits extended the area of basics to important concepts and processes and a small number included instructional strategies *a la* Piaget.

Second, the calculator and its sophisticated distant relative, the computer, were finding a place in the mathematics classroom. By 1975, hand-held calculators were inexpensive enough to be owned by many high school students. Whether the mathematics teacher approved or not (and many did not!), the calculator was being used to complete calculations. However, contrary to predictions of the 1960s, computer technology was still far too expensive to intervene widely into mathematics instruction. Nonetheless an increasing number of schools participated in time-sharing systems at nearby universities, industries, or regional educational centers. Programming in the BASIC language and problem solving via computer programs became the focus of an elective computer science course in some schools.

Third, the gap between the understanding of mathematics and the ability to use, or even appreciate the use of, mathematics led to an interest in teaching the nature of mathematical models. The mathematization of the social sciences, medicine, and business as well as the traditional natural sciences resulted in a spurt of college-level courses on mathematical models. At the other end of the spectrum, mathematics educators such as Max Bell (1972) saw in mathematical models a link to the everyday world of students. An increasing number of articles in professional journals on ecology, wind chill, sports car rally directions, and even scuba diving were evidence of increasing interest in ways to implement instruction in mathematical models.

Finally, there was once again a surge of interest in interrelating mathematics and science in schools. In particular on the junior high level, some popular science curricula (such as ISCS, the Intermediate Science Curriculum Study) were designed to interweave mathematics skills and concepts throughout the chapters. Several SMSG texts that used science laboratory experiences to introduce mathematical concepts and rules were offered as supplementary mathematics curricular material.

Unfortunately, all four of these trends did not receive equal attention. The results of the first National Assessment of Educational Progress, with data collected in 1973, were reported in the national press by 1977, with publication of the full report with analysis by mathematics educators in 1978. The popular press ran scare headlines on the poor calculation skills of students. Subsequently, the public demanded that teachers emphasize these skills and reincorporate drill and practice. The results of the second assessment conducted in 1978, with analysis published by NCTM in 1981, showed that calculation skills had improved significantly. This seemed to indicate that teachers had been responsive to this societal force. However, data from this same assessment showed a lack of understanding of basic concepts and processes and difficulty with nonroutine or multistep problems. Thus, the **Reaction** had become an **Overreaction**.

A Crisis of Mediocrity

In 1980, the National Council of Teachers of Mathematics reacted to the results of NAEP studies, as well as to surveys of teaching and reports from international studies of mathematics achievement in a report entitled *An agenda for action: Recommendations for school mathematics of the 1980s*. First among the eight recommendations was the statement that problem solving should be the focus of school mathematics in the 1980s. The writers made it clear that they were talking about the problem solving processes needed in all applied fields, such as analysis, conceptualization, data gathering, and hypothesizing. The writers also insisted on the importance of learning basic skills; however, they defined basic skills as more than the ability to calculate. Articles, lectures and a NCTM yearbook, *The Agenda in Action*, illustrated lesson ideas that would reflect the recommendations found in the report.

Meanwhile, the public became more aware of the problems of education as a result of a widely published report, *A Nation at Risk* (1983). Although the committee was commenting on education in general, their characterization of American education, as a "rising tide of mediocrity," captured the headlines. Other national reports followed, with one specifically devoted to the need for citizens literate in mathematics and science. This last report, *Educating Americans for the 21st Century* (1983) was sponsored by the National Science Board and read almost like a call to return to the early post-Sputnik days, in terms of its emphasis on content. Some reactors warned the mathematics and science education community not to forget the lessons of the post-Sputnik period. Overemphasis on good mathematics had produced texts that mathematicians found acceptable. However, lack of emphasis on research on human learning, cognitive development of students, and education of teachers in strategies based on this interface had led to little change in the classroom. As Begle is supposed to have said, the curriculum revolution may have resulted in the teaching of better mathematics; but it did not result in better teaching of mathematics.

Responses   At the national level, Congress began to approve legislation that increased the funding available to develop curricula, create inservice mathematics teacher education programs, and initiate research programs. However, the grants were not of the same magnitude as that of the immediate post-Sputnik era. Thus, large-scale national projects have not been the norm. Instead there have been many smaller curriculum projects, often aimed at a unit within a course; some innovative materials financed by industry; state-funded curriculum projects; and sourcebooks and curricular modules published commercially and by the National Council of Teachers of Mathematics. We have elected to highlight one example in each of these categories.

The University of Chicago School Mathematics Project, directed by Zalman Usiskin, is being funded by grants from industries and the National Science Foundation. The project is producing textbooks, teacher's guides, training materials and resource materials for both primary and secondary school mathematics. Teachers are involved in the development, evaluation, and implementation of project material. Each set of texts goes through an extensive tryout, formative evaluation, and revision phase before the summative evaluation and final revision is completed. The director cites the need to integrate calculators and computers into the curriculum, to emphasize applications, to maximize the acquisition of skills and understanding, and to eliminate outmoded mathematics from the curriculum. A newsletter is produced to keep interested mathematics educators updated on the progress of the project.

New York State's Three-Year Sequence for High School Mathematics was collaboratively produced by groups of classroom teachers and university faculty, under the supervision of members of the Bureau of Mathematics Education of the NYS Education Department. After extensive formative evaluation and revision, a curriculum guide was printed and distributed in 1976. The guides for Courses II and III went through a similar process, with the present curriculum guide for Course III being printed in 1978. As of this date, a revision of Course I is being printed and is to be distributed in the fall of 1988. This high school sequence is notable in its attempt to break down the traditional barriers between algebra and geometry. Three major strands, symbolic logic, transformation geometry, and probability and statistics, were introduced into the courses. These curriculum guides have been the subject of controversy by some college faculty who decry what they see as lack of practice on algebraic manipulations and by some classroom teachers who dislike the emphasis on transformation geometry and the accompanying de-emphasis on typical synthetic geometry proofs in grade ten.

New York State has recently revised its seventh and eighth grade curriculum guides to support the new high school sequence. The seventh and eighth grade guides, which highlight problem solving as a major goal of the curriculum, are more extensive documents than the high school guides and, thus, are good sources for teaching ideas.

An innovative project funded by the Phillips Petroleum Company is titled "The Challenge of the Unknown." The project consists of a series of seven films, available on videotape, and a teaching guide. The entire set of films is aimed at teaching problem solving skills, by reference to the real applications and the use of zany cartoon characters. The teaching guide contains specific teaching suggestions, additional background reading for the teacher, interesting exercises and projects for the students and an annotated bibliography. As an example, the film on Estimation contains a segment called *Sharks: One if by air...Two if by sea*; another called *China census: Everyone counts* and a third titled *Avalanche: Snow job*. It is easy to teach students about the interface of mathematics and science with these films. The films can be borrowed from Phillips by a school district, for the purpose of dubbing on videotape. There is no charge for the loan. The guide is available from W. W. Norton at a small cost.

An example of a set of modules published commercially is *Contemporary applied mathematics*, published by Janson. The five books in the series are *Glyphs*,

Queues, Graph theory, Mathematics and medicine, and *Dynamic programming.* A teacher's manual was designed to help the teacher integrate the modules into the curriculum, identify difficult concepts, extend the ideas in the modules and provide additional background. These books provide excellent examples of the use of mathematical models in real world situations.

It would take pages to describe the sources available from the National Council of Teachers of Mathematics. We list here a sample of the most recent yearbooks that include responses to recent forces and issues: the 1988 yearbook, *The ideas of algebra, K–12,* the 1987 yearbook, *Learning and teaching geometry: K–12,* the 1985 yearbook, *The secondary school mathematics curriculum,* the 1984 yearbook, *Computers in mathematics education,* the 1982 yearbook, *Mathematics for the middle grades (5–9),* and the 1981 yearbook, *Teaching statistics and probability.*

Information technology and mathematics   By 1980, personal computers were being touted as the tool that would transform teaching. There was a flurry of activity at school and college levels to train teachers, usually mathematics teachers, so that they might teach courses in computer literacy, computer programming, and computer math. At the same time there was considerable debate over the definitions of computer literacy and computer math. School districts, through small grant programs, purchased microcomputers and set up computer labs—in many case, with little idea of what to do with the technology once it was in place. In less than five years, microcomputers have become incredibly sophisticated; educational software has begun to move beyond the "drill and practice" variety; and a generation of students are already quite familiar with joysticks, keyboarding, mouses, and the like. In response to changing needs and changes in technology, many instructors of college and inservice computer education courses have de-emphasized the teaching of programming, and emphasized ways to evaluate and adapt software for use in mathematics lessons.

However, change takes place very slowly in classrooms. Surveys of the use of microcomputers in mathematics classrooms (McDonald, 1987) have shown that most mathematics teachers (72%, $n = 264$) agree that integration of microcomputers into the mathematics classroom is a desirable goal, but only 27% of these same teachers felt that they had been successful in accomplishing this goal. Less than 24% of the respondents felt that the mathematics departments in their schools had been successul in reaching this goal. Lack of time in the curriculum, lack of knowledge on the part of teachers and lack of hardware for class use were cited by these teachers as major factors impeding progress.

The perceptive commentaries by mathematics educators at a conference on computing and mathematics identify the basic stumbling blocks to more integration of information technology into the mathematics classroom (Fey, 1984). In separate chapters on algebra, geometry, calculus, and discrete mathematics, the writers called for a major restructuring of the curriculum to make education responsive to changes already in place in industry, government, and science. In an illustration from the chapter on algebra, the roots of a quadratic equation are found by using a simple BASIC program.

```
10 INPUT A,B,C
20 FOR X=A TO B STEP C
30 PRINT X, (X−5)*X+3
40 NEXT X
```

The student who inputs −5,5,1 and types RUN, will be using the method of successive approximation to estimate the roots of $x^2 - 5x + 3$. The RUN will yield:

−5,5,1	
−5	53
−4	39
−3	27
−2	17
−1	9
0	3
1	−1
2	−3
3	−3
4	−1
5	3

As the authors pointed out, the data provide not only a good idea where the zeros are, but give a good idea of the minimum point of the polynomial and solutions of the inequality $x^2 - 5x + 3 > 0$ and $x^2 - 5x + 3 < 0$. A new search within the interval from 0 to 1 will yield a better estimation of the roots. The authors extended this idea to show how the graphic capability of the computer can be used to get a graph of the function. As the authors noted, some mathematics teachers may argue against this use of a "guess and try" strategy, rather than the standard quadratic algorithm. However, these writers presented a powerful case for the naturalness of the successive approximation strategy and its usefulness in many simple and complex situations. They outlined a possible sequence of subtopic instruction in the quadratic, in which concrete approaches would allow the students to solve complex real world problems early in instruction. Only later, and possibly only for advanced students, would formal analysis of the quadratic, relations between coefficients and roots, nature of roots, factoring and the quadratic formula be taught.

It seems clear that the vision of the mathematics educators at this conference will affect the curriculum and instruction of the future. When? As we have seen in the brief history of mathematics education presented thus far, forces outside the education community can either hinder or promote that vision.

The Standards and the Future

In 1987, a commission appointed by the National Council of Teachers of Mathematics released a draft version of a document entitled *Curriculum and evaluation standards for school mathematics*. The *Standards* is a response to current issues and forces in mathematics education. These include societal concerns over the growing mismatch between what is taught in school mathematics and what is needed in college mathematics, the comparative data on American students and those from other industrialized nations (McKnight, Crosswhite, Dossey, Kifer, Swafford, Travers, & Cooney, 1987), the underrepresentation of ethnic and cultural minorities in advanced mathematics courses and the achievement differences between these populations and those of the white majority, as well as between girls and boys. In an effort to address these concerns, the writers produced standards that include emphasis on problem solving, communication, and reasoning, as well as on specific major conceptual strands in mathematics and on attitudes. The document includes specific illustrations of ways in which these standards might be met. Suggested strategies are explained in terms of research on the cognitive development of students and the learning of mathematics. For example, at all grade levels, the importance of small group work, student-to-student interaction, is stressed. Indeed, it is acknowledged that even the formal reasoner profits from concrete approaches in the development of new concepts. In addition, there is explicit attention to instruction that reflects the processes and products of mathematics. The writers suggest that calculators be used to perform tedious computations and that the role of paper and pencil practice of algorithms be de-emphasized. Similarly, computer technology is viewed as important for its capability as an interactive tool whose graphic and data reduction and data analysis capabilities may be used to promote problem solving. The *Standards* writers were obviously in agreement with much of the vision expressed by the mathematics educators at the conference on information technologies and mathematics education.

After widespread discussion of the document, response back to the writers, and revision by the commission, a final document is to be distributed in 1988–1989. The final version of the *Standards* and the expected subsequent development of corresponding curricular materials could have a dramatic impact on the school mathematics you will teach in the next decade. Much depends on the commitment of schools and the public to a significant change in their schools.

9.3 IMPLICATIONS FOR THE MATHEMATICS TEACHER

Think back to the Introductory Activity. You were asked to compare a recent algebra text with a text typical of the curriculum revolution. You should have found the threads of emphasis on axiomatics, structure, precise language, and so on, throughout the newer text. Thus, the first major implication of the curriculum reforms of recent decades resides in their impact on all curricular materials produced since 1970. There is no turning back, despite the cry of "Back to Basics," but modifications of the emphases of varying projects are possible and already in full swing.

This means that the texts you may be expected to use should correspond to a contemporary view of mathematics, a view your own mathematical background ought to reflect. Hence, you'll understand the basic mathematics well enough to reinterpret it for the students you teach. Right? Wrong! Under the best of circumstances, the *learning* of college mathematics does not require that the student translate mathematical concepts and principles into everyday situations, rephrase definitions in his or her own words, or explain the reasonableness of a definition or assumption. Under the worst of circumstances, the college student often succeeds in mathematics by dutifully grinding out responses and regurgitating proofs or problem solutions previously demonstrated in class. In the latter case, the college student suddenly (often painfully) realizes that he or she just doesn't understand great chunks of mathematics. "Ask me to differentiate anything! I'm a whiz! But don't ask me why it works or what it's good for or what it depends on ...." If this is your plight, you might well question the mathematics instruction that allowed you to be stamped as "passed." More to the point, you need to start re-educating yourself, and some of the best source books for that purpose are those of curriculum projects such as SMSG or UICSM. Read the text material, work out the exercises, and constantly seek answers to "why?" as well as "how?" Moreover, even those luckier mathematics majors who did learn much of their mathematics meaningfully need to begin to work at the problem of communicating mathematics without distorting it. The teacher's commentaries accompanying each SMSG text are one source of potential help. For each topic in the student text, the teacher's commentary includes a parallel consideration but adds background material, gives a justification for the mode or sequence of presentation, and may refer the reader to other in-depth sources. Each of the other curriculum projects described earlier are similar sources of background material for the prospective teacher. Finally, while novice teachers are rarely in a position to select new texts for a class, they should be constantly seeking resource ideas to add life and meaning to lessons.

Don't overlook texts from the nineteenth or early twentieth century. One such text, *Concrete Geometry* by Hornbrook (1895), contains nothing but questions, among them several excellent paper-folding and cutting activities. Many of our students are so convinced of the value of these old texts that they haunt second-hand book stores and look for old algebra, arithmetic or geometry texts. Next, take note of the curricular projects of the revolution. They are a gold mine of ideas, to be selectively extracted from the project and modified as necessary.

For example, the authors of SMSG's *Intermediate Mathematics* text present logarithms in terms of the areas under a curve (Figure 9.1). Then, the exponential function is defined as the inverse of the logarithmic function (Figure 9.2). The properties of the exponential function and the usual "laws of exponents" are developed as a natural outgrowth of the work with logarithms. For example, from the graph the value of $E_a(0) = 1$; while $E_a(1) = a$ since $y = E_a(x)$ is the inverse

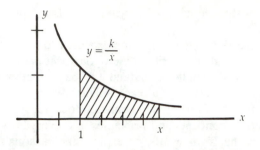

Fig. 9.1 The shaded area is used to define the log function.

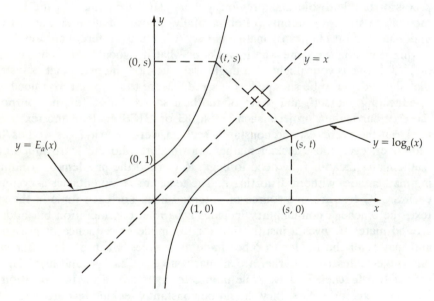

Fig. 9.2 A log function and its inverse.

of $y = \log_a x$. We recommend this atypical approach to the logarithmic function *providing that* the teacher gives the students some reason for the sudden interest in areas under curves and a justification for tagging a label like "logarithm" on certain areas under the curve $y = k/x$. The SMSG text omits this entirely but your own memory of integral calculus should provide a clue. Yes, it is up to you to make intelligent selections and to modify where needed.

The SMP materials are rich in concrete illustrations of many kinds. Here is just one example from Book H. A spinner (Figure 9.3) is used to initiate questions about probability.

1. What is the probability that the arrow will stop on a red sector?

2. If we spin the arrow 1000 times and succeed in obtaining "red" 609 times, what is our success fraction?

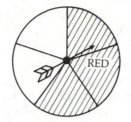

Fig. 9.3 Spinner with three red sectors.

First Spin   *Second Spin*   *Outcome*

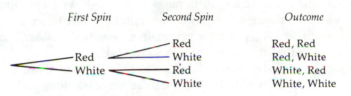

		Red	Red, Red
	Red	White	Red, White
	White	Red	White, Red
		White	White, White

Fig. 9.4 Tree diagram for red-white spinner.

3.   What is the probability the arrow will stop on the same color in two consecutive spins? in four consecutive spins?

In order to answer the more complicated questions, tree diagrams are used. The tree diagram showing possible outcomes for two consecutive spins on the red-white spinner is depicted in Figure 9.4.

One goes from tree diagrams to mathematical models in one easy step, or so it seems, as the SMP authors model a traffic situation by means of a specially designed spinner (Figure 9.5).

Number of commercial vehicles	In k sets of 10 vehicles
0	8
1	9
2	14
3	7
4	2
5	0

Fig. 9.5 Data and model for traffic survey.

The table represents data obtained by counting the number of commerical vehicles (for example, trucks and buses) in every set of 10 vehicles traveling on a particular highway. In all, 40 sets of 10 vehicles (400 vehicles) were counted. The table indicates that 8 sets included *no* commercial vehicles while each of 9 sets contained 1 commercial vehicle. The appropriate spinner can be designed by constructing the sectors so that the probability that the arrow will stop at 0 is 8/40, at 1 is 9/40, and so on. The students are asked to verify the 72° angle in the diagram, to find the other angles, to construct such a spinner and use it to simulate the actual traffic count.

The previous illustration is just one of many in the SMP texts, but don't stop there in your search for laboratory/demonstration/visual/everyday ideas. We especially recommend the two sets of books produced by the University of Illinois Arithmetic Project staff. Teachers with whom we work have used the *Motion Geometry* ideas from middle school through senior high with appropriate modifications upward in language for senior high students. *Stretchers and Shrinkers* seemed to work for students in their general mathematics classes. The teachers were delighted with this different approach to fractions.

Don't expect to find a section labeled "Labs" in any of these materials. In most cases you have to read with care and extract laboratory and demonstration ideas from the texts. Even the spinner illustration from the SMP text does not specifically say: "*Show* the students a large spinner. *Have* individuals *spin* the arrow." It is up to the teacher to realize that here is an idea for both a demonstration and a laboratory activity and that one or both modes are essential *before* asking the students to predict results.

As a result of increased attention to the implications of Piaget's data, a large number of paperback pamphlets, hardcover texts, and articles in professional journals have focused on activities suitable for laboratory activities or demonstrations. These sources are treasure houses of instructional ideas. Some, like *Geoboard Geometry* (Farrell, 1971), give examples of the use of one manipulative device—in this case, a 5×5 pegboard—at several grade levels and within several topics.

A source book with multiple aids, activities and strategies for the teacher of mathematics has been recently revised by Sobel and Maletsky (1988/1975). Pull-out teaching sections are a regular feature of *Arithmetic Teacher, Mathematics Teacher*, and the NCTM Newsletter. A similar kind of feature is produced by the EQUALS CONSORTIUM. As part of the CONSORTIUM's dedication to equal access in mathematics education for minority and ethnic groups, they devote considerable attention to improving instruction for all students. Each issue of the newsletter contains a sequence of developmental lessons on one major concept or kind of reasoning ability. One of the most recent such lessons (See December, 1987 newsletter), later used by one of our graduate student/inservice high school teachers, was a pre-algebra lesson. She modeled her lesson after the one we had worked on in our graduate class and divided her class into pairs. Each pair was given a copy of the Fishbowl sheet, containing several problems like the one below, and a supply of goldfish (goldfish crackers), catfish (doggie biscuits) and guppies (navy beans). After a demonstration by the teacher, they set to work solving the problems and eventually creating their own fishbowl problem.

Sample Fishbowl Problem

1. This fishbowl contains: 16 fish

A fourth of them are goldfish

Two-thirds of the rest are guppies

These are just a few of the ideas to be found in curriculum materials. We encourage you to investigate your college library to locate ones mentioned in this chapter. Then browse thoughtfully for ideas, presentations, interesting problems, information on history of mathematics, laboratory activities and demonstrations that might be useful when you are teaching. Don't ignore cartoons to be found in some texts, in the daily newspaper, in professional journals, or even mathematics calendars. Jacobs (1982/1970) makes especially good use of these to teach mathematics.

9.4 SUMMARY AND SELF-CHECK

In this chapter we identified the major milestones in the history of school mathematics, the forces behind some events, and the issues which continue to affect mathematics teaching. The characteristics of the curriculum revolution of the 1960s were delineated and seven projects of that era were outlined. We examined the reaction to the curriculum revolution and the swing of the pendulum back to emphasis on "basic skills." Then we referred to the reports of comparatively low achievement of American youngsters, the spate of national reports criticizing education, and the swing of the pendulum back towards emphasis on the so-called "hard" sciences. We briefly considered the potential that information technology has to offer mathematics education and the impact it could have on mathematics curriculum. Finally, we examined some of the recommendations of the *Standards* and the forces that seemed to influence these recommendations.

The title of this chapter has the subtitle: Learning from the Past. To the beginning teacher, the fact that changes in school mathematics have sometimes been made on the basis of powerful public reaction is startling. *"You mean that the texts I'm teaching from may not be based on our expanding knowledge base and on a consideration of an instructional model such as the one the we have been studying?"* It surely is possible, if past history is an indication. Thus, we have emphasized the importance of a rich bank of ideas in your resource file. Ideas that do correspond to the instructional model in this text will help you get beyond a static, outdated text. Here the past can assist you again. For the project materials, old textbooks, journal articles, handbooks and paperback resource books are sources of those ideas. We gave examples of a few of these. Many more can be found within the covers of each of the sources cited in this chapter.

At this point you should be able to:

1. Identify some of the forces and issues that have repeatedly affected school mathematics.

2. Describe the major characteristics of at *least four* major projects of the curriculum revolution.

3. Describe the two-pronged nature of the "new" math as seen by the curriculum writers/teachers of the 1960s.

4. Identify two specific ways information technology may affect mathematics curriculum and instruction.

5. Select ideas from curriculum projects, yearbooks and pamphlets cited in this chapter that would be appropriate supplements to any curriculum that you are assigned to teach.

9.5 SIMULATION/PRACTICE ACTIVITIES

A. Choose a topic from secondary (7–12) mathematics. Research the approach to that topic in *one* of the curriculum projects described in Section 9.2. Then answer the following questions:

  1. What prerequisites do the authors of the chosen text assume as a basis for the selected topic?

  2. In what ways and to what extent are the processes and products of mathematics illustrated by the text presentation?

B. Read **two** of the following and write a summary of the author's position.

Cooney, T. J. (1988). "The issue of reform: What have we learned from yesteryear?" *Mathematics Teacher*, **81** (5), 352–363.

Dossey, J. A. (1988). "Learning, teaching, and standards." *Mathematics Teacher*, **81** (4), 290–293.

Ralston, A. (1985). "The really new college mathematics and its impact on the high school curriculum." In C. R. Hirsch (Ed.), *The secondary school mathematics curriculum* (1985 Yearbook). (pp. 29–42). Reston, VA: National Council of Teachers of Mathematics.

Usiskin, Z. (1985). "We need another revolution in secondary school mathematics." In C. R. Hirsch (Ed.), *The secondary school mathematics curriculum* (1985 Yearbook). (pp. 1–21). Reston, VA: National Council of Teachers of Mathematics.

C. The 1963 Cambridge Conference report, *Goals for School Mathematics*, outlines a possible secondary school curriculum for 1990. Read the outline of that 7–12 curriculum. Would your mathematics background be sufficient preparation if you were to teach such a program? Why or why not? How does the proposed curriculum differ from the mathematics program you will teach?

D. Read *An Agenda for Action*, (1980) report of the National Council of Teachers of Mathematics. Then review the *Curriculum and Evaluation Standards for School Mathematics* (1988) from the National Council of Teachers of Mathematics. Compare the recommendations of these two groups on problem solving, on the use of calculators, and on the use of computer technology.

E. Locate two or more exercises in pre-1950 textbooks that would be interesting to today's students.

F. In the Introductory Activity, 9.1, you were asked to examine problem sets for stereotyping of activities. When our students did this, they found that contemporary junior high texts had a good mix of activities with males and females engaged in like roles.

However, they found that the senior high texts seldom included exercises that mentioned humans. Review a section from Jacobs, H. R. (1982) *Mathematics: A human endeavor* (2nd ed.). San Francisco, CA: W. H. Freeman & Co. and identify the ways Jacobs has illustrated that mathematics is an activity of **humans**.

SUGGESTIONS FOR FURTHER STUDY

Hirsch, C. R. (Ed.). *The secondary school mathematics curriculum* (1985 Yearbook). Reston, VA: National Council of Teachers of Mathematics.

In addition to issue articles such as those listed in Exercise B, this yearbook contains idea articles for various sections of the curriculum.

Jones, P. S. and Coxford, A. F. (Eds.). (1970). *A history of mathematics education in the United States and Canada* (32nd Yearbook). Washington, DC: National Council of Teachers of Mathematics.

This yearbook has served as the major source for the pre-1979 material in this chapter. It is an excellent source of reference material for further details on forces and issues in the evolving history of school mathematics.

Addresses of Some of the Sources Cited in this Chapter

The Challenge of the Unknown Film Series (free)
Phillips Petroleum Company
Bartlesville, OK 74003

The Challenge of the Unknown Teaching Guide (minimal cost)
W. W. Norton
500 Fifth Ave.
New York, NY 10110

EQUALS—Sharing Resources Newsletter (free)
Jean Stenmark, Editor
Lawrence Hall of Science
University of California
Berkeley, CA 94720

Mathematical Sciences Calendar
A yearly calendar with historical information, cartoons, quotes—ideas that can be used in the classroom. (minimal cost)

Rome Press Inc.
Box 31451
Crabtree Valley Station
Raleigh, NC 27622

National Council of Teachers of Mathematics
1906 Association Drive
Reston, VA 22091

Send to NCTM for the **catalog of educational materials** for a listing of all of the current available resource material. Members pay less for items.

CHAPTER TEN

THE MATHEMATICS, SCIENCE AND EVERYDAY WORLD INTERFACE

Communication and Cooperation

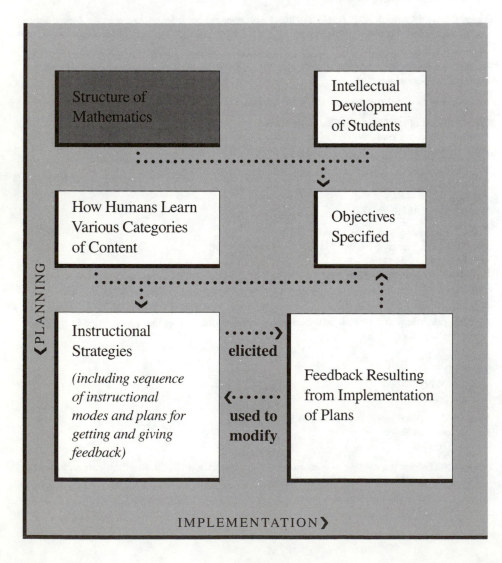

Few who are aware of the recent history of mathematics in the secondary school propose that it be taught primarily for the very few students who will become professional mathematicians. Fewer yet of those alert to the temper of the times and the needs of contemporary society recommend treating school mathematics as an island unto itself. In fact, the goal of mathematical literacy for every citizen has been steadily gaining support among mathematics educators for over a decade. Not all who cherish this goal agree on the exact meaning of the term *mathematics literacy*. However, there are common grounds of agreement that are likely to persist and these merit the attention of all mathematics teachers.

Students, as well as teachers, agree that it makes sense to consider the implications of mathematics for everyday life, but why single out the interrelationships with science? Doesn't mathematics have some important connections with many other school subjects? We think it does, and in this chapter we sketch a few of them. However, we have chosen to concentrate on science for a number of reasons. First, mathematics is the lifeblood of modern science. The concepts and thought models of mathematics are interwoven in every secondary school science course that *your* students will be studying. Your students should *not* be learning that the algebra taught by the mathematics teachers differs significantly from that used in science classes. Second, the history of mathematics and the history of science illustrate the long and fruitful union of mathematics and science. The contributions of Newton, Galileo, and others were cited in Chapter 4 as sources of teaching ideas for the mathematics class. Third, the science teacher's academic background typically includes a substantial amount of mathematics. This ought to facilitate talking to and working cooperatively with colleagues in science education. You should be able to depend on their expertise to help you design relevant, interesting, science-based mathematics lessons. Fourth, science teachers also need *your* help in finding ways to use mathematics, rather than to abuse it. Thus, a profitable *quid pro quo* arrangement is highly feasible. Finally, one has to start somewhere in helping students cross those artificial watertight compartments that too often isolate one school subject from another and separate school learning from out-of-school life.

Successful cooperation with science teachers can lead you to explore similar possibilities with those who teach your students subjects such as social studies, English, industrial arts, and fine arts. Communication and cooperation among teachers can go a long way toward overcoming the feelings of isolation and frustration which too frequently engulf teachers and students alike.

We have shaded in the "Structure of Mathematics" portion of the instructional schema to call attention to the mathematics/science interface so often overlooked in the literature. Authors of many journal articles that deal with the use of science in mathematics instruction treat it as interesting, supplementary material to incorporate in lessons, if time allows. We recommend a more serious and deliberate approach based on a careful analysis of the nature of the two disciplines, the structure of school curricula, and the application of out-of-school life. Both

Table 10.1
Selected Science-Based Questions for the Mathematics Classroom

Questions	The related science course or level
1. How are a doorknob, a set of stairs, a screwdriver, a baseball bat and an egg beater related?	JHS Physical Sciences and Physics
2. What shape are the compartments in a honeycomb? Would some other shape be more efficient (in terms of the survival of the bee)?	Biology
3. An impala can jump 30′ to 40′; a large jack rabbit, about 25′; a kangaroo, 25′ to 30′; a cricket-frog only an inch long can jump 3′. What is the record for humans in horizontal jumping? How does it compare with the data given above? (Be sure to consider the relative size of the human versus the animals cited.)	JHS Life Science
4. How could you estimate your volume? Think of at least two ways. Use the figures you obtain and your weight to calculate your specific gravity. (This is likely to vary a bit depending on the figures used.)	JHS Physical Science

the Introductory Activity and other sections of the chapter are designed to start you thinking along these lines.

10.1 INTRODUCTORY ACTIVITY

Ivory towers are lonely places these days.

You may need to consult a high-school science text in order to complete activity A.

A.   Table 10.1 contains a set of science-based questions that can be used by the mathematics teacher to introduce or develop understanding of certain mathematical concepts or rules.

   1.   For each question, give at *least two* reasons why the question was paired with the level or kind of *science* discipline listed next to it in Table 10.1. (If you're having trouble coming up with specifics, consult a related secondary school text. Also ask a science major to help you, but don't be surprised if he or she pleads ignorance!)

   2.   Identify specific mathematics concepts/principles that could be introduced or developed by means of instructional strategies that incorporate ways to answer *each* question.

B.   Table 10.2 contains a set of questions that can be used to introduce or develop understanding of mathematical concepts or rules. These questions are drawn from the everyday world of potential interests of the students.

   1.   Answer questions 1, 4, and 5 from the table.

   2.   List the steps a class would need to take to obtain prerequisite information related to questions 2 and 3.

Table 10.2
Selected Everyday-World Questions for the Mathematics Classroom

Questions	Everyday world of:
1. What kinds of numbers appear on soup labels, cereal boxes, the odometer of the family car, a light bulb? What is the largest and smallest number in each case?	the home
2. If all the litter found in one week in the square block area around the school were recycled, how much and how many different kinds of trash could be salvaged?	ecology and the school
3. Tyrus Cobb, a former baseball player, had a lifetime batting average of .367. Compare this with the top batting average of this year's World Series players and the top batting average of your school's varsity players.	sports
4. Winning at pool is said to depend on a combination of skill and use of geometry. What uses of geometry?	sports
5. Obtain a snapshot and an enlargement of the photo. Tape these on a sheet of paper. Show how lines connecting corresponding points can be used to locate a center of enlargement. Sketch a still larger photo by extending the pattern lines.	hobbies

3. For *each* question in Table 10.2, write additional spinoff questions that could be used to enhance the mathematics being taught.

After comparing your responses to these activities with those of other classmates, you may find that you need additional background references on certain questions. If so, check through the references provided in the final section of this chapter. When you're fairly clear about the potential uses of the questions in Tables 10.1 and 10.2, then you're ready to sink your teeth into the sections that follow.

10.2 MATHEMATICS THROUGH SCIENCE

You don't have to have a second field in one of the sciences in order to teach mathematics through the vehicle of science-based ideas. You do have to understand the *concept* of a mathematical model. In all of science—theoretical or applied, elementary-school level to graduate school, biological or physical—mathematical models are used to describe something going on in the world, to explain and predict events, and to suggest solutions to complicated problems. Thus, the natural (counting) numbers are appropriate mathematical models for describing the number of planets but inadequate models for describing the size of bacteria, a virus, and a molecule. Does that use of mathematical model seem to be a far cry from the sophisticated mathematical models found in college-level physics texts and advanced biology texts? It should. However, it's exactly that simpler view of modeling that is the key to the ideas presented in this section.

Fig. 10.1   Potential "cells" for comb.

Let's start with an activity based on question 2 in Table 10.1. In a junior high class, the teacher can show the students a picture of a cross-section of a honeycomb or, better yet, pass around (and project on the overhead) a portion of a real honeycomb. Don't assume that all the students have seen a honeycomb. Many supermarkets sell only jars of honey, minus honeycomb. Next the problem posed in the question has to be spelled out. What is meant by "efficient" in this case? (Here's a good place to involve a science colleague directly in the class, or indirectly as a resource person. Be sure to ask that science teacher about the two aspects of the bee's behavior: building the comb and storing the honey. Also seek your colleagues' assistance in alerting students to the dangers of thinking about the bee's behavior in terms of human attributes and reversed cause and effect relationships. Don't feel guilty about asking for this kind of assistance since your science colleagues will certainly need your help in assisting students to make proper use of mathematics in their science classes.) The "efficiency" question should eventually get restated so that quantitative techniques can be used. Students should be helped to see that there are two main issues.

1.   What other shape(s) would "fill the plane"?

and

2.   Given a fixed surface area to use for a cell wall, which shape provides for maximum volume of the enclosed space?

Figure 10.1 depicts some common shapes that could be considered as the students try to model the situation of a comb.

Multiple congruent cutouts of each of the shapes could be used to answer question 1. The students might be asked to "tile a floor" and, as a result, to identify those shapes that make good tiles and to determine the number of such tiles needed around a point. It is a good idea to include large (such as 10 cm on an edge) and small (such as 4 cm on an edge) sets of each shape. Then, elicit from the students conclusions, such as "six equilateral triangles fit around a point whether the triangles enclose a large or a small region." A table like Table 10.3 can be used to record data.

Protractors can be made available if students have forgotten (or are just beginning to investigate) the angle measures of some of the shapes. The students can be encouraged to find patterns in the data, such as the recurring product of 360° (6 × 60°, 4 × 90°, 3 × 120°), and the increasing number of sides coupled with the decreasing number of tiles around a point. Ask the students to look at the pattern under the "No. of tiles around a point" column and explain why that

Table 10.3
A Partially Completed Data Table

Shape of tile	No. of sides	Fills the plane	No. of tiles around a point	Measure of one angle
Circular	NA	No	3	NA
Equilateral triangle	3	Yes	6	60°
Square	4	Yes	4	90°
Regular pentagon	5	No	3+	108°
Regular hexagon	6			

pattern "tells" us to end the investigation. If the pattern of a product of 360° holds, then no wonder the regular pentagon wasn't a useful tile: 108° would have to be a factor of 360° and it isn't. Don't miss the opportunity to point out the inexactness of measurement and the differences between the cell of the comb, the cutout hexagonal shape, and the mathematical thought model, the hexagon. Finally, emphasize the processes of inductive reasoning (looking for patterns, extending patterns) and of deductive reasoning (explaining the significance of the 360° product of angles) that were being used by the students throughout this investigation.

The results of this part of the investigation make the construction of the comb even more puzzling. Surely, it would be easier to build a three- or four-walled cell rather than a six-walled cell! Perhaps the solution of the second problem we posed originally will help here. Although the students could use the same cutout shapes and simply compute areas, we've found that a laboratory activity designed to produce a three-dimensional visual solution is far more productive. You can use old manila folders (or other suitable substitutes), which you will need to cut into strips 2 cm by 12 cm. Students working in groups of two or three should be asked to construct a cross-section of a comb. Some groups should construct a comb with hexagonal cells; others, a comb with square cells; and the rest, a comb with triangular cells. In *all* cases, the surface area of the wall of any *single* cell will be the same, 2 cm × 12 cm. Each group will need a supply of strips (8 to 10), tape, a scissors, and a metric ruler. (The group constructing square cells won't need a ruler. Why not?) The teacher needs to remind the class that combs do not contain double-walled cells. Furthermore, the teacher will need to precede this laboratory with a demonstration of the construction of a single cell and the subsequent attachment of an adjacent cell. As students work through the laboratory, and then compare results visually by placing one kind of honeycomb cell over another, the capacity-advantage of the hexagonal cell over either of the others should be unmistakable.

The "combs" in Figure 10.2 were produced by groups in one class. The combs were taped to the board, and all the students observed the structural problem, which had been commented on earlier by several small groups. "The triangle is a rigid figure" became a meaningful statement to all the observers. (Then, why

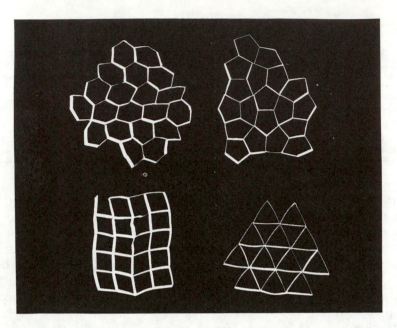

Fig. 10.2   Models of combs.

don't the hexagonal cells droop in the honeycomb? If you're not sure, check with a science colleague.)

Shape, space-filling, perimeter/area/volume, and structural rigidity relationships are important to multiple fields of science. Any of the following questions can help to promote mathematical understanding in a science setting.

1. A person coming out of a bath or shower carries a film of water which makes him or her 1 percent heavier. For your own weight, what weight of water could this be? What volume? (1 g of fresh water is very close to 1 cc.)

2. A human is about five thousand times as heavy as a mouse. Approximately how much does a mouse weigh? Haldane (See Newman [1956] in the Suggestions for Further Study) says a wet mouse will carry a film of water about equal to its own weight. Why would that be true? How could we compare the *surface area* of a mouse with that of a human? (Hint: An average mouse is about 4 inches long—if we ignore its tail. Assume that an average adult human is about 68 inches tall.)

3. Why is it very difficult for a fly to escape from a puddle of water?

These are just a few of the area/volume relationships that are crucial to an understanding of certain science relationships. Many more will be found in sources cited in the final section of this chapter.

Beyond the relationships of size and shape are the manifold properties represented by a class of mathematical models known as curves. *Pitch, frequency,*

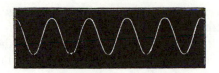

Fig. 10.3   The trace of a vibrating tuning fork.

and *period* are terms associated both with properties of sound and of the sine curve. The trace of a vibrating tuning fork is depicted in Figure 10.3. The sine curve stands out vividly.

The soda straw clarinet laboratory is designed to introduce the concepts of frequency and pitch and the mathematical relationship between them through the medium of music. The teacher must obtain a supply of soda straws, some single-edged razor blades, and a metric ruler. Measure a 3 cm length from one end of a straw and carefully make a horizontal crease at that point. Then flatten the shorter portion of the straw as shown in Figure 10.4. To complete the construction of the reed of the clarinet, cut two congruent right triangles out of the reed about 2.5 cm from the end of the straw. Now try the clarinet.

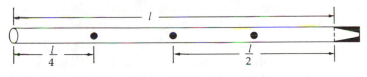

Fig. 10.4   Soda straw clarinet.

The reed vibrates as air is blown through the straw, which acts as a wind tunnel. The sound will not be very musical, but it represents the basic note of that clarinet. Each student's clarinet may sound slightly different (a good place to ask "Why?"). Be sure that each one is able to produce a sound before proceeding further. You may need to suggest that a sharper crease be made at the end of the reed or that the trapezoidal mouth of the reed be opened more so that air will circulate into the straw. (Paper straws may have become too wet, while some plastic straws are difficult to flatten.)

The next step is to alter the clarinets so some variable sounds can be heard. The teacher must demonstrate how to cut a hole *on the top* (this is important!) of the straw and halfway down the air column (see Figure 10.4). Then have each student "tune-up" and alternately open and close the hole with a finger to produce the basic note and the new note. The new note should sound higher; ideally, it will be pitched twice as high as the basic note. What happens when new holes are cut at the one-quarter and three-quarter marks? Let the students try these and produce the resulting sounds. The class is now ready to play their own music. They should be encouraged to do so and to listen to the effects caused by changing the length of the air tunnel.

From here to inverse variation is an easy step. Length of air column can be related to wavelength produced by the vibrating air within that column. The *time it takes to produce a single wave* is called *the period*. If the class is studying the sine function, the teacher has a good opportunity to identify the period of $\sin x$ as 2π radians, of $\sin 2x$ as π radians, and so on. The teacher can point out that time, usually expressed in seconds, is used to define period in the case of sound and time is used again to define *frequency* as *the number of complete vibrations in a second*. Experiments have demonstrated that whether executed as a loud or soft sound, a pitch of middle C on a tuning fork will result in 262 vibrations per second. Moreover, a frequency of 262 will produce a pitch of middle C for all musical sounds. For example, if 262 teeth of a steam-saw cut into a log every second, middle C is produced. Many more examples of the relationship of frequency to pitch are given in Jeans's essay "Mathematics of Music" in Volume 4 of *The World of Mathematics* (see Newman [1956] in the Suggestions for Further Study). The relationship of frequency, and thus pitch, to wavelength is equal to the velocity of sound. Is the amplitude of the sound curve somehow related to what we hear? Definitely, and your students who know about amplifiers can probably guess how. That's right—a louder sound will result in higher curves. A middle C on the piano will sound like middle C as long as that key is played but as the pressure on the key changes, the sound curve reflects this in a shifting amplitude.

There are many additional questions that are spinoffs from the clarinet laboratory.

1. Who in class plays a drum, a violin, or a trumpet? Where is the vibrating air column in each of these instruments? How are changes in pitch created? (This is an excellent place to use the expertise of the music teacher, as well as that of the physics or physical science teacher.)

2. What is the mathematical relationship of any note to a note an octave lower or higher? Compare your answers with the data from your own experiment with the clarinet. What numerical relationships are tied to notes within an octave?

3. According to the *Guinness Book of World Records* (McWhirter & McWhirter, 1976), the amplification for the rock group Deep Purple attained 117 decibels in London's Rainbow Theatre in 1972. Three members of the audience were said to become unconscious as a result. What is a decibel? What kind of input power is required to produce an output of 117 decibels? What is the relation of energy to perception of loudness? See Jeans's essay (Newman, 1956) for information on loudness, the threshold of pain, and the scale of sound intensity.

The clarinet laboratory is one with long-term possibilities—for interrelating mathematics and science and for interrelating mathematics and music. This kind of triple benefit is not unusual. The honeycomb laboratory, like Ms. Blumenstalk's lab on estimating the area of irregularly shaped plane figures described in

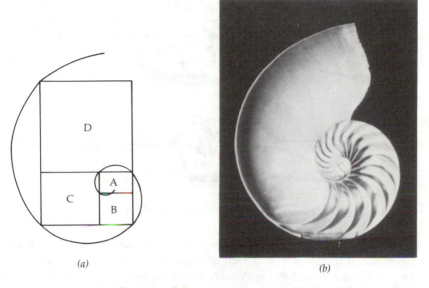

(a)

(b)

Fig. 10.5 Examples of the equiangular, or logarithmic, spiral.

Chapter 3, may lead to additional excursions into geometric plane-filling patterns used by artists in Moslem tile work or those found in E. M. Escher prints.

The well-known Fibonacci sequence (1,1,2,3,5,8,...) can be introduced by sketching the family tree of a male bee. (Why *male*? Check with a biology colleague.) However, it can also be related to the golden rectangle, a rectangle whose sides are in the ratio of 1 to $(\sqrt{5}+1)/2$, and to the uses of that rectangle in architecture and art. The spiral illustrated in a family of golden rectangles (Figure 10.5a) is an example of an equiangular, or logarithmic, spiral which is vividly displayed in the shell of the chambered Nautilus (Figure 10.5b). Wait a minute! The logarithmic spiral, like all other mathematical curves, is a *mathematical model*, so the shell of the chambered Nautilus is a *physical model* with the characteristics of the logarithmic spiral. If your students are in a second-year algebra course, you might explore with them the extent to which this mathematical model is a good fit for the curved shape of the shell of the Nautilus. After all, the needle on a moving phonograph record describes a spiral quite different in appearance from the logarithmic spiral and, it turns out, different mathematically. However, the logarithmic spiral *is* the best fit model for the shell of the chambered Nautilus as is evident from an analysis of its structure. Before asking a science colleague to explain this, do Simulation Exercise B. You may find yourself in the position of "science teacher."

Notice how each of the activities suggested thus far has interfaced with everyday world interests of students. Questions about musical groups the kids enjoy are likely to capture their attention. Avid beachgoers and shell-collectors

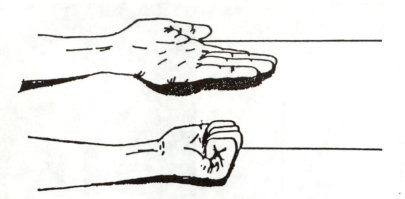

Fig. 10.6 Muscle fatigue laboratory.

are usually interested in the relationship of the Fibonacci sequence to the chambered Nautilus if the shell is displayed and questions are raised about the shapes of other shells that they have collected. Don't be worried about needing to be an instant expert. Learn together by consulting a field guide, such as Abbott, R. T. (1968). *A guide to field identification: Seashells of North America.* New York: Golden Press. Ask students to voluntarily explore the possible relationships for other shells. These are classroom-tested ways to instruct so as to work toward affective objectives.

The illustrative questions following the honeycomb lesson directed attention to the "here and now" interests of students, in particular, their own bodies. In like manner, the laboratory lesson described in the following paragraphs exploits student interest in muscular prowess. The lesson, entitled Muscle Fatigue, is fully described in the SMSG text, *Mathematics and living things* (See the Suggestions for Further Study for the complete reference.). It is one of several lessons intended to help the mathematics teacher teach mathematics through science.

The class is challenged, perhaps by the latest feats of school athletes or by stories of national champion weight lifters or interviews with winners of international events. They've probably seen TV coverage of the exhausted marathon runners as they stagger across the finish line. All of these familiar experiences are the basis for introducing the question of the effect of a simple exercise on fatigue, of a brief rest on the quality of subsequent performance, and of differences in the quality of performance from student to student. The teacher demonstrates the exercise in question. With one arm on the desk, elbow to hand touching the desk and palm of that hand facing up, the teacher clasps and unclasps the hand. Each time the fingers must touch the palm and then the desk, while the entire arm remains on the desk (Figure 10.6). The goal is to do this as fast as possible within a period of 90 seconds, rest for 30 seconds, and resume the exercise for another 90 seconds.

Table 10.4
Lab Sheet for Muscle Fatigue Activity

Name _____			Rt. or left-handed _____		
Time Period	Time in Seconds	Total Count Rt. Hand	Right Hand	Total Count Lt. Hand	Left Hand
1st	30				
2nd	30				
3rd	30				
Rest	30				
4th	30				
5th	30				
6th	30				

The only equipment needed for this activity is one large wall clock with a second hand (or sufficient watches with second hands for each lab group) and lab sheets for each student (See Table 10.4).

The class is divided into groups of three. One person does the exercise for the right hand, and then for the left; one counts aloud the number of flexes from the starting to the stopping signal; the third person starts and stops the exercise and records the number of flexes at 30 second intervals on a lab sheet. The teacher will have to tour to be sure that students are performing the exercise correctly. As soon as one member of a lab group completes the exercise for both hands, a second member of that lab group begins the exercise. When all members of the class have completed the exercise, the teacher should ask the students to compare the individual data from the first 30 seconds to the second and then to the third 30 second period, and for the periods after the rest. Finally, each student can compare the data for the left hand to the data for the right hand. Each student can be asked to compute a mean of the data for each hand before and after the rest period. Individual data and the means of the class can be graphed. This is one place when the students may expect the performance of the boys to exceed the performance of the girls. Collect the means by gender and graph these data. Percent of increase and decrease, range, and extrapolation of the data beyond that collected—all of these are potential topics that can be explored. This is a good example of the use of mathematical techniques and models to interpret biological data.

Have the students talk about the location of the muscles that tired. Work with the science teacher on ways to explain how muscles work. (There is a brief explanation in the teacher's commentary to *Mathematics and living things*. See Suggestions for Further Study.) Some of the following questions might be asked:

1. How might a physical therapist use data of this kind to be able to better help a patient?

2. Did you "recover" fully in the 30-second rest period?

3. Did right-handed people show an advantage for use of the right hand?

As the foregoing illustrations demonstrate, the world around us provides us with a limitless source of data that can be used to teach mathematics. Moreover, the science teacher can become a key resource person if you ask the right questions. Most mathematics majors know that high-school physics and chemistry involve considerable mathematics, but they seldom think of biology or the various junior high science courses as an arena for mathematics/science cooperation. Furthermore, mathematics teachers often fail to ask their science colleagues specific questions. Since many science teachers are just as vague about the background of the mathematics concepts and rules they use, the result of misguided attempts to communicate is often frustration. We've found that both parties are amazed by data such as that displayed in Table 10.5 and Table 10.6. Now each has specific topics that can be used as starting points for planning ideas, for ironing out mutual problem areas, and so on.

After examining these tables, the mathematics teacher might ask a science colleague one of the following questions.

Table 10.5
Selected Mathematics-Biological Science Interrelationships in Grades 7–9

Math grade level	Mathematics topics	Some science examples
7–9	Area and volume	Limits on cell size, water loss by leaves
7–9	Simple probability	Transmission of inherited traits
9	Mixture problems	Concentration of solutions
9	Functions	Growth curves of all types
7–9	Graphing	Population studies
7–9	Percentage	Genetics, population studies, diffusion of molecules
7–9	Rate and ratio	Enzyme action rates, ratios of elements in compounds
7–9	Metric units of measure	Centimeter, meter, gram, liter
7–9	Big and small numbers	Size of cells
7–9	Symmetry	Classification of organisms
7–9	Statistics: counting, data collecting, histograms, mean, mode	Predicting offspring types

Table 10.6
Selected Mathematics-Physical Science Interrelationships in Grades 7–9

Math grade level	Mathematics topics	Some science examples
9	Function	Solubility
7–9	Geometric structures and figures	Crystal structure, shell in model of atom
7–9	Graphs	Distance-time, potential energy
7–9	Percentage (solution/mixture problems)	Percentage composition
7–9	Scientific notation	6.02×10^{23} (Avogadro's Number)
9	Slope of line	$a = \Delta v / \Delta t$
7–9	Metric units of measure	Kilogram, calorie, centimeter, liter
7–9	Variation (direct proportion; inverse proportion	Law of lever, other simple machines
8–9	Volume	Boyle's law, Charles's law
7–9	Big and small numbers	Distance to planets
7–8	Symmetry	Crystals
7–9	Equations (solving)	Chemical equations (balancing)

1. I'm teaching scientific notation and I need some very large and very small sizes or distances as illustrative examples. Would you give me some examples and some background information, perhaps distance to planets and size of cells? What's Avogadro's number, by the way? Who was he?

2. We're starting work on graphs of parabolas next week. I'd like to use some science illustrations that yield that kind of curve. What distance/time or velocity/time problems would be good to use?

The science teacher may suggest some unwieldy numbers from your point of view. Real-life measures are seldom "nice," and it is important for the mathematics teacher to introduce an awareness of this fact. However, you might explain to your science colleague that you'll use the unwieldy numbers in the later stages of your work but need to begin with comparatively simple numbers (few significant digits) so as to keep the students' attention on the *process*, rather than on all the details. They'll understand since they do the same thing when introducing a scientific principle. Moreover, if you're careful to share what each of you would like the students to learn from the graphs referred to in question 2, you'll find that the science teacher can't understand why mathematics students automatically divide the sheet of graph paper into four quadrants. The graph of $s = (1/2)gt^2$

(the formula for the distance of a freely falling object where distance in feet is expressed as a function of time in seconds and g is the gravitational constant, $32'/\sec^2$) doesn't make much sense when t is negative. What kind of relationships might result in the use of more than one quadrant in graphs? Temperature problems or problems involving distances above and below sea level come to mind immediately. These are just a few examples of the potential for science/mathematics cooperation. See the resources listed at the end of this chapter as you begin to add teaching ideas to each of the folders in your resource file.

10.3 MATHEMATICS AND THE EVERYDAY WORLD

As we have seen, lessons designed to emphasize the interface of mathematics and science often include attention to the everyday world. However, it is possible to interface mathematics with the everyday world in ways that do not necessarily emphasize science. When we talk about the "everyday world," we mean the *here-and-now* world of *the students*. Recall the list of potential interests of teenagers given in Chapter 7. These areas represent starting points, with your own future students providing clues as to additional areas of interest. Although attention getting and keeping alone would be sufficient reasons to concentrate on the everyday world, there is another reason. The vast majority of your students (97 to 98 percent) will *not* be majors in mathematics but they *will* be citizens in a world whose events are increasingly described in quantitative terms and where decisions are based on the application of mathematical models ranging from simple odds to complex statistical systems. Thus, the everyday world of school, home, hobbies, sports, summer jobs, music, design, and the like makes sense to the teenager and helps give meaning to the mathematics of their present and possibly future use.

In the Introductory Activity we introduced you to some potential sources of everyday data that could be used to teach mathematics. How can a survey of litter on the school ground be used to teach or apply mathematics? You probably thought of the need for classifying and tabulating data, and perhaps sampling the presentation of data in graphic form. A bar graph would be an ideal way to represent data on numbers of all soda cans, beer bottles, papers, matchbooks, and miscellaneous trash. However, a histogram would *not* be an appropriate way to picture such data. Why not? Remember the continuous bars of a histogram? That's right, they must touch so that continuous data (for example, age ranges from birth to age 16) can be depicted. However, kinds of litter represent discrete data as do color of eyes, a collection of TV shows, a group of rock records, and so on. Litter suggests the area of ecology, but isn't that science? Yes, it is. Just as the physics of sound was found to relate to music, so much of the everyday world of the students may have science ties *if* we look for them.

Literature is another field with rich possibilities for teaching mathematics. Even before *The Hobbit* became popular, a creative mathematics student teacher (Feldt,1977) decided to use ideas drawn from Tolkien's fantasy in order to develop applications of ratio and proportion in a ninth-grade algebra class. The students were introduced to that particular part of the adventure in which the

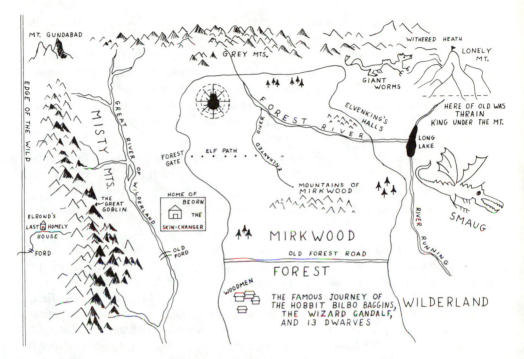

Fig. 10.7   The journey of the hobbit.

From C. C. Feldt, "Ratios and proportions with a little help from J. R. R. Tolkien," *New York State Mathematics Teachers Journal* 27 (Winter 1977): 26–27. Reprinted by permission of the editor and author.

hobbit, Bilbo Baggins, 13 dwarfs, and a wizard undertake a pilgrimage to obtain the riches belonging to the dwarf Thrain. Each student was given a copy of an adaptation of Tolkien's map in color and a set of 15 questions that developed the story line and required the application of ratio and proportion principles. An artist's version of the Feldt map (see Figure 10.7) and the first 7 questions that the students were to answer are reproduced to illustrate how the teacher wove the story line through a sequence of mathematical exercises.

1.   To begin, if you are curious as to the height of Bilbo the hobbit and his dwarf companions, use the following information: The ratio of the height of Bilbo to that of the wizard Gandalf is $1:2$ and the ratio of the height of Gandalf to that of the average dwarf is $4:3$. How tall are Bilbo and the average dwarf if Gandalf is 6 feet tall?

2.   Find the ratio of the height of Bilbo to that of the average dwarf.

3.   The goal of the far-wandering group is to reach Lonely Mountain where the ancient dwarf king Thrain has left his riches. How many miles high is the highest peak of Lonely Mountain (as indicated by the flag)?

4. After a last good home-cooked dinner at Elrond's Last Homely House, the party must cross the Misty Mountains. Using the straight-line distance, how far is it from Elrond's front door through the mountains to the old ford?

5. But while crossing the tunnels of the Misty Mountains, the adventurous group is surprised by goblins—big goblins, great ugly-looking goblins! And Gandalf, the wizard, is nowhere to be found. That leaves 14 brave little souls in the party. If there are 6 goblins to every dwarf and 2 goblins for Bilbo, find the total number of goblins to be fought.

6. To find the height of an average goblin, go back to the information concerned with dwarfs in problem (1) and note that the ratio of the heights of a dwarf to that of a goblin is 6:7.

7. What is the ratio of the height of a hobbit to that of a dwarf to that of a goblin?

Ratio and proportion could also be introduced by studying the relationship between the number of teeth on gear arrangements and the revolutions of the gears. Why not start with an example from the world of many teenagers, a bike with gears? We recommend that you locate a three-speed bike, or use the first, intermediate and highest gears on a bike with ten or more gears. Why does first gear allow you to pedal with relative ease when biking up a steep hill? Turn the bike upside down and have one student turn the pedals. The number of revolutions of the pedals and the corresponding number of revolutions of the rear wheel need to be recorded for first, second, and third gear (lowest, intermediate, highest) respectively. Does the ratio change if the rider goes at a faster pace? Why or why not? If you're working with a junior high class, a simple laboratory with cardboard gears would be a good way to help them understand this application of proportion. Figure 10.8 depicts models of two different gears (30 teeth and 15 teeth), which may be copied and traced on sturdy cardboard, such as the backs of tablets. After the models have been cut out, they should be fastened to a cardboard backing by means of paper fasteners through the center of each gear. The students move the gears so that the starting points touch and then move the larger gear through a complete revolution while counting the number of revolutions of the smaller gear. A data table is completed (Table 10.7) and the students are asked to predict the number of revolutions of the smaller gear for 5, 6, and 12 revolutions of the larger gear.

The students are thus guided to compute the ratio of the number of teeth of the two gears, perhaps *before* the term *ratio* is known. There are one-half as many teeth in gear B as in gear A. What would happen if a still smaller gear with 10 teeth were meshed with the larger gear? An extension of the laboratory would be a fine way to explore the students' conjectures; or, if time became a problem, a demonstration on the overhead projector could be used to answer the question. Spirograph gears make excellent overhead projector models for this purpose as long as the teacher first selects gears with numbers (of teeth) that are factors of one another.

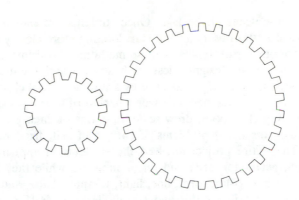

Fig. 10.8   Gear models.

Table 10.7
Data Table for Gear Laboratory

Gear A No. of turns	Gear B No. of turns	No. turns A No. turns B
1	2	1/2
2	4	2/4 = 1/2
3	—	—
4	—	—

Cartoons from the daily or Sunday paper are a source of teaching ideas that capture student attention immediately. An overhead transparency of a cartoon can be used to start a lesson in logic. In a recent Ziggy cartoon strip, Ziggy told the reader to stop everything and pay attention, but then realized that if the reader did stop everything, he or she must stop reading the comic strip. Ziggy can't figure his way out of the paradox. Cartoons, ads and promotional messages are excellent starting points for class interaction on the reasoning written into the various messages. If the class is studying symbolic logic, then the message in the cartoon can be analyzed by means of symbolic logic tools.

Cartoons and pictures are also potential sources of ideas for transformation geometry lessons. One recent one showed a swimming pool with mice on the diving board and a sign that read

NOW NO
SWIMS
ON MON

The reader was told that there was something unusual in the picture, other than the mice around the pool, and asked to identify it. A slide of a lake in New Zealand, called MIRROR LAKE because the lake is so clear, shows a sign printed with the mirror image of the name of the lake. The name itself can be seen reflected in the water of the lake. Once students are shown examples like these, they become better observers and start looking more closely at signs, logos, pictures, and cartoons for examples of these mathematical transformations.

Some teachers have designed lessons based on architectural concepts. A unit called Classroom Re-Design was used by a middle school class who involved a local architect as a resource person. Over a period of seven weeks, the students analyzed the existing classroom, drew scale diagrams of each piece of furniture and the floor plan; discussed problems of entry and exit, fixed perimeter, storage needs,.... The entire project involved the students in applying concepts of ratio, proportion, perimeter, area and linear measure while they learned about design elements such as color, form, line, light, texture, shape, and space. (Refer to *MARA* for more details on this and related lessons. *MARA* is listed in the Selections for Further Study).

The world of crafts is a good source of lesson ideas. One of our graduate students, who teaches high school, designed a lesson on symmetry groups in which she used samples of basic quilting designs. She brought in patches from her own work and asked the students to identify the basic (unit) pattern and the symmetries of each design.

Sports are a rich source of mathematics ideas. Get a scale drawing of a girls' basketball court from a *Basketball Guide* such as the one produced by the National Association of Girls' and Women's Sports. Distribute that to the students and engage the students in all or some of the following activities.

Have them measure their own average pace and then have them pace off the home court. Next they should convert the measure in paces to meters and compute the area of the home court, the areas of the minimum and maximum courts allowed by NAGWS, and the percentage of difference between the areas of the home court and the minimum and maximum courts. Spectators, and sometimes players, wonder why the ball seems to hover over the hoop and then fail to go in. Have the students compute the area of the circular basket hoop and the area of the great circle of the basketball. Compare the difference. Records of the home team's win/loss record can be kept and percentages computed. Some students can be asked to interview the coach to find out how "high percentage shots" for individual players are computed. Let your imagination and the curiosity of your students take over and provide more ways to extend this interface of mathematics and the world of sports.

There is really no end to the possibilities for teaching mathematics by using the everyday world. Table 10.8 lists additional types of everyday material and questions to introduce or review some related mathematics concepts/principles.

By this point you should have noticed that sources of everyday materials are all around us *if* we are diligent observers. Those data tables and graphs in the local newspaper, photos of geometrically designed architecture found in last year's calendar or taken on your last vacation trip, the Peanuts cartoon on base two addition, sports records in the school newspaper, the pine cones you found outside (Count the bracts and look at the spirals!)—these are all potential sources

Table 10.8
Selected Everyday Ideas as Sources of Mathematics Instruction

Everyday ideas	Mathematics questions
1. Statistics on deaths by car accident and/or motorcycle accident involving teenage drivers over a particular holiday weekend (see *Time* or *Newsweek* or check with National Safety Council).	1. Over the past three years, what are the trends in type of accident (graphs, ratio)? Predict the number of deaths per type of accident for this year, for each holiday. What factors might alter the chances of your predictions occurring?
2. Obtain a completed scoring sheet from a bowling game.	3. Write a flow chart that would tell a non-bowler exactly how to compute a friend's score.
3. Obtain a city map that can be clearly projected. Mark the well-known locations (school, churches, city hall, stadium, city park, etc.)	4. Have students give the coordinates of specified locations, using map indices. Have them locate their homes and name the coordinates. Why are such maps usually indexed by letter and number, rather than by two numbers?
4. My size, my height, my weight—how do I compare with my classmates? A young child?	5. Estimation uses are unlimited. Make out a personal chart with your height in meters, the length of your fingernail in cm, the length of your shoe in cm, the distance from your elbow to the tips of your fingers in cm, and your weight in kg. Compare the weight of a paper clip and a penny in g. Use your table to estimate the dimensions of your desk, the height of the door, the dimensions of the hockey rink, and the weight of a softball, football, or basketball.

of teaching ideas. If they are to be on hand when you need them, they must be systematically stored in your resource file, annotated as to potential use, and able to be readily retrieved when needed. *Now* is the time to start!

10.4 SUMMARY AND SELF-CHECK

Although constant references to students' interests have been made throughout this chapter, the authors chose to shade in only the "Structure of Mathematics" portion of the instructional schema. Why? We wanted to emphasize the products and processes of mathematics in their relation to other subjects and other areas of everyday life. Thus, we provided examples of simple mathematical models such as the hexagon in relation to the cells of a honeycomb. Moreover, we suggested strategies designed to *introduce* mathematical concepts and rules, as well as strategies designed to promote retention and transfer through applications in situations novel to the students.

We emphasized the everyday world of the students, in contrast to applications of the work world. We did so, not because the latter are unimportant, but because for many students, these adult applications are not real to them. Once again, note the influence of Piagetian theory. If we are to convince students that mathematics is relevant for them, the connections must be concrete and familiar. Once these connections have been made, we agree on the interest-potential of applications from the field of medicine, avalanche control, the criminal justice system, genetic research, and so on. However, these must be presented in an understandable and interest-catching manner. Materials such as *Contemporary Applied Mathematics*, referenced in Chapter 9, is a good source of teacher idea material.

Throughout the various illustrations, the reader was reminded to consider the intellectual developmental stage of the students, to be alert to the dangers of overgeneralization, and to cooperate with science colleagues in an intellectually honest presentation of the mathematics/science interface.

Now you should be able to:

1. Describe several ways in which mathematics teachers can use scientific settings in the teaching of mathematics.

2. Give *at least three* reasons to support an emphasis on the mathematics/science interface in mathematics classes.

3. Describe ways in which several areas other than science can be used to teach mathematics.

4. Cite *at least four* sources of science-related materials that have potential for teaching mathematics.

5. Cite *at least four* sources of everyday-world materials that have potential for teaching mathematics.

6. Add to your resource file ideas that use science, other school subjects, and everyday phenomena in the teaching of mathematics.

10.5 SIMULATION/PRACTICE ACTIVITIES

A. Obtain a contemporary high school biology text. Select *one* of the following topics from mathematics: probability, functions, graphing, rate and ratio, or symmetry; and research the ways in which that topic is referred to and used in the biology text. What differences (similarities) in treatment from that typically given in a mathematics class are reflected? In what ways could you, the mathematics teacher, assist in transfer of these mathematics concepts/rules in the context of biology?

B. The logarithmic, or equiangular spiral, is a property of dead tissues rather than living tissues, according to D'Arcy Thompson (1917/1961). In his book *On Growth and Form* he provided details on the chambered Nautilus and listed several other examples of structures that display the equiangular spiral: a snail's shell, an elephant's tusk, a beaver's tooth, a cat's claws, a canary's claws, and a ram's horn. Study any of these structures by observing the varied lines of growth in one of the structures or in a good photograph. Compare the organism at various stages of growth with the spiral shown in Figure 10.5a. Next, look up a definition of the logarithmic spiral in a mathematics dictionary. Finally, read Thompson's explanation in Chapter 6 of *On Growth and Form* (See Suggestions for Further Study) to compare your ideas with his.

Based on your observations and reading, outline a presentation that might be used with a second-year algebra class.

C. An easy way to help a junior high class understand that the triangle is a rigid figure is to give them equal lengths of plastic straws and straight pins. Have them construct equilateral figures of 3, 4, 5, 6, 7, and 8 sides. Project sample models on the overhead. Then display the picture of a golfer shown in Figure 10.9 and ask the students to find the triangles and to explain how these shapes help in preserving the stability needed in golf.

Fig. 10.9   The golfer.

Locate pictures of other sports that reflect the use of the triangle to promote stability. Then locate pictures of manmade structures (e.g. bridges, houses under construction) that also make use of the triangular shape. Identify ways you would use these resources in a junior high class as well as in a geometry class.

D. Read **two** of the sports-related articles listed here and write brief reviews of each:

Dunkin, D. R., & Litwiller, B. H. (1977). "Statistics in the classroom: Examples from football." *New York State Mathematics Teachers' Journal*, 27, 77–79.

Fitting, M. A. P. (1974). "SCUBA: Some challenging un-boring arithmetic." *Arithmetic Teacher*, 21 (4), 294–297.

Martin, W. G., & Ponte, J. (1985). "Measuring the area of golf greens and other irregular shapes." *Mathematics Teacher*, 78, 385–389.

Sloyer, C. W. (1975). "Play a cool pool." *School Science and Mathematics*, 75, 185–190.

E. Find examples of photos, slides, clippings or cartoons that might be used to teach students something about the interface of mathematics and science or mathematics and the everyday world. Be sure to write a brief explanation of the way(s) the item might be used in a lesson.

SUGGESTIONS FOR FURTHER STUDY

Boehm, D. A. (Ed.). (1988). *Guinness book of world records*. New York: Sterling Publications Co., Inc.

This paperback is regularly updated to incorporate the latest records set by both pros and amateurs. The authors have more than once illustrated ways in which such data might be used to teach mathematics. We encourage you to browse through the latest edition and be alert for ways to teach ratio, measurement, volume concepts, and so on.

Bureau of Curriculum Development, (1982). *MARA: Mathematics/architecture related activities*. Albany, NY: The State Education Department.

A lesson from this paperback book was outlined in this chapter. Complete details for several lessons, a glossary of terms and a set of additional resources is included.

House, P. A. (1980). *Interactions of science and mathematics*. Columbus, OH: ERIC Clearinghouse for Science, Mathematics, and Environmental Education.

This book contains a variety of science investigations requiring minimal equipment. The investigations are designed to help the mathematics teacher respond to that typical question by students—Why do we need to know this? The activities do not require any particular background in science on the part of the teacher or students. They are both interesting and relevant.

Jacobs, H. R. (1982). *Mathematics a human endeavor* (2nd ed.). San Francisco, CA: W. H. Freeman.

The subtitle says it all: "A textbook for those who think they don't like the subject." Both novice and experienced teachers have found that Jacobs knows what he's talking about. In the course of two pages, one finds questions using information about ice crystals, viruses, the planetary system, and playing-card designs. We recommend the text as a source of multiple teaching ideas for all levels of mathematics.

Kastner, B. (1978). *Applications of secondary school mathematics*. Reston, VA: National Council of Teachers of Mathematics.

Kastner treats topics such as optics, music, and the geometry of molecules in this valuable paperback book. Chapters are cross-referenced to the level of secondary mathematics needed to work through the questions. Supplementary exercises, lists for further reference, and answers to questions are included.

Newman, J. (Ed.). (1956). *The world of mathematics* (Vol. 1, 2, 3, 4). New York: Simon and Schuster.

This set of four volumes includes essays on the mathematics of "gifted" birds, the kinetics of gases, crystals, mathematics in golf and gambling, and mathematics in war and art. Two essays, Jeans's and Haldane's, are particularly valuable as sources of mathematics/science ideas. We encourage you to visit these texts often. You will find multiple ways to relate mathematics to science, to technology, and to the everyday world.

Petit, J. (1985). *The adventures of Archibald Higgins* (Transl. by I.Stewart). Providence, RI: Janson Publications, Inc.

We recommend two books in this series as particularly appropriate in terms of the mathematics/science interface—*Everything is relative* and *The black hole*. Bright senior high students will find the cartoon approach to complex ideas from physics and mathematics both challenging and enjoyable.

Polya, G. (1963). *Mathematical methods in science* ("Studies in Mathematics," Vol. 11). Stanford, CA: School Mathematics Study Group.

Polya's paperback guides the reader through the struggles of Newton, Galileo, Kepler, and others. He describes the way monumental results were developed on the basis of simple mathematical concepts. The book abounds with examples of the contiguous development of mathematics and science and is highly recommended.

Sharron, S. (Ed.). (1979). *Applications in school mathematics* (1979 Yearbook). Reston, VA: National Council of Teachers of Mathematics.

This sourcebook contains applications that we would call "here and now" applications, as well as those more related to the world of science, society and technology. See especially Pagni's chapter on

Human Variability and Swift's on *Capture-Recapture Techniques*. An annotated bibilography provides information on other sources.

SMSG. (1965). *Mathematics and living things* (Rev. ed.). Stanford, CA: School Mathematics Study Group.

A student text and teacher's commentary are available under this title. This valuable paperback is aimed at students who either do not like or do not understand mathematics. The approach is to begin with some interesting life science activities and to present the mathematics concepts and rules as the need arises. The science activities require only commonly available or homemade apparatus. The mathematics ideas are developed inductively for the most part by finding common patterns in the data. Main topic titles include: "Leaves and Natural Variation," "Natural Variation—Us," "Muscle Fatigue," and "Size of Cells." Our student teachers and cooperating teachers rate this set as A-1.

SMSG. (1964). *Mathematics through science* (Rev. ed.). (Parts 1, 2, and 3). Stanford, CA: School Mathematics Study Group.

This three-volume set includes a student text and teacher's commentary under each of the following titles: Part 1—"Measurement and Graphing," Part 2—"Graphing, Equations and Linear Functions," and Part 3—"An Experimental Approach to Functions." The content coverage is exactly what the three titles lead one to believe and mathematics teachers will find a wealth of ideas to enrich mathematics classes from grades 6–9. The required equipment is very common and simple—rules, string, coat hangers, marbles, washers, and the like. The texts are loaded with gems!

Steinhaus, H. (1969). *Mathematical snapshots*. (3rd ed.). New York: Oxford Press.

"What does a mathematician do?" Steinhaus answers that question by presenting mathematical phenomena as they relate to the real world in photographs and diagrams. His illustrations include the analysis of chess strategies, the scale used for measuring shoe sizes, the patterns formed by dried mud, the properties of soap bubbles and the paths squirrels follow up a tree. This is a highly recommended source which you should put at the top of your list.

CHAPTER ELEVEN

RESOURCES FOR MATHEMATICS INSTRUCTION

Gold Is Where You Find It

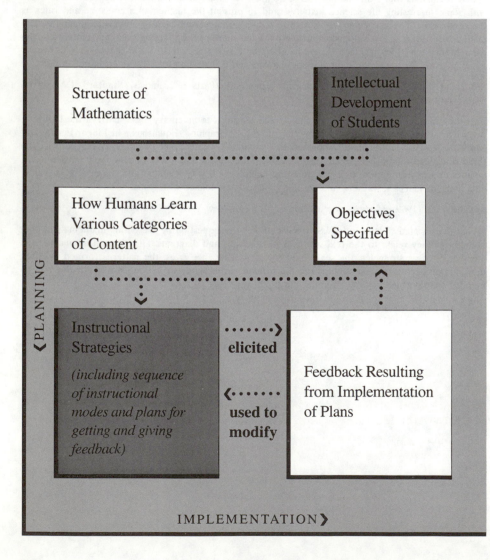

If you've been interacting with the text, you have no doubt realized that Chapters 1–8 comprise a cycle of instruction with each chapter focused on one or two components of the instructional model. Chapter 9 was designed to help provide perspective to the teacher—a perspective that at one and the same time sheds light on the past and the present and points the way to intelligent uses of contemporary curricular materials. Chapter 10 played a complementary role in that you were alerted to the instructional potential of other school subjects and non-school areas—areas outside the academic aspects of subject matter *per se*. These last two chapters were intended to add depth and breadth to the integrated approach to instruction that evolved in Chapters 1–8. Now you should be ready to use that approach in planning and teaching.

Why have we devoted an entire chapter to resources? Any why so late? After all, we did recommend that you begin collecting resource ideas as early as Chapter 4. Moreover, we continually provided illustrations of a variety of references. Then what is the focus of this chapter?

In this chapter, we look at the everyday world of concrete objects, movable devices, people and issues to see how they might relate to mathematics instruction. We know that all too often by the time the teacher sits down to plan a lesson on functions, or spatial perception, or statistics, there is a frantic last-minute search for concrete materials that could be used in a demonstration. Then, the teacher remembers the "junk" thrown away last week that might have been used in this lesson or the TV program that could have been taped to use as an advance organizer. This chapter, then, is based on the premise that part of the long-term planning that supports meaningful instruction depends on storing in a Resource File the mathematics teacher's collectibles. Our students have found that they become better collectors after they have had some teaching experience; thus, this chapter is presented late in the text. We are also cognizant of the life-long study of teaching in which the best inservice teachers continually engage. So in the final section of the chapter, we briefly outline some of the resources available through professional associations, through associations devoted to work on contemporary issues and through teacher participation in research.

Why did we elect to shade in the "Instructional Strategies" and the "Intellectual Development of Students" portions of the instructional model? The reason for the first choice is probably obvious to you since instructional modes are key elements in strategy design. If you recall that research on adolescent reasoning demonstrates the essential role of concrete experiences in learning abstractions, then the rationale for shading in the second box becomes clear. For this same reason, we ask you to begin your interaction with the ideas in this chapter by engaging in the concrete experience that follows.

11.1 INTRODUCTORY ACTIVITY

Seeing is not the same as observing.

Go to a multipurpose store (such as Woolworth's or K-Mart). Visit the hardware, toy, notions, stationery, sewing, pet, and household departments.

A. Make a list of all inexpensive items that are potential pieces of teaching equipment. Specify the projected use of each item. For starters, think of the materials included in previous illustrations in this text.

B. Compare your list with that of two or more other classmates.

C. Keep this list handy and modify it as needed after you finish studying this chapter.

11.2 INEXPENSIVE EQUIPMENT AND SUPPLIES

If you were surprised at the length of the lists compiled by you and your class-mates, you are in good company. As soon as you begin to observe the teaching potential of all you encounter, the most mundane objects take on mathematical characteristics. For example, a wine bottle cork may be perceived as a truncated cone or a weight for a pendulum lab. Table 11.1 lists items like the wine bottle cork. Some may be purchased, but most may be found in the garage, the kitchen cupboard, the sewing basket, and even en route to the trash can. As you read the list in Table 11.1, try to concoct one or two ways in which each item could contribute to a lesson.

Don't be overly concerned if you draw a blank on some items at first. We have provided illustrations of the uses of a few of these. After interacting with the reading, make a second attempt to identify uses of items that stumped you on the first go-around. Then be on the alert for other potentially useful pieces of "junk" and add these to your collection.

In addition to these multipurpose everyday-world materials, there are rel-atively inexpensive kinds of equipment that are directly related to teaching and particularly useful for the teaching of mathematics. Some of these, such as class-size sets of protractors, are requisitioned through the mathematics department and should be available for use during student teaching. (However, the mathe-matics department may own only 35 protractors, so plan ahead if you expect to use them on a particular day.) Other items, such as geoboards, *might* be owned by the mathematics department but, if not, *can* be easily constructed with the aid of finishing nails, a hammer, and squares of plywood. In Table 11.2 we list class-room equipment and materials that have been found to be particularly useful in the teaching of mathematics. We have included some typical items, such as rulers, but notice that they must be metric. (It is important to reinforce the adoption of the metric system in the United States by using it at every opportunity.) We've also included items, like geoboards and geo-d-stix, that may be purchased under a commerical label but that may also be homemade.

Table 11.1
Usable "Junk"

Bags and baggies (plastic)	Needles (sewing): assorted sizes
Bags: assorted sizes (paper)	Paper clips
Balloons: assorted sizes	Paper fasteners
Balls: ping pong, golf, baseball	Pins: common
Bicycle inner tube	Pipe cleaners (white and colored)
Boxes: assorted sizes (cardboard)	Plastic tape
Buttons: assorted sizes	Plastic covers from cans: assorted
Cans: assorted sizes	sizes
Carpenter's ruler	Poker chips
Cards: 3 x 5, 4 x 6, 5 x 8	Razor blades
Cartons: milk (1/2 pt., pt., 1/2 gal.)	Reinforcements (paper)
Clay (modeling) or putty	Sand
Cloth: misc. pieces and colors	Sandpaper
Clothespins (pincer type)	Scales (balance)
Coat hangers (wire)	Scissors: class set
Computer pinhole strips	Scrabble game
Contact paper, transparent	Screws: assorted
Cotton: roll or balls	Shirt cardboards
Corks: assorted sizes	Soda straws
Cups (paper)	Sponges: assorted sizes
Dowels (wooden)	Springs: assorted sizes
Dress snaps	Stopwatch
Egg cartons (colored)	String
Elastic thread	Styrofoam
Felt scraps	Tape: adding machine
Flashlight bulbs and receptacles	Thermometer
Foil (aluminum)	Tongue depressors
Funnels	Toothpicks
Household chemicals: sugar,	Toy car: both battery-operated
food coloring	and not battery-operated
Jars: baby food, both sizes,	Tubes (cardboard) from wax paper
with tops	rolls, saran wrap, etc.
Jars: pint and quart size	Thread
with screw tops	Velcro swatches
Magnets	Washers (metal): assorted sizes
Marbles	Waxpaper
Mirrors: plane	Wire ties
Masking tape	Yarn (colored)

Although some would argue that computers cannot be called *inexpensive*, we have included these items because their importance in the mathematics classroom is without question. There are grants and discounts available to schools for the purchase of computer equipment. Before a major purchase of this kind is undertaken, the teacher (and preferably the entire mathematics department) should study the advantages and disadvantages of the proposed computer system, the kinds of educational software available for the system, and its potential for diversification in instruction. Bramble and Mason (1985) provide some specific

Table 11.2
Mathematics Equipment and Materials

Abacus	Geoboard for overhead use
Acetates for overhead	Geo-d-stix
Angle-mirror	Georule
Calculators (class size set)	Hypsometer-clinometer
Calculator (overhead model)	Mira (class size set)
Chalk, semipermanent	Pencils (#2) in quantity and in
Compasses (class size set)	colors
Compasses for chalkboard	Pens for overhead in colors
(use chalk on a string)	Protractors (class size set)
Compass for overhead use	Protractor—board size
(Circle Master Compass)	Protractor (transparent) for
Computer(s) and related	overhead use
hardware and software	Rulers (metric) and meter sticks
Geoboards—rectangle grid	Tangram set
(class size set & large demonstration)	Transit
Geoboards—circular grid	Weights (metric)

pre-purchase ideas in their chapter, *Getting started* in *Computers in schools* published by McGraw Hill. A field trip by the mathematics teachers to one or more schools using microcomputers—to talk with other teachers, to see classroom uses and to try out the system—is one viable way of getting specific information before making a major purchase.

If any item in the list seems unfamiliar, check one of the equipment sources listed in the Suggestions for Further Study section of this chapter. However, don't expect to find semipermanent chalk on sale in any typical catalogue of equipment. That's something you must concoct by using the recipe in Figure 11.1. After chalk is treated in the way described in the recipe, it becomes very soft and *cannot* be used to draw a *fine* line. However, the lines made with this chalk do not erase, although they fade over time and can easily be washed off a chalkboard. The potential is enormous. (See the next section for one example.)

---

4 or 5 sticks of soft colored and white chalk
2 jars with tight-fitting covers (peanut butter jars are fine)
A supply of lukewarm tap water
3 or 4 paper towels
A supply of table sugar

- -

Half fill one jar with water. Add sugar and stir *until* sugar will no longer dissolve. (Obtain a supersaturated solution.) Immerse chalk in solution. Take out after bubbles stop forming. Lay chalk on paper towel for a *few* minutes to blot up excess water. Store treated chalk in other jar. Be sure cover is on tight.

- -

Solution can be used again *if* stored in tightly covered jar. Check its effectiveness after 2–3 months.

Fig. 11.1   Recipe for semipermanent chalk.

11.3 USES OF COLLECTIBLES IN THE MATHEMATICS CLASSROOM

In the paragraphs that follow, selected uses of equipment from Tables 11.1 and 11.2 are outlined as they pertain to specific instructional modes or activities used in conjunction with one or more of these modes.

Demonstration

For example, if you don't have a microcomputer available for use in a lesson on the quadratic function, then use semipermanent chalk to draw the axes, write the scale, and draw a basic curve, say $y = x^2$. Other curves, $y = 2x^2$, $y = (1/2)x^2$, $y = x^2 + 2$, and $y = x^2 - 2$, can be drawn, compared, and erased at will without disturbing the treated part of the diagram.

A little string, some buttons, and two shirt cardboards are all that's needed if you want to construct a string polyhedron. Draw the same polygon on the two cardboards and cut each out carefully (see Figure 11.2). Make puncture holes near each vertex and thread equal lengths of string through a large button. Thread the ends through two vertices of both layers of the polygon. Next thread each end through a small button and knot. From pyramid to prism is one easy step. Just move one polygonal shape up. Oblique prisms can be quickly demonstrated by sliding one polygon horizontally away from the other. A twist of the wrist will send the prism into a double-napped pyramid. Once you begin to manipulate this inexpensive string model, you will discover many more uses.

What on earth can you do with plastic coffee can covers? We're sure you thought of their use as circular discs, but not very many people consider their potential as overhead projector models. Draw the shape of an equilateral triangle on the cover with a flare pen. Carefully cut out the shape with a safety razor blade. Two congruent plastic shapes may be used to teach a lesson on similarity. Place one on the lighted stage of an overhead projector. Then walk to the screen to try to fit one of the cutout shapes over the projected image of the second congruent shape. By means of the visual matching, you can help the students conclude that corresponding angles are congruent regardless of the distance of the projector from the screen. Don't throw away the remaining part of the cover. That, too, can be used in a demonstration on the overhead. The cover becomes a stencil. You'll find it helpful to make cover stencils of the most common shapes you work with, such as the equilateral triangle, the square, and the regular hexagon.

A carpenter's rule can be folded to form various polygonal shapes. Form a rhombus. Have a student move the rhombus to form a rhombus of maximum area and one of minimum area. Compare the shapes. What changes? What remains the same? Form an equilateral triangle and illustrate the rigid nature of the structure. A georule could be used to illustrate the same ideas and has the advantage of being brightly colored and wider than the typical carpenter's rule.

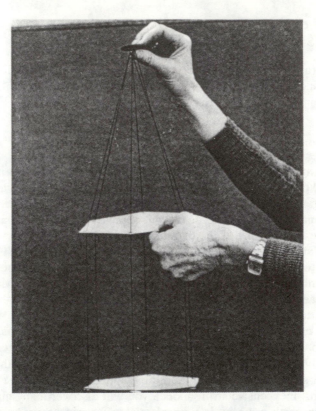

Fig. 11.2 String polyhedron.

Buffon's problem can be replicated by a laboratory, prefaced as always by a demonstration. In this case, the demonstration makes use of the projection properties of the overhead projector. Count Buffon was an eighteenth century naturalist, whose name was given to a geometric probability problem that is related to the irrational number, π. Before class, prepare an acetate sheet with parallel lines ruled about 6 cm apart. Then obtain a number (20 for each lab group and 20 for the demonstration) of small sticks, about 5 cm long. (Toothpicks will serve as a good approximation.) Holding your hands high, drop the sticks onto the acetate sheet. Have the students help count the cases where sticks cross the lines. If a stick does not fall on the sheet at all, drop it again. They should record the number of crosses so that the ratio of crosses to the total number of sticks can be calculated. Have the students talk about the varied possible orientations of any stick with respect to the bars on the sheet. The fact that a particular stick might rotate as it falls should bring to mind a circle and the possibility that π is related to this ratio. Next, have groups of students repeat the demonstration at least 40 times, tabulate the data from all groups, and obtain the ratio of the number of sticks crossing the lines (c) to the total number (N). The ratio of

c/N has been shown to be equal to $2k/\pi a$, where k = the length of a stick, a = the distance between a pair of parallel lines, and $a > k$. Therefore, $\pi = 2kN/ac$. Thus, the results of the lab can be used to obtain an empirical value of π, in this case, $\pi \approx 2(5)N/6c$. For an explanation of this finding that your advanced students would enjoy reading, see Gamow (1947, pp. 210–213).

Laboratory

Wax paper, pencils, and a few straightedges comprise the essential equipment for a paper-folding laboratory. In the Introductory Activity in Chapter 3, Section 3.1, you were asked to complete a paper-folding laboratory that yielded one of the conics, the parabola. Refresh your memory on the directions for this lab and the series of questions we posed. We hope that you saw the enormous potential of this lab for developing the locus definition of a parabola as the locus of all points equidistant from a fixed line and a given point not on that line. The concepts of focus (the given point), directrix (the fixed line) and family of tangents (the folds) are given concrete meaning and the folding process itself seems to simulate the dynamic mathematical process of *generating a curve*.

If you complete this laboratory with *your* students, don't ignore the opportunity to investigate other physical models of the parabola and paraboloid—flashlights, floodlights, automobile headlights, the path of a projectile, the water gushing out of a fountain. A followup take-home lab to construct the ellipse and the hyperbola yield added benefits. To construct a paper-folded ellipse, draw a circle and place a point within the circle, but *not* at the center. Match the given point to the points on the circle (Figure 11.3a). A circle is also drawn as the first step in hyperbola construction but now a point is placed *outside* the circle. Again the fixed point is matched to points on the circle (Figure 11.3b).

Feedback can be obtained the next day very quickly by placing a correct model (one of the student's or your own) on the overhead projector. The wax paper model shows up quite clearly on the screen and is an easy way for students to check their efforts. Be sure to keep your personal model of each conic handy.

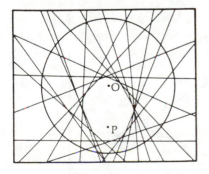

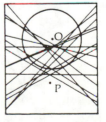

(a)   The ellipse.   (b)   The hyperbola.

Fig. 11.3   Wax paper ellipse and hyperbola.

You will find multiple uses for these in geometry (locus), algebra (quadratics), and analytic geometry (conics).

An interesting laboratory activity, which gets at such important concepts as variation, frequency, range, and norm, involves the use of sunflower seeds. Give each pair of students about 200 seeds and 14 paper cups labeled 0 through 13. Instruct them to count the number of black stripes on both sides of each seed and then place each seed in the correspondingly numbered cup. Total class results are compiled by emptying the paper cups into 14 numbered hydrometer jars (borrow these from the science department) or tall, thin, olive jars lined up on the front desk. This activity is a golden opportunity to teach students the difference between the graphing of discrete and continuous data. The sunflower seed bar graph is a concrete example on which to base developmental questions and subsequent exercises on graph paper. (See Sample Card on this lab in the Resource File Assignment in the Appendix.)

Individual Projects

Straws, coat hangers, cardboard, and styrofoam chunks are the raw material from which student-designed models can be constructed. Straws, cut in equal lengths, can be joined with pipe cleaners or fastened with straight pins to build complex geometric structures, such as the great dodecahedron. Geo-d-stix kits may be used for the same purpose. Stellated polyhedra and a representation of a fourth dimensional cube are challenging to construct. Models of the five regular Platonic solids are an excellent starting point for a comparison of faces, edges, and vertices and an exploration of the concept of duality. (See Cundy and Rollett, referenced in the Suggestions for Further Study section, for further details.)

Ask students to construct mechanical models illustrating locus problems. Some elastic, cardboard, glue, and a nail with a large head were used to construct the locus model in Figure 11.4.

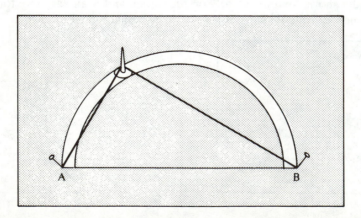

Fig. 11.4 Locus model of vertex of right angle of right triangle with fixed hypotenuse.

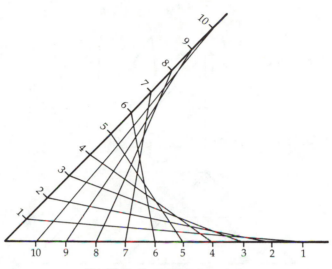

Fig. 11.5 Curve-stitched parabola.

With thread or yarn, a needle, and cardboard, the students can design and build beautiful models using curve stitching. The simplest patterns are obtained by joining holes that are equally spaced on line segments or circles. On the reverse side of the cardboard, the thread must be taken to the next hole on the pattern; on the right side of the cardboard, the thread is taken across to the next unoccupied hole on the far side of the design. Explaining this process to students is easier if they are told to number the holes on each side of an angle as depicted in Figure 11.5. The same numerals appear on both arms but are reversed on one arm. Then have them connect hole one with hole one, hole two with hole two, and so on, following the rules given earlier.

Perhaps you're wondering if curve stitching could be used as a laboratory. The answer is an emphatic "Yes!" In fact, many of the demonstrations outlined earlier can be developed as laboratories, just as most laboratory activities have promise as demonstrations. Continue thinking of multiple uses as you read the sections that follow.

Bulletin Boards

A corkboard surface, a wall, a chalkboard, or even a square of poster board can be used as the backdrop for a static or movable display. Use loops of masking tape on movable colored cutout shapes and transform an unused section of chalkboard into a vertical demonstration table. Have students bring in clippings that illustrate uses of integers and make a collage of their examples. Titles are readily constructed by "writing" in yarn with the aid of a stapler or by twisting pipe cleaners into the shape of letters. Student progress records on the "Problem

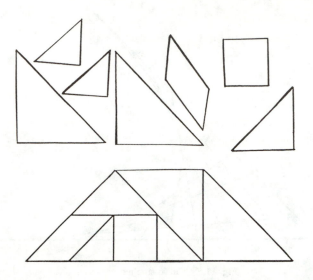

Fig. 11.6 Tangram problem.

of the Week" can be designed as a chart and posted on the wall. Students then record their own progress by pasting a silver star for an attempt and a gold star for success. Maps of the city can be hung from chart clips and used to initiate a lesson in distance problems, scale drawing, map reading, or even coordinate work.

If you want to manipulate shapes as a basis for developing a formula, such as the area of a parallelogram, a feltboard (or a velcro board) is useful. Cover one side of a sheet of plywood with felt or velcro. (Ask the industrial arts teacher for help.) Staple it securely to the reverse side. Use light poster paper to trace and cut out the shapes you want to move. Paste a piece of flannel or a piece of velcro on each cutout shape, depending on the type of board you've constructed. Then place the shapes on the board; move them to different positions, move them again. Some teachers use this kind of board in a classification task. First the board is separated, perhaps by two large yarn enclosures. Then the movable shapes (e.g. parallelograms and non-parallelograms) are moved by the students into the correct enclosure. A board of this type can be used to show the results of dissection problems, perhaps with prepared tangrams. Figure 11.6 shows the result of rearranging a tangram set to cover a given shape. We suggest that each tangram piece be a different color so that the class can identify the location and changed orientation of each shape.

We encourage you to *use* bulletin board displays as a basis for demonstrations, as a basis for a problem-solving lesson, as a cue card for review lessons, or as an attention-getter for a unit. The topics that follow are just a few which might be the subject of a bulletin board display.

1. The Catenary—What Is It?

2. The Snowflake and Geometry

3. Magic Squares

4. Linkages—Watt's Linkage

5. Clocks and Calendars

6. The Googol and Googolplex

7. Alice in Wonderland Mathematics

8. Spirals in Nature

9. The Biggest and the Smallest

10. Music and Mathematics

11. A Flow Chart on the Solution of an Equation

12. $(a + b)(a + b) = a^2 + 2ab + b^2$ "Move the shapes and see for yourself."

13. Our School's Basketball Statistics

14. The Weather and Probability

15. Advertising and Fallacious Reasoning

Games and Competitions

Perhaps pleasant past experiences cause students to equate a game with fun. Whatever the reason, a well-designed and well-organized game has the potential for getting and keeping attention. When you visited the toy and games department as part of the Introductory Activity, you probably noted commercial games and kits that could be used in the mathematics classroom. Some that we have found useful are:

Forecast	Hexogram
Tuf	Chess
Numble	Checkers
Spirograph	Battleship
Dominoes	Scrabble

Most of the above games are suitable for use by at most two or three students at a time. Keep them in mind when you plan diversified activities but be prepared to modify them for class-size groups. The commercial game of Battleship, for example, uses pegs on two plastic grids but with the aid of graph paper and the use of pencilled symbols to represent different kinds of ships, the entire class can play in subgroups of two. See the *School Mathematics Project Book A* for a description of the game played in quadrant I.

In similar fashion, you can modify other games not originally designed for the mathematics classroom. Watch any of the popular game shows on television and take notes as to the essential features of the game—the rules, the penalties, the kind of game board, and so on. Cross-wits becomes a combination of a crossword puzzle and a "less than 20-questions" game. If your puzzle were projected on the overhead, the entire class could follow the game. The contestants might be filling in names of concepts, formulas, or trigonometric identities, or citing reasons for some geometric assertions. There are no holds barred on the content of the individual items or the key question related to the individual clues. Moreover, the entire class could play the game if two teams were designated and appropriate rules for deciding the order of the contestants were outlined.

The game of Trivia can be adapted for use in the classroom with the help of the students. Ask each one to prepare trivia cards, by topic, about mathematicians and their contributions, or perhaps about the relationship of a concept or rule to some real world application. A student committee might take the responsibility of screening all cards and getting decks ready for classroom use. More cards or decks could be added during the year.

Finally, don't forget the games of childhood. Twenty questions, Who dunnit? and What's my question? are always ready to be adapted for a quick review or a probing, challenging exploration.

11.4 NONTYPICAL USES OF AUDIOVISUAL AND TECHNOLOGICAL AIDS

Cassette audiotape recorders can be used to bring a wide variety of sounds into the classroom, such as the sounds of the countdown at a space center, parts of a speech by a famous mathematician, and radio commercials. Some teachers have also recorded their own mini-lectures designed to accompany a demonstration, filmstrip, or slide presentation. Recall the student teacher's use of a tape recorder to give directions in a lesson on use of the compass in Chapter 7. The unusual use of a tape recorder not only got attention, but also freed the teacher to move about the class observing individual student psychomotor learning. Furthermore, if repetition of instructions is needed, the tape recorder will faithfully repeat verbatim. Teacher preparation needs to include (1) speaking slowly and clearly with pauses built in and (2) asking someone else to listen to the tape and try to follow the instructions.

Homemade charts are easy to make and valuable to have. Obtain some of those outdated pull-down maps from the social studies department. Turn them over and you have blank charts that one of your artistically inclined students can convert into custom designed visuals.

If you have access to a microcomputer with a scanner, you can scan cartoons, pictures, graphs and the like and transfer these to class handouts to be xeroxed.

The uninterrupted and unaltered viewing of a motion picture film is not always the most effective use of this medium. Shut off the projector at key points and question students as to (1) the major points developed thus far and (2) their predictions of what will happen next. Turn off the sound and supply your own audio when the commentary is either too sophisticated or too childish for your students. Reverse the film, start it again, and ask students to observe a sequence a second time. Moreover, don't overlook the possibility of making a motion picture of your own design. Many schools own a good quality motion picture or video camera. Typically it is signed out to the athletic department on a semipermanent basis, but since it is school property, you should be able to arrange to use it.

Filmstrips and slides also lend themselves to imaginative use. Students who have been absent for several days can be put in one corner of the room with projector, filmstrip, and teacher's guide while you are busy with other students. After viewing the strip and reading the guide, the catch-up session with the teacher will be facilitated. Some filmstrips may contain only a dozen relevant frames. Cut these out and mount them in empty 35 mm slide mounts available from any photographic supply store. Homemade filmstrips are easily produced by turning a 35 mm camera on its side while photographing the scenes. Then simply instruct the developing house to "Develop only. Do not cut into separate frames." Making your own sets of instructional slides is even easier. The yearbook advisor is the likely custodian of a school-owned 35 mm camera which you can arrange to borrow. Students in the photography club can be enlisted to instruct you in its use or to supply both the camera and skilled labor to get the job done. Also, investigate some of the slide sets available from mathematics supply houses. Some can be projected on the chalkboard with room lights on so teacher and students can add labels, auxiliary segments and graph lines with chalk. These are designed to promote an inquiry approach and many of them are quite effective.

Overhead projectors have become the most common visual aid in the schools. Typically their use is limited to projecting acetate-based images on a screen, but they do have additional uses. Trace or "bake" (use a thermofax or xerox machine) a complicated diagram on acetate, project it on the chalkboard after school, go to the board, and trace the lines with a soft lead pencil. The lines will be visible to you, but not to the students, as you chalk over each in turn during a lecture and question/answer session in class the next day. Also, some demonstrations are more effective if projected on a screen. We've already noted the uses to which coffee can covers might be put. Another example involves placing on the stage a polygon made from soda straws joined with pipe cleaners and flexing it to illustrate the lack of rigidity of non-triangular shapes. Overhead projectors can be used to project large screen computer displays when the appropriate hardware is wired to the computer and placed on the stage. The MacViewFrame is one such example of liquid crystal display (LCD) technology. An image as large as 15 feet can be projected onto a wall or screen. Color changes in various demonstrations are also easier to see if the glass containers are set on the lighted stage of an overhead projector. In this case it is helpful to cover the projection lens with dark cloth or a cardboard mask.

A slide projector may also be used as a light source for all kinds of demonstrations. Obtain a model of a cube. Darken the room and set up the slide projector. Then adjust the distance between object and lens so as to obtain a sharp image on the wall or screen. Have the students conjecture as to the shape that will be projected as you hold the cube so that a face is parallel to the wall and then when one of the major diagonals is perpendicular to the wall. Most will be amazed at the hexagonal shape obtained in the latter case. Objects of other familiar shapes can be manipulated in like manner to introduce the students to orthographic projection drawings or even to problems dealing with various cross-sectional slices.

Television equipment is now available in almost every school and offers many unique opportunities for teachers. Mathematics-related programs can be recorded from commercial television during evenings or weekends for class viewing during regular school hours. (Care must be taken not to violate copyright laws.) It is also easy to record phenomena from field trips and laboratory work and play the tape back in slow or stop motion. One experienced teacher used a camcorder to film a portion of a video game that was then used to introduce a sequence of story problems related to the game. Another videotaped the compass demonstration originally outlined in Chapter 7.

These are just a few ideas to start you thinking about seldom-used audiovisual and technological techniques. We made no attempt to tell you how to thread, set up, or focus these devices. Each make is a bit different, and each comes with instructions for its use. The easiest way to learn the mechanics of these devices is to have someone show you how and supervise your first attempt.

11.5 FIELD TRIPS

Field trips have high potential for contributing to important goals of mathematics instruction *if* they are carefully planned and effectively executed. Among the possible goals are generating interest in the subject, collecting data for further study in class, and observing the use of mathematics in an applied area. Some examples of field trips oriented toward senior high mathematics students are (1) visiting the drafting department of a nearby company to see and hear about the geometric and algebraic relationships being used, (2) demonstrating the use of the transit, hypsometer-clinometer, and angle mirror in an outdoor setting, (3) touring the computer center of a nearby industry or university, and (4) visiting the set design area of a college or local theater to learn about the mathematics related to design problems. Trips to a state environmental center to collect data by means of sampling techniques, a bank to learn about the mathematics involved in savings accounts, the athletic fields to obtain data on the dimensions and shapes involved, and the wooded area outside school to collect leaves for a surface area project have proved valuable for junior high mathematics classes.

Thorough and detailed planning far in advance of the trip is essential. *You* must take the proposed trip, time it, and construct a guide sheet for students to use both before and during the trip. Safety rules, appropriate clothing, and any special student behaviors need to be specified on the guide sheet and reinforced verbally. These rules and the purposes of the trip should also be included in the parental permission slips that are to be signed and returned prior to the day of the trip. Such slips carry little legal status in a court of law but they do establish consent and often generate parental understanding and support for your efforts. Don't forget to consult the principal's office about arrangements for students who forget to return permission slips. Every school has its own set of regulations governing field trips, and these must be followed from the earliest planning stage through the culmination of the trip.

All trips must be carefully supervised. Here's the time to enlist parental assistance and wider support of your efforts. Followup activities include written reports, laboratory work on collected data, class discussions, and letters of appreciation to those who made the trip possible. A brief oral report to the principal and department chairperson is in order and may well insure cooperation when future trips are planned.

11.6 HUMAN RESOURCES

Don't overlook the human resources available to you for the asking. We have repeatedly referred to the science teacher as a resource person and we encourage you to seek out that expertise and to reciprocate as needed. All of the other teachers in the school are also potential human resources. For example, the art teacher can demonstrate and explain the relationship of perspective in paintings to proportion in mathematics. A parent who is a carpenter can explain the mathematics used before the actual cutting of lumber needed for a bookcase. Architect's plans, scale diagrams, and a photo of the finished product can be provided by a local architect and displayed on the bulletin board. A student's older sister home for a college vacation may be willing to talk about her mathematics major requirements with interested students. A local research mathematician or college professor might be willing to consult with a talented student pursuing a mathematics fair project. The president of an amateur photography or radio club could send a member to talk about the mathematics related to each of these hobbies. The local meteorologist may be willing to explain the computation of the probabilities associated with weather forecasting. There are many laboratory technicians in nearby industries and hospitals who could talk about their work and the training required for such careers.

Then, too, don't forget your students. Many of them will have hobbies and skilled training in mathematics-related areas. Musicians, philatelists, skiers, golfers, model car- and plane-builders, orienteerers, sailing enthusiasts, and puzzle enthusiasts are but a few of the many human resources often overlooked. It is probably obvious that model car and plane hobbyists have been working with scale models, but what can be done with future sailors? Think in terms of vectors and forces!

11.7 SAFETY AND LEGAL ASPECTS

Teachers are legally responsible for the welfare of students under their supervision. Attendance books have been subpoenaed for evidence in courts of law and teachers have been called upon to testify as to the accuracy of these records.

Teachers have been sued for liability when injuries were sustained while the teacher stepped out in the hall for a few moments. Negligence actions have been won against teachers who allowed students to use faulty equipment, perform laboratory exercises that included undue safety hazards, or work without using proper safety devices.

We are not lawyers and thus cannot give legal advice. However, we are experienced teachers and supervisors and can offer tips about how to avoid trouble:

1. Keep accurate attendance records for every class period. Put a written reminder in the "Routines" section of each lesson plan and put a checkmark next to the notation after you do it.

2. Present a model of correct performance while doing demonstrations. Call attention to both the techniques used and the reasons for using them.

3. Write specific safety precautions (as needed) on each laboratory guide sheet and verbally remind students of these before they begin work.

4. Check all equipment before distributing it to students and instruct them to notify you at once if anything seems to malfunction.

5. Know your state safety laws thoroughly and enforce them religiously.

6. Train the students to report *all* accidents to you immediately. You, in turn, should report these in writing according to the established policy in your school.

7. Supervise actively and thoroughly. No one expects you to be standing next to every student at the same instant, but correcting papers while youngsters work unattended is an invitation to trouble.

11.8 DIFFERENTIATING INSTRUCTION

Sometimes teachers or administrators try to make the best of the difference in needs, interests, and abilities of the human resources of their students by diverse grouping arrangements. Many secondary schools use some kind of homogeneous grouping system, for example, sections for the college-bound and noncollege-bound or classes designated as honors, average, and basic. Regardless of these attempts to subdivide students according to such criteria as IQ scores, reading test scores, grade-point averages, or teacher recommendations, even a casual observer soon notices wide differences in a supposedly homogeneous group of students. For this reason, we believe that differentiation of instruction must take place in *every* class. Again we call attention to the saying: "Different strokes for different folks!" On a day-to-day basis, the teacher can work at this by (1) assigning individual projects that span a wide range of interests and skills, (2) dividing the class into several heterogeneous groups so that a variety of talents may be shared, or using more homogeneous groups, each assigned different activities, (3) initiating a "buddy" system where pairs of students work together at stated times (seek the advice of your cooperating teacher before deciding who will be paired with whom), (4) designing homework assignments with built-in choices, and (5) allowing individual students to browse through mathematics-related reading on a classroom shelf, work on a project, spend more time checking work on a calculator, and so on while the teacher and the rest of the class continue a lesson. Doesn't that kind of instruction require a lot of planning time? You bet it does! However, if the payoff for the time and energy you've expended is student learning, then the extra effort is worth it.

If you've realized that the success of such activities also depends heavily on the accurate diagnosis of student talents and weaknesses, then you've taken the first step toward differentiating instruction. Thoughtful observation of selected students followed by conferences with their other teachers will help to sharpen your observation skills. At the same time you need some broad guidelines relative to atypical students. Novice teachers generally find it most helpful to focus on those who are labeled the "slow learner" and the "academically talented."

We remind you that characteristics of these categories of students were outlined in Chapter 3. Moreover, other individual differences in reasoning and approaches to problems were presented in that chapter. It is a good idea to return to that section when you are faced with the diagnosis of learning difficulties of one or more of your students.

An increasingly popular way to individualize instruction within a heterogeneous classroom is by the use of structured small groups working within the guidelines of cooperative learning (Slavin, 1987). In cooperative learning groups, students share ideas and take responsibility for their own learning and for their teammate's learning. Some teachers have used such groups for a single lesson, or a group of lessons.

11.9 THE MATHEMATICS TEACHER IS A LEARNER, TOO

There is life after student teaching! and after graduation! However, as you will soon realize, there is always more to learn about the teaching of mathematics. Much will be learned from your colleagues; perhaps more, from your students. In this section we emphasize three other kinds of resources that are of great help to the career teacher of mathematics.

Professional associations Throughout this text we have referenced many sources published by the National Council of Teachers of Mathematics, the major professional association for the United States and Canada. We encourage you to take out a membership in this association and your state or regional association as early as possible. Members get discounts on publications, receive free copies of position papers, and receive journals and newsletters as part of the dues. Find out when and where the annual or regional meetings of these associations are being held. Find out school policy on attending such meetings and whether some or all of your expenses might be paid. Teachers repeatedly sing the praises of such meetings for the learning and sharing of ideas that takes place and the renewed vigor with which they return to classes. We also believe that one of the first steps toward helping teaching become a profession is for teachers to be active members of their professional associations.

Exploring issues   In Chapter 3, we referred to some of the research on gender differences in achievement in mathematics and some of the possible factors affecting differential achievement and differential attitudes. Both gender and equity issues continue to be an important area of concern for all teachers, although they seem to be particularly of concern to mathematics and science teachers. This is one area that might be addressed through inservice education, or even in mathematics department meetings. Activities suggested in Cheek, H. N. (Ed.). (1984). *Handbook for conducting equity activities in mathematics education*. Reston, VA: National Council of Teachers of Mathematics might be reviewed and a departmental project selected. The mathematics faculty might discuss an article on equity issues, such as that by Taylor (1983) or one that also includes attention to gender issues, such as the research article by Reyes & Stanic (1988). Both of these articles are listed in the References. See the Suggestions for Further Study for a list of resource groups related to this issue.

In Chapter 9, we outlined some of the curricular issues facing mathematics teachers. Among these were the curricular revisions that would be possible if technology were integrated into the classroom The mathematics teacher needs to read about this issue, study the implications for change, and be open to potential major changes in the curriculum. We identified major sources of reading in Chapter 9. Frequent updates will be found in the journals of the National Council of Teachers of Mathematics.

Related to the integration of technology into the classroom are a host of social, ethical and equity issues. See, for example, articles by McDonald (1985) or Kreidler (1986) listed in the References. Such articles can serve as a starting point for a faculty discussion of ways these issues affect their own classroom instruction.

Teacher partners in research   Inservice teachers are sometimes asked to collect data, administer tests, or release students for interviews by college faculty researchers. However, more and more often, there are opportunities for interested teachers to be active members of research teams. Research networks have been started in some parts of the country (In New York State, there is a Mathematics and Science Education Research Network.), expressly to encourage cooperative efforts across disciplines, between faculty at different colleges and between faculty in schools and colleges. Such teams usually come together because all wish to explore one particular area of concern. In meetings, existing research background, special problems of conducting research in schools, appropriate collection methods and the like are discussed. Some teacher participants want to learn interview techniques and become the skilled collectors of data; others are interested in analysis of data; and still others prefer to work on the managerial tasks associated with a project. Team presentations at professional meetings are an exciting way of sharing the team's experiences with other teachers. For those who like to write, jointly authored articles or project booklets are a satisfying result of thoughtful collaboration.

11.10 SUMMARY AND SELF-CHECK

In the present chapter we extended the earlier work on the importance of a rich collection of resources. We emphasized the use of simple and inexpensive materials in innovative ways, atypical uses of Audiovisual and Technological Aids (ATA's), guidelines for field trips, safety in mathematics teaching, and the human resource pool. Then we turned to the need to individualize or differentiate instruction for the various levels of students in the same class. We referred to the use of cooperative learning teams to accomplish this goal. Finally, we asked you to look beyond student teaching to the continual learning characteristic of effective teachers. We highlighted the resources available to members of mathematics education professional associations, faculty discussion and work on contemporary issues and involvement in research teams.

Now you should be able to:

1. Collect a wide variety of free and inexpensive materials and project specific uses for each item in mathematics instruction.

2. Cite atypical uses of ATA's in teaching mathematics.

3. Identify specific human resources and the ways in which they might assist in mathematics instruction.

4. Expand your resource file to include the total range of resources needed to teach both typical and atypical students.

5. Plan and conduct field trips in a manner consistent with both safety and educational considerations.

6. Plan and conduct mathematics learning experiences that are in accord with sound safety procedures.

7. Identify two or more ways practicing mathematics teachers can use resources to continue their education.

11.11 SIMULATION/PRACTICE ACTIVITIES

A. Obtain one of the sources of ideas listed in the final section of this chapter.

  1. Locate *two* manipulatives, *not* specifically described in this chapter, that have potential use in a junior high class. Outline projected use. Indicate topic, specific subject matter content objectives, and teacher and/or student use.

  2. Locate *two* manipulatives that would enhance a lesson in geometry, second-year algebra, or trigonometry, and outline the use of each as indicated in A.1.

B. Each of the films/videos/slide sets in the following list has been successfully used in mathematics instruction. Locate *each* in the appropriate film catalogue. List, for each, the cost of rental or purchase, color or black and white, time, the content, and the grade level toward which the visual is directed. Preview as many as possible.

Film	Company
1. Adventure in Science: The Size of Things	Bailey Film Associates
2. The AHA! Box	W. H. Freeman and Co.
3. Dance Squared	International Film Bureau
4. Donald in Mathmagic Land	Walt Disney
5. Geometry in Our World	National Council of Teachers of Mathematics
6. Infinite Acres	Modern Learning Aids
7. Optical Illusion Slide Show	Dale Seymour Publishers
8. The Paradox Box	W. H. Freeman and Co.

C. The major national professional association for mathematics teachers is the National Council of Teachers of Mathematics (NCTM). Active state and regional organizations also exist throughout the country. Each of these associations can be of service to beginning teachers.

1. Research the purposes, membership fees, publications and services of the NCTM.

   a. What special student membership and conference registration fees are offered?

   b. What types of publications are provided and at what costs? Specify the titles of *at least one* of each type.

   c. Obtain information on the location and scope of all NCTM meetings being held during this academic year.

   d. What employment/placement services are offered to members?

2. Answer all of the above questions for one other mathematics teaching organization in your state or region.

D. In Section 11.2 we included a short list of commercially produced games. Obtain *two* such games and read and follow the instructions. (You may need to obtain one or more coplayers.) After playing the games, respond to the following questions for *each* game.

1. What math topics might be appropriate ones for use of the game? Explain.

2. What grade level(s) and type of students seem most appropriate for use of game? Defend your decision.

3. Estimate the time needed to both learn and play the game. For you? For your students?

4. What problems might be encountered if this game were used, as directed, in a classroom? What revisions or modifications might alleviate these problems?

E. Research some sources aimed at the talented and the slow learner. Prepare *at least five* cards (for your resource file) directed at enrichment for the talented student and *at least five* others directed at adapting instruction for the slow learner.

F. Identify *two* locations in your geographical region that would be appropriate places for a field trip in your content area. For each location, outline:

1. the instructional objectives of such a trip,

2. the preparation the students would need prior to the trip,

3. the followup classroom activities related to the objectives, and

4. anticipated problems relative to this field trip.

G. Read one of the following articles and report on the ideas presented and the way in which they could be used in mathematics instruction.

Evered, L. (1987). "Tape constructions." *Mathematics Teacher*, **80** (5), 353–356.

Lennie, J. L. (1986). "Producing videos from microcomputers" (In *Sharing teaching ideas*). *Mathematics Teacher*, **79** (9), 708–709.

Lovell, R. (1986). "Flip and twist, shuffle, snap, and compose." *Mathematics Teacher*, **79** (3), 636–638.

SUGGESTIONS FOR FURTHER STUDY

Catalogues of manipulatives and visual resource material

It is worth getting on the mailing list for each of the catalogues listed here. Be sure to ask for both elementary and secondary catalogues, if available. Frequently, manipulatives in the elementary catalogue are readily adapted for secondary school use.

Creative Publications
Order Department: 5005 West 110th St., Oak Lawn, IL 60453

Dale Seymour Publications
P.O. Box 10888, Palo Alto, CA 94303

Cuisenaire Co. of America, Inc.
12 Church St., Box D, New Rochelle, NY 10802

W.H. Freeman and Co.
660 Market St., San Franciso, CA 94104

Janson Publications, Inc.
222 Richmond St., Suite 105, Providence, RI 02903

Midwest Publications
P.O. Box 448, Pacific Grove, CA 93950

NASCO
901 Janesville Ave., Fort Atkinson, Wisconsin 53538

J.Weston Walch, Publisher
P.O. Box 658, Portland, Maine 04104-0658

Computers and calculators

Coburn, T. (1987). *How to teach mathematics using a calculator: Activities for elementary and middle school*. Reston, VA: National Council of Teachers of Mathematics.

Teachers have found the calculator activities very classroom adaptable and are especially pleased with the use of the calculator to develop concepts and assist in building problem-solving skills.

Goldberg, K. P. (1982). *Pushbutton mathematics*. Englewood Cliffs, NJ: Prentice-Hall.

See abstract in Chapter 1.

Martin, K. & Bearden, D. (1985). *Mathematics and LOGO: A turtle trip through geometry*. Englewood Cliffs, NJ: Prentice-Hall.

This teacher's guide is designed for middle school teachers who are experienced in LOGO and whose students know LOGO.

Miller, D. (1977). *Calculator explorations*. St. Cloud, MN: St. Cloud State University.

This inexpensive paperback book contains pages of inventive keystroke sequences that are designed to lead students to generalize, invent their own algorithms, and practice standard algorithms.

Petit, J. P. (1985). *The adventures of Archibald Higgins: Computer magic*. (Trans. by I. Stewart). Providence, RI: Janson Publications, Inc. (Originally published in 1980).

This is another of the clever Archibald Higgins series in which Archibald learns about computers. Bright students who already are computer-knowledgeable will enjoy the escapades in this cartoon book.

Williams, D. E. (1984). *Mathematics teacher's complete calculator handbook*. Old Tappan, NJ: Prentice-Hall.

This book contains exercises, challenges and clasroom activities.

Demonstration and laboratory idea sources

Bruni, J. V. (1977). *Experiencing geometry*. Belmont, CA: Wadsworth Publishing Co., Inc.

This entire text is based on a laboratory approach to geometry, with the laboratory equipment being inexpensive and easy to obtain. Here you will also find atypical uses of audiovisual aids to produce images of conic sections.

Cundy, H. M., & Rollett, A. P. (1961). *Mathematical models* (2nd ed.). London: Oxford University Press.

This text is a classroom-tested guide book to the construction of simple models from linkages to stellated polyhedra. The authors provide information on needed materials and some background on the related mathematics. This is a classic that belongs in your personal library.

Farrell, M. (1971). *Geoboard geometry*. Palo Alto, CA: Creative Publications.

This book contains activities that range from kindergarten to twelfth grade for the 25 pin geoboard. Proofs, concepts and problem solving are highlighted.

Gillespie, N. J. (1973). *MIRA activities for junior high school geometry*. Palo Alto, CA: Creative Publications.

We consider many of these activities equally appropriate for senior high geometry. Blank microscope slides can be substituted for the commercially produced MIRA, which is the instrument used in this series of laboratory exercises. While the activities are designed to develop further fundamental concepts of congruence, symmetry and the like, many can also be used in a unit or course on transformation geometry.

Hess, A. L. (1982). *Mathematics projects handbook* (2nd ed.). Reston, VA: National Council of Teachers of Mathematics.

The book contains useful ideas for secondary school teachers and students who are developing projects. There is an extensive bibliography.

Krulik, S. A. (1971). *A handbook of aids for teaching junior-senior high school mathematics*. Philadelphia, PA: W. B. Saunders Co.

The title says it. Here are included directions and diagrams of "equipment" such as Napier's Bones, "materials" such as magic squares, and games. All are easily constructed with inexpensive materials.

—————— (nd). *MIRA math activities for high school*. New Rochelle, NY: Cuisenaire Co. of America, Inc.

Topics in this book include properties of perpendicular lines, reflection, and symmetry. The activities are gradually sequenced from grade 7 up through geometry problems found in senior high school. Like the Gillespie book the labs require a MIRA, or a comparable substitute.

Seymour, D. (1971). *Tangramath*. Palo Alto, CA: Creative Publications.

This pamphlet describes demonstration and laboratory activities based on the seven-piece tangram puzzle. Similarity, congruence, and properties of polygons are some of the topics.

Exploring issues: gender and equity issues

Cheek, H. N. (Ed.) (1984). *Handbook for conducting equity activities in mathematics education*. Reston, VA: National Council of Teachers of Mathematics.

This source includes descriptions of intervention programs, workshops for teachers and information on the status of minorities in mathematics and science classes.

Truely, W. G. & Bilski, V. (n.d.) *A winning formula: A program to promote sex equity in mathematics and science*. Brooklyn, NY: New York City Board of Education.

This program guide contains ideas for the classroom teacher and essays on the underrepresented minorities. Valuable lists of resources—materials, ATAs, and human—are included in the guide.

Resource Organizations

Assocation for Women in Mathematics (AWM), Women's Research Center, Wellesley College, 828 Washington St. Wellesley, MA 022181

Math/Science Network, c/o Math Science Resource Center, Mills College, Oakland, CA 94613

Women & Mathematics Education (WME), c/o Education Department, George Mason University, 4400 University Drive, Fairfax, VA 22030.

Women's Educational Equity Act Publishing Center. Education Development Center, Inc., 55 Chapel St. Newton, MA 02160. (Send for their current catalogue of resources for educational equity.)

Exploring issues: computers and calculators

Fey, J. T. (Ed.) (1984). *Computing and mathematics*. Reston, Va: National Council of Teachers of Mathematics.

This report of a conference was described in Chapter 9. It is included here as excellent background reading on present and future issues in mathematics education.

Hansen, V. P. (Ed.). (1984). *Computers in mathematics education* (1984 yearbook). Reston, VA: National Council of Teachers of Mathematics.

This yearbook includes chapters on issues, as well as those containing classroom teaching ideas. An annotated bibliography of further ideas is included.

Howson, A. G. & Kahane, J. P. (Eds.). (1986). *The influence of computers and informatics on mathematics and its teaching*. Cambridge, MA: Cambridge University Press.

The editors report on a symposium held in March, 1985. Selected papers from that meeting dealing with the influence of the computer on mathematics curriculum, teaching and learning are included.

Taylor, R. (Ed.) (1980). *The computer in the school: Tutor, tool, tutee*. New York: Teachers College Press, Columbia University.

This book of readings contains sometimes provocative essays by early leaders in computer education: Alfred Bork, Thomas Dwyer, Arthur Luehrmann, Seymour Papert and Patrick Suppes.

Resource Organizations

CONDUIT
P.O. Box 388, Iowa City, IA 52244

Minnesota Educational Computing Consortium (MECC)
2520 Broadway Drive, Saint Paul, MN 55113

Problems and puzzles idea sources

Adler, I. (Ed.). (1972). *Readings in mathematics* (Books 1 and 2). Lexington, MA: Ginn and Co.

These short articles can be read with profit by teacher and a wide range of students. The topics range from deciphering a cryptogram left by Captain Kidd to the atom and its nucleus.

Barr, S. (1969). *Secondary miscellany of puzzles, mathematical and otherwise*. London: Collier-Macmillan, Ltd.

This collection of puzzles can be solved with elementary arithmetic, algebra, or geometry along with a good measure of common sense. Many of these puzzles are appropriate for the typical high-school student. Look for those that demand a little more of the students.

Bureau of Mathematics Education. (1978). *Creative problem solving*. Albany, NY: The State Education Department.

Although the preface includes a statement that the ideas in this pamphlet are suitable for kindergarten through eighth grade, we have found the insightful approach useful for the secondary school classroom.

Farrell, M. A. (Ed.) (1988). *Imaginative ideas for the teacher of mathematics grades K–12*. Reston, VA: National Council of Teachers of Mathematics.

This book of readings includes some of the best of Ernest Ranucci's work. The material has been categorized into five sections: Patterns, Mathematics in the World, And Then There Was Space!, Inventiveness in Geometry, and Games to Learn By.

Burns, M. (1975). *The I hate mathematics! book*. Palo Alto, CA: Creative Publications.

This cartoon approach to the student who dislikes math has appeal for the slow learner and may even interest some mathematical "kooks." There are laboratory and pencil-and-paper activities. The mathematics ranges from basic skills in disguise to recreational mathematics.

Kasner, E., & Newman, J. (1940). *Mathematics and the imagination*. New York: Simon and Schuster.

This classic is a source of a host of fascinating ideas. It can be read by the talented student or used by the teacher to initiate projects or to teach some mathematical concepts (such as, π, e, logarithm) to the "average" group of students.

Gardner, M. (1971). *Martin Gardner's sixth book of mathematical games from Scientific American*. San Francisco, CA: W. H. Freeman.

As always, Martin Gardner is able to stimulate our imagination and pique our curiosity with puzzles, paradoxes, illustrations from nature, and photos of phenomena. This is just one of the excellent source books for both the talented student and the teacher who needs ideas for the so-called "average" class.

Ransom, W. R. (1955). *One hundred mathematical curiosities*. Portland, ME: J. Weston Walch.

This inexpensive paperback is a treasury of riddles, paradoxes, and problems. All are mind boggling at first, although the difficulty level varies from easy to hard.

Salkind, C. T. (1966). *The MAA problem book II*. New York: Random House.

This paperback contains problems (with solutions) from the annual high-school contests sponsored by the Mathematical Association of America in 1961–1965. Solutions are included.

Seymour, D. (1971). *Aftermath* (Books 1–4). Palo Alto, CA: Creative Publications.

These books consist of collections of puzzles and problems presented by cartoon characters. Mathematical material is appropriate for seventh- through ninth-grade mathematics. They have been successfully used with slow learners as well as the average student.

Selected Journals

Published by the National Council of Teachers of Mathematics (NCTM):

Arithmetic Teacher, *Mathematics Teacher* and *Journal for Research in Mathematics Education*

The first two journals are devoted to the improvement of mathematics teaching through idea articles, issue essays, sample lessons and special columns. Recent issues of the *Mathematics Teacher* have carried a calendar for the month with the box for each date filled with a puzzle, fact from the history of mathematics, or a question. Both of these journals contain reviews of courseware, software, texts and programs. Recent issues of both journals include articles on the use of calculators and computers to teach mathematics concepts. Although the *Arithmetic Teacher* is officially designated for K–9 teachers, many of the classroom activities have been used, with little or no modification, by senior high teachers. The *Mathematics Teacher* is directed toward teachers in secondary school and two year colleges and mathematics education faculty in colleges and universities. The third journal will be of most interest to the inservice teacher who wishes to learn about or become involved in research.

Published by the Central Association of Science and Mathematics Teachers (CASMT):

School Science and Mathematics features articles on the teaching of the two separate disciplines. Recent issues have also included a column devoted to lessons that would integrate mathematics and science.

Published by the Association of Teachers of Mathematics of Great Britain:

Mathematics Teaching is one of the best sources of ideas for creative secondary mathematics teachers. Articles tend to reflect the psychological frame of reference that has been part of our integrated approach to mathematics teaching.

*There are also some excellent journals published by state mathematics teachers associations, as well as a number of international journals that are devoted to theoretical or research articles.

**In addition to the articles and columns on technology and information processing to be found in any of the journals listed above, there are also some recent journals devoted to computers and education. Three of these are listed here:

Computing Teacher, *Journal of Computers in Mathematics and Science Teaching*, and *Mathematics and Computer Education*.

Check all other chapters, but especially Chapters 9 and 10 for additional idea references.

CHAPTER TWELVE

DISCIPLINE

Control or Chaos In Your Classroom

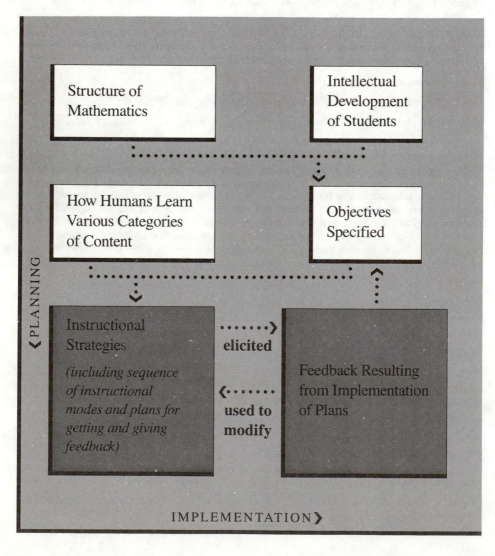

Some prefer to call this topic *pupil management*, while others insist that *instructional leadership* is the proper term. Choose whichever title pleased you most, but what they all boil down to is *control or chaos in your classroom*. Yes, yours. After all, you, the teacher, are supposed to be the adult in charge—the one legally responsible for the safety of students and professionally accountable for providing an environment for learning.

Make *no* mistake. Someone will be the leader in your class, and the choice is up to you as to whether it is you or one or more of the students. Some type of atmosphere for learning will prevail as a result of that leadership. The question here is the suitability of that climate for learning, both in the sense of promoting intellectual understanding and as a positive response to reasonable rules designed to protect the rights of all. These two goals, intellectual understanding and the protection of the rights of all, are the keys to the two boxes shaded in on the opening page of this chapter. The emphasis intended by shading the boxes, "Instructional Strategies" and "Feedback," is that a positive classroom atmosphere depends on careful planning and consistent, thoughtful responses to feedback during the class period. What should and can be done about this problem?

In general, there are two approaches that work in the classroom; in the real world of the classroom *both* are needed. The first, like preventive medicine, must be employed whenever possible; the second, like surgery, is effective only in specific cases and for limited time spans. But before going into the details of either of these approaches, we should first agree on operational definitions of terms used frequently to characterize "good" versus "poor" discipline.

12.1 ATTENTION VERSUS NOISE

An *absolute* prerequisite to comprehending most of the terms used to describe classroom management is firm knowledge of the operational definitions of instructional modes as found in Chapter 1. Why is this the case? It should be fairly obvious that specific expectations for student behavior vary according to the mode being used at the moment. Thus it will be well worth the effort to run a quick self-check on these prerequisites prior to reading any further. Be aware of the fact that the classroom management terms considered in this section are limited to those which seem to be most useful to the novice teacher.

Appropriate noise level   Immediately after a classroom observation we are frequently asked, "Was my class too noisy today?" In our judgment, the *kind* of noise should be the primary concern, but more on that later. The noise level is appropriate for a lecture or a quiz if *the sounds from students approach zero (very, very closely)* and the noise level is appropriate for Q/A if *students speak one at a time with volume enough for all to hear*. Why does this description of appropriate noise level make sense? Note the specific ties to the particular mode being used at given points in the class period, and proceed to construct your own operational definitions of appropriate noise level for each of the other common modes of instruction. An obvious nonexample would be if students in a small discussion group were screaming to each other in order to communicate over the shouting level being used by another group. Suppose that the inappropriate noise level of this group had been, in turn, caused by their need to hear each other over the alternately loud and quiet conversations of yet another group. Some novices fail to recognize this as a problem if all talk is relevant to the task at hand. Then they are surprised that one group is soon forced to escalate its volume further to hear themselves over the other groups.

Appropriate kind of noise   Like the previous set of operational definitions, this one is tied specifically to the particular instructional mode being used at various points in the class period. During lecture there should be *only the sound of the teacher's voice.* However, during Q/A *one-at-a-time talk on the topic by both teacher and students is desired.* During laboratory work appropriate kinds of noises include *the sound of footsteps, student-to-student and teacher-to-student conversation on procedures and content topics, the manipulation of equipment, and clean-up sounds.* Obvious nonexamples include talk about dates and the sounds of breaking glassware, equipment falling on the floor, or chairs being knocked over. Now consider the other instructional modes and construct your own operational definitions for the kind of noise appropriate for each.

Positive student attention signs   What would be some kinds of feedback which a trained observer in your classroom would characterize as positive student attention signs? *Students facing front, being quiet, and occasionally writing in notebooks would be positive attention signs during that portion of a class period when the teacher was lecturing from the front of the room.* Similarly *many hands raised with relevent questions and answers being volunteered are positive signs during a question/answer session.*

Negative student attention signs   Quiet may be very desirable during a lecture, quiz, or while viewing a motion picture, but *silence should be interpreted as a negative attention sign during certain modes such as discussion, question/answer, and small-group laboratory work.* Similarly, *spitball throwing, manufacturing paper airplanes (with accompanying test flights), note passing, students eyeing the clock, reading of books hidden from the teacher's view, eating lunches, or sticking neighbors with pins can rarely be considered anything other than negative attention signs regardless of the instructional mode in use.* Now extend the list to include more of the subtle varieties and ask an experienced teacher to check it out for completeness. Be sure to include such signs as *students' gaze fixed on the spot where the teacher used to be and many requests that the teacher repeat questions.*

We have observed examples of student behavior listed in this section in many classrooms. In our experience, it is fatal for a teacher to overlook or ignore repeated instances of inappropriate level and kind of noise or negative student attention signs. The introductory activity, which follows, is designed to start you thinking seriously about teacher behaviors characteristic of both effectively and ineffectively managed classrooms.

12.2 INTRODUCTORY ACTIVITY

Get it straight from the horse's mouth.

In order to perform this activity, you will need to locate three to five secondary school students. Interview each of them individually to get their perceptions regarding the characteristics of good and bad teaching. Ask each student to record reactions on a form such as the one in Figure 12.1.

After collecting your data, compare it with that collected by your classmates who have interviewed different students. Look for patterns in the data, talk about these patterns with your classmates, and be prepared to discuss the matter further with your instructor.

A successful interview requires preparation as well as follow-through. One does not just walk into a secondary school and stop students in the hallway. You should talk with your instructor, who is knowledgeable about local school and college/university policies, regarding any permissions and protocol. Once the arrangements for interviewing have been made, you must duplicate the form in a neat, easily readable fashion. During the interview, you may need to give operational definitions of terms which may not be clear to younger students. Encourage them to ask questions about any statement which is not clear to them. *Refuse to allow the student to use the name of any particular teacher, either on the form or in conversation with you.* Observe closely to be sure that the directions are being followed and be sure to thank the students and all school personnel who made the interviews possible.

12.3 AN OUNCE OF PREVENTION

If the data that you obtained in the introductory activity matches that which students have given us, then the notion of trying to survive in a poorly managed class probably frightens you as much as it does us. We know of no teacher who is pleased about the possibility of being in a chaotic class. It's clear that the wise teacher does all in his or her power to *prevent* such a situation, and the first line of defense is to be found in the quality of the lesson!

Planning and Implementation of the Lesson

Getting student attention *on the lesson* is a prime consideration in the development of any lesson plan. The number and variety of ways to accomplish this are limited only by the teacher's imagination. An interesting demonstration is one of the most productive ways to accomplish this end. What makes an interest-catching demonstration? Seek one that seems to defy "common sense" or one that focuses attention on an unfamiliar (to the student) aspect of a common phenomenon. If you can locate one that combines both ingredients, so much the better. Other serviceable ideas include laboratory activity (Remember we mean by this, *student manipulation of materials!*) having the same characteristics as described for demonstration, a controversial statement written on the chalkboard

TO THE STUDENT

I am interested in learning to be a good teacher. I believe that student judgments about good and poor teaching can be helpful to me. Thus, I am asking you to record your honest reactions on this form. Do not sign your name. Your reactions will be kept confidential and will be added to those of other students to give me a picture of what many students think about good and poor teaching.

First, think in terms of one or two of the very best teachers *YOU* have had. Use the column on the left under the word BEST and place a check mark in one of the five boxes to indicate whether your best teacher(s) had a particular characteristic never, rarely, sometimes, frequently or always. Do this for each of the ten characteristics listed.

After you have finished rating all ten characteristics in terms of your best teacher(s), start again at the top of the list and place a check in the boxes in the right column which describe the worst teacher(s) *YOU* have had.

MY BEST
TEACHER(S)

MY WORST
TEACHER(S)

Never Rarely Sometimes Often Always		Never Rarely Sometimes Often Always
☐☐☐☐☐	1. Made the subject interesting.	☐☐☐☐☐
☐☐☐☐☐	2. Made the subject easy to learn.	☐☐☐☐☐
☐☐☐☐☐	3. Kept many students participating in class.	☐☐☐☐☐
☐☐☐☐☐	4. Had only a few rules for student behavior in class.	☐☐☐☐☐
☐☐☐☐☐	5. Had many rules for student behavior in class.	☐☐☐☐☐
☐☐☐☐☐	6. Enforced whatever rules he or she had for student behavior in class.	☐☐☐☐☐
☐☐☐☐☐	7. Treated all students fairly.	☐☐☐☐☐
☐☐☐☐☐	8. Threatened students.	☐☐☐☐☐
☐☐☐☐☐	9. Punished only those who misbehaved.	☐☐☐☐☐
☐☐☐☐☐	10. Punished the whole class for the misbehavior of a few students.	☐☐☐☐☐

Fig. 12.1 Student reaction form.

prior to class, or a totally restructured classroom environment that connects to the lesson (chairs and desks arranged in a circle or small clusters). The illustrations found in Chapters 1–11, as well as the references cited in Chapters 9, 10, 11, are rich sources of ideas for such activities.

Keeping student attention on the lesson is a more difficult task. This cannot even be approached unless the teacher *first gets attention*. Let us assume that this has been done. One obvious way to keep attention is to vary the teaching modes. If the class began with a teacher-performed demonstration coupled with question/answer, the teacher might switch to short lecture, then small-group discussion or short lecture with note-taking and/or a combination of student board work and seat work. Relevance to the "here-and-now" interests of students should be worked in as quickly as possible and emphasized throughout the class period. The increasing use of divergent questions as the period progresses will also help maintain attention. "Dead time" in the lesson is an invitation to trouble. When planning the lesson keep asking yourself, "Is there something constructive for every student to be doing every minute of the class period?" If the teacher cannot answer "yes," potential problems surely lie ahead. In addition, many novices beg for trouble by not informing students what they should be doing every minute of the class period. Even more make the error of not informing students *how* they are to perform the instructional tasks. Now might be a good time to refer back to "The Events of Instruction" in Chapters 2 and 7. Here our emphasis is prevention of management problems; in those chapters the emphasis was on ways to plan and implement a meaningful lesson. Notice how one depends on the other.

Students will work just so long without feedback on their efforts. They need to know how they are doing. Nothing is quite so satisfying as success coupled with knowledge of success. What can be more frustrating than failure or thinking you are doing a task correctly only to find out too late that you have been practicing errors? Refer back to Chapter 2 on feedback, which contains many specific suggestions on this point.

"It is a smart person who knows when to give up." Many students get lost when the teacher has failed either to control the pace or to ensure that each step in the lesson is based upon prerequisite learnings actually achieved by the students. This kind of teacher behavior breeds frustration, then a "what's the use" attitude, followed by student activities of their own design—often at odds with what the teacher had in mind. The work of many researchers in the reasoning of adolescents and the conditions affecting learning provides important guidelines for how to avoid these problems and is well worth referring to once again (see Chapters 3 and 6).

Effective and Efficient Handling of Routines

Attendance must be taken every class period. The class attendance records of a teacher are legal documents subject to examination in a court of law. The teacher must take care of this detail daily without allowing the procedure to constitute "dead time." It is important that the class session get off to a fast and interesting beginning. A seating chart is a must until the teacher knows at a glance who is absent and can record the same without taking any class time for this important routine. Useful techniques include checking attendance at the start of the period while (1) some students put answers to homework on the board and others check answers at their seats, (2) all take a quiz, or (3) the teacher conducts a five-minute question/answer review of yesterday's lesson. Sometimes a student volunteer can perform the mechanics of attendance taking, but the teacher must check the accuracy of the record at some convenient point during the period.

Collecting and passing out papers must also be reduced to a routine. Students respond readily to habit in this regard if the teacher establishes a set procedure at the beginning of the year and consistently uses it. For example, the teacher might hand all papers for a given row to the student sitting on the right end of that row. That student passes the papers to the left. Likewise, papers might always be collected by having students pass them to the left end of the row and then to the front left seat. Some teachers have a box near the door for routine collection of homework papers as students enter class. The main idea is to establish a procedure and make it automatic so that it does not interrupt the flow of the lesson.

The distribution and collection of working materials should be similarly handled. A key consideration here is preventing jam-ups (and consequent pushing, arguing, and so on) by planning efficient distribution patterns. Dividing materials into four sets available at the four corners of a classroom makes much sense. On the other hand, asking an entire class to clean up materials at one desk during the final three minutes of class is an invitation to chaos.

Administration of a quiz or test should begin by getting complete attention from all students and following the routines for passing out papers. Then the teacher belongs in the rear of the room, on his or her feet with eyes and ears alert. Do you see why? If a student were to cheat, what is the first thing that student would have to do? That student would have to look around to find out where the teacher is—thus attracting the teacher's attention. Students with questions should be instructed to raise their hands and the teacher should follow procedures designed to avoid disturbing nearby students when attending to individual requests for clarification. As in supervised practice, the teacher must listen to a question while glancing around frequently at other students, whisper in response to a question, and insist that students speak at the same quiet level. Unlike supervised practice, during a test, the teacher must refuse to respond to students who seek assistance with the content. Beginning teachers are often trapped into giving the cues they would have provided in a supervised practice situation. Students soon learn that those who ask, receive! The complaints of unfair treatment are well deserved and the teacher is on the road to a self-imposed discipline problem. See the section on Administration of the test in Chapter 8 for further details on preventing undesirable behavior on the part of the test-takers.

Teaching students to respond to nonverbal signals is relatively easy and quite effective. Try switching the lights on and off in a class or laboratory where students are talking and/or working away at some activity. It works the first time and will work on successive occasions *if it is taught* as a signal that (1) it is time to stop work and clean up, (2) the noise has inadvertently gotten a bit too loud for the present activity, and (3) it is not used for every little disturbance. Effective instructors teach students to respond to a whole range of other nonverbal signals such as a snap of the fingers, the closing of the classroom door, or a finger touched to the lips of the teacher. Observe a real "pro" to pick up a whole repertoire of other signals to which students can be taught to respond.

Praise/Reward for Correct Behavior

Few teachers give enough attention to praising and rewarding students for behavior they wish to foster. Most attend only to inappropriate behavior and ignore that which they would like to promote. To be effective, the praise must be sincere, justly deserved, and not embarrassing to student recipients. Effective teachers use techniques such as (1) telling the entire group what a good job they did with today's lesson, (2) congratulating all for the fine results on yesterday's unit test, (3) calling attention to the thought-provoking quality of the question just raised by one student, and (4) asking a student's permission to read a particularly outstanding homework answer to the rest of the class. Also, nonverbal praise in the form of teacher smiles, hand signals, and gestures is very effective.

Other rewards often further increase the effects of praise. For example, the teacher can point out that because work progressed so effectively during the first 30 minutes today, the class can devote the final 15 minutes to an interesting educational game. Similarly, at the end of a particularly effective supervised study or practice session, the teacher can announce cancellation of the previously announced written homework problems as there now appears to be no need for further practice. It is quite important to insure that students understand that the reward is a consequence of their good work, not a capricious act on the teacher's part.

One of the biggest mistakes we all tend to make in using praise/reward is the tendency to withhold these until student performance reaches some peak of perfection. We must learn to give encouragement for small steps in the right direction without overdoing it (and thus finding nothing left to connect with the final level of performance desired). Another all-too-common error of novices is to mistake a punishment for a reward. The typical student does not view doing problems 11–20 as much of a reward for having correctly solved problems 1–10 faster than the rest of the class! Sometimes the teacher can offer an incentive to the class when attention to the task begins to lag. One way to do this is by application of "Grandma's Rule."

What rule is that? Grandma might have said, "Yes, you certainly may have a portion of ice cream, as soon as you finish your meat and vegetables." Thus, Grandma's Rule occurs when you make the satisfaction of someone else's wants dependent upon first achieving what you desire. When the teacher tells the class that those who complete the set of practice problems in class will have no home-work tonight while everyone else will have to complete the exercises and hand them in tomorrow, that teacher is using Grandma's Rule. Another example of a teacher using Grandma's Rule was the response of Mr. Norris to his seventh-graders. As the students entered his classroom, they began coaxing him to let them continue playing the educational game in progress at the end of yesterday's lesson. Mr. Norris's response was that if all students worked effectively on the new lesson, they should have 10 to 15 minutes left for the game. Every teacher needs to master this approach because it works and because students react posi-tively to its use when properly employed.

Conveying the Teacher's Enthusiasm for the Subject

It is a truism that one can't convey what one does not have. Some prospective teachers have learned mathematics as a stagnant body of "facts" and complicated rules or principles. They can recite these flawlessly to the class (provided they re-memorized the details the night before) and can work stereotype problems faster than all but their brightest students. But that is it; there isn't any more! Those who recognize the above as a self-description are in deep trouble in trying to deal with students. "Death-warmed-over" won't work. What are these prospec-tive teachers to do?

Self-education here and now is the *only* way out. Understanding the struc-ture of ideas and processes for generating knowledge in mathematics can be gleaned from the sources cited and activities suggested in Chapter 4. A rich store of interesting applications to the real-world and the "here-and- now" interests of students is to be found in Chapters 10 and 11. Once the teacher becomes enthu-siastic about the subject matter, then it is probable that he or she will find ways to demonstrate it to students. The obvious techniques include incorporating a wide variety of atypical examples, television commercials, labels from food and drug packages, newspaper articles, cartoons, and other objects brought in from the outside world. Appropriate nonverbal signals such as the gleam in the eye, spring in the step, or excited tone in the voice of the teacher are hard to describe and prescribe; but these are very important. Observe an enthusiastic teacher at work and try to incorporate some of these aspects that are compatible with your own personality and classroom style.

The Quiet, Insistent, Consistent, Business-like Approach

Screaming simply does not work! In fact, some students make a game out of seeing how quickly and often they can elicit this kind of response from their teachers. They will respect the calm, cool approach if the lesson is well planned and interesting. Students expect the teacher to act like an adult, not a tantrum-throwing child or an insecure teenager. This quiet approach, used consistently, has the same certain results as erosion that reduces boulders to sand grains over time.

Business-like does not mean the teacher never smiles or laughs with the students when something genuinely humorous happens. On the other hand, when we have all enjoyed our laugh, it's time to get back to work. Incidentally, it is unpardonable to laugh if it is at the expense of a student or group of students. No student respects a teacher who does this, but all admire a teacher who is big enough to laugh at himself or herself on occasion.

Neither this nor any other approach will work, however, if you, the teacher, present poorly prepared lessons that students perceive as dull or disjointed. A firm prerequisite to effective long-term classroom management is the planning and implementation of lessons that are both interesting and understandable. You will find that one of the most potent forces at work in the classroom is *peer pressure*. If the majority of the students are convinced that something worthwhile and interesting happens in your class, they will use very effective sanctions against the one or two whose actions tend to get out of line.

Remember that *consistency is imperative*. Words and deeds must match, and the teacher cannot allow rules to be violated for the first half of the lesson and then come on with thunder and lightning about the same breaches in conduct during the final minutes of the period. Appearances to the contrary, teenagers are really very conservative in many respects. They are creatures of habit and like to know which rules are to be enforced.

Establishing a Few, Simple, Reasonable Rules

If there are too many rules, the class atmosphere is repressive and students can't remember half of them in any case. If the rules are too complicated, most students will find avoidance behavior a more appealing alternative than trying to follow the rules. If the rules seem arbitrary and codifications of the teacher's whims, it will take more time and effort to enforce them than any teacher of an academic subject can afford to devote to nonacademic matters.

Some advocate spelling out all rules the first day, but our experience suggests a different approach in order to emphasize the "no rule without a good reason" guideline. For example, on the first day of class students usually will enter and automatically take a seat. Suppose at the instant the bell rings, a cartoon relevant to mathematics is projected on the overhead and students are asked to raise their hands if they cannot see. They are then told they can keep their chosen seats as long as they can see, hear, and behave where they are today. They are requested, however, to keep the same seat for at least the first few weeks so the teacher can learn all of their names quickly. Suppose, too, that a question/answer session is woven in with the opening attention-getter. Then the first time several students call out in a mixed chorus, one nonparticipating student is asked if he or she agrees with the answer given and why. After he or she admits confusion, the request for hand raising is made. Then students will understand that the rule is for the benefit of all. As the question/answer continues, another mixed chorus response is likely to occur and this time the teacher should call on someone who raised a hand and did not shout out. Consistent teacher behavior leads quickly to desired student behavior without recourse to threats, screams, or punishment. Other simple rules, such as that no one talks while another (student or teacher) has the floor, are similarly taught as the occasion arises. Nonverbal signals, such as those described earlier, are very helpful both in establishing and maintaining the reasonable, rule-governed behavior which sets humans apart from lower animals.

12.4 THE BIG CULPRITS

The suggestions in the previous section are designed to help you eliminate the major sources of discipline problems faced by the novice. We call these sources the "big culprits" because we have seen them trap and destroy student teachers. In many situations the student teacher is deceived as to the destructive nature of these teacher behaviors because they see no apparent disastrous effects in the classrooms of experienced teachers. What novices fail to observe are the many counterbalancing moves by experienced teachers. If you would avoid the usually impossible task of regaining control once it has been lost, you must learn to recognize and avoid the big culprits.

Accepting responses of students who do not raise their hands The teacher tells the students to raise their hands and wait to be called upon prior to answering or asking questions. Shortly thereafter, someone calls out a correct answer and the teacher says "Right." What effect does this action have on the students who did raise their hands and did wait for the teacher's signal to answer? What would you do if you held your hand up while others who ignored the teacher's directions were rewarded by being recognized? The slowest student quickly realizes that the teacher's actions and words do not match. This realization leads to an increasing number of students who shout out in response to the teacher's questions. Finally, the teacher gets upset, "reams-out" the class, and proceeds further down the road to disaster by going right back to inconsistency of words and deeds. This reaction often is paired with the second big culprit.

Inviting the chorus response Sometimes there are several students calling out the *same answer* at the same time (if the teacher is lucky or everyone knows the material anyway). There are two big problems with this unison chorus.

First, it is inevitable that only the vocal segment of the class will continue to respond while the majority sits quietly. But will the quiet ones think along with the teacher and the minority, or will they find some other quiet activity to engage in while the show goes on?

Second, how long can this situation continue before it becomes a mixed chorus of shouts? Soon two or three different responses occur at once. How does the teacher pick the one to respond to with "Right," "O.K.," or "Good"? Typically the teacher only hears what is expected and ignores the other responses. Imagine the plight of the quiet and attentive student who wonders which of three answers is being identified as "Good." Now put yourself in the role of the teacher who wants to get feedback on group thinking and reinforce correct responses. Certainly, inadvertent promotion of the second big culprit is not the way to do it. Furthermore, the resultant student confusion fostered by this type of teacher behavior frequently leads to the third big culprit.

Teacher talks over student-to-student talk Inviting the chorus response not only results in student boredom but is the leading correlate of student- to-student $(S \leftrightarrow S)$ talk. Students ask neighbors, "What did he say?" "How can that be if this is... ?" "I thought she told us yesterday... ," and so on. Typically, the teacher caught in his or her own web either remains unaware of the $S \leftrightarrow S$ talk or ignores it so as not to squelch the responsiveness of the class (perhaps only 4 to 10 students out of 25). When the murmur becomes a roar, the novice teacher senses that all is not well with the class and comes down hard with recriminations, threats, or slogans that are the direct opposite of what has been reinforced by previous events. Good luck to this teacher! Experienced supervisors call this practice "pushing the self-destruct button." Some novice teachers insist on continually pressing this button, and their supervisor's unhappy dilemma becomes the identification of the kindest and gentlest way to counsel them out of teaching.

Threats the teacher cannot or will not carry out   "If you do not...immediately, I will... ." Is the teacher sure he or she can carry out the threat? Too often the novice teacher hasn't the foggiest idea how he or she can make good while the students are reasonably sure that the teacher can't or won't make the ultimate decision. Usually the students know more than the novice teacher about a particular school's policies. After all, they have been playing the game of school for eight to eleven years in this very system while the teacher has been here only a few weeks and *doesn't even know that the principal never sees troublemakers who are sent to the office*. Those foresighted novice teachers who look up the school policy may find out that the vice-principal sees discipline cases. The student is thoroughly chastised by the vice-principal and returns to class a reformed student, right? Wrong! In more cases than we'd care to count, the student cools his or her heels in an outer office and continues the disruptive behavior for the benefit of the school secretary and visitors and peers who stroll by. When, at last, he or she confronts the vice-principal, there may be a brief heart-to-heart talk with a finale in which the student glibly promises to do better. Now who has punished whom? The student returns from the wars as a veteran with a story to tell, and you may be sure that it will be told.

There may be a time when one student must be removed from the class for the benefit of others, but the teacher must determine where that student can be sent, follow up the removal, and treat this kind of action as a final step with serious consequences.

Musical chairs   This variation of the popular child's party game is often played by teachers who are really a bit old for this game. The game begins when the teacher moves a troublesome student to another seat away from his or her friends. If the character in question is the class clown, the typical move to a front seat provides a wider audience for future antics. Who has fooled whom? Then, too, what has the teacher unwittingly done to the cooperative student who previously enjoyed the front seat? One could hardly say that this student was rewarded for good behavior by being forced to change seats. What is the teacher's next move when Charley's (the clown's) behavior deteriorates again? Too often another student is forced out of his or her seat in order to relocate Charley a second time. Frequently other students now join in the sport, the game gets more complicated, and the class slips further away from the control of the teacher.

This is *not* to say that judicious moving of one or two students is valueless. A move can be quite effective if the teacher (1) separates students who can't seem to get along together, (2) avoids creating even worse combinations (usually requires teacher homework ahead of time such as a trip to the guidance office and/or consultation with other teachers of these same students), and (3) makes clear to all concerned that their next seat change will have to be to somewhere other than in this classroom. Obviously the teacher must check the school policy thoroughly and be prepared to follow through.

Rewarding inappropriate behavior   The sixth big culprit creeps in when the teacher inadvertently reinforces the very behavior he or she is trying to extinguish. For example, one teacher told the class that those who worked effectively and efficiently on the worksheet during the period would have time to work at the micro. Sam wasted time and distracted others. The teacher reprimanded him several times during the first 30 minutes of class time. Finally the teacher took away Sam's half-finished worksheet and told him to begin work on the micro. What did this teacher's action tell those students who had worked diligently at the assigned task? What did it tell Sam?

Suppose the teacher has some students who do not wish to be in class. They are there only because (1) they had too many study halls and thus the guidance officer put them in algebra class or (2) parents insisted that they take geometry. Is it reward or punishment for these students to be expelled from a class they have tried to escape taking in the first place? There is no denying that it may occasionally be in the best interest of all concerned to remove such a student from class. However, let's neither mislead ourselves that this is a punishment nor try to sell the students on this as a punitive measure. They simply won't buy it!

Inconsistent teacher behavior   Yesterday the teacher angrily reprimanded the class when several students poked neighbors and disturbed other students during a paper folding lab. Today, the teacher ignored this same behavior without so much as a verbal reminder. What will be the teacher's reaction to similar student behavior tomorrow? Is it any great wonder that inconsistent student behavior develops and that students come to view rules of order as capricious whims of their teacher?

Teacher's words and deeds do not match   This culprit is very closely related to inconsistent teacher behavior, but it is common and important enough to deserve special emphasis. It also overlaps many other categories of culprits identified here. For example, minutes after stating that students must raise their hands and wait to be recognized, the teacher falls into the pattern of accepting shouted-out answers. Another common error occurs when the teacher announces that there will be absolute quiet during the test and then finds it necessary to make numerous oral announcements, corrections, and clarifications throughout the period. A third common invitation to breakdown in morale is the practice of admonishing students to do neat and accurate work and then passing out teacher-made handouts that are almost impossible to read.

Using subject matter as punishment or threat of punishment   "If this class doesn't quiet down immediately, we will have three extra homework problems for tonight." Such a statement has the same effect on student attitude toward the subject as "Because there's so much noise, we'll have a quiz right now." It is a well-known truism that students who are interested in the subject matter or "turned on" by the way the teacher presents ideas attend to the lesson and *not* to disruptive activities. Now the harassed teacher has destroyed the goal toward which he or she is working. What must students think of quizzes that are planned on the basis of noise rather than on teacher assessment of feedback on lessons? The predictable reaction of the students is undisguised grumbling, comments on the lack of fairness of the teacher, and an increased dislike for mathematics that must be practiced for punishment, rather than need.

Pleading for personal favors   One of the most difficult roles for the novice teacher is that of acting like a thoughtful, responsible leader in the classroom. During initial lessons, the beginning teacher's unwillingness to accept this responsibility is exhibited by verbal patterns such as "Would you please be quiet?" or "Keep it down, please," usually offered in a pleading, hesitant tone. The students quickly sense the teacher's failure to lead and begin taking over the reins of the classroom. Such a teacher tends to describe the situation by statements such as *"They* were very good today" or *"They* were noisy so I couldn't accomplish anything!" The students have been given the decision-making role here and have not been helped to greater self-control. Student caprice determines the days of apparent cooperation.

    If this initial behavior of the teacher isn't altered fast, the observer soon is treated to the spectacle of abject pleading: "Please be quiet!" "Help me out, please!" The teacher who reaches this stage must change or withdraw from teaching, for he or she is doing irreparable harm to the students in the process of losing his or her own human dignity.

Punishing all students for the misdeeds of a few   "If the person who threw the spitball doesn't confess, everyone will stay after school for one hour." What does this treatment tell students who have been behaving as desired? They might as well get into the act, since it is likely they will be punished anyway! This also tells students that the teacher is not capable of controlling the situation. This teacher has convicted all students as accessories to the misbehavior. Students cry "Foul play" deservedly. The teacher has gained many enemies and has helped to solidify the class in opposition to him or her. The odds of 25 students to 1 teacher are very difficult ones for any teacher to overcome.

The inappropriate teacher behaviors illustrated in these sections are those which seem to occur repeatedly and with immediate negative consequences in the classrooms of those who are unable or unwilling to accept their responsibility for ensuring a positive atmosphere. But suppose a teacher has been attending to all the suggestions and has been alert to early signs of erosion—does that teacher ever find it necessary to react to disorder? If so, what are some alternatives? Some of the ills for which you may need a cure and some classroom-tested cures are described in the following section.

12.5 A POUND OF CURE

The day of the hickory stick in public-school classrooms is long gone. It is true that some teachers lament its demise and a few attribute many of our present educational problems to its passing. Nonetheless, the fact of the matter is that there are very few schools today (public or private) where teachers are allowed to punish students with either fists or physical objects—the substitutes for the bygone hickory stick. Contemporary teachers must find more appropriate ways to get and maintain control over events in their classrooms.

The experiences of effective teachers, department chairpersons and student teachers indicate that the approach to take is the *elimination of the need* for punishment. Careful and consistent attention to the recommendations made previously in Sections 12.3 and 12.4 have proved to be 90 to 95 percent effective. But aren't there situations where punishment is called for in spite of the best efforts of the teacher? Yes, unfortunately. Remember above all else that any alternative will work if and only if the teacher has been trying, and continues to try, to implement the positive approach. We can hold out little or no hope that anything will work out for the teacher who has consistently and over a period of time ignored the "ounce of prevention" approach.

What is and is not considered punishment? *Punishment is the presentation of aversive stimuli.* Aversive to whom? The offender, of course. Anyone who hopes to use punishment effectively must remain alert to the fact that what is aversive to one student may actually be perceived as positively reinforcing to another. A loud and stern lecture on proper behavior delivered to the boy who craves attention is hardly punishment for him—particularly if it is done in the presence of his peers. Similarly, the lonely and lovesick girl sentenced to spend an hour after school with a handsome young male teacher doesn't perceive her predicament as the worst of all possible fates. Effective use of punishment, like so many other aspects of instruction, is dependent on the teacher's knowledge of individual differences among students.

Be forewarned. Punishment, negative reinforcement, seems to have less predictable effects on behavior than a positive, preventive approach, (Skinner, 1953) and it often results in fostering poor attitudes toward school, mathematics, and the teacher. "O.K., but what am I to do when I *must* punish?" Let's consider some general guidelines and their application within the framework of realities set by typical school situations.

The first order of business is to *find out both the school and the department policy on discipline*. It is a rare school that doesn't have such policy statements written down somewhere. Often the department has more specific guidelines designed to fit within the general school policy. Seek these out and learn them before the first day you teach a class. Armed with this knowledge you should then be able to question experienced teachers regarding those all-important "unwritten" policies that everyone, including the students, knows—that is, everyone except you. It is too late to find out these things after you have embarked on a course of disciplinary action and find yourself in the embarrassing position of having to back down.

Warn only once. Then act. This is easy to carry out provided you catch "little things" that, if ignored, will rapidly grow into major problems. For example, if you notice Paul is writing definitions for his English vocabulary list during supervised practice in mathematics class, tell him in a whisper to put away that assignment and work on the assigned problems. The next time you see him exhibit this type of misbehavior, either during the same or any subsequent class session, don't say anything to him. Simply pick up his paper, put it in your desk drawer, and refuse to discuss the matter during class. When he appears at the end of the period to plead for his paper, tell him you will deliver his paper to the English teacher with an explanation of how it got into your hands. If Paul repeats this type of behavior a third time, immediately tear up the paper, drop it in the wastebasket, and refuse to discuss the matter.

Immediacy is vital if the consequence (punishment) is to be connected in the student's mind to the cause (the act of misbehavior). Note in the illustration in the preceding paragraph that the punishment was initiated within seconds of the time the offense came to the teacher's attention. Suppose you had opted for telling Paul a second time not to do other homework in this class and you had sentenced him to stay after school to make up one period of class time. The time span between the undesired act and its consequence now becomes hours instead of seconds. Further, you are now punishing yourself by giving up after-school time needed to help slower students and to prepare materials for tomorrow's lesson. Also consider that staying after school may not be much punishment for Paul if he normally just hangs around after school with little to occupy his time. Then, too, in many school situations it is impossible to keep certain students the same day. For example, bus students must have a day's advance notice, band students cannot be kept from after-school rehearsals on Tuesdays and Thursdays, and varsity athletes are immune on game dates. By the time you get some students in after school, both you and they will barely remember the purpose! Experienced teachers learn to use staying-after-school punishment with discretion.

"Praise in public and punish in private" is an old slogan that retains quite a bit of applicability to the contemporary school scene. For example, once you have told Sue and Kathy (persistent whisperers) to see you immediately after class, go right on with the lesson. Steadfastly refuse to respond to their pleas of "We weren't doing anything." Such a conversation in the presence of other students will only serve to waste class time, divert other students' attention from the lesson, and provide an audience for whom Sue and Kathy feel compelled to provide an "act." Further, this matter is no one's business except yours and the offending students. Experienced teachers also know that Tommy Tough Guy frequently becomes reasonable when dealt with in private and Mary Martyr climbs down from her cross when no audience of peers is around to appreciate her performance.

The punishment must fit the crime—both in kind and in severity—if it is to achieve maximum effect. An effective consequence of littering the floor with bits of paper is to arrange for the offender to spend some of his or her own spare time picking up similar debris by hand in several classrooms. Similarly, more than one desk carver has been cured by the experience of hand-sanding and refinishing the object back to its original condition (by all means, check school policy first on this one). Consider also the case of Spitting Sam, who was caught doing his act from the front row of the balcony during an assembly program. Immediately after school he was handed a beaker, informed of the biology classes' need for 100 cc of saliva for tomorrow's laboratory experiment, and told he could leave when that need had been fulfilled. Interim drinks of water could not be allowed since the need was for saliva, not water. One nonexample of the point being made here is the practice of having students write "I must not talk out of turn during class" some horrendous number of times. Typically this serves more to develop an aversion to writing than anything else!

It is the act that must be punished, not the person. All of us must make certain we communicate this message to students when we administer punishment. Words alone help some, and making the kind of punishment match the kind of behavior at issue often helps even more. But it is the teacher's behavior toward the offending student *after* the punishment that can clinch the point. Every effort and means must be used to project attitudes such as "Your mistake is over and done with, and I bear you no grudge" and "I expect you have changed and no recurrence of the problem is anticipated." A student who is left with the impression that he or she is a marked person whom the teacher will seek opportunities to pick on is very likely to become a repeat offender due to a "what's the use" attitude.

Consider three different approaches to handling collusion during a test. One approach is to tear up the offenders' papers and record zeros in the grade book. A second is to allow the offenders to complete the test believing they are undetected, score their papers, take the higher score, and award half to each paper in question—justifying this in private conversation with these students as the fairest way you could devise since you don't know who contributed which proportion of the correct information. A third approach is to do or say nothing about it this time and prepare two identical-looking but varying forms of the next test. The easiest way to do this is to vary the order of choices for each multiple-choice question. Identify the two test versions only by a period after the test title on one form, stack the papers so alternate forms are distributed to students sitting next to each other, proctor as usual; then collect, sort, score, and return the papers. Which of the three approaches best matches what has been pointed out about punishment thus far? In which do guilty students catch and punish themselves? If you chose the third approach, you agree with us. You should also have noticed that the third approach avoids the trap of requiring that the teacher "prove" the students cheated if irate parents phone the principal.

Consistency from day to day and from student to student is vital. You must learn to resist the tendency to overlook an infraction when perpetrated by Bright Bill and yet to come down hard on Slow Sally for the same breach of conduct. Student morale suffers badly if they even suspect their teacher is playing favorites. Likewise, tolerating loud and boisterous behavior during laboratory work one day and punishing it the next confuses students about the teacher's expectations. Developing a consistent approach takes a conscious effort on the part of most teachers, but the results are well worth the effort.

Suppose you have tried various means to deal with Terrible Tim, but nothing seems to work in his case. You have reached the end of your rope. He simply cannot be allowed to continue disrupting the lessons. Should you call for help, or would this be admitting to students, parents, and school administrators that you are incapable of handling the class? If you have done everything expected of a competent teacher, you should appeal to your cooperating teacher first and next, through the cooperating teacher, to the department chairperson. A regular teacher who has this problem has some additional options to explore if the problem persists. He or she could go for outside assistance at this point. A recommended sequence of actions would be to phone the parents, describe the evolution of the problem, tell them what he or she has tried to do to date, impress upon them the teacher's responsibility to others in the class, and ask for their assistance in correcting the situation. If this doesn't lead to resolution of the problem, the teacher could ask the guidance counselor to schedule a conference including the parent, the teacher, and the counselor. Should these measures fail, the next step is to remove the student from class and turn the matter over to the department chairperson for resolution with the vice-principal or principal. Many school systems now have access to the services of a school psychologist, who may be called into the situation at various points in the process. A student teacher may proceed through all of these steps but only in concert with the cooperating teacher. The cooperating teacher is ultimately responsible for the learning of the students and needs to be perceived by the parents as a continuing force in the education of their children. In any case, the phone call or conference is bound to be more effective if it is a cooperative effort of two colleagues, the cooperating teacher and the student teacher. Above all else, doublecheck the school policy *before* you initiate the first steps that could ultimately lead to the removal of a student from class, as this is a very serious matter.

In any case involving punishment it is critical to be sure you have first identified the right student(s) as targets for corrective action. This seems obvious, doesn't it? For example, Ms. Smith turned from writing on the board just in time to see Marge slap Walt, who sat behind her. Marge was kept after class and lectured to on everything from the evils of distracting others to standards of ladylike behavior. Ms. Smith raved on at such a pace that Marge could not get a word in edgewise. By the time Marge was given a chance to speak, she was so angry that she refused to say anything. Her anger flared even more when, after being dismissed by Ms. Smith, she heard Wiley Walt bragging to his friends about how he had gotten away with jabbing her with a compass. What a difference it would have made if Ms. Smith had asked Marge the reason for her behavior prior to starting the aversive lecture!

Some techniques for catching those guilty of copying neighbors' test answers have already been described. But how can the teacher catch litterbugs and desk carvers when five different classes use the same room during a day? Let's assume Mr. Johnson finds carving on a certain desk as he is trying out a demonstration activity after school. Which of the five students who sit at that desk is the guilty one? Mr. Johnson need only take a quick tour of the area during the last minute of *each* class period for a day or so to find out. When additional embellishments are added, his question is answered. Think through other possible instances when it may not be obvious which student or students are the actual offenders and consider alternative ways of identifying the individuals at fault. This kind of thinking ahead should be excellent preparation for the moment when actual decisions will have to be made.

12.6 SO YOU'RE A TEACHER

Are you sure you want to be a mathematics teacher? What kind of person will you become? Must you stop smiling, never make mistakes, always behave in the "proper" way? In the early twentieth century citizens required their teachers to adhere to certain rules and regulations. One list given to New York City teachers admonished them against courting on weekdays, frequenting barbershops, and using curses or other foul language. Today it's a rare community that has written rules of behavior for teachers, although some still cling to unwritten rules. You should check out such unwritten rules with experienced teachers before you accept a job in the community.

But, more important than any rules are the human characteristics that encourage that positive atmosphere in which students are able to learn. We've said often that you must be able and willing to be effective and consistent. Are you willing, or are you plagued by doubts about the teacher image? Let no one tell you that students and parents will ignore the teacher who gets noisily drunk in the local inn as they ignore the similar behavior of their favorite auto mechanic. The mechanic will often service the family car with no loss of effectiveness, but the teacher may be forced to deal with in-class misbehavior as a consequence of the teacher's actions outside of school. How strange! Authors of some articles in popular magazines seem to imply that teachers don't have to worry about serving as adult models, that today's students don't want their teachers to play this role. Ask a student teacher who has just given an anonymous attitudinal survey to the class about the nature of student responses to class management. The great majority of students regularly reiterate their desire to have a class environment suitable for learning and their belief that the teacher is the one to ensure that this is the case. Statements such as the following are often made: "You should have told the kids who talk to shut up," "You let the kids get away with too much noise," "It's not fair to the ones who are trying to work when other kids clown around. You should stop them," or "I study for tests, but you let other kids cheat." These statements speak loud and clear. *You* are supposed to be the leader. It's your job to see that all are given an equal chance. The students look to you to exercise that leadership.

A little thought will also convince you that teenagers want adult models desperately and are today sometimes deprived of them by well-meaning, confused parents and teachers—the two classes of adults who have the most contact with teenagers. Both parents and teachers sometimes try to be friends, just like Lynn or Carolyn. But most teenagers have plenty of friends their own age with whom they can share secrets, exploits, and misdeeds. They occasionally want the very advice they seem to ignore—for example, the firm decision about curfew and the consequences that follow when that curfew is ignored. Tony, a sophisticated eleventh-grader who never did any homework and had a record of numerous "cuts" and failing grades, was inspired to do one unusual homework assignment by a thoughtful student teacher. The next day he told that student teacher how both his parents expressed pleasure that he had brought a schoolbook home and was doing homework. "But," said Tony, "they never told me before that they cared whether I did homework. If they'd told me how upset they were, I would have done it earlier." There's a moral in the above true story for all who work with teenagers. Attempting to reduce the barriers between student and teacher by becoming "just one of the gals or guys" may actually create a barrier so high that no student will seek out your advice, accept your leadership, or try to attain the goals you set.

Will you accord your students the same measure of respect that you want demonstrated toward you? Will you listen thoughtfully when students are responding to a question even when they are stumbling with both ideas and words? Will you encourage students to try without fear of a verbal put-down if they make an honest error? Some teachers mistakenly believe that they are preserving the integrity of mathematics by insisting on precision and exact answers even during the early stages of the development of a topic. In fact they discourage insight, do harm to the understanding of the content, and present an uncompromising personality.

Students have bad days, too! When Bonnie, usually a cooperative, pleasant student, suddenly erupts and spits out a defensive remark, the thinking teacher won't lash out in return, but may quietly, and for Bonnie's eyes only, signal a "calm down." That teacher will probably remember to unobtrusively seek Bonnie out at the end of class—not as a punishment, but to find out if help is needed. But beware! We all have an aversion to the classic "do-gooder." A teacher's help *cannot* be forced on a student.

If students have a right to make an honest error, to try different approaches to a problem, and to expect that there should be a reason why they are required to learn something, then teachers also have a right to make an honest mistake, to admit they don't have all the answers, or to say that question never occurred to them. None of the above teacher behaviors will diminish the respect of the students for him or her if such behaviors are appropriately followed up. Ms. Steyer says she has no idea why the symbol for integration is $\int$, but admits that that's a reasonable question and says that she will find out and answer it tomorrow. Mr. Mapes was asked the same question, but he countered with, "That's a question you should all be able to answer! Since you asked, Barry, your assignment is to look up the answer and report to all of us tomorrow." Which response adds to the teacher's stature? You may be sure that Barry has learned not to ask curious, relevant questions of this teacher. Notice that the word *relevant* was used in the previous sentence. Students come in all flavors, and you'll be missing the spice of life if you are never faced with one or more good-humored clowns, with their irrelevant and funny questions. It is up to you to discriminate between the good-humored clown and the so-called troublemakers. Neither one must be allowed to steal the time of other students, but your response to each differs significantly. Reread Section 12.5 and try to identify differences. In no case should you try the game of one-upmanship! Once a teacher begins to respond to a funny remark with a funny remark, the class is off in a contest of wits which has nothing to do with the lesson. Nine times out of ten the teacher is no match for the student, and even the one time the teacher wins, he or she has lost. The students have learned that the teacher is fair game and the traps will be set with repeated frequency.

Are you sure you want to be a teacher? Yes, you *can* smile and you *will* make mistakes, but you must realize that you will be seen as a model. If you are able to roll with the punches, to keep your enthusiasm for teaching mathematics despite long, hard hours of work, and to find satisfaction in the long-term accomplishments of your students, then you are the kind of person who can help your students become all they are capable of becoming.

12.7 SUMMARY AND SELF-CHECK

Whether we use the words *control*, *discipline*, or *management*, we are labeling a set of competencies that are a necessary but not a sufficient prerequisite to instruction. In other words, if a teacher is unable to promote and maintain an environment for learning, no other instructional competencies the teacher may possess will be realized. However, the reverse is not true! The ability to stave off chaos does not automatically include the ability to instruct in an interesting and meaningful manner. The development of worthwhile lessons will require further work on all the components of the instructional model.

You would be well advised to remind yourself of the "big culprits" as you gain experience in teaching. Experienced teachers have told us that this chapter is a gold mine of practical ideas that they have found helpful. All of us at times fall into a comfortable rut of bad habits—habits that may prove to be disastrous in a new class.

At this point you should be able to:

1. Give illustrations of negative and positive student attention signs—indicators of time-on task.

2. Identify instances of negative and positive student attention signs and of either a "live" or recorded lesson and state reasons for your judgments.

3. Identify instances of the "big culprits" during either a "live" or recorded lesson and describe the teacher reactions to the "big culprits" and consequences that occurred as a result of those teacher behaviors.

4. List four to five preventive measures that should be part of each teacher's behavior pattern.

5. Explain how you could apply Grandma's Rule, given a specific description of a class situation.

6. Describe remedial steps you would take to solve a specific misbehavior problem and be able to justify your decisions.

In the following exercises you are given an opportunity to test your ability to meet some of the above objectives. Be sure to check your responses with those of your classmates and your instructor. Perhaps more than any other area treated in this text, management requires more than an intellectual response. You must learn to know yourself, the attitudes you project in the classroom, and the effects of your behavior on students. You must respect both yourself and your students. It is a lifelong study for those who want to be students of teaching.

12.8 SIMULATION/PRACTICE ACTIVITIES

A. The first day Mr. Atkinson met his class, two students arrived a half-minute late. On the second day three students were a minute late and Mr. Atkinson waited to begin class until they were in their seats. By the end of the week he was delaying the start of class until five minutes after the bell because the students continued to trickle in throughout this time interval.

1. What do you predict will be the situation by the end of the second week? Why?

2. What alternatives are open to Mr. Atkinson for Monday of the second week?

3. Which of the alternatives identified in your response to 2 are likely to lead to a worse situation? Why?

4. Which of the alternatives identified in your response to 2 are likely to lead to improvement? Why?

B. Ms. Brown complains that her class sessions begin quite promptly but that trouble starts about the middle of the period and the situation rapidly degenerates to obvious chaos by the end of the class. When asked to specify the nature of the problem, she replies that the students have no manners and such poor attention spans that even frequent switches of teaching modes get her nowhere. A check of her lesson plans reveals well-sequenced lessons, frequent change of modes, adequate plans for getting and giving feedback, many practical applications, and good relevance to the "here-and-now" interests of students. Plans for pacing seem adequate and there is an excellent match of strategies and stated objectives. On paper she looks great!

1. Assume you are going to observe Ms. Brown in action. What would you focus on in this observation? Why?

2. What is (or are) the most likely problem(s) you would expect to find?

3. Cite specific suggestions you would make based upon the data you would expect to gather in 1.

C. Mr. Forgette's class proceeds smoothly as long as the modes employed are short lectures, question/answer, or teacher demonstration. Whenever he uses laboratory or small-group discussion, or sends students to the board, discipline disintegrates.

1. What are possible causes of the problem?

2. Which of the possible causes is the most probable? Why?

3. What is the basic cure for the cause cited in 2?

D. The students in Ms. Klutz's class are busily working—that is, all but Pete and Harry. Ms. Klutz, a pretty first-year teacher, hears a sound and glances up just in time to see a note being passed from Pete to Harry. She stalks down the aisle and loudly demands the note. The rest of the students stop work and watch as Harry obsequiously hands Ms. Klutz a folded paper. Ms. Klutz threatens, "If this note is so important, maybe I should read it to the entire class!" Pete smirks and says, "Go ahead." When Ms. Klutz looks at the paper, she is horrified to find an obscene remark directed at her.

1. It is clear that Ms. Klutz has already firmly entrapped herself. Describe the best alternative(s) at this point.

2. If Ms. Klutz had it to do over, what effective approach(es) could she have used from the instant she spotted the note? Be sure to consider the limitations of each alternative approach you suggest.

E. Barbara approached Mr. Zillis after class and invited him to attend a party at her house following the Friday night pep rally and bonfire. Mr. Zillis is a young unmarried teacher with no previous commitment for that evening.

1. Describe a few potentially troublesome situations Mr. Zillis might be getting into if he accepts this invitation.

2. What further information should he seek, and from whom, prior to deciding whether to attend?

SUGGESTIONS FOR FURTHER STUDY

Cooper, C. R., & Petrosky, A. (1976). *Secondary school students' perceptions of math teachers and math classes. Mathematics Teacher*. **69** (3), 226–233.

The authors report on the results of a nationwide survey of secondary school students in which the students describe their worst and best classes, as well as their perceptions of their high school's best and worst attributes. Excerpts from student essays dramatically identify the mathematics teacher characteristics that students perceive as either helping or hindering their learning. Every mathematics teacher and student teacher would profit from reading this article and reflecting on the insights the students reveal.

APPENDIX

Modular Assignments

RESOURCE FILE MODULE

A. Objectives

   1. To build an organized resource file for *one* of the major units in a course you will teach (or for a course you are presently teaching).

   2. To begin an organized resource file for *each* of the other units in the course selected in A-1.

   3. To devise an organizational scheme that will serve as a pattern for developing resource files for other courses.

B. Enabling activities

   1. Study the syllabus, a widely used text, and teacher's handbook for the chosen course, in order to identify the major objectives for the unit selected for A-1 and for the entire course referred to in A-2.

   2. Consult the annotated references in the Suggestions for Further Study section at the end of each chapter in this text.

   3. Look for additional idea sources in the college or university library, the public library, the professional and school libraries at the secondary school where you will student-teach (or are teaching), supermarkets, department stores, garages, newspapers, and popular magazines. Some suggested areas where you will need resource ideas are educational games, pictures and sketches of bulletin boards, ideas for projects, supplementary readings on a range of reading levels, transparency ideas, directions for constructing homemade equipment or models, field trip possibilities, and laboratory activities.

C. Directions

   1. Whether you are storing your resource file on a computer disk or in a file drawer, you will need to prepare 8–12 file folders. Label each with the topic of a unit in the selected course. As the storehouse of ideas increases, you will find it helpful to add subtopics to each folder. (If you

Moose, C.A. (1953). "A normal curve of distribution illustrated in sunflower seeds." *The Science Teachers Bulletin*, **23**, 7–8.

Idea: Give each team of two Ss 15 baby food jars, labeled with the numbers from 1 to 15 and approximately 100 sunflower seeds. Have Ss classify seeds by # of stripes per seed and separate into the appropriately labeled jar. As the baby jars are filled, have the students empty them into numbered tall, thin olive jars or hydrometer jars borrowed from the physical science teacher. Be sure to arrange the large jars in a single row in numerical order.

Purpose: Lab to introduce topics of variation in nature and the normal curve and/or to provide illustrations of a "living" bar graph.

Modification: Precede by a demo so Ss will count stripes correctly.

Fig. A-1   Sample card from a resource file folder.

are using manila folders, subdivide within a folder via colored divider sheets as the store of ideas increases.) Even with a computer system, you will need to provide for storage of adjunct materials, such as physical models in labeled boxes or a file cabinet.

2. As you find a potentially useful idea, record the bibliographic data and a **summary** under **Idea** on a resource file card (See Figure A-1). It is seldom productive to simply copy pages of an article and file them. A resource file is not very helpful if, at a later date, you must go back to the original source, reread it to see why you selected it, and then try to retrieve your original intent. Make exact copies of only those diagrams, reading material, and references that would be lost in a summary.

3. Return to the cards you have begun and now identify projected classroom **purpose(s)** of the idea (for example, an attention getter in a lesson on _____ , an enrichment assignment in _____ for more capable Ss, a lab to introduce the rule _____ , and so on). Be sure to briefly summarize details of that use. For example, indicate whether the lab, demo or other mode will be used to **introduce** a concept or **give practice in** a rule.

4. Finally, be sure to note any **modifications** needed for the class you will be teaching (for example, rewriting at a lower reading level). Sometimes you will add modifications after testing out the idea with one class.

5. The set of 8–12 folders should be sprinkled liberally with items that emphasize:

   a) Mathematics/science interrelationships, as well as those to other content area.

   b) Content related to the Ss "here and now" interests.

c) Ideas from *at least two* national and/or international curriculum projects.

d) Ideas from *at least three* different teaching journals in your content area (as well as the interrelated mathematics/science journals).

LEARNING HIERARCHY MODULE

According to mathematicians, experienced teachers, and cognitive psychologists, the discipline of mathematics is a tightly hierarchical structure. Unfortunately many novice teachers view their subject matter discipline as a massive collection of facts and an arbitrary set of rules with few connections. Moreover, secondary school students are unlikely to learn anything about the structure of the subject matter unless relationships and connections are made explicit by their teacher often and in various ways. Thus, the planning of instruction consistent with the structure of the subject matter requires serious homework by the novice teacher. It is to that end that this module is directed.

A. Objectives

1. To construct a learning hierarchy for one of the major units you will teach.

2. To write a sample test item for each objective in the learning hierarchy.

B. Enabling activities

1. Study both content sequences and exercises in the syllabus, a widely used text, and teacher's handbook and identify the major objectives of the unit and some of the assessment measures found in those sources.

2. Study the learning hierarchies diagrammed in Chapter 6 of this text.

3. Study the guidelines proposed in the "Task Analysis" section of Chapter 6 to sequence the set of objectives listed in the same section.

C. Directions

1. Select a unit comprising two to three weeks of instruction.

2. Write five to seven *major (important)* cognitive instructional objectives and one sample corresponding test/quiz item per objective. Each objective and its corresponding test item should appear on a separate index card. Arrange these in a learning hierarchy by clipping or taping cards to a large sheet and adding appropriate arrows.

3. Then analyze *each of the* major objectives to identify prerequisite objectives not already written. (It is possible that one of the major objectives may be prerequisite to another major objective.) Write these additional instructional objectives and corresponding sample test/quiz items on index cards. Insert these in appropriate locations in the learning hierarchy and change arrows as needed.

4. Finally, write four to six *future* objectives (that is, from units to be taught after the selected one), for which the original major objectives are prerequisites. Write corresponding sample test items. Again adjust the learning hierarchy arrangement and arrows so as to correctly depict the overall sequence. Key the three types of objectives by a color code or diverse shapes. Identify the unit and grade level on the final chart.

REFERENCES

Adi, H., & Pulos, S. (1980). "Individual differences and formal operational performance of college students." *Journal for Research in Mathematics Education*, **11**, 150–155.

Adler, I. (Ed.). (1972). *Readings in mathematics* (books 1 & 2). Reston,VA: National Council of Teachers of Mathematics.

Ausubel, D. P. (1963). *The psychology of meaningful verbal learning: An introduction to school learning*. New York: Grune & Stratton.

Ausubel, D. P. (1968). *Educational psychology: A cognitive view*. New York: Holt, Rinehart & Winston.

Ausubel, D. P. (1979). "Education for rational thinking: A critique." In A. E. Lawson (Ed.), *The psychology of teaching for thinking and creativity* (pp. 174–190). Columbus, OH: ERIC Clearinghouse for Science, Mathematics and Environmental Education, The Ohio State University.

Bandura, A. (1969). *Principles of behavior modification*. New York: Holt, Rinehart & Winston.

Bell, E.T. (1937). *Men of mathematics*. New York: Simon and Schuster.

Bell, E.T. (1951). *Mathematics: Queen and servant of sciences*. New York: McGraw Hill.

Bell, M. S. (1972). *Mathematical uses and models in our everyday world*. (Studies in Mathematics, Vol. 20). Stanford, CA: School Mathematics Study Group.

Bidwell, J. K., & Clason, R. G. (Eds.). (1970). *Readings in the history of mathematics education*. Washington, DC: National Council of Teachers of Mathematics.

Bloom, B. S. (Ed.) (1956). *Taxonomy of educational objectives, Handbook I: Cognitive domain*. New York: David McKay.

Boyer, C. B. (1968). *A history of mathematics*. New York: John Wiley & Sons Inc.

Bramble, W. J., & Mason, E. J. (1985). *Computers in schools*. New York, NY: McGraw-Hill Book Co.

Brown, C. A., Carpenter, T. P., Kouba, V. L., Lindquist, M. M., Silver, E. A., & Swafford, J. O. (1988). "Secondary school results for the fourth NAEP assessment: Discrete mathematics, data organization and interpretation, measurement, number and operations." *Mathematics Teacher*, **81** (4), 241–248.

Brownell, W. A. (1935). "Psychological considerations in the learning and the teaching of arithmetic." In W. D. Reeve (Ed.), *The teaching of arithmetic* (10th Yearbook of the National Council of Teachers of Mathematics). (pp. 1–31). New York: Bureau of Publications, Teachers College, Columbia University.

Brownell, W. A. (1987). "Meaning and skill: Maintaining the balance." *Arithmetic Teacher*, **34** (8), 18–25. (Originally published in 1956).

Bruner, J. S. (1960). *The process of education*. Cambridge, MA: Harvard University Press.

Bruner, J. S. (1966). *Toward a theory of instruction*. New York, NY: W. W. Norton.

Budd-Rowe, M. (1973). *Teaching science as continuous inquiry*. New York: McGraw Hill.

Budd-Rowe, M. (1978). "Wait, wait, wait, ..." *School Science and Mathematics*, **78** (3), 207–216.

Buerk, D. (1982). "An experience with some able women who avoid mathematics." *For the Learning of Mathematics*, **3** (2), 19–24.

Bushaw, D., Bell, M., Pollak, H. O., Thompson, M., & Usiskin, Z. (1980). *A sourcebook of applications of school mathematics*. Reston,VA: National Council of Teachers of Mathematics.

Callahan, L. G., & MacMillan, D. L. (1981). "Teaching mathematics to slow-learning and mentally retarded children." In V. J. Glennon (Ed.), *The mathematical education of exceptional children and youth: An interdisciplinary approach* (pp. 146–190). Reston, VA: NCTM.

Carpenter, T. P. (1980). "Research in cognitive development." In R. J. Shumway (Ed.), *Research in mathematics education* (pp. 146–206) Reston, VA: NCTM.

Carpenter, T., Coburn, T. G., Reys, R. E., & Wilson, J. W. (1978). *Results from the first mathematics assessment of the National Assessment of Educational Progress*. Reston, VA: National Council of Teachers of Mathematics.

Carpenter, T. P., Corbitt, M., Kepner, H. S., Lindquist, M. M., & Reys, R. E. (1981). *Results from the second mathematics assessment of the National Assessment of Educational Progress*. Reston, VA: National Council of Teachers of Mathematics.

CASDA. (1985–1986). "High school students discuss attitudes of young women toward the study of math and science." *Albany, NY: CASDAIDS Newsletter*, **24** (1), 6–7.

Colburn, W. (1970). "Teaching of arithmetic." In J. K. Bidwell & R. G. Clason (Eds.), *Readings in the history of mathematics education* (pp. 24–37). Washington, DC: National Council of Teachers of Mathematics. (Originally given as a lecture in 1830; reprinted from a 1912 article in the *Elementary School Teacher*, **12**, 463–480).

Commission on Standards for School Mathematics. (1987). *Curriculum and evaluation standards for school mathematics*. (Draft). Reston, VA: National Council of Teachers of Mathematics.

Corcoran, M., & Gibb, E. G. (1961). "Appraising attitudes in the learning of mathematics." In D. A. Johnson (Ed.), *Evaluation in mathematics* (26th yearbook) (pp. 105–122). Washington, DC: National Council of Teachers of Mathematics.

Davidson, N. (1980). "The small group discovery method: 1967–1977." In J. G. Harvey & T. A. Romberg (Eds.), *Problem-solving studies in mathematics* (pp. 33–57). Madison, WI: University of Wisconsin Monograph Series.

Davis, R. B. (1984). *Learning mathematics: The cognitive science approach to mathematics education*. New Jersey: Ablex Publishing Corporation.

Dewey, J. (1910). *How we think*. Boston, MA: Heath.

Dewey, J. (1965). *Democracy and education*. New York: The Macmillan Co. (Originally published in 1916).

Dienes, Z.P. (1960). *Building up mathematics*. New York: Hutchinson Educational Ltd.

Duncker, K. (1945). "On problem-solving." *Psychological Monographs*, **58** (5), 1–111.

Erb, C. (1971). *A formative evaluation of an experimental teacher education project for juniors in mathematics education at the Ohio State University*. (Doctoral dissertation, The Ohio State University, 1970). Dissertaion Abstracts International, 32, 4464A.

Eves, H. (1963). *A survey of geometry* (Vols. 1, 2). Boston, MA: Allyn and Bacon, Inc.

Fajemidagba, O. (1983). *The relationship between Piagetian cognitive developmental stages of concrete and formal operations and achievement on mathematical ratio and proportion problems*. (Doctoral dissertation, State University of New York at Albany, 1983), Dissertation Abstracts International, 43, 3497A .

Farmer, W. A. (1983). *Cognitive development of gifted middle school students*. Paper presented at the Regional Conference of Association for the Education of Teachers in Science. Teaneck, N. J.

Farmer, W. A., & Farrell, M. A. (1986). *Teaching math/science concepts K–6: A sampler of classroom tested ideas*. Albany: State University of New York at Albany.

Farrell, M. A. (1967). *Pattern centering and its relation to secondary school geometry teaching: The formation of hypotheses*. (Doctoral dissertation, Indiana University, 1967). Dissertation Abstracts International, 28, 3552-3553A.

Farrell, M. A. (1970). "Area from a triangular point of view." *Mathematics Teacher*, 63 (1), 18–21.

Farrell, M. A. (1971). *Geoboard geometry*. Palo Alto, CA: Creative Pub.

Farrell, M. A., & Farmer, W. A. (1985). "Adolescents' performance on a sequence of proportional reasoning tasks." *Journal of Research in Science Teaching*, 22 (6), 503–518.

Fawcett, H. (1938). *The nature of proof*. (13th Yearbook of the National Council of Teachers of Mathematics). New York: Bureau of Publications, Teachers College, Columbia University.

Feldt, C. C. (1977). "Ratios and proportions with a little help from J. R. R. Tolkien." *New York State Mathematics Teachers Journal*, 27, 25–31.

Fennema, E. (1975). "Spatial ability, mathematics, and the sexes." In E. Fennema (Ed.), *Mathematics learning: What research says about sex differences* (pp. 33–45). Columbus, OH: ERICSMEAC.

Fennema, E., & Sherman, J. A. (1978). "Sex-related differences in mathematics achievement and related factors: A further study." *Journal for Research in Mathematics Education*, 9 (3), 189–203.

Fey, J. (1979). "Mathematics teaching today: Perspectives from three national surveys." *Mathematics Teacher*, 72, 490–504.

Fey, J. (Ed.). (1984). *Computing and mathematics*. Reston, VA: National Council of Teachers of Mathematics.

Fremont, H. (1969). *How to teach mathematics in secondary schools*. Philadelphia: W. B. Saunders Company.

Gagné, R. M. (1963). "Learning and proficiency in mathematics." *Mathematics Teacher*, 56, 620–626.

Gagné, R. M. (1970). *The conditions of learning* (2nd ed.). New York: Holt, Rinehart and Winston.

Gagné, R. M. (1977). *The conditions of learning* (3rd ed.). New York: Holt, Rinehart & Winston.

Gagné, R. M. (1979). "Learnable aspects of human thinking." In A. E. Lawson (Ed.), *The psychology of teaching for thinking and creativity* (pp. 1–27). Columbus, OH: ERIC Clearinghouse for Science, Mathematics and Environmental Education, The Ohio State University.

Gagné, R. M., & Briggs, L. J. (1979). *Principles of instructional design* (2nd ed.). New York: Holt, Rinehart & Winston.

Gamow, G. (1947). *One two three...infinity*. New York: NY: The New American Library of World Literature, Inc.

Geeslin, W. E. (1973). *An exploratory analysis of content structure and cognitive structure in the context of a mathematics instructional unit*. (Doctoral dissertation, Stanford University.)

Hall, G. S. (1883). "The contents of children's minds." *Princeton Review*, 11, 249–272.

Hart, K. (1978). "The understanding of ratio in the secondary school." *Maths in School*, 7 (1), 4–6.

Heath, T. L. (Trans.) (1956). *The thirteen books of Euclid's elements* (Vol I, 2nd ed., rev. ed.). New York: Dover Pub. Inc.

Hornbrook, A.R. (1895). *Concrete geometry*. New York: American Book Co.

Howson, G, Keitel, C., & Kilpatrick, J. (1981). *Curriculum developments in mathematics*. New York: Cambridge University Press.

Inhelder, B., & Piaget, J. (1958). *The growth of logical thinking from childhood to adolescence*. New York: Basic Books.

Jacobs, H. R. (1982). *Mathematics: A human endeavor* (2nd ed.). San Francisco, CA: W. H. Freeman and Co. (Originally published in 1970).

Jones, P. S., & Coxford, A. F. (Eds.). (1970). *A history of mathematics education in the United States and Canada* (32nd Yearbook). Washington, DC: National Council of Teachers of Mathematics.

Karplus, R., & Karplus, E. (1972). "Intellectual development beyond elementary school III: Ratio: A longitudinal study." *School Science and Mathematics*. 72 (8), 735–742.

Karplus, R., Lawson, A. E., Wollman, W., Appel, M., Bernoff, R., Howe, A., Rusch, J. J., & Sullivan, F. (1977). *Science teaching and the development of reasoning* (Volumes for Biology, Chemistry, Earth Science, General Science and Physics). Berkeley, CA: The University of California.

Karplus, R., Pulos, S., & Stage, E. K. (1983). "Early adolescents' proportional reasoning on 'rate' problems." *Educational Studies in Mathematics*, 14, 219–233.

Kell, C. L., & Corts, P. R. (1980). *Fundamentals of Effective Group Communication*. New York: Macmillan.

Kline, M. (1972). *Mathematical thought from ancient to modern times*. New York: Oxford University Press.

Krathwohl, D., Bloom, B., & Masia, B. (1964). *Taxonomy of educational objectives, Handbook II: Affective domain*. New York: David McKay.

Kreidler, W. J. (1986). "Teaching computer ethics." In D. O. Harper & J. H. Stewart (Eds.), *Run: Computer education* (pp. 223–226). Monterey, CA: Brooks/Cole Publishing Co.

Krist, B. J. (1981). *The programmable calculator in senior high school: A didactical analysis*. (Doctoral dissertation, SUNY at Buffalo, 1980), Dissertation Abstracts International, 41A, 2982.

Krulik, S. (Ed.). (1980). *Problem solving in school mathematics* (1980 Yearbook). Reston, VA: National Council of Teachers of Mathematics.

Kulm, G. (1980). "Research on mathematics attitude." In R. J. Shumway (Ed.), *Research in mathematics education*. (pp. 356–387). Reston, VA: National Council of Teachers of Mathematics.

Larkin, J. H. (1977). *Problem solving in physics*. (Working Paper), University of California, Berkeley, Group in Science and Mathematics Education and Department of Physics.

Libeskind, S. (1980). "Development of a unit of number theory for use in high school, based on a heuristic approach." In J. G. Harvey & T. A. Romberg (Eds.), *Problem-solving studies in mathematics* (pp. 59–66). Madison, WI: R & D Center for Individualized Schooling.

Lockhard, J. D. (Ed.). (1976). *Seventh report of the International Clearinghouse on Science and Mathematics Curricular Developments*. College Park, MD: Science Teaching Center, University of Maryland.

Lovell K. (1971). "The development of the concept of mathematical proof in abler pupils." In M. F. Rosskopf, L. P. Steffe & S. Taback (Eds.), *Piagetian cognitive-development research and mathematical education* (pp. 66–80). Reston, VA: NCTM.

Lowry, W. C. (Ed.). (1972). *The slow learner in mathematics* (35th Yearbook of the National Council of Teachers of Mathematics). Washington, D.C.: NCTM.

Matthews, W. (1984). "Influences on the learning and participation of minorities in mathematics." *Journal for Research in Mathematics Education*, 15 (2), 84–95.

McBride, J. W., & Chiappetta, E. L. (1978). *The relationship between the proportional reasoning ability of ninth-graders and their achievement of selected math and science concepts.* ERIC Reports (ED 167 351).

McDonald, J. L. (1982). *The role of cognitive stage in the development of cognitive structures of geometric content in the adolescent.* (Doctoral dissertation, State University of New York at Albany, 1982). Dissertation Abstracts International, 43, 733A.

McDonald, J. L. (1985). "Computer ethics. Do we practice what we teach?" *New York State Mathematics Teachers Journal,* **35** (1), 134–135.

McDonald, J. L. (1987). "Results of the 1986 AMTNYS survey of computer use in the mathematics classroom." *New York State Mathematics Teachers Journal,* **37** (2), 124–131.

McKnight, C. C., Crosswhite, F. J., Dossey, J. A., Kifer, E., Swafford, J. O., Travers, K. J., & Cooney, T. J. (1987). *The underachieving curriculum: Assessing U.S. school mathematics from an international perspective.* Champaign, IL: Stipes.

McWhirter, N., & McWhirter, R. (1976). *Guinness book of world records.* New York: Bantam Books.

National Advisory Committee on Mathematical Education. (1975). *Overview and analysis of school mathematics grades K–12.* Washington, DC: Conference Board of the Mathematical Sciences.

National Commission on Excellence in Education. (1983). *A nation at risk: The imperative for educational reform.* Washington, DC: U.S. Government Printing Office.

National Council of Teachers of Mathematics. (1969). *Historical topics for the mathematics classroom* (31st Yearbook). Reston, VA: NCTM.

National Council of Teachers of Mathematics. (1980). *An agenda for action: Recommendations for school mathematics of the 1980s.* Reston, VA: NCTM.

National Science Board Commission on Precollege Education in Mathematics, Science and Technology. (1983). *Educating Americans for the 21st century.* Washington, DC: National Science Foundation.

Neimark, E. D., DeLisi, R., & Newman, J. L. (Eds.). (1985). *Moderators of competence.* Hillsdale, NJ: Lawrence Erlbaum Assoc.

Newman, J. (Ed.). (1956). *The world of mathematics* (Vol. 1, 2, 3, 4). New York: Simon and Schuster.

Novak, J. D., & Gowin, D. B. (1984). *Learning how to learn.* New York: Cambridge University Press.

O'Connell, R. O. (1984). *The influence of content organization and relevant prior knowledge on the cognitive structure and achievement of sixth grade science students* (Doctoral dissertation at the State University of New York at Albany).

Peterson, P. L., & Fennema, E. (1985). "Effective teaching, student engagement in classroom activities, and sex-related differences in learning mathematics." *American Educational Research Journal,* **22** (3), 309–335.

Piaget, J. (1971). *Science of education and the psychology of the child* (D.Coltman, Trans.). New York: The Viking Press. (Originally published in two parts 1935 and 1965).

Piaget, J., & Inhelder, B. (1969). *The psychology of the child* (H. Weaver, Trans.). New York: Basic Books. (Original work published 1966).

Polya, G. (1962). *Mathematical discovery* (Vol. 1). New York: John Wiley & Sons.

Ranucci, E. R., & Teeters, J. L. (1977). *Creating Escher-type drawings.* Palo Alto, CA: Creative Pub.

Reeve, W. D. (1936). "Attacks on mathematics and how to meet them." In W. D. Reeve (Ed.), *The place of mathematics in modern education* (11th Yearbook of NCTM). (pp. 1–21). New York: Bureau of Publications, Teachers College, Columbia.

Resnick, L. B., & Ford, W. W. (1981). *The psychology of mathematics for instruction*. Hillsdale, NJ: Lawrence Erlbaum Assoc.

Reyes, L. H. (1984). "Affective variables and mathematics education." *The Elementary School Journal*, **84** (5), 558–581.

Reyes, L. H., & Stanic, G. M. A. (1988). "Research into practice: Gender and race equity in primary and middle school mathematics classrooms." *Arithmetic Teacher*, **35** (8), 46–48.

Rickover, H. G. (1960). *Education and freedom*. New York: E. P. Dutton & Co., Inc.

Ridge, H. L., & Renzulli, J. S. (1981). "Teaching mathematics to the gifted and talented." In V. J. Glennon (Ed.), *The mathematical education of exceptional children and youth* (pp. 191–266). Reston, VA: NCTM.

Romberg, T. A., & Carpenter, T. P. (1986). "Research on teaching and learning mathematics: Two disciplines of scientific inquiry." In M. C. Wittrock (Ed.), *Handbook of research on teaching* (3rd ed.). (pp. 850–873). New York: Macmillan Pub. Co.

Rosskopf, M. F. (1953). "Transfer of training." In H. F. Fehr (Ed.), *The learning of mathematics* (21st Yearbook). (pp. 205–227). Washington, DC: National Council of Teachers of Mathematics.

Russell, B. (1929). *Mysticism and logic*. New York: W. W. Norton.

Sawyer, W. W. (1964). *Vision in elementary mathematics*. Baltimore: Penguin.

Schoenfeld, A. H. (1979). "Explict heuristic training as a variable in problem solving performance." *Journal of Research in Mathematics Education*, **10** (3), 173–187.

Senk, S. (1985). "How well do students write geometry proofs?" *Mathematics Teacher*, **78** (6), 448–456.

Shavelson, R. J. (1974). "Methods for examining representations of a subject-matter structure in a student's memory." *Journal of Research in Science Teaching*, **11** (3), 231–249.

Shayer, M., & Wylam, H. (1978). "The distribution of Piagetian stages of thinking in British middle and secondary school children, 11–14 to 16 year olds and sex differentials." *British Journal of Educational Psychology*, **48**, 62–70.

Shulman, L. S. (1970). "Psychology and mathematics education." In E. G. Begle (Ed.), *Mathematics education* (69th Yearbook of the National Society for the Study of Education). (pp. 23–71). Chicago, IL: University of Chicago Press.

Silver, E. A. (Ed.). (1985). *Teaching and learning mathematical problem solving: Multiple research perspectives*. Hillsdale, NJ: Lawrence Erlbaum Assoc., Pub.

Skinner, B. F. (1953). *Science and human behavior*. New York: The Free Press.

Skinner, B. F. (1968). *The technology of teaching*. New York: Appleton.

Slavin, R. E. (1980). "Cooperative learning." *Review of Educational Research*, **50** (2), 315–342.

Slavin, R. E. (1987). "Cooperative learning and individualized instruction." *Arithmetic Teacher*, **35** (3), 14–16.

Smith, D. E. (1925). *History of mathematics* (Vols. 1, 2). New York: Dover Pub.

Sobel, M. A., & Maletsky, E. M. (1988). *Teaching mathematics: A sourcebook of aids, activities, and strategies* (2nd ed.). Englewood Cliffs, NJ: Prentice Hall.

Suydam, M. N. (1980). "Untangling clues from research on problem solving." In S. Krulik (Ed.), *Problem solving in school mathematics* (1980 Yearbook of the National Council of Teachers of Mathematics). (pp. 34–50). Reston, VA: NCTM.

Taylor, B. R. (1983). "Equity in mathematics: A case study." *Mathematics Teacher*, **76** (1), 12–17.

Thompson, A. G. (1985). "Teachers' conceptions of mathematics and the teaching of problem solving." In E. A. Silver (Ed.), *Teaching and learning mathematical problem solving: Multiple research perspectives.* (pp. 281–294). Hillsdale, NJ: Lawrence Erlbaum Assoc., Pub.

Thompson, D. W. (1961). *On growth and form.* (Abridged ed.). Cambridge: The University Press. (Originally published in 1917).

Thorndike, E. L. (1921). *New methods in teaching arithmetic.* New York: Rand-McNally.

Thorndike, E. L. (1922). *The psychology of arithmetic.* New York: Macmillan Co.

Thorndike, E. L. (1923). *The psychology of algebra.* New York: Macmillan Co.

Wagner, S., Rachlin, S., & Jensen, R. (1984). *Algebra learning project: Final report*, NIE Research Contract No. 400-81-0028.

Wertheimer, M. (1959). *Productive thinking* (Enl. ed.) New York: Harper & Row. (Original work published in 1945).

NAME INDEX

Abbey, D., 44
Abbott, E., 103
Abbott, R., 278
Adi, H., 64, 346
Adler, I., 70, 188, 316, 346
Appel, M., 61, 349,
Ausubel, D., 129, 130–132, 145, 147, 346

Bandura, A., 141, 346
Barr, S., 316
Bearden, D., 314
Beberman, M., 252
Begle, E., 155, 252, 256, 351
Bell, E., 90, 346
Bell, M., 103, 201, 255, 346, 347
Bernoff, R., 61, 349
Bidwell, J., 251, 346, 347
Bilski, V., 315
Binet, A., 48
Bloom, B., 112, 117, 158, 346, 349
Boehm, D., 290
Bolyai, 75, 251
Boyer, C., 83, 164, 346
Bramble, W., 295, 346
Braswell, J., 243
Briggs, L., 133, 140–141, 348
Brown, C., 179, 346
Brownell, W., 46, 129, 130, 153, 249, 346
Bruner, J., 129, 130, 132, 147, 153, 155, 346
Bruni, J., 314

Budd-Rowe, M., 9, 346, 347
Buerk, D., 54, 347
Buffon, 298
Bureau of Curriculum Development, 290
Bureau of Mathematics Education, 243, 257, 316
Burns, M., 316
Bushaw, D., 201, 347

Callahan, L., 65, 347
Campbell, P., 103
Carin, A., 27
Carpenter, T., 46, 90, 179, 243, 346, 347, 351
CASDA, 142, 347
Cheek, H., 310, 315
Chiappetta, E., 62, 350
Clason, R., 251, 346, 347
Coburn, T., 243, 313, 347
Colburn, W., 46, 130, 249, 347
Commission on Standards for School Mathematics, 208, 347
Cooney, T., 260, 266, 350
Cooper, C., 341
Copes, W., 99, 257–258
Corbin, M., 243
Corbitt, M., 347
Corcoran, M., 234, 347
Corts, P., 13, 349
Coxford, A., 247, 267, 349
Crosswhite, F., 260, 350
Crouse, R., 103
Cundy, H., 300, 314

Davidson, N., 15, 347
Davis, R., 61, 64, 155, 251, 347
DeLisi, R., 56, 350
Dewey, J., 46, 130, 139, 249, 347
Dienes, Z., 129, 130, 147, 153, 251, 347
Dossey, J., 260, 266, 350
Duncker, K., 138–139, 347
Dunkin, D., 289

Educational Testing Service (ETS), 228
Einstein, A., 76
Euler, L., 98
Erathosthenes, 82
Erb, C., 102, 347
Euclid, 75–76, 180, 250
Evered, L., 313
Eves, H., 80, 347

Fajemidagba, O., 61, 347
Farmer, W., 56, 61, 67, 348
Farrell, M., 56, 61, 63, 99, 264, 314, 316, 348
Fawcett, H., 63, 348
Fehr, H., 155, 253, 351
Feldt, C., 282, 283, 348
Fennema, E., 64, 348, 350
Fey, J., 251, 258, 315, 348
Fitting, M., 289
Ford, W., 64, 147, 149, 351
Fremont, H., 140, 142, 201, 348

Gagné, R., 41, 44, 132–138, 140–141, 142, 146, 147, 166, 180, 348

Galois, 66–67
Gamow, G., 299, 348
Gardner, M., 316
Garofalo, J., 153
Gauss, 75
Geeslin, W., 144, 348
Gibb, E., 234, 347
Gillespie, N., 314
Glennon, V., 71, 347
Goldberg, K., 27, 314
Gorman, R., 71
Gowin, D., 144, 350
Greenwood, I., 248
Grinstein, L., 103

Haldane, J., 274
Hall, G., 46, 348
Hansen, V., 315
Harper, D., 27, 349
Hart, K., 61, 348
Harvey, J., 347, 349
Heath, T., 101, 348
Hess, A., 314
Hirsch, C., 267
Hornbrook, A., 261, 348
House, P., 290
Howe, A., 61, 349
Howson, G., 251, 316, 349
Hunkins, F., 27

Inhelder, B., 48–49, 51, 62, 349, 350

Jacob, S., 71
Jacobs, H., 265, 267, 290, 349
Jeans, J., 276
Jensen, R., 60, 352
Johnson, D., 347
Jones, P., 247, 267, 349

Kahane, J., 316
Karplus, E., 61, 349
Karplus, R., 61, 349
Kasner, E., 316
Kastner, B., 290
Kaufman, B., 253
Keitel, C., 251, 349
Kell, C., 13, 349
Kepner, H., 243, 347
Kifer, J., 260, 350
Kilpatrick, J., 251, 349
Kline, M., 80, 251, 349
Kouba, V., 179, 346
Krathwohl, D., 117, 349

Kreidler, W., 310, 349
Krist, B., 63, 349
Krulik, S., 142, 201, 315, 349, 351
Kulm, G., 234, 349

Larkin, J., 148, 349
Lawson, A., 61, 346, 348, 349
Legendre, 67
Leibniz, 74
Lennie, J., 313
Libeskind, S., 63, 349
Lindquist, M., 179, 201, 243, 346, 347
Litwiller, B., 289
Lobachevsky, 75, 251
Lockhard, J., 252, 349
Lovell, K., 63, 349
Lovell, R., 313
Lowry, W., 65, 71, 349

MacMillan, D., 65, 347
Mager, R., 124
Maletsky, E., 264, 351
Mann, H., 248
Martin, K., 314
Martin, W., 289
Masia, B., 117, 349
Mason, E., 295, 346
Mathematical Association of America (MAA), 250
Matthews, W., 141, 349
Mc Bride, J., 62, 350
McDonald, J., 56, 64, 144, 258, 310, 350
McKnight, C., 260, 350
McWhirter, N., 176, 276, 350
McWhirter, R., 176, 276, 350
Miller, D. , 314

National Advisory Committee on Mathematical Education (NACOME), 251, 350
National Assessment of Educational Progress (NAEP), 179, 255, 256

National Commission on Excellence in Education, 350
National Council of Teachers of Mathematics (NCTM), 75, 103, 129, 138, 202, 250, 251, 256, 258, 260, 264, 266, 309, 350
National Science Board Commission on Precollege Education in Mathematics, Science and Technology, 256, 350
National Science Foundation (NSF), 250, 256
Neimark, E., 56, 350
Newman, J., 274, 276, 290, 316, 350
Newman, J. L., 56, 350
Newton, I., 74, 269
Novak, J., 144, 350

O'Connell, R., 144, 350

Paige, D., 252
Pavlov, 133
Perl, T., 103
Peterson, P., 64, 350
Petit, J., 104, 290, 314
Petrosky, A., 341
Piaget, J., 46, 48–49, 51, 56, 57, 62, 127, 136, 140, 349, 350
Picard, A., 125, 243
Playfair, 76
Pollak, H., 201, 347
Polya, G., 104, 142, 184, 202, 290, 350
Ponte, J., 289
Pulos, S., 61, 64, 346, 349

Rachlin, S., 60, 352
Ralston, A., 266
Ransom, W., 317
Ranucci, E., 54, 251, 350
Reeve, W., 250, 346, 350
Renzulli, J., 67, 351
Resnick, L., 64, 147, 149, 351
Reyes, L. , 64, 310, 351
Reys, R., 243, 247

Rice, J., 248
Rickover, H., 250, 351
Ridge, H., 67, 351
Riemann, 76, 251
Rollett, A., 300, 314
Romberg, T., 46, 90, 347, 349, 351
Rosskopf, M., 152, 349, 351
Rusch, J., 61, 349
Russell, B., 77, 351

Saccheri, 76
Sacco, W., 99, 257–258
Salkind, C., 317
Sawyer, W., 61, 104, 202, 251, 351
Schoenfeld, A., 142, 183, 351
Senk, S., 63, 351
Seymour, D., 315, 317
Sharron, S., 291
Shavelson, R., 144, 351
Shayer, M., 56, 351
Sherman, J., 64, 348
Shulman, L. , 152, 155, 351
Shumway, R., 347, 349
Silver, E., 142, 179, 346, 351, 352
Skinner, B., 132, 141, 333, 351
Slavin, R., 183, 309, 351
Sloyer, C., 99, 103, 257–258, 289
Smith, D., 83, 351
Sobel, M., 251, 264, 351
Souviney, R., 202
Stage, E., 61, 349
Stanic, G., 310, 351
Stark, R., 99, 257–258
Steffe, L., 349
Steinhaus, H., 291
Stewart, J., 27, 349
Sullivan, F., 62, 349
Sund, R., 27, 125, 243
Suydam, M., 138, 243, 351
Swafford, J., 179, 260, 346, 350

Taback, S., 349
Taylor, B., 310, 351
Taylor, R., 316
Teeters, J., 54, 350
Thompson, A., 91, 252

Thompson, D., 288–289, 352
Thompson, M., 201, 347
Thorndike, E., 128, 132, 249, 352
Travers, K., 260, 350
Truely, W., 315

Usiskin, Z., 201, 256, 266, 347

Wagner, S., 60, 352
Wertheimer, M., 130, 155, 352
Wilder, R., 104
Williams, D., 314
WIlson, N., 244
Wilson, J., 243, 244, 347
Wittrock, M., 351
Wollman, W., 61, 349
Wylam, H., 56, 351

SUBJECT INDEX

Academically talented, 66–68, 253, 254, 309

Advance organizer, 145–146, 151, 167

Affective domain, 111, 117–120, 187
  assessment, 221, 233–236, 239
  taxonomy, 118
  (also see Attitudes)

Agenda for Action, 138, 256–262, 266

Algebra, 16, 17, 24, 80–83, 87–88, 91, 94–96, 97, 261–262, 282–284
  research on, 60–61
  solution problems plan, 177–178
  translation, teaching of, 174–175, 178
  type problems, 41, 175–178
  unit plan on systems of equations, 195

Architecture and mathematics, 286

Area, 113–114, 137, 297, 302
  concept, 52–54
  examples from science, 272, 273, 274

Attention getting and keeping, 16, 37, 41, 167, 176, 189, 191–192, 201, 277, 302, 303, 321, 323

Attitudes, 183, 236, 252
  conditions for learning, 141, 188
  instructional strategy, 188, 190
  operational definition, 140–141
  research, 141, 234
  (also see Affective domain)

Audiovisual and technological activities (ATAs), 5, 20–22, 186, 187, 257, 284, 285, 297, 299, 304–306

Axiomatic chain, 75, 99, 131, 179, 180, 250, 253, 260
  (also see Proof)

Basic skills, 249, 250, 254–255, 256, 260

Beliefs about mathematics, 54, 91, 120

Buffon's needle (lesson), 298–299

Bulletin boards, 301–303

Calculator, 5, 16, 21, 27, 91, 109, 255, 257, 313–314, 315–316
  (also see ATAs, Information technology)

Cambridge Conference, 253, 266

Cartoons used in lessons, 220, 234, 252, 256, 265, 285, 286

Chambered Nautilus, 277, 278, 288–289

Cheating, 225, 226, 334–335

Cognitive domain, 111–117, 119–120, 150
  assessment, 208–233
  taxonomy, 112, 151, 182, 211, 213, 217

Cognitive style, 56, 63–64, 65

Collectibles, uses of, 297–304
  (also see Usable junk)

Committee of Ten, 251

Compass skills, 120–121, 186–187

Computers and microcomputers, 16, 20, 27, 29, 31, 42, 63, 69, 220, 255, 257, 260, 295–296, 297, 313–314, 315–316
  (also see ATAs, Information technology)

Concept, 77–78
  cognitive developmental schema, 53
  conditions for learning, 136, 165
  instructional strategy, 166, 190, 287
  kinds, 76, 77, 78
  operational definition, 78
  primes and composites plan, 161–164

Concept mapping, 143–145, 193–194

Conics, 16, 17, 47–48, 139, 299–300

Cooperative learning, 183, 309
  (also see Grouping for instruction)

Curriculum and Evaluation Standards in School Mathematics, 260, 266

Curriculum (projects), 250, 251–254, 255

Comprehensive School Mathematics Program (CSMP), 253–254
Intermediate Science Curriculum Study (ISCS), 255
Madison Project, 253, 254
New York State Three Year Sequence for High School Mathematics, 257
School Mathematics Project (SMP), 253, 254, 262–264, 303
School Mathematics Study Group (SMSG), 252–253, 255, 261–262, 278, 279, 291
Secondary School Mathematics Curriculum Improvement Study (SSMCIS), 253
University of Chicago School Mathematics Project (UCSMP), 256–257
University of Illinois Arithmetic Project, 252, 254, 264
University of Illinois Committee on School Mathematics (UICSM), 252, 261
Curve stitching, 301

Demonstration, 4, 15–16, 174, 177, 186, 264, 278, 284, 297–299, 302, 314–315, 321
Developmental questioning, 8, 9, 18, 32
Diagnosis and remediation, 13, 39–40, 59, 63, 213, 215, 231–233, 309
Discipline (see Management)
Discovery learning (teaching), 42, 131–132, 252, 253
Discrimination learning, 135–136
Discussion, 3–4, 11, 12–15, 182, 236
  management of, 13–15, 319–320
  (also see Cooperative learning)
Drill (see Practice)

Educating Americans for the Twenty-first Century, 256
Elastic clause, 160, 169
Equipment and materials, 294–296
Equity, 65, 260, 264, 310, 315
  (also see Gender)
Escher patterns, 54, 277
Evaluation, 205, 227, 239
  diagnostic, 205, 206, 215, 237
  formative, 205–206, 213, 256
  summative, 205, 206, 237, 256
  (also see Test)
Events of instruction, 41, 189, 323

Feedback, 6, 29–31, 108, 159, 320
Feedback getting, 6–7, 15, 18, 20, 21, 31–39, 59, 109, 110, 127, 136, 165, 166, 173, 187, 299, 328
  in homework post-mortem, 25, 36–38, 39–40
  in laboratory, 34–36
  in supervised practice, 33
  in test/quiz post-mortem, 12, 36, 37–38
Feedback giving, 6–7, 15, 18, 20, 21, 22, 40–42, 63, 187, 235, 236, 323, 328
  (also see Model of correct performance)
Feedback using, 6–7, 25, 39–40, 325
Fibonacci sequence, 277, 278
Field trips, 306–307
Films, slides, 20, 21, 187, 304–306, 312
Fishbowl activity, 264–265
Formulas and algorithms, 78, 79, 137, 176
  (also see Planning, daily)

Games, 225, 303–304, 326
Gender, 64–65, 247, 266–267, 279, 310
  (also see Equity)
Geoboard, 16, 17, 70, 264, 294, 296
Geometry, 15, 16, 17, 47–48, 52–54, 56–57, 69, 75–77, 78, 80–82, 86–87, 99, 113–114, 197–198, 271, 277, 300
Gestalt, 132, 138, 147, 249–250
Golden rectangle, 277
Grading, 219, 226–228, 237–239
Grandma's rule, 134, 325–326
Grouping for instruction, 308–309
  (also see Discussion)

"Here-and-now" interests, 192, 271, 276, 277–278, 282–287, 288, 323, 326
Heuristics, 181, 184–185
Hierarchy, 111–112, 117, 133
Histogram, 150, 282
History of mathematics (ideas), 164, 167
  Circumference of the earth, 82–83
  Euler's network problem, 97–98
  Greek dissection problems, 80–82
  Invention of calculus, 74
  Non-Euclidean geometry, 75–76
  Sine, cosine, tangent, 93–94
History of school mathematics, 246–260
Homework, 5–6, 23–25, 36–38, 39–40
Human resources, 307

Individual differences, 25, 46, 55–57, 63–68, 308, 338
  (also see Grouping for instruction)

Individual student projects, 5, 18–20, 66, 183, 300–301
Information processing, 64, 147–149
Information technology, 258–259, 310
Inverse variation (proportion), 62, 67, 276
Item analysis, 228–233, 238
  item difficulty, 220, 229, 231
  item discrimination, 220, 229–231

Journals, 264, 317–318

Könisgsberg bridge problem, 98

Laboratory, 4–5, 13, 16–18, 34–35, 70, 81–82, 86–87, 91–92, 132, 161–164, 168, 264, 272, 273, 275, 279, 284, 298, 299–300, 301, 314–315, 320
Language/symbolism, 54, 64, 65, 80, 166–167, 174–175, 251, 252, 254, 260, 272
  (also see Verbal association)
Learning
  definition of, 127
  hierarchy, 142–143, 153, 154, 193, 194, 197, 344–345
  meaningful, 59, 129–132, 146, 167, 177, 179
  research, 128, 129–130, 132, 138–139, 141, 146, 152
  rote, 129, 130, 146
Learning types, Gagné's, 133–140
Lecture, 3, 7, 32, 58, 59–60, 131, 319, 320
Likert-type scales, 234–235
Litter lesson, 271, 282
Logarithmic spiral, 277, 289

Management, classroom, 9, 10, 15, 18, 20–22, 23–24, 134, 187, 212, 224–225, 306, 307, 319–321, 323–336, 337, 339
Mathematical system, 77, 90, 91, 99
Mathematics, invented or discovered, 73–74, 88, 89, 91, 100
Mathematics processes, 74–75, 80–88, 89, 96–100, 164–165, 179, 181, 216, 219, 251, 256, 260, 281, 287
Mathematics products, 74–80, 88, 89, 91–96, 179, 181, 251, 260, 287
Mathematics/science interface
  biological science examples, 15, 234, 274, 277, 278, 280
  comparison of the disciplines, 90, 269, 280, 281–282
  honeycomb, 272–274
  muscle fatigue lesson, 278–280
  physical science examples, 281

science-based questions, 270
soda straw clarinet, 275–276
sound (music), 274–276
structure, rigid, 273–274, 289, 297
Measurement activities, 16, 17, 86, 91, 168, 272, 286
Model
  instructional, 2, 25, 29, 38, 68, 73, 87, 88, 127, 146, 157, 204, 246, 265, 269, 287, 293, 319, 339
  mathematical, 79–80, 87, 88, 169, 255, 263, 271, 274, 277, 278, 282, 287
  of correct performance, 41, 173, 308
  of the nature of mathematics, 89–90, 97–98, 100
  physical, 15, 16, 17, 76, 77, 78, 87, 88, 89, 100, 165, 277, 284, 285, 299
  thought, 78, 88, 89, 146, 149, 273
Modes, instructional, 2
  (also see ATAs, Demonstration, Discussion, Homework, Individual student projects, Laboratory, Lecture, Question/answer, Supervised practice)

A Nation at Risk, 256
"New Math", 247, 251
Nonverbal signals, 16, 22, 34, 40–41, 324–325, 328, 338

Objectives, instructional, 196–197
  affective domain, 117–120, 236
  cognitive domain, 112–117, 225
  cognitive domain-verbs, 117
  operational definition, 110
  psychomotor domain, 120–122, 238–239
Observation scales, 208, 236, 237

Paper-folding, 17, 47–48, 260, 299–300
Pascal's triangle, 97, 184
Patterns, analysis, 12, 18, 24, 84–86, 91–92, 94–96, 97, 272–273
Pi (π), 87
  lesson ideas, 17, 86–87, 168–172, 298–299
Piagetian theory, research, 48–60, 61, 64, 78, 136, 167, 251, 253, 260, 264, 288
  adaptation, 59–60
  cognitive interaction, 46, 57–58, 59, 183
  concrete operational reasoning, 50–54, 56, 95, 144, 165
  conservation, 50, 52, 53
  formal operational reasoning, 50–54, 56, 63, 144
  nested stages model, 54–57, 112, 146

social interaction, 57, 58, 183
Planning, daily, for
  attitudes, 187–188
  concepts, 160–166
  formulas and algorithms, 168–174
  novel problem solving, 182–185
  proof, 179–181
  psychomotor learning, 186–187
  rules/principles, 168–181
  type problems in algebra, 41, 175–179
  vocabulary and symbolism, 166–167
Planning, long-range, for a
  course, 196–199
  unit, 192–196
Postulate, 76–77, 78, 89
Practice, 22–23, 24, 52, 66, 67, 128,
  149–151, 173, 178–179, 249, 255, 258
Praise and reward, 10, 15, 18, 35, 36,
  41–42, 66, 135, 160, 164, 204, 325–326
Primes and composites, 17, 161–165, 188
Probability and statistics, 4, 34–35, 53, 56,
  70, 222, 262–264, 279, 286, 298
Problem solving, novel, 254, 302, 316–317
  conditions for learning, 15, 139–140
  difference from type problems, 138
  instructional strategy, 183, 190
  sample examples, 113, 138, 139, 185
  research, 138, 142, 183
  (also see Heuristics)
Professional associations, 309–310
Proof, 12, 51–52, 54, 56–57, 76–77, 85, 87,
  88, 90, 97, 101, 141, 152, 197, 250
  research, 63
  (also see Theorems)
Proportional reasoning
  Mr. Tall and Mr. Short, 61–62, 67, 69
  research on, 53, 61–62, 67
  (also see Ratio and proportion)
Psychomotor domain, 111, 120–122, 135
  assessment, 221, 236
  instructional strategy, 187, 190
  learning of motor skills, 134–135, 150
Punishment, 24, 160, 164, 325, 329, 330,
  331, 332–336
Pythagorean theorem, 69, 70
Pythagorean triples, 75

Question/answer, 3, 7–11, 32, 39, 165, 320,
  327–328

Ratio and proportion, 61–62, 298–299
  bicycle lesson, 284–285
  The Hobbit lesson, 282–284
  (also see Proportional reasoning)

Reasoning
  deductive, 51, 63, 77, 80, 83–84, 87, 97,
    99, 273
  inductive, 51, 80, 83–85, 86, 87, 88, 95,
    96–97, 273
  research on, 60–63, 144, 148, 293
  (also see Piagetian theory, research;
    Individual differences)
Reliability, 207, 218
Report card, 236–239
Representation, cognitive, 49, 57, 61, 64,
  78, 88, 98, 114, 130, 139, 144, 148,
  149
Resource file, 101, 185, 187, 188, 193, 194,
  195, 223, 265, 282, 311, 342–344
Retention, 61, 62, 64, 65, 66, 67, 128, 129,
  131, 139, 146, 147–149, 287
  (also see Information processing)
Role models, 65, 141, 331, 336–338
Rules/principles
  conditions for learning, 138
  instructional strategy, 169, 190, 287
  operational definition, 78
  sample plan for rule of $C = \pi d$,
    170–172
  types of, 78–79, 168

Safety and legal aspects, 306, 307–308
Sampling, 7, 11, 15, 31, 32, 109, 204, 208,
  209, 224
  (also see Test, sampling)
Semantic differential, 233–234
Semi-permanent chalk, 296, 297
Sequencing, 127, 142, 168, 173, 194,
  197–199
Signed numbers, 60, 94–96
Slow learners, 65–66, 252, 254, 309
Sports and mathematics, 87, 271, 278, 286,
  287, 289
Sputnik, 131, 247, 250, 252, 254, 256
Straw vote or poll, 10, 32, 33, 38
Structure of discipline, 130, 145, 194, 252,
  253, 260
Sunflower seed lab, 300, 343
Supervised practice, 5, 22–23, 33, 224,
  324, 325
Symbolism (see Language/symbolism)

Table of specifications, 221–223
Task analysis, 142–143
Taxonomy, 111, 112, 113, 114, 117–118,
  119, 122
Test, 196, 205, 206

administration of, 225–226, 324,
    334–335
assessing results of, 226–228
criterion-referenced, 221
norm-referenced, 221
post-mortem, 12, 36, 37–38, 231–232
review lesson, 224–225, 302
sampling, 211, 215
unit test, 220–224
Test items
completion, 212–213
credit assignment, 219
long response, 217–219
matching, 215–217
modified true-false, 211–212
multiple choice, 213–215
storage and retrieval, 220
true-false, 210–211
Theorems, 75, 77, 79, 89, 90, 99
analysis, 179–180, 181
planning, rules/principles, 179–181
planning, novel problem solving,
    188–189
synthesis, 180–181
Transfer, 63, 146, 147, 151–152, 179, 287
Transformation geometry, 252, 257,
    285–286
Trigonometry, 91–94, 115–116, 128, 149,
    276

Usable "junk", 295
    (also see Collectibles)

Validity, 207, 219, 238
Verbal associations, 128, 135, 136, 166,
    173
conditions for learning, 135
instructional strategy, 167, 190
    (also see Language/symbolism)
Visualization (pictorial), 56, 61, 65, 149,
    174–175, 178, 273
    (also see Representation, cognitive)
Volume, 49, 50, 53, 54
examples from science, 272, 274

Wait-time, 9
"Word" problems (see Algebra, Planning)